WORD
BIBLICAL
COMMENTARY

General Editors
David A. Hubbard
Glenn W. Barker †

Old Testament Editor
John D. W. Watts

New Testament Editor
Ralph P. Martin

WORD
BIBLICAL
COMMENTARY

Volume 23A

Ecclesiastes

ROLAND E. MURPHY

THOMAS NELSON
Since 1798

NASHVILLE   DALLAS   MEXICO CITY   RIO DE JANEIRO

Word Biblical Commentary
Ecclesiastes
Copyright © 1992 by Thomas Nelson, Inc.

Library of Congress Cataloging-in-Publication Data
Main entry under title:

Word biblical commentary.

    Includes bibliographies.
    1. Bible—Commentaries—Collected works.
BS491.2.W67   220.7'7   81-71768
ISBN 10: 0-8499-0222-3 (v.23a) AACR2
ISBN 13: 978-0-8499-0222-2

Printed in Mexico

Translations of the Scripture text appearing in italic under the heading *Translation* are the author's own.

8 9 10 11 12 EPAC 15 14 13 12 11

To the congenial
faculty colleagues, students, and staff
of the Divinity School
and Graduate School of Religion
at Duke University

Contents

Preface

Another commentary on Qoheleth? What has the current spate of commentaries to offer, compared to some of the great ones of the past, such as those of E. Podechard and the late R. Gordis? Even if Podechard was mistaken in detecting several authors within this baffling book, his work remains indispensable after some eighty years. Since that time there have been original insights proffered by A. G. Wright, M. Fox, N. Lohfink, and D. Michel, among others. But certain works remain classic, even if they are dated. The present commentary rests on the shoulders of previous scholars, Jerome included, while trying to remain faithful to the thought of Qoheleth and to avoid what can only be described as pet theories.

Qoheleth never ceases to attract students, but perhaps no other book in the Bible has so steadfastly defied analysis and refused to be typed. In presenting this commentary to the public, the author remains painfully aware of its limitations. It aims at succinctness and accuracy within the format adopted by the Word series. It is one interpretation among many: somewhere between Qoheleth the preacher of the absurd and Qoheleth the preacher of joy—not that he himself sought a middle way (thus, contrary to a common interpretation of 7:16–18). Qoheleth remains as mysterious as his name, as the wisdom he sought (and failed, 7:23) to capture.

Posterity was kind to him, if I understand 12:9–14 correctly, but less so are many modern interpreters, whatever be the reason. His work is often hailed as the bankruptcy of wisdom and invidiously compared with the chimera of pure orthodox faith, whether of Israel or of the Church. This is more than ironic. Qoheleth has as much to say about the quality of faith as does any other biblical work. He tells us that faith means accepting God on God's terms.

The author has obligations to many people, first and foremost to a good friend, David Hubbard, the General Editor of the Word Biblical Commentary. Because of his multifarious activities, he relinquished his plan to write the commentary on Ecclesiastes—long a favorite work of his, to judge from earlier studies. I am grateful to the personnel of WBC, from John Watts who read the typescript to Melanie McQuere who copyedited it. The work would never have been written without the efforts of the dedicated ladies of the Duke Divinity School secretarial pool. It was also enriched by the challenge of my former students at Duke University and by the collegial atmosphere of its faculty members. Hence the dedication.

Washington, D. C.   ROLAND E. MURPHY, O. CARM.
May 1992

Editorial Preface

The launching of the *Word Biblical Commentary* brings to fulfillment an enterprise of several years' planning. The publishers and the members of the editorial board met in 1977 to explore the possibility of a new commentary on the books of the Bible that would incorporate several distinctive features. Prospective readers of these volumes are entitled to know what such features were intended to be; whether the aims of the commentary have been fully achieved time alone will tell.

First, we have tried to cast a wide net to include as contributors a number of scholars from around the world who not only share our aims, but are in the main engaged in the ministry of teaching in university, college, and seminary. They represent a rich diversity of denominational allegiance. The broad stance of our contributors can rightly be called evangelical, and this term is to be understood in its positive, historic sense of a commitment to Scripture as divine revelation, and to the truth and power of the Christian gospel.

Then, the commentaries in our series are all commissioned and written for the purpose of inclusion in the *Word Biblical Commentary.* Unlike several of our distinguished counterparts in the field of commentary writing, there are no translated works, originally written in a non-English language. Also, our commentators were asked to prepare their own rendering of the original biblical text and to use those languages as the basis of their own comments and exegesis. What may be claimed as distinctive with this series is that it is based on the biblical languages, yet it seeks to make the technical and scholarly approach to a theological understanding of Scripture understandable by—and useful to—the fledgling student, the working minister, and colleagues in the guild of professional scholars and teachers as well.

Finally, a word must be said about the format of the series. The layout, in clearly defined sections, has been consciously devised to assist readers at different levels. Those wishing to learn about the textual witnesses on which the translation is offered are invited to consult the section headed *Notes.* If the readers' concern is with the state of modern scholarship on any given portion of Scripture, they should turn to the sections of *Bibliography* and *Form/Structure/Setting.* For a clear exposition of the passage's meaning and its relevance to the ongoing biblical revelation, the *Comment* and concluding *Explanation* are designed expressly to meet that need. There is therefore something for everyone who may pick up and use these volumes.

If these aims come anywhere near realization, the intention of the editors will have been met, and the labor of our team of contributors rewarded.

General Editors: *David A. Hubbard*
Glenn W. Barker †
Old Testament: *John D. W. Watts*
New Testament: *Ralph P. Martin*

Abbreviations

CChrSL   Corpus Christianorum (Series latina)
CF   Collectanea Friburgensia
CJT   *Canadian Journal of Theology*
ConBOT   Coniectanea biblica (Old Testament)
CUASST   Catholic University of America Studies in Sacred Theology
DBSup   *Dictionnaire de la Bible, Supplément*
DNEB   Die Neue Echter Bibel
EBib   Etudes bibliques
ED   *Euntes Docete*
EF   Erträge der Forschung
EI   *Eretz Israel*
EJM   Etudes sur le Judaïsme Médiévale
EphCarm   *Ephemerides Carmeliticae*
EstBíb   *Estudios bíblicos*
ETL   *Ephemerides theologicae lovanienses*
EvQ   *Evangelical Quarterly*
EvT   *Evangelische Theologie*
ExpTim   *Expository Times*
FC   Fathers of the Church
FGLP   Forschungen zur Geschichte und Lehre des Protestantismus
FOTL   The Forms of the Old Testament Literature
GKC   *Gesenius' Hebrew Grammar*, ed. E. Kautzsch, tr. A. E. Cowley (Oxford: Clarendon, 1910)
GL   *Geist und Leben*
HAR   *Hebrew Annual Review*
HAT   Handbuch zum Alten Testament
HBC   *Harper's Bible Commentary*, ed. J. L. Mays (San Francisco: Harper & Row, 1988)
HKAT   Handkommentar zum Alten Testament
HS   *Hebrew Studies*
HSAT   Die Heilige Schrift des Alten Testaments
HTR   *Harvard Theological Review*
HUCA   *Hebrew Union College Annual*
IBS   *Irish Biblical Studies*
ICC   International Critical Commentary
Int   *Interpretation*
ITQ   *Irish Theological Quarterly*
IW   *Israelite Wisdom: Theological and Literary Essays in Honor of Samuel Terrien*, ed. J. G. Gammie and L. Perdue (Missoula: Scholars Press, 1978)
JAAR   *Journal of the American Academy of Religion*
JAOS   *Journal of the American Oriental Society*
JETS   *Journal of the Evangelical Theological Society*
JBL   *Journal of Biblical Literature*
JNES   *Journal of Near Eastern Studies*
Joüon   P. Joüon, *Grammaire de l'hébreu biblique* (Rome: Pontifical Biblical Institute, 1947)
JQR   *Jewish Quarterly Review*
JSOT   *Journal for the Study of the Old Testament*

JSS	*Journal of Semitic Studies*
JTS	*Journal of Theological Studies*
KAT	Kommentar zum Alten Testament, ed. E. Sellin
KB³	L. Köhler, W. Baumgartner, et al. *Hebräisches und aramäisches Lexikon zum Alten Testament,* 3rd ed., 4 vols. (Leiden: Brill, 1967–90)
KeH	Kurzgesasstes exegetisches Handbuch zum Alten Testament (2nd ed., 1893)
KHC	Kurzer Hand-Commentar zum Alten Testament
KPG	Knox Preaching Guides
Lat	*Lateranum*
LD	Lectio divina
LUÅ	Lunds universitetsårsskrift
MU	Mainzer Universitäts-Reden
MUSKTF	Münchener Universitätsschriften Katholisch-Theologische Fakultät
NCBC	New Century Bible Commentary
NJBC	*The New Jerome Biblical Commentary,* ed. R. E. Brown et al. (Englewood Cliffs, NJ: Prentice Hall, 1990)
NRT	*La nouvelle revue théologique*
OBO	Orbis biblicus et orientalis
OLA	Orientalia lovaniensia analecta
OLP	Orientalia lovaniensia periodica
OLZ	*Orientalistische Literaturzeitung*
OTG	Old Testament Guides
OTL	The Old Testament Library
OTP	*The Old Testament Pseudepigrapha,* ed. J. Charlesworth (Garden City, 1983–85)
PAAJR	*Proceedings of the American Academy of Jewish Research*
PG	J. Migne, *Patrologia graeca*
PL	J. Migne, *Patrologia latina*
POS	Praetoria Oriental Series
PSB	*Princeton Seminary Bulletin*
PTMS	Pittsburgh Theological Monograph Series
RB	*Revue biblique*
RHPR	*Revue d'histoire et de philosophie religieuses*
RivB	*Rivista biblica*
RQ	*Revue de Qumran*
RSR	*Recherches de science religieuse*
RTP	*Revue de théologie et de philosophie*
SagAT	*La Sagesse de l'Ancien Testament,* ed. M. Gilbert, BETL 51 (Leuven: Leuven UP, 1979)
SAIW	*Studies in Israelite Wisdom,* ed. J. L. Crenshaw (New York: KTAV, 1976)
SANT	Studien zum Alten und Neuen Testament
SAT	Schriften des Alten Testamentes
SB	La Sacra Bibbia
SBLASP	Society of Biblical Literature Abstracts and Seminar Papers
SBLDS	Society of Biblical Literature Dissertation Series
SBLMS	Society of Biblical Literature Monograph Series
SBLSCS	Society of Biblical Literature Septuagint and Cognate Studies

SBTh	*Studia Biblica et Theologica*
ScC	*Scuola Cattolica*
ScEs	*Science et Esprit*
Sef	*Sefarad*
SFEG	Schriften der finnischen exegetischen Gesellschaft
SGFWW	Schriften der Gesellschaft zur Förderung der Westfälischen Wilhelms-Universität zu Münster
SIANE	*The Sage in Israel and the Ancient Near East*, ed., J. G. Gammie and L. G. Perdue (Winona Lake, IN: Eisenbrauns, 1990)
SPIB	Scripta Pontificii Instituti Biblici
SThU	*Schweizerische theologische Umschau*
SubBib	Subsidia Biblica
SUNT	Studien zur Umwelt des Neuen Testaments
SWBAS	The Social World of Biblical Antiquity Series
SZ	*Stimmen der Zeit*
TBC	Torch Bible Commentary
TD	*Theology Digest*
TI	Text and Interpretation
TOTC	Tyndale Old Testament Commentaries
TQ	*Theologische Quartalschrift*
TRu	*Theologische Rundschau*
TTZ	*Trierer theologische Zeitschrift*
TV	*Theologia Viatorum*
TZ	*Theologische Zeitschrift*
UF	*Ugaritische Forschungen*
VD	*Verbum domini*
VF	*Verkündigung und Forschung*
Von Kanaan	*Von Kanaan bis Kerala*, FS J. van der Ploeg, ed. W. C. Delsman et al., AOAT 211 (Neukirchen-Vluyn: Neukirchenev, 1982)
VS	Verbum salutis
VT	*Vetus Testamentum*
VTSup	Vetus Testamentum, Supplements
Wagner	M. Wagner, *Die lexikalischen und grammatikalischen Aramaismen im altestamentlichen Hebräisch*, BZAW 96 (Berlin: Töpelmann, 1966)
WB	Die Welt der Bibel
WF	Wege der Forschung
Williams	R. J. Williams, *Hebrew Syntax: An Outline* (Toronto: Toronto UP, 1976)
WMANT	Wissenschaftliche Monographien zum Alten und Neuen Testament
WUNT	Wissenschaftliche Untersuchungen zum Neuen Testament
WW	*Word & World*
WZLGS	*Wissenschaftliche Zeitschrift der Karl-Marx Universität Leipzig Gesellschafts- und sprachwissenschaftliche Reihe*
ZAS	*Zeitschrift fur Ägyptische Sprache und Altertumskunde*
ZAW	*Zeitschrift für die alttestamentliche Wissenschaft*
ZDMG	Zeitschrift der deutschen morganländischen Gesellschaft
ZDPV	*Zeitschrift des deutschen Palastina-Vereins*
ZTK	*Zeitschrift für Theologie und Kirche*

ANCIENT VERSIONS

Aq	Aquila
OL	Old Latin
Sym	Symmachus
Tg	Targum
Theod	Theodotion
Vg	Vulgate

MODERN TRANSLATIONS

Eü	Einheitsübersetzung
KJV	King James Version
NAB	New American Bible
NEB	New English Bible
NIV	New International Version
NJB	New Jerusalem Bible
NJV	New Jewish Version (Tanakh)
NRSV	New Revised Standard Version
REB	Revised English Bible
RSV	Revised Standard Version
TEV	Today's English Version
TOB	Traduction Oecumenique de la Bible

BIBLICAL AND APOCRYPHAL BOOKS

OLD TESTAMENT

Gen	Genesis		Cant	Canticles,
Exod	Exodus			Song of Solomon
Lev	Leviticus		Isa	Isaiah
Num	Numbers		Jer	Jeremiah
Deut	Deuteronomy		Lam	Lamentations
Josh	Joshua		Ezek	Ezekiel
Judg	Judges		Dan	Daniel
Ruth	Ruth		Hos	Hosea
1–2 Sam	1–2 Samuel		Joel	Joel
1–2 Kgs	1–2 Kings		Amos	Amos
1–2 Chr	1–2 Chronicles		Obad	Obadiah
Ezra	Ezra		Jon	Jonah
Neh	Nehemiah		Mic	Micah
Esth	Esther		Nah	Nahum
Job	Job		Hab	Habakkuk
Ps(s)	Psalm(s)		Zeph	Zephaniah
Prov	Proverbs		Hag	Haggai
Eccl	Ecclesiastes		Zech	Zechariah
			Mal	Malachi

APOCRYPHA

Add Esth	Additions to Esther	Pr Azar	Prayer of Azariah
Bar	Baruch	Pr Man	Prayer of Manasseh
Bel	Bel and the Dragon	Sir	Ecclesiasticus or
1–2 Esdr	1–2 Esdras		The Wisdom of Jesus
4 Ezra	4 Ezra		Son of Sira
Jdt	Judith	Sus	Susanna
Ep Jer	Epistle of Jeremiah	Tob	Tobit
1–4 Kgdms	1–4 Kingdoms	Wis	Wisdom of Solomon
1–4 Macc	1–4 Maccabees		

NEW TESTAMENT

Matt	Matthew	1–2 Thess	1–2 Thessalonians
Mark	Mark	1–2 Tim	1–2 Timothy
Luke	Luke	Titus	Titus
John	John	Phlm	Philemon
Acts	Acts	Heb	Hebrews
Rom	Romans	Jas	James
1–2 Cor	1–2 Corinthians	1–2 Pet	1–2 Peter
Gal	Galatians	1–3 John	1–3 John
Eph	Ephesians	Jude	Jude
Phil	Philippians	Rev	Revelation
Col	Colossians		

MISCELLANEOUS

chap.	chapter
ed(s).	editors(s), edited by
esp.	especially
et al.	and others
ET	English translation
FS	Festschrift
hap. leg.	*hapax legomenon*
MS(S)	manuscript(s)
MT	Masoretic text
NT	New Testament
OT	Old Testament
pace	despite the interpretation of
passim	elsewhere
s.v.	*sub voce*
tr.	translator, translated by
UP	University Press

Main Bibliography

References to commentaries are by name only; pages are given when the reference does not obviously deal with the chapter and verse under consideration.

COMMENTARIES

Allgeier, A. *Das Buch des Predigers oder Koheleth.* HSAT. Bonn: Hanstein, 1925. **Alonso Schökel, L.** *Eclesiastes y Sabiduria.* Los Libros Sagrados 17. Madrid: Ediciones Cristiandad, 1974. **Barton, G. A.** *Commentary on the Book of Ecclesiastes.* ICC. Edinburgh: T. & T. Clark, 1908. **Barucq, A.** *Ecclésiaste.* VS 3. Paris: Beauchesne, 1968. **Bea, A.** *Liber Ecclesiastae.* SPIB 100. Rome: Pontifical Biblical Institute, 1950. **Bonaventure.** "Commentarius in Ecclesiasten." In *Doctoris Seraphici S. Bonaventurae Opera Omnia.* Florence: Quaracchi, 1893. 6:3–103. **Brenz, J.** *Der Prediger Salomo: Faksimile-Neudruck der ersten Ausgabe Hagenau 1528.* Stuttgart: Frommann, 1970. **Buzy, D.** "L'Ecclésiaste." In *La Sainte Bible.* Ed. L. Pirot and A. Clamer. Paris: Letouzey et Ané, 1946. 6:191–280. **Cohen, A.,** tr. "Ecclesiastes." In *Midrash Rabbah.* Ed. H. Freeman and M. Simon. London: Soncino, 1939. **Collins, J. J.** *Proverbs, Ecclesiastes.* KPG. Atlanta: John Knox, 1980. **Crenshaw, J. L.** *Ecclesiastes.* OTL. Philadelphia: Westminster, 1987. **Delitzsch, F.** *Commentary on the Song of Songs and Ecclesiastes.* 1891. Reprint. Grand Rapids: Eerdmans, 1982. **Eaton, M.** *Ecclesiastes.* TOTC. Downers Grove: InterVarsity, 1983. **Fonzo, L. di.** *Ecclesiaste.* SB. Rome: Marietti, 1967. **Fuerst, W. J.** "Ecclesiastes." In *The Five Scrolls.* CBC. London: Cambridge, 1975. **Galling, K.** "Der Prediger." In *Die fünf Megilloth.* 2nd ed. HAT 18. Tübingen: Mohr/Siebeck, 1969. **Gietmann, G.** *Commentarius in Ecclesiasten et Canticum Canticorum.* Paris: Lethielleux, 1890. **Ginsberg, H. L.** *Koheleth.* Jerusalem: Newman, 1961. **Ginsburg, C. D.** *The Song of Songs and Coheleth.* Reprint. New York: KTAV, 1970. **Glasser, E.** *Le procès du bonheur par Qohelet.* LD 61. Paris: Cerf, 1970. **Gordis, R.** *Koheleth—The Man and His World.* 3rd ed. New York: Schocken, 1968. **Graetz, H.** *Kohelet oder der Salomonische Prediger.* Leipzig, 1871. **Haupt, P.** *The Book of Ecclesiastes.* Baltimore: Johns Hopkins, 1905. **Hertzberg, H.** *Der Prediger.* KAT 17,4. Gütersloh: Mohn, 1963. **Hubbard, D.** *Beyond Futility.* Grand Rapids: Eerdmans, 1976. **Hugh of St. Victor.** "In Salomonis Ecclesiasten Homiliae." PG 175:113–256. **Jastrow, M. Jr.** *A Gentle Cynic.* Philadelphia: Lippincott, 1919. **Jerome.** "Commentarius in Ecclesiasten." In *S. Hieronymi Presbyteri Opera.* Ed. M. Adrianen. CChrSL 72. Turnholti: Brepols, 1959. 1:249–361. **Kidner, D.** *A Time to Mourn, and a Time to Dance: Ecclesiastes and the Way of the World.* Leicester: InterVarsity, 1976. **Kroeber, R.** *Der Prediger.* Schriften und Quellen der alten Welt, 13. Berlin: Akademie-Verlag, 1963. **Kuhn, G.** *Erklärung des Buches Koheleth.* BZAW 43. Giessen: Töpelmann, 1926. **Lauha, A.** *Kohelet.* BKAT 19. Neukirchen-Vluyn: Neukirchener, 1978. **Levy, L.** *Das Buch Qoheleth.* Leipzig: Hinrich's, 1912. **Loader, J. A.** *Ecclesiastes: A Practical Commentary.* TI. Grand Rapids: Eerdmans, 1986. **Lohfink, N.** *Kohelet.* DNEB. Würzburg: Echter, 1980. **Luther, M.** "Notes on Ecclesiastes." In *Luther's Works.* Ed. J. Pelikan. St. Louis: Concordia, 1972. 15:3–187. **Lys, D.** *L'Ecclésiaste ou Que vaut la vie?* Paris: Letouzey et Ané, 1977. **Maillot, A.** *La Contestation: Commentaire de l'Ecclésiaste.* Lyon: Cahiers de Reveil, 1971. **McNeile, A. H.** *An Introduction to Ecclesiastes.* Cambridge: UP, 1904. **Neher, A.** *Notes sur Qohélét (L'Ecclésiaste).* Paris: Minuit, 1951. **Nötscher, F.** *Kohelet.* Echter-Bibel 4. Würzburg: Echter Verlag, 1954. **Nowack, W.,** and **Hitzig, F.** *Der Prediger Salomo's.* KeH 7. 2nd ed. Leipzig: Hirzel, 1883. **Odeberg, H.** *Qohaelaeth.* Uppsala: Almquist & Wiksells, 1929. **Ogden, G.** *Qoheleth.* Sheffield: JSOT Press, 1987. **Ploeg, J. van der.** *Prediker.* BOT 8. Roermond: Romen & Zonen, 1952. **Plumptre, E. H.** *Ecclesiastes.* CBSC. Cambridge: UP, 1881. **Podechard, E.** *L'Ecclésiaste.* EBib. Paris: Gabalda, 1912. **Rankin, O. S.** "Ecclesiastes." In *The Interpreter's Bible.* Nashville: Abingdon, 1956. 5:3–88. **Rashbam.** *The Commentary of R. Samuel Ben Meir Rashbam on*

Qoheleth. Ed. S. Japhet and R. Salters. Jerusalem-Leiden: Magnes/Brill, 1985. **Ravasi, G.** *Qohelet.* Milano: Edizioni Paoline, 1988. **Ryder, E. T.** "Ecclesiastes." In *Peake's Commentary on the Bible.* Ed. M. Black and H. H. Rowley. New York: Nelson, 1962. 458–67. **Sacchi, P.** *Ecclesiaste.* Rome: Edizioni Paoline, 1976. **Scott, R. B. Y.** *Proverbs. Ecclesiastes.* AB 18. Garden City: Doubleday, 1965. **Siegfried, C. G.** *Prediger und Hoheslied.* HKAT 2:3,2. Göttingen: Vandenhoeck & Ruprecht, 1898. **Strobel, A.** *Das Buch Prediger (Kohelet).* Die Welt der Bibel. Düsseldorf: Patmos, 1967. **Volz, P.** "Betrachtungen des Kohelet." In *Weisheit.* SAT 3/2. Göttingen: Vandenhoeck & Ruprecht, 1911. 230–58. **Whybray, R. N.** *Ecclesiastes.* NCBC. Grand Rapids: Eerdmans, 1989. **Wildeboer, G.** "Der Prediger." In *Die fünf Megillot.* KHC 17. Freiburg i. Br., 1898. 109–68. **William, A. L.** *Ecclesiastes.* CBSC. Cambridge: UP, 1922. **Wright, A. G.** "Ecclesiastes (Qoheleth)." *NJBC.* 490–95. **Wright, C. H. H.** *The Book of Koheleth.* London: Hodder & Stoughton, 1883. **Zapletal, V.** *Das Buch Koheleth.* CF, n.f. 7. Freiburg: O. Gschwend, 1905. **Zimmerli, W.** *Das Buch des Predigers Salomo.* ATD 16/1. Göttingen: Vandenhoeck & Ruprecht, 1962. 123–253.

GENERAL STUDIES

Barucq, A. "Qohéleth (ou livre de l'Ecclésiaste)." *DBSup* 10. 610–74. **Bickerman, E.** *Four Strange Books of the Bible.* New York: Schocken, 1967. **Braun, R.** *Kohelet und die frühhellenistische Popularphilosophie.* BZAW 130. Berlin: de Gruyter, 1973. **Childs, B. S.** *Introduction to the Old Testament as Scripture.* Philadelphia: Fortress, 1979. **Duesberg, H.** and **Fransen, I.** "La critique de la sagesse par le Qoheleth." In *Les scribes inspirés.* Maredsous: Editions de Maredsous, 1969. 537–92. **Ellermeier, F.** *Qohelet I/1: Untersuchungen zum Buche Qohelet.* Herzberg: Jungfer, 1967. **Ellul, J.** *Reason for Being: A Meditation on Ecclesiastes.* Grand Rapids: Eerdmans, 1990. **Fox, M. V.** *Qohelet and His Contradictions.* BLS 18. Sheffield: Almond, 1989. **Gammie, J.**, and **Perdue, L.** *The Sage in Israel and the Ancient Near East.* Winona Lake, IN: Eisenbrauns, 1990. **Gilbert, M.**, ed. *La Sagesse de l'Ancien Testament.* BETL 51. Leuven: UP, 1979. **Harrison, C. R.** *Qoheleth in Social-historical Perspective.* Ann Arbor: UMI, 1991. **Loader, J. A.** *Polar Structures in the Book of Qohelet.* BZAW 152. Berlin: de Gruyter, 1979. **Loretz, O.** *Qohelet und der Alte Orient: Untersuchungen zu Stil und theologischer Thematik des Buches Qohelet.* Freiburg: Herder, 1964. **Michel, D.** *Qohelet.* EF 258. Darmstadt: Wissenschaftliche Buchgesellschaft, 1988. ————. *Untersuchungen zur Eigenart des Buches Qohelet* (mit einem Anhang von R. G. Lehmann, Bibliographie zu Qohelet). BZAW 183. Berlin: de Gruyter, 1989. **Murphy, R. E.** *Wisdom Literature.* FOTL 13. Grand Rapids: Eerdmans, 1981. ————. *The Tree of Life: An Exploration of Biblical Wisdom Literature.* ABRL. New York: Doubleday, 1990. **Pedersen, J.** *Scepticisme Israélite.* Cahiers de *RHPR.* Paris: Alcan, 1931. **Preuss, H. D.** *Einführung in die alttestamentliche Weisheitsliteratur.* Urban-Taschenbücher 383. Stuttgart: Kohlhammer, 1987. **Rad, G. von.** *Wisdom in Israel.* Nashville: Abingdon, 1972. **Renan, E.** *L'Ecclésiaste.* Paris: Levy, 1890. **Schmid, H. H.** *Wesen und Geschichte der Weisheit.* BZAW 101. Berlin: Töpelmann, 1966. **Sheppard, G.** *Wisdom as a Hermeneutical Construct.* BZAW 151. Berlin: de Gruyter, 1979. **Trible, P.** "Ecclesiastes." In *The Books of the Bible: The Old Testament.* Ed. B. W. Anderson. New York: Scribner's, 1989. 1:231–39. **Vogels, W.** "Performance vaine et performance saine chez Qohélet." *NRT* 113 (1991) 363–85. **Whitley, C. F.** *Koheleth: His Language and Thought.* BZAW 148. Berlin: de Gruyter, 1979. **Whybray, R. N.** *Ecclesiastes.* OTG. Sheffield: JSOT Press, 1989. **Wright, A. G.** "The Riddle of the Sphinx: The Structure of the Book of Qohelet." *CBQ* 30 (1968) 313–34 (= *SAIW,* 245–66). ————. "The Riddle of the Sphinx Revisited: Numerical Patterns in the Book of Qoheleth." *CBQ* 42 (1980) 38–51.

Introduction

Introductory Questions

Bibliography

Every commentary (e.g., R. Gordis, A. H. McNeile, E. Podechard, C. H. Wright) devotes some attention to the introductory questions of date, canon, text, and versions. The following studies should also be noted:

Author, Date, and Canonicity:

Audet, J. -P. "A Hebrew-Aramaic List of Books of the Old Testament in Greek Transcription." *JTS* 1 (1950) 135–54. **Crüsemann, F.** "The Unchangeable World: The 'Crisis of Wisdom' in Koheleth." In *God of the Lowly.* Ed. W. Schotroff and W. Stegemann. Maryknoll: Orbis, 1985. 57–77. **Dahood, M.** "The Phoenician Background of Qoheleth." *Bib* 47 (1966) 264–82. **Gordis, R.** "The Social Background of Wisdom Literature." *HUCA* 18 (1943/44) 77–118. **Hertzberg, H. W.** Palästinische Bezüge im Buche Kohelet." *ZDPV* 73 (1957) 113–24. **Humbert, P.** *Recherches sur les sources égyptiennes de la littérature sapientiale.* Neuchâtel: Delachaux & Niestlé, 1929. **Kaiser, O.** "Judentum und Hellenismus." *VF* 27 (1982) 68–88. **Lohfink, N.** "*melek, šallît* und *mōšēl* bei Kohelet und die Abfassungszeit des Buchs." *Bib* 62 (1981) 535–43. **Loretz, O.** "Zur Darbietungsform der 'Ich-Erzählung' im Buche Qoheleth." *CBQ* 25 (1963) 46–59. **Michel, D.** *Untersuchungen zur Eigenhart des Buches Qohelet.* BZAW 183. Berlin: de Gruyter, 1989. 1–4, 112–26. **Reif, S. C.** "A Reply to Dr. C. F. Whitley." *VT* 32 (1982) 346–48. **Salters, R.** "Qohelet and the Canon." *ExpTim* 66 (1974/75) 339–42. **Schunck, K.** "Drei Seleukiden im Buche Kohelet?" *VT* 9 (1959) 192–201. **Strothmann, W.** *Erkenntnisse und Meinungen.* Ed. G. Wiessner. Wiesbaden: Harrassowitz, 1973. 189–238. **Whybray, R. N.** *The Intellectual Tradition of the Old Testament.* BZAW 135. Berlin: de Gruyter, 1974. ———. *Ecclesiastes.* OTG. Sheffield: JSOT Press, 1989.

Text and Versions:

Barthélemy, D. *Les devanciers d'Aquila.* VTSup 10. Leiden: Brill, 1963. **Bertram, G.** "Hebräischer und griechischer Qohelet." *ZAW* 64 (1952) 26–49. **Holm-Nielsen, S.** "On the Interpretation of Qoheleth in Early Christianity." *VT* 24 (1974) 168–77. **Hyvärinen, K.** *Die Übersetzung von Aquila.* ConBOT 10. Lund: Gleerup, 1977. **Kamenetzky, A.** "Die Pšita zu Koheleth textkritisch und in ihrem Verhältnis zu dem masoretischen Text, der Septuaginta und den andern alten griechischen Versionen." *ZAW* 24 (1904) 181–239. **Lane, D. J.** "Ecclesiastes." In *The Old Testament in Syriac II,5.* Leiden: Brill, 1979. **Muilenburg, J.** "A Qoheleth Scroll from Qumran." *BASOR* 135 (1954) 20–28. **Murphy, R. E.** "On Translating Ecclesiastes." *CBQ* 53 (1991) 571–79. **Schoors, A.** "Kethib-Qere in Ecclesiastes." In *Studia Paulo Naster Oblata.* OLA 13. Leuven: Peeters, 1982. 215–22. ———. The Peshitta of Koheleth and Its Relation to the Septuagint." In *After Chalcedon: Studies in Theology and Church History.* FS A. van Roey. OLA 18. Leuven: Peeters, 1985. 345–57.

AUTHOR, DATE, AND CANONICITY

In both Jewish and Christian traditions, the work is known by the epithet of its putative author, Hebrew "Qoheleth," whose Septuagintal rendering yielded the familiar name "Ecclesiastes." All that can be said about the person so designated must be inferred, somewhat precariously, from the book itself. In the editorial postscript we are informed that Qoheleth was a חכם (ḥākām, "sage"), who occupied himself diligently with the study of proverbial materials (משלים, mĕšālîm) and taught "knowledge" (דעת) to the people (12:9). We are ignorant, though, of any specific circumstances of his academic work and teaching. The first-person style in which he wrote is not to be confused with modern "autobiographical" narrative, as though one could derive from it personal data concerning the life or psychological history of the author (see O. Loretz, CBQ 25 [1963] 46–59). He is not to be thought of as "melancholic," in the fashion of Soren Kierkegaard, Friedrich Nietzsche, or Franz Kafka.

The editorial superscription to the book in 1:1 entitles the book "the words of Qoheleth" and further describes the author as "the son of David, king in Jerusalem." The author introduces his own work in 1:12, describing himself somewhat more cryptically as "king over Israel in Jerusalem." The peculiar epithet קהלת (qōhelet) and the identification with "David's son" call for further comment.

The precise meaning of קהלת has eluded scholarly research. The word is construed semantically as masculine, but it is the qal feminine singular active participle of the root קהל. Verbal usage is well attested for both the nipal, in the sense "gather together, congregate," and the hipil, meaning "convoke an assembly"; but apart from the form קהלת, the qal is unattested. The definite article appears with the term in two of its seven occurrences (7:27, emended text, and 12:8), which would suggest that it is a professional title or designation of office rather than a proper name. The broadest meaning of the term indicates one who has something to do with a קהל, "assembly, or congregation." Hence various interpretations have been proposed, such as "collector (of sayings)," "convoker (of an assembly)," "speaker (to an assembly)." The last suggestion underlies the common English rendering "Preacher," which goes back to Luther's Prediger and Jerome's concionator. But this rendering is over-specific; קהל does not mean "preach." Perhaps the best explanation recognizes that the feminine participle indicates an office associated with an assembly and that this term is used secondarily as a proper name. Analogies can be found in the ancestral names Hassophereth (one who prepares leather) and Pochereth-hazzebaim (one who tends gazelles) in Ezra 2:55–57. Such proper names were apparently derived from specific offices and professional titles.

"David's son" in the superscription (1:1) is the basis for the long-standing tradition of the book's Solomonic authorship. This identification is more specific than the statement in 1:12, in which the author tells us merely that he "was king of Israel in Jerusalem." The claim in both forms seems to stem primarily from the Solomonic aura of chap. 2 where Qoheleth describes his experiment with riches. The real question is: why did he adopt the identity of a king? Since wisdom is usually associated with royalty, and Solomon had a great reputation for wisdom (1 Kgs 5:9–12[4:29–34]), the adoption of the king fiction is intelligible (as in the case of the Greek Wisdom of Solomon). However, the king fiction is not the self-understanding of Ecclesiastes throughout the book. His attitude to kingship is distant, if not critical, as in the observations about injustice in 3:16; 4:1–2; and 5:7. The comments about royalty in 8:2–4 and 10:4–7, 16–17, 20 stem from one who appears to know more about how to deal with a king than how to rule.

Indeed, these passages lend some credibility to the claim that he is talking about situations in a foreign court, and hence about the post-exilic period. In short, both the tenor of the book and the language in which it is written render impossible the identification with Solomon or any Hebrew. The author of the epilogue was right: Qoheleth was a sage (חכם, 12:9).

But even this designation does not tell us very much. What did a sage do and when did he do it? Are the sages a monolithic class through the history of the OT? R. N. Whybray (*The Intellectual Tradition of the Old Testament*, BZAW 135 [Berlin: de Gruyter, 1974]; see also M. Fox, *Qohelet*, 330–32) has even questioned the existence of a class of sages, disputing the common interpretation of Jer 8:8–9 and 18:18 that seem to consider them a class. The sociological background to the wisdom literature, and hence to the sages, has always been difficult to describe, but this has not daunted scholars who are prone to build theories out of unproven assumptions. The most successful theory has been that of R. Gordis (*HUCA* 18 [1943–44] 77–118), who proposed that the sages belonged to the upper class. The alleged connection between the royal court and court schools (cf. the "men of Hezekiah" in Prov 25:1) helped to make this a popular view. But there is little hard evidence for such a generalization. Formal education is not a prerequisite for wisdom. One need only recall the famous observation of Ptah-hotep, the Egyptian sage: "Good speech is more hidden than the emerald, but it may be found with maidservants at the grindstones" (*ANET*, 412). Moreover, the wisdom literature spans a long period (some ten centuries), during which various sociological conditions obtained.

The arguments for the sociological background of Qoheleth are adduced largely from silence. Thus Gordis writes: "As a Wisdom teacher Koheleth was closely identified with the upper-class groups of Jewish society by vocation. It is, of course, possible that he was of lowly origin, and had won his place among the successful groups by his superior abilities, but we should then have expected, in one as sensitive as Koheleth, a greater degree of reaction to social injustice and oppression than we find in this book. It therefore seems most probable that Koheleth belonged to the upper classes by birth and position, for we find no indications that he ever suffered poverty and want. Apparently he enjoyed the benefits of travel and other opportunities that were denied to the poor" (Gordis, *Koheleth—The Man and His World*, 77). The only reply to such a hypothetical reconstruction is to test it against the text of Ecclesiastes. An extreme position has been proposed by F. Crüsemann ("The Unchangeable World: The 'Crisis of Wisdom' in Koheleth," 57–77). He regards Qoheleth as an aristocrat: "We should not dissociate the increasing alienation of the aristocracy and its interest from those of almost all the rest of the people (as manifested, for example, in the absorption of the aristocracy into the system of state monopoly, which makes them agents of foreign overlords) from the ideological alienation represented by Koheleth" (65). One must ask for more evidence than is provided to support this kind of reconstruction.

Scholarly opinion has attempted to determine the place where Ecclesiastes was written. Again, this has to be a matter of inference from the text. Thus P. Humbert (*Recherches sur les sources égyptiennes de la littérature sapientiale*, 113) analyzed the natural phenomena described in 1:5–7 and concluded that they pointed to Egypt as the locale of the author. For example, the idea of the sun going back to its place of origin (1:5) is an Egyptian concept. Hertzberg (42–43; cf. also *ZDPV* 73 [1957] 113–24) rightly responded that even if this is correct, it says nothing about where the book was composed. He went on to argue that the writing took place in Palestine, and probably in Jerusalem. His arguments are respectable. Reservoirs (Eccl 2:6), leaky roofs (10:18), wells (12:6), the farmer's attention to the wind (11:4)—all these are matters easily understood in Palestine. Moreover, the Temple seems to be referred to in 4:17 and 8:10. But when these and other arguments are assessed, one is left with the wisdom of Hertzberg's own reply to Humbert: they do not really prove where the book was written. Nor can one conclude with M. Dahood ("Canaanite-Phoenician Influence in Qoheleth," *Bib* 33 [1952] 30–52, esp. 34) that the nature of the language leads to the conclusion that Qoheleth lived in northern Palestine, "a resident of a Phoenician city." All in all, Palestine seems more reasonable than Egypt, but there is no compelling evidence either way.

Neither can a certain date be assigned to the book of Ecclesiastes. There is general consensus among critical scholars that the language and thought of the book point to the post-exilic period (R. N. Whybray, *Ecclesiastes*, 15–22). A *terminus ante quem* in the mid-second century B.C. is provided by textual fragments of the book found in Cave IV at Qumran (Muilenburg, *BASOR* 135 [1954] 20–28). If one were to allow with Hertzberg (45–49) and many others that Ben Sira (writing about 180 B.C.) made use of Ecclesiastes, that date can be pushed back further to about 200. The absence of any reference relative to the Maccabean troubles would be another sign that 200 is a suitable date for the *terminus ante quem.*

Arguments in favor of the Persian or the Greek period compete with each other, and current scholarship is inclined to favor the Hellenistic era, around 250 B.C. (D. Michel, *Qohelet*, 114). But there are no compelling reasons. Efforts have been made on the basis of certain passages (e.g., 4:13–16; cf. also 8:2–4; 9:13–15; 10:16–17) to discover references to the contemporary scene (K. Schunck, *VT* 9 [1959] 192–201). But these are rather typical happenings, not contemporary events that are described. The text is simply too vague to support historical reference. At the most, one may grant that there is a Hellenistic coloring to the types of courtly characters mentioned in the book. N. Lohfink (*Bib* 62 [1981] 535–43) points out that Qoheleth uses different vocabulary for those in power—for a king (in Alexandria), and for Hellenistic kings in general—and takes this as a sign that one should distinguish the royal court from other courts that offered career possibilities to members of the Jewish upper-middle class. Of course, if one grants the thesis that there is definite Hellenistic influence upon the book, a date in the middle of the third century would be appropriate.

C. F. Whitley (*Koheleth*, 119–48) has assigned the composition of Ecclesiastes to a date between 152 and 145 on the basis of historical and linguistic arguments. However, these are very fragile. If the dependence of Sirach upon Ecclesiastes is difficult to prove, the other way round is out of the question. The linguistic evidence adduced by Whitley has been refuted by S. Reif (*VT* 31 [1981] 120–26) and O. Kaiser (*VF* 27 [1982] 68–88, esp. 74–78). There is no way of showing that the language of Qoheleth "seems to be later" than that of Daniel, or that Ecclesiastes was composed "in a period when the Mishnaic tongue was beginning to be widely used," or that Mishnaic Hebrew "must have been used extensively as a literary medium" by the year 140 B.C. (see Whitley, *Koheleth*, 136, 141, 144).

Ecclesiastes was included in the five "scrolls" (*mĕgillôt*), which were placed together in the *kĕtûbîm* ("writings") as early as the fifth century A.D. In most MSS it is the fourth of five scrolls, to be read on the fourth liturgical feast, Tabernacles. Scholars have inferred that the identification of Qoheleth with Solomon was the reason for the canonization, but we are in total ignorance of the nature of the canonical process. One may not infer from the supposed use of Ecclesiastes by Ben Sira that it was recognized as canonical in the second century B.C. Neither do fragments found at Qumran, dated about 150 B.C., indicate that it had canonical standing among the Essenes (see R. E. Brown, *NJBC*, 66:36–37, pp. 1040–41).

It can be said that the book was already considered canonical when controversy arose concerning it in the time of Rabbi ʿAqiba (d. *circa* A.D. 135). Then it was affirmed that Ecclesiastes, as well as the Song of Songs, did "pollute the hands," i.e., that it is canonical, despite the questions that had been raised. The opinion of the school of Hillel prevailed over that of the school of Shammai: "All the holy writings render unclean the hands. The Song of Songs and Ecclesiastes render unclean the hands. R. Judah says, The Song of Songs renders unclean the hands, but there is a dispute about Ecclesiastes. R. Jose says: Ecclesiastes does not render unclean the hands, but there is a dispute about the Song of Songs. R. Simeon says: (the ruling about) Ecclesiastes is one of the leniencies of Beth Shammai and one of the stringencies of Beth Hillel. R. Simeon B. ʿAzzai said: I received a tradition from the seventy-two elders on the day when they appointed R. Eleazar B. ʿAzariah head of the academy that the Song of Songs and Ecclesiastes render unclean the hands. R. ʿAkiba said: Far be it! No one in Israel disputed about the Song of Songs (by saying) that it does not render unclean the hands. For the whole world is not as worthy as the day on which the Song of Songs was given to Israel; for all the writings are holy but the Song of Songs is the holy of holies so that if they had a dispute, they had a dispute only about Ecclesiastes. R. Johanan B. Joshua the son of the father-in-law of R. ʿAkiba said: In accordance with the words of Ben ʿAzzai, so they disputed, and so they reached a decision" (*Yadayim* 3.5; cf. *The Babylonian Talmud Seder Tohoroth*, ed. I. Epstein [London: Soncino, 1948] 558–59).

The book of Ecclesiastes is mentioned in the earliest canonical lists among the Christian community, such as that of Melito of Sardis (d. about 190). His enumeration is Proverbs, Ecclesiastes, Canticle, the same sequence that is found in another second-century list (J.-P. Audet, *JTS* 1 [1950] 135–54). The opposition of Theodore of Mopsuestia is doubtful, although it is often alleged as fact. According to W. Strothmann, "for Theodore, Ecclesiastes is unquestionably a book of the Old Testament canon. Through his commentary the Bishop of Mopsuestia influenced the exegesis of Qoheleth for centuries in both the Syriac Churches" (W. Strothmann, *Erkenntnisse und Meinungen*, 225–27). The *notarii* of the Emperor at the fourth session of the fifth ecumenical council of Constantinople are responsible for the contrary interpretation by their bowdlerization of a portion of Theodore's introduction, and by the addition of the phrase "he of his own person" (*ipse ex sua persona*, an indication that Solomon spoke of his own accord and not through divine inspiration). Strothmann points out that the commentary of Theodore omits no sections of the book, avoids allegorism, and investigates the literal meaning.

TEXT AND VERSIONS

The Hebrew text of Ecclesiastes seems to have been transmitted rather faithfully. The text can be traced back through Jerome and the Vulgate, through the fragments from Qumran, and through the Greek tradition. The differences between the traditional Hebrew and these ancient versional witnesses arise in many instances from the peculiar nature of the language and the complexity of thought rather than from serious differences in the *Vorlage.*

The fragments of Qoheleth from Qumran (Muilenburg, *BASOR* 135 [1954] 20–28) do not contribute notably to a knowledge of the textual form of the book. They are characterized, as might be expected, by a freer use of *scriptio plena.* But the textual variants are not compelling, e.g., ואם לוא in 6:6 for MT ואלו; שׂ[מחה in 7:2 for MT משׂחה. The most interesting variant is תעזר, found in fourteen Kennicott MSS and reflected in LXX βοηθήσει, in 7:19, where MT has תעזר.

From a study of qere-ketib readings A. Schoors (*Studia Paulo Naster Oblata*, 215–22) concluded that the qere is the preferable reading except for Eccl 5:10 and probably 10:20. But only in 9:4 (יחבר for יבחר) and 12:6 (ירתק for ירחק) is the meaning affected. In the present translation and commentary relatively few changes in the Hebrew text have been adopted, and these have been indicated in the translation by the use of brackets. But the real difficulties in Ecclesiastes lie elsewhere. Even when one can "justify" a given translation of the Hebrew text, it must be frankly admitted that the translation is simply uncertain (R. E. Murphy, *CBQ* 53 [1991] 571–79). The text of Ecclesiastes puts severe strain on the rules of classical Hebrew. The uncertainty of a translation need not derive from a corrupt text, but from ignorance or the inherent obscurity with which Qoheleth has expressed his thought. One can give many examples: 2:3 (למשׁוך); 2:15 (אז יותר); 2:25; 3:15 (נרדף); 3:17 (שׁם); see also 4:15–17; 5:6, 8, 17; 6:8, 10; 8:10, 12; 9:1–2; 9:4; 10:1, 10; 12:3–6; 12:13.

The Greek translation of Ecclesiastes, as found in the traditional Septuagint, has been the occasion of much discussion. This version was marked by the same literalness that characterized what was known of the hexaplaric fragments attributed to Aquila. While the version of Aquila (about A.D. 130, a disciple of Rabbi ʿAqiba) could not be simply identified with the Septuagint, there was talk of "editions" of Aquila, one of which was the traditional Septuagint form. Such was the view expressed by A. H. McNeile (115–68) and by G. A. Barton (8–13). The implication was that the Greek Septuagint version of the book dates from the end of the first century A.D. However, no firm decision derived from the discussions that took place decades ago (see E. Podechard, 201–7).

The current state of the question has been affected by the studies of D. Barthélemy of the so-called *kaige* recension of the Bible (*Les devanciers d'Aquila*). A test case for the identification of Aquila's translation has been his well-known treatment of את, the sign of the accusative in Hebrew. Aquila rendered this untranslatable Hebrew particle as σύν, "with," followed by the accusative, although this is contrary to Greek usage. Barthélemy has analyzed the translation of the traditional "Septuagint" rendering of Ecclesiastes in the light of this mechanical correspondence and other signs. He concluded (30) that Aquila's hand was at work: "It is the translation of Aquila that has represented the book of Ecclesiastes in the Septuagint of the Greek church—and this before the time of Origen who was probably not aware of the fact. He then put it in the Septuagint column of the hexapla.

But he had no Aquila version to put in the third column which was its usual place, so he put in another version. Those who used the hexapla, accustomed to find Aquila in the third column, took this version as being by Aquila." It appears that the supposed version of Aquila (in the third column of Origen's hexapla) betrays characteristics associated with the version attributed to Symmachus. For example, הבל (*hebel*, "vanity") is rendered ματαιότης in the "Septuagint," and this correspondence is typical of what has been preserved of Aquila in other parts of the Bible. The rendering ἀτμός or ἀτμίς, "breath," regularly corresponds to הבל in the translation of Symmachus.

According to Barthélemy, Qoheleth would have been the last of the *mĕgillôt*, or scrolls, to be translated. This is suggested by the well-known debate about its canonicity, and also by the fact that in the diaspora the book of Baruch was apparently read on the Feast of Tabernacles. Although Baruch was not "canonical" for the Palestinians, they had to settle the dispute about the canonicity of Qoheleth before any change could be made in the choice of reading for the feast (*Les devanciers d'Aquila*, 159–60).

However, another study has disputed Barthélemy's conclusions about Greek Ecclesiastes. K. Hyvärinen points to some translation examples that do not fit the theory. His view is that the "old Septuagint" was a few decades before Aquila's version: "The LXX version of Ecclesiastes, from the point of view of the history of the text, is one of the recensions inspired by the rabbis, which also shows the remarkable translation of the *nota accusativi*, without its being therefore to be considered a version by Aquila. It was done under the leadership of R. Akiba, possibly translated in the 70s, and later perhaps revised by Aquila" (K. Hyvärinen, *Die Übersetzung von Aquila*, 99).

The uncertainty about the identity and origins of the "Greek" translation of Ecclesiastes contributes to a murky assessment of the nature of this translation. G. Bertram claimed that the Greek translation gives "witness to an orthodox interpretation that overcomes, in the light of Old Testament religious belief, the inclination of Qoheleth to a pessimistic world view, and hence it made possible the theological acknowledgment of the work" (*ZAW* 64 [1952] 26–49, esp. p. 28). He proposed ten features of the Greek in favor of his thesis. Not all of these are satisfactory. Thus, the rendering of נפש by ψυχή, or "soul," is a mechanical correspondence in the Greek Bible without real theological significance; it remains a problem for the modern translator as can be seen in renditions of Ps 104:1. It is true that the rendering of הבל by ματαιότης does not bring out the evanescent quality of human existence. But neither does it necessarily point in the direction of sinful human nature, as Bertram claims. A more challenging example (Bertram, *ZAW* 64 [1952] 47–48) of a change of meaning is the προαίρεσις πνεύματος ("purpose" or "choosing" of spirit?) for the frequent רעות רוח (e.g., Eccl 1:14). It is not easy to say just what the translator had in mind, but it might well be an honest effort that is inept rather than tendentious. When the general trend of the Greek translation is examined, it is difficult to establish the spiritualizing and moral tendency recognized by Bertram and by S. Holm-Nielsen (*VT* 24 [1974] 170–71). There are too many of the provocative passages of Qoheleth (e.g., 3:18–21; 7:13–14; 9:1–3) that remain untampered with in the Greek translation, thus belying the claim of tendentious translator(s). The theological standpoint of the Greek translation remains yet to be worked out.

The Peshitta text of the OT is the standard Syriac translation from the Hebrew, comparable to the Latin Vulgate in the Western world. However, it is the work of several translators from various historical periods, certainly before A.D. 400. It betrays in part the influence of the Septuagint, and it is debated whether the work was achieved under Jewish or Christian auspices. A critical edition of the text of Ecclesiastes has been published by D. J. Lane *(The Old Testament in Syriac, 2:5)*. For a comparison of the Syriac readings with the Hebrew and Septuagint, one can have recourse to the tables in Gordis (140–43). He seems to be in agreement with the earlier study of A. Kamenetzky *(ZAW* 24 [1904] 181–239) that the Syriac derives from the Hebrew text despite showing influence from the Greek tradition.

Jerome made two Latin translations. The one contained in his commentary (about 389), originally destined for Blesilla, is somewhat eclectic. Although he translated from the Hebrew, he explicitly states (1:249) that he adapted it to the Septuagint in instances that were not much different from the Hebrew, and that he also took into account the other Greek translations. Commenting on 4:13–16 he mentions that a certain Jew read Ecclesiastes with him. The translation in the Vulgate (around 398) is, along with Proverbs and Canticle ["the books of Solomon"], a work of three days *(PL* 28:1305). This text is also found, allowing for a few variants, in the so-called *bibliotheca divina (PL* 28:1339–52). Jerome may also have composed an emended Latin version of the Hexaplaric Greek text of Ecclesiastes, but it has not been preserved (J. N. D. Kelly, *Jerome* [New York: Harper & Row, 1975] 158–59).

The Targum, or Aramaic paraphrase of the Hebrew Bible, is often important for textual criticism. However, the Targum of Ecclesiastes is so periphrastic as to make it "virtually an Aramaic midrash" (Gordis, 138), and hence of little value for the textual criticism of this book. Similarly, the Coptic and other ancient translations have little bearing on correction of the received Hebrew text.

Language, Style, and Form

Bibliography

A list of *hapax legomena* and of late words is found in the commentaries of F. Delitzsch (190–96) and C. H. H. Wright (488–500). A grammatical analysis of forms and syntax, followed by basic stylistic observations, is given in the commentary by C. G. Siegfried (13–23). Vocabulary, literary characteristics, and wisdom topoi are discussed by O. Loretz *(Qohelet,* 135–217). Vocabulary and idiomatic peculiarities are studied by C. F. Whitley *(Koheleth,* 4–105). See also the studies of Fredericks, Isaksson, Delsman, and du Plessis noted below. A form-critical analysis of the entire book is provided in R. Braun, *Kohelet,* 153–59; F. Ellermeier, *Qohelet I/1,* 48–93; R. E. Murphy, "Ecclesiastes (Qohelet)," in *Wisdom Literature,* FOTL 13 [Grand Rapids: Eerdmans, 1981]. See also R. F. Johnson, "A Form-Critical Analysis of the Sayings in the Book of Ecclesiastes" (Diss., Emory University, 1973); J. Loader, *Polar Structures in the Book of Qohelet,* BZAW 183 [Berlin: de Gruyter, 1979] 18–28; 115–16.

Ackroyd, P. "Two Hebrew Notes." *ASTI* 5 (1967) 82–86. **Archer, G. L.** "The Linguistic Evidence for the Date of 'Ecclesiastes,'" *JETS* 12 (1969) 167–81. **Ausejo, S. de.** "El género literario del Ecclesiastés." *EstBib* 7 (1948) 394–406. **Ceresko, A. R.** "The Function of Antanaclasis (*ms²* 'to find'//*ms²* 'to reach, overtake, grasp') in Hebrew Poetry, Especially in the Book of Qoheleth." *CBQ* 44 (1982) 551–69. **Dahood, M. J.** "Canaanite-Phoenician Influence in Qoheleth." *Bib* 33 (1952) 30–52, 191–221. ———. "Qoheleth and Recent Discoveries." *Bib* 39 (1958) 302–18. ———. "Qoheleth and Northwest Semitic Philology." *Bib* 43 (1962) 349–65. ———. "The Phoenician Background of Qoheleth." *Bib* 47 (1966) 264–82. ———. "Hebrew-Ugaritic Lexicography." *Bib* 49 (1968) 335–65. ———. "Three Parallel Pairs in Ecclesiastes 10,18." *JQR* 62 (1971/72) 84–87. ———. "Ugaritic-Hebrew Parallel Pairs." In *Ras Shamra Parallels: The Texts from Ugarit and the Hebrew Bible 1.* Ed. L. Fisher. AnOr 49. Rome: Pontifical Biblical Institute, 1972. 71–382. **Davila, J. R.** "Qoheleth and Northern Hebrew." *Maarav* 5–6 (1990) 69–87. **Delsman, W. C.** "Zur Sprache des Buches Koheleth." In *Von Kanaan.* AOAT 211. 349–65. **Driver, G. R.** "Problems and Solutions." *VT* 4 (1954) 225–45, esp. 225–35. **Fredericks, D. C.** *Qoheleth's Language: Re-evaluating Its Nature and Date.* ANETS 3. Lewiston, NY: Mellen Press, 1988. **Ginsberg, H. L.** *Studies in Koheleth.* New York: Jewish Theological Seminary, 1950. ———. "Koheleth 12,4 in the Light of Ugaritic." *Syria* 33 (1956) 100. **Gordis, R.** "The Original Language of Qoheleth." *JQR* 37 (1946/47) 67–84. ———. "Was Koheleth a Phoenician? Some Observations on Methods in Research." *JBL* 74 (1955) 103–14. ———. "The Translation Theory of Qohelet Re-examined." *JQR* 40 (1949/50) 103–16. ———. "Koheleth—Hebrew or Aramaic?" *JBL* 71 (1952) 93–109. ———. Qoheleth and Qumran: A Study of Style." *Bib* 41 (1960) 395–410. **Isaksson, B.** *Studies in the Language of Qoheleth.* AUU.SSU 10. Uppsala: Almquist & Wiksell, 1987. **Joüon, P.** "Notes de syntaxe hébraique: 2. L'emploi du participe du parfait dans l'Ecclésiaste." *Bib* 2 (1921) 225–26. ———. "Notes philologiques sur le texte hébreu d'Ecclésiaste." *Bib* 11 (1930) 419–25. **Klostermann, E.** *De Libri Coheleth Versione Alexandrina.* Kiel: Schmidt & Klaunig, 1892. **Loretz, O.** *Qohelet und der Alte Orient.* Freiburg: Herder, 1964. 145–217. ———. "Altorientalische und Kanaanäische Topoi im Buche Kohelet." *UF* 12 (1980) 267–78. **Michel, D.** *Qohelet.* 46–51; 76–81. **Ogden, G. S.** "The 'Better'-Proverb (*Tob-Spruch*), Rhetorical Criticism, and Qoheleth." *JBL* 96 (1977) 489–505. ———. "Qoheleth's Use of the 'Nothing is Better'-Form." *JBL* 98 (1979) 339–50. **Piotti, F.** "La lingua dell'Ecclesiaste e lo sviluppo storico dell'ebraico." *BeO* 15 (1973) 185–95. ———. "Osservazioni su alcuni usi linguistici dell'Ecclesiaste." *BeO* 19 (1977) 49–56. **Plessis, S. du.** "Aspects of Morphological Peculiarities of the Language of Qoheleth." In *De Fructu Oris Sui.* FS A. van Selms. Leiden: Brill, 1971. 164–80. **Savignac, J. de.** "La sagesse de Qoheleth et l'épopée de Gilgamesh." *VT* 28 (1978) 318–23. **Schoors, A.** *The Preacher Sought to Find Pleasing Words: A Study of the Language of Qoheleth.* OLA 41. Leuven: Peeters, 1992. **Shaffer, A.** "The Mesopotamian Background of Qohelet 4:9–12." *EI* 8 (1967) 246–50. ———. "New Light on the 'Three-Ply Cord.'" *EI* 9 (1969) 138–39, 159–160. **Wagner, M.** *Die lexikalischen und grammatikalischen Aramaismen im alttestamentlichen Hebräisch.* BZAW 96. Berlin: Töpelmann, 1966. **Whitley, C. F.** "Koheleth and Ugaritic parallels." *UF* 11 (1979) 611–24. **Whybray, R. N.** "The Identification and Use of Quotations in Ecclesiastes." In *Congress Volume, Vienna, 1980.* Ed. J. Emerton. VTSup 32. Leiden: Brill, 1981. 435–51. **Wise, M. O.** "A Calque from Aramaic in Qoheleth 6:12; 7:12; and 8:13." *JBL* 109 (1990) 249–57. **Zimmermann, F.** "The Aramaic Provenance of Qoheleth." *JQR* 36 (1945/46) 17–45. ———. "The Question of Hebrew in Qoheleth." *JQR* 40 (1949/50) 79–102.

The statement of F. Delitzsch remains a classic: "If the Book of Koheleth were of old Solomonic origin, then there is no history of the Hebrew language" (190). There is general agreement that the language is late; it is usually characterized as pre-Mishnaic, representing the state of the language before it developed into the Mishnaic Hebrew found in the Talmud. D. C. Fredericks has challenged this view recently, maintaining that Qoheleth's language "should not be dated any later than the exilic period, and no accumulation of linguistic evidence speaks against a pre-exilic date" (*Qoheleth's Language*, 267). The statistical nature of his argumentation does not beget much confidence. The peculiarities of the language are far from being resolved; cf. A. Schoors, *The Preacher*, 222.

The majority of scholars thinks that Qoheleth wrote his work originally in Hebrew. At one time this was an issue of vigorous debate, when F. Zimmerman and H. L. Ginsberg argued that it was a translation from Aramaic. They were effectively answered by R. Gordis (*JQR* 37 [1946/47] 67–84; *JBL* 71 [1952] 93–109). The whole controversy has practically died out, especially since the discovery of Hebrew fragments at Qumran. This leaves little room, reckoning backward from the second century, for an alleged Aramaic original and its translation. Probably the most telling argument, however, is the weakness of the grammatical reasoning put forth in favor of an Aramaic original. There is no clear case of a text in Ecclesiastes being an example of a mistranslation from the Aramaic. Moreover, the paronomasia and other tricks of style in the Hebrew text are more easily understood of one writing in a native language than of a translator. The entire episode, however, is symbolic of the mystery of the language of this book, which still remains puzzling.

In 1952 M. Dahood opened a new approach to the language, arguing that it was originally written in Phoenician orthography *(scriptio defectiva)* and that in morphology, syntax, and vocabulary it showed a strong Canaanite-Phoenician influence. Although Dahood kept adding to the examples of evidence that he had amassed, the theory has not been accepted (see Gordis, *Bib* 41 [1960] 395–410; Whitley, *Koheleth*, 111–18). But it has been supported in part by J. R. Davila, (*Maarav* 5–6 [1990] 69-87), who argues that Qoheleth's Hebrew "was influenced by a northern dialect of Hebrew" (87). G. L. Archer (*JETS* 12 [1969] 167–81) has accepted Dahood's arguments, and postulated a "gifted tenth century Hebrew author" (181).

Did Qoheleth write in prose or in poetry? He could hardly have been like Monsieur Jourdain in Molière's play who was surprised to learn after many years that he had been speaking prose all along. The answer to the question lies in the definition of poetry in biblical Hebrew. There is widespread agreement that the psalms are written in "poetic lines," and that the sayings in Proverbs should be set off as poetry. But in the case of Ecclesiastes there is a striking difference of opinion. E. Podechard (137) thought that in the main Ecclesiastes was written in prose, indeed in "une prose assez mauvaise." Before him, no less a figure than R. Lowth had issued a similar judgment: "The style of this work is, however, singular; the language is generally low, I might almost call it mean or vulgar; it is frequently loose, unconnected, approaching to the incorrectness of conversation; and possesses very little of the poetical character, even in the composition and structure of the periods: which peculiarity may possibly be accounted for from the nature of the subject" (*Lectures on the Sacred Poetry of the Hebrews* [Lecture 24; Boston: Buckingham, 1815] 342–43).

Many translators set the book up almost entirely in prose paragraphs (NEB) or a kind of "free verse" (A. Lauha; D. Michel, *Kohelet*, 127–68). But most recognize a mixture of prose and poetry (the latter being present especially in chaps. 7 and 10). The problem remains, because it is not easy to set up criteria for the distinction. Recently, J. Kugel (*The Idea of Biblical Poetry: Parallelism and Its History* [New

Haven: Yale UP, 1981]) has raised serious question about the definition of biblical poetry, and especially the role of parallelism. Yet, whatever the answer be on a theoretical level, one can hardly deny the existence of some poetic lines in the book (not only 3:2–8, but 11:1–4).

While judgment about the peculiar grammatical characteristics of the language is still out (cf. W. D. Delsman, S. du Plessis, B. Isaksson, D. C. Fredericks), there can be no doubt about the distinctiveness of Qoheleth's literary style. The poem on the repetition of events in 1:4–11 is as it were a symbol of this style; repetition is its trademark. This repetition is manifest in vocabulary and also in a phraseology that is almost formulaic, as the following statistics illustrate.

The favorite words in Eccl 1:4–12:7, whether occurring as verbs or in related forms, are the following (see O. Loretz, *Qohelet*, 167–80):

עשׂה	*ʿśh*	do (62)
חכם	*ḥkm*	wise (51)
טוב	*ṭwb*	good (51)
ראה	*rʾh*	see (46)
עת	*ʿt*	time (37)
שׁמשׁ	*šmš*	sun (33)
עמל	*ʿml*	trouble (33)
ראה	*rʾh*	evil (30)
הבל	*hbl*	vanity (29, in all 38)
כסיל	*ksyl*	fool (18)
שׂמח	*śmḥ*	joy (17)
אכל	*ʾkl*	eat (15)
ישׁ	*yš*	there is (15)
יתר	*ytr*	profit (15)
סכל	*skl*	fool (13)
רוח	*rwḥ*	wind (as parallel to *hbl*) (13)
מות	*mwt*	die (13)
רשׁע	*ršʿ*	wrongdoing (12)
צדק	*ṣdq*	just (11)
ענה	*ʿnh*	trouble (10)
רעות/רעיון	*rʿwt/rʿywn*	chase (10)
שׁלט	*šlṭ*	power (9)
זכר	*zkr*	remember (8)
חלק	*ḥlq*	portion (8)
כעס	*kʿs*	vexation (7)
חפץ	*ḥpṣ*	affair (7)
הלל	*hll*	folly (7)
כשׁר	*kšr*	succeed (5)

The statistics compiled by O. Loretz (*Qohelet*, 179) are astounding. Out of all the words appearing in chaps. 2–11 there is a variation of between 29.1 percent (chap. 2) and 14.1 percent (chap. 11) for the favorite words: "Among the 2643 words (Qoh 1,4–12,7) we count 562 favorite words, thus 21.2%."

Besides the use of individual words, there is the phenomenon of repetition of set phrases:

הבל	*hbl*	in various formulae, e.g., this also is vanity (38)
שתה/אכל	*ʾkl/šth*	eat/drink (5)
עמל	*ʿml/ʿml*	toil (8)
כל/המעשה אשר נעשה	*kl/hmʿśh ʾšr nʿśh*	all/deeds that are done (9)
תחת השמש	*tht hšmš*	under the sun (27)
מי-יודע	*mî yōdēaʿ*	who knows? (4)

Several terms have been subjected to careful analysis by D. Michel. The verb ראה, "see" occurs forty-six times, and twenty-one of these in the first person (Michel, *Eigenart*, 24–28, 35–38). In passages like 2:13, 24 it does not mean merely the experience of seeing, but rather critical observation (*prüfend betrachten*). The point is not that Qoheleth is registering an empirical datum, an object of his vision. It is a critical evaluation of what he has perceived. Such is often the meaning of ראה (cf. 2:12–15). For this reason, among others, Michel (*Qohelet*, 33) argues that Qoheleth was not an empiricist: "Qoheleth is no empiricist who engages in various and contradictory experiences and notes them down, but a thinker (more exactly, an epistemological skeptic)." But M. Fox writes, "Qohelet has an essentially empirical methodology: he seeks both to derive knowledge from experience and to validate ideas experientially" (*Qohelet*, 80). The difference between the two interpreters may be only verbal. Both Fox and Michel agree that Qoheleth is a philosopher, and for Fox, the general approach of the sages is not "empirical"; for them "experience is simply an occasion for thought" (91). When the sage saw a ruined field, he was moved to think about the reason: laziness (Prov 24:30–34). Qoheleth uses experience to support his conclusions (the events in 1:4–7 justify the conclusion of 1:9 that nothing new happens under the sun). Michel seems to base his conclusions on his analysis of later stages of Qoheleth's thought: how Qoheleth moves with his various observations.

Another favorite word is יש, "there is": 1:10; 2:21; 4:8, 9; 5:12; 6:1–11; 7:15 (twice); 8:6, 14 (three times); 9:4; 10:5. Michel (*Eigenart*, 184–99) points out that the word is used in Proverbs especially to introduce paradoxes (Prov 11:24; 13:7; 14:22, etc.), or in the case of Ecclesiastes, "limit situations" (*Grenzfälle*). For example, 2:21 introduces an observation that happens: the wise leave the fruits of their toil to those who have not toiled (cf. the question in 2:19). This does not always happen, but it does occur—it is a limit case, that Qoheleth finds convincing and worthy of emphasis.

Michel (*Eigenart*, 200–212) has subjected Qoheleth's use of the ever elusive כי, ("indeed," "because," "when," etc.) to a sharp analysis. When, for example, it is used four times in two verses (8:6–7; 9:4–5) or thrice in three verses (7:4–5; 2:24b–26), one almost despairs of catching the nuances, and it is difficult to find any agreement among translators. Michel's contribution is to emphasize that כי is also a deictic or strengthening particle. In this function it is a signal of some subordination. Thus, 8:6–7 can be translated: "Now (deictic כי) for every deed there is a time and judgment; to be sure (deictic כי) an evil thing weighs on humans, for (causal כי) they know not what will be, because (causal כי) who can tell them how things will turn out?" There are many deictic usages of כי elsewhere, exemplified by Michel for 7:7; 6:8; 9:4–5; 2:24b–26; 2:21–23; 11:1–2; 11:6; 8:12b; 9:11–12.

The use of אֲשֶׁר as the relative particle is so common in Hebrew that its other and puzzling uses are not always noticed. Michel (*Eigenart*, 213–44) points out the sense of "namely" in 9:1 ("I considered all this: namely the just and the wise and their works are in the hand of God"). More important is his analysis of אֲשֶׁר in 7:28 (see the *Comment* below on 7:25–29). The particle does not have a relative function, connecting 28a with v 27 (as this is usually translated). Rather, it serves to make a subject out of a sentence, so that one should translate: "What I have still sought but not found is (this): One man out of a thousand, etc." In other words, Qoheleth denies the validity of the statement about one man and no woman among the thousand.

Qoheleth is fond of cognate accusatives: "the toil at which one toils" (2:18, 22; 5:17; 9:9); "the deed that is done": 1:9, 13–14; 2:17; 4:3; 8:9, 17; 9:3, 6. There are sixteen examples of the comparative use of טוֹב מִן: 4:3, 6, 9, 13; 5:4; 6:3, 9; 7:1, 2, 3, 5, 8; 9:4, 16, 18; in four other cases טוֹב is to be understood (cf. G. Ogden, *JBL* 98 [1979] 339–50). The identity of Aramaisms is hard to establish; those that are alleged will be pointed out in the commentary.

There is no satisfactory solution to the literary form of the book. "Royal Testament" (G. von Rad, *Wisdom in Israel* [Nashville: Abingdon, 1972] 226) will not do, since the king fiction disappears after chap. 2. F. Ellermeier (*Qohelet I/1*, 49) seriously proposes *māšāl* as the genre, but admits at once that it is not very helpful. R. Braun (*Kohelet*, 36, 165, 179) and S. de Ausejo (*EstBib* 7 [1948] 394–406) both proposed the Hellenistic diatribe as the proper form of the book. A diatribe is a literary form cultivated among the Cynics and adopted by the Stoics. The form continued into the Roman period, as can be seen in the *Discourses* of Epictetus. It seems to have been influential on the style of the Pauline letters, and also known by the author of the Wisdom of Solomon (cf. Wis 13:1–9). The contents of the diatribe are ethical philosophy, the daily human existence with which the authors were preoccupied. Nothing was preserved of the writings of Bion, the earliest of these writers, but fragments of Teles have been published. The notable characteristic of the diatribe is the dialogue that the writer holds with an interlocutor, real or fictitious. This feature seems to be the main argument for describing Ecclesiastes as a dialogue. However, one may well question if this is adequate to the complexities of the book. Ultimately the book is not a dialogue, even if Qoheleth inevitably had in mind certain thinkers and their views.

Characteristic of Ecclesiastes is the genre called "reflection" by F. Ellermeier (*Qohelet I/1*, 89–92) and R. Braun (*Kohelet*, 153–59). This designates the particular form in which Qoheleth develops his thought. Ellermeier distinguishes between a critical reflection that is unified (e.g., 3:16–22; 4:1–3) and a critical "broken" reflection. The first begins with a negative observation in order to criticize an optimistic view (3:16–22); the second starts from a neutral point, and goes on to make its critique (1:4–11). He also describes a third type, which begins with a negative observation and arrives at establishing a relative value (4:4–6). These subtle distinctions are not as important as the term itself; reflection is what Qoheleth is clearly doing. The terminology of R. Braun is different. He distinguishes among the considered reflection (*betrachtende Reflexion*), in which the theme is stated; the consideration (*Betrachtung*), in which empirical points are indicated; instruction (*Belehrung*), with warning and challenge;

considered teaching *(betrachtende Belehrung)*, consisting of consideration, reasons, and challenge. Again, the differences between one kind of reflection and another seem subtle and even unnecessary, but Braun analyzes the entire twelve chapters in this fashion (*Kohelet*, 155–58). Fortunately, the reflection is easier to recognize than to describe. It has a loose structure; it begins with some kind of observation, which is then considered from one or more points of view, leading to a conclusion. Within it one may find sayings or proverbs, employed to develop or round out the thought (e.g., 1:12–18).

Qoheleth of course utilized the typical forms of his trade, such as the saying and the instruction (R. E. Murphy, *Wisdom Literature*, 4–6). The saying is a statement most often in the indicative mood, which generalizes on experience. Usually it is formulated in a pithy, succinct way, and if it gains currency among the community it attains the stature of a real proverb. The saying may be purely observational, merely telling "the way it is," as in Prov 10:24, or Eccl 7:11; 10:3. Other sayings appear to be observational, but they are slanted toward a judgment. For example, "One who pays heed to the wind will not sow, and one who watches the clouds will never reap" (Eccl 11:4). Implicitly there is a warning to the hearer that inaction is disastrous. The sayings in Ecclesiastes are found especially in chaps. 7 and 10, but they are also scattered through the work. The instruction form is a mode of persuasion, especially employing command or admonition. This can be seen in 4:17–5:6. The "example story" *(Beispielserzählung)* cultivated by the sages is also to be found in 4:13–16 and 9:13–16.

Integrity and Structure

Bibliography

Were all twelve chapters written by Qoheleth? Did he give a visible structure to his book? Nearly every commentary on Ecclesiastes gives some attention to these questions. In addition, note the following in particular:

Barucq, A. "Qoheleth." *DBSup* 10. 654–61. **Castellino, G.** "Qohelet and His Wisdom." *CBQ* 30 (1968) 15–28. **Coppens, J.** "La structure de l'Ecclésiaste." In *SagAT*. 288–92. **Ellermeier, F.** *Qohelet I,1.* 129–41. **Fox, M. V.** *Qohelet.* 19–28. ————. "Frame-Narrative and Composition in the Book of Qohelet." *HUCA* 48 (1977) 83–106. ————. "The Identification of Quotations in Biblical Literature." *ZAW* 92 (1980) 416–31. **Loader, J. A.** *Polar Structures in the Book of Qohelet.* BZAW 152. Berlin: de Gruyter, 1979. 4–9. **Michel, D.** *Qohelet.* 9–45. **Lys, D.** "Être et le Temps." In *SagAT*. 249–58. **Mulder, J. S. M.** "Qohelet's Division and Also Its Main Point." In *Von Kanaan*. 341–65. **Rousseau, F.** "Structure de Qohélet I 4–11 et plan du livre." *VT* 31 (1981) 200–17. **Schoors, A.** "La structure littéraire de Qoheleth." *OLP* 13 (1982) 91–116. **Whybray, R. N.** *Ecclesiastes.* OTG. Sheffield: JSOT Press, 1989. 29–49. ————. "The Identification and Use of Quotations in Ecclesiastes." In *Congress Volume, Vienna, 1980.* VTSup 32. Leiden: Brill, 1981. 435–51. **Wright, A. G.** "The Riddle of the Sphinx: The Structure of the Book of Qoheleth." *CBQ* 30 (1968) 313–34. (= *SAIW*, 245–66). ————. "The Riddle of the Sphinx Revisited: Numerical Patterns in the Book of Qoheleth." *CBQ* 42 (1980) 38–51. ————. "Additional Numerical Patterns in Qoheleth." *CBQ* 45 (1983) 32–43. **Zimmerli, W.** "Das Buch Kohelet—Traktat oder Sentenzensammlung?" *VT* 24 (1974) 221–30.

INTEGRITY

There is widespread agreement that 12:9–14 constitutes an epilogue to the book, even if commentators differ on the number of hands involved in the composition of these verses (see *Comment* on 12:9–14). In contrast to the style in the body of the work, Qoheleth is referred to in the third person, and a report is given about his teaching activity. Moreover, this epilogue follows immediately upon 12:8, which forms an *inclusio* with 1:2. The inclusion may be editorial, since the superlative, "vanity of vanities," is not used elsewhere in the book. Again Qoheleth is spoken of in the third person.

The opening poem on toil (1:3–11) is a strong beginning, for it deals with a key concept in the book, עָמָל *ʿāmāl*, "toil," and it affirms that there is no "profit" (יִתְרוֹן, another important term) from human toil. This poem is clearly marked off from the motto in v 2, and the "beginning" in 1:12, where the writer introduces himself in the first person as a king. The poem is a self-contained unit, a kind of prologue. The examples drawn from nature exemplify the monotonous and futile course that nature follows (vv 3–7), and the application to the human scene occurs in vv 8–11.

The real issue for integrity is not the prologue and epilogue, but the presence of glosses or interpolations, which supposedly were not written (better, could not have been written) by Qoheleth. The tensions in the book are clear even to the casual reader. On the one hand, Qoheleth laments that the wise man dies as well as the fool, and therefore he loathes life (2:16–17). On the other hand, "a live dog is better than a dead lion" (9:4). Such "contradictions" in his thinking gave rise to the view that the work must contain several "hands" or "voices." The history of exegesis of the book (see "History of Interpretation" below) shows that early on interpreters who accepted Solomonic authorship explained such passages as Solomon in dialogue with himself or with others. In more recent times, this yielded to the view that the dissonance was created by glosses or interpolations from later hands. A typical example, somewhat extreme, is the view of C. G. Siegfried.

In 1898 C. G. Siegfried (2–12) proposed a far-reaching and influential interpretation by recognizing several glossators: a Sadducean who favored Epicureanism (Q²), a wise man or חכם *ḥākām* (Q³), and a pious person or חסיד (Q⁴). In addition there was a group of glossators that were responsible for further insertions (Q⁵). This approach concentrated on the alleged contradictions in the book, and it eliminated these in favor of a "pure" and dour Qoheleth. But difficulties with this methodology remain. First, the contradiction is sometimes more in the interpretation given to the text than in the text itself. Second, the passage in question may not be so out of harmony with the rest of the work that it must be attributed to a glossator. There is danger of imposing an a priori judgment on what constitutes Qoheleth's thought.

At the beginning of this century, the approach of Siegfried was espoused in various forms in the leading commentaries (e.g., G. Barton, E. Podechard, and A. H. McNeile). Recently the trend has been away from this tendency, but many commentators (K. Galling, H. Hertzberg, A. Lauha, et al.) frequently have recourse to glosses. There is no unanimity in the determination of specific glosses. The most "troublesome" texts seem to be those that suggest judgment: 3:17;

8:12b–13; 11:9 (see the *Comment* on these texts). But other texts also are singled out for elimination (e.g., 3:17; 5:18; 7:18b) by various scholars. It is hard to escape the impression that the interpreter's subjectivism is at work. It is preferable to explain the book as generally of one piece (so R. Gordis, J. Loader, W. Zimmerli [except 11:9b], among others), with the obvious exception of the epilogue.

Those who defend the integrity of the book have recourse to certain stylistic features and exegetical moves as a reply to the division into various glossators. The boldest method is that of M. V. Fox who simply recognizes contradictions within the book (*Qohelet*, 19–28). H. W. Hertzberg (30) proposed an exegetical solution: the recognition of the "yes, but" saying *(zwar-aber Tatsache)*. This indicates a qualification, if not denial, of a point that has just been made, as in Eccl 2:13–14a, which speaks of the superiority of wisdom. These verses are followed by vv 14b–15, which question the advantage of wisdom. Hertzberg listed several such passages: 1:16–18; 2:3–11; 2:13–15; 3:11; 3:17–18; 4:13–16; 7:7, 11–12; 8:12b–15; 9:4–5; 9:16; 9:17–10:1; 10:2–3, 5–7. W. Zimmerli (130–31) acknowledged such shifts in the thought of Qoheleth. On the other hand, F. Ellermeier (*Qohelet I/1*, 125–28) stoutly refused to recognize the *zwar-aber* mentality. Whether or not one uses this terminology, most interpreters of Ecclesiastes acknowledge that the complex nature of Qoheleth's thought does appear to embrace certain contradictions. The settlement of this question must be left to the exegesis of a concrete text as well as to the general construal of Qoheleth's thought.

Another solution akin to the "yes, but" saying is the recognition of quotations in the book (R. Gordis, 95–108; R. N. Whybray, *Ecclesiastes*, OTG, 35–40). Gordis described quotations as "passages that cite the speech or thought of a subject, actual or hypothetical, past or present, which is distinct from the context in which it is embodied" (96). A clear example of this is Eccl 4:8, in which the description of the solitary toiler concludes with "for whom am I toiling. . . ?" Whether this is a question he asks himself (so NEB), or fails to ask himself (so Gordis), it is certainly a quotation, pointedly employed by Qoheleth to heighten the futile situation of the solitary person. R. N. Whybray (VTSup 32 [1981] 435–51) has continued the study of quotations, attempting to determine whether or not Qoheleth is citing a traditional wisdom saying. If so, how is the citation used, how does it function? The proof that a quotation is present is not easy to provide. M. V. Fox has called for stricter criteria in identifying quotations in biblical literature (*ZAW* 92 [1980] 416–31); they must be marked in some way: explicitly, e.g., by a verb of speaking, or implicitly, such as by a change in grammatical number and person. No matter the issue of proof, some lines simply have the ring of proverbial sayings that are being quoted, such as Eccl 4:5–6, or vv 15 and 18 in the complex of 1:12–18. Whybray examined some forty examples from the point of view of form, theme, and language. His rigid criteria led to the conclusion that there were eight clear examples (2:14a; 4:5; 4:6; 7:5; 7:6a; 9:17; 10:2; 10:12). One might be inclined to be less strict than Whybray in the establishing of criteria. In any case, he claimed that when Qoheleth has used traditional wisdom material (such as in these eight instances), "His purpose in quoting these sayings was not to demonstrate their falsity. He quoted them because he accepted their truth" (450). At the same time, Qoheleth modified them in the direction of pessimism. The general point made by Whybray fits well the dialogical character of the book.

STRUCTURE

If one accepts the basic integrity of the book of Ecclesiastes, it might be expected that some general agreement about its structure could be reached. But there is hardly one commentator who agrees with another on the structure; some simply adopt or modify the structure proposed by others. Almost all have recourse to a conceptual or logical analysis. The variation of opinion can be quickly gauged by perusing the surveys of A. G. Wright (*CBQ* 30 [1968] 315–316) and F. Ellermeier (*Qohelet I/1*, 129–41), to which the following later examples can be added:

A. Barucq (16–18) does not attempt a logical division of the work, but he recognizes thirteen divisions within 1:4–12:8.

R. Braun (*Kohelet,* 165) divides the book into 1:2–11, introductory considerations; 1:12–2:12, the king fiction; 2:12–4:16, reflection; 4:17–11:10, teaching; 12:1–8, concluding consideration.

The analysis of structure by J. Coppens ("La structure de l'Ecclésiaste," 288–92) is based on logical development. The basic work develops the theme of vanity in two parts: 1:12–2:16 records the personal experiences of King Solomon. 3:9–10:7 contains his views on life, but it has been interrupted by several insertions of *logia* from classical wisdom, which have little relation to the theme of vanity; these would total over eighty verses. The rest of the book is shaped by redactional additions (e.g., 1:4–11) and appendices (e.g., 12:9–14).

L. di Fonzo (9–10) distinguishes a prologue (1:1–3) and five parts: vanity of nature and history (1:4–11); the general vanity of life and its values (1:12–2:26); the enigmas of human life (3:1–6:12); practical conduct for life (7:1–11:6); youth and old age (11:7–12:8). These are followed by the epilogue (12:9–14).

K. Galling, in his revised 1969 commentary (76–77), recognizes an introduction (1:1–3) and two epilogues (12:9–14), between which are arranged twenty-seven statements of Qoheleth.

E. Glasser (179–84) sees the following steps in the movement of the book: introduction (1:12–18); Qoheleth's personal analysis of happiness (2:1–26); his analysis of the happiness of other human beings (3:1–9:10); an exhortation to embrace the happiness that is possible for humans (9:11–12:7). The work is a kind of "philosophical essay" (187).

A. Lauha (4–7) takes a position similar to K. Galling. While having conceptual and stylistic unity, the work is basically a collection composed of thirty-six units.

N. Lohfink (10–11) thinks the book is "almost a philosophical treatise" and divides it into a cosmology (1:4–11), anthropology (1:12–3:15), social criticism (3:16–6:10, with a critique of religion in 4:17–5:6), a critique of ideology (6:11–9:6), and ethics (9:7–12:7), plus two additions by way of epilogue.

D. Lys, in his unfinished commentary (65), recognizes two general divisions between the introduction and conclusion: a treatment of the human condition (1:4–4:3) and a renewed treatment of this topic (4:4–12:7).

F. Rousseau (*VT* 31 [1981] 200–17) analyzes 1:4–11 in almost mathematical detail on the basis of the pairing or *"jumelage"* of stichs. The same principle, along with the recognition of the sevenfold refrain to enjoy life, is applied to structure the rest of the book, which divides into seven parts, apart from the prologue and epilogue: Solomon's "confession," 1:12–2:26; the sage's ignorance of God's plan in general, 3:1–13; the sage's ignorance of what is after death, 3:14–22; various deceptions (הבל *hebel*) and exhortations, 4:1–5:19; various deceptions and exhortations, 6:1–8:15; weakness of the sage, 8:15–9:10; deceptions and exhortations, 9:11–11:10.

A. Schoors (OLP 13 [1982] 91–116) reviews the structures proposed by several authors and remarks that they are all based on content. He allows (98) that the structure worked out by A. G. Wright "seems to be the best one can find," but ultimately it does not satisfy the logical progression of ideas, nor the set expressions and formulae that keep reappearing. He proposes his own outline, which is based both on logical progression and the constant repetitions (catch words, inclusions, etc.) that are scattered through the book. For example, he finds the מה יתרון, "what profit,"question of 1:3 answered in 2:11; hence 1:3–2:11 is a redactional unit. However, his structural outline rests as much upon content as upon literary characteristics.

J. L. Crenshaw (47–49) characterizes his analysis as "tentative" and resembling "in many respects that of Schoors." He ends up with twenty–five units and recognizes several glosses.

G. Ogden (11–13) holds that the "profit" question (1:3), its answer (negative), and the response that flows from that form the framework for chaps. 1–8. The final discourse (9–12) appraises the value of wisdom in the light of life's enigmas.

R. N. Whybray (*Ecclesiastes*, OTG, 46–47) makes no claim for one outline of the structure more than another. He simply presents thirty-one thematic units, based on content.

M. V. Fox (*Qohelet*, 161–62; *HUCA* 48 [1977] 83–106) expresses his general agreement with the views of W. Zimmerli and A. Schoors (with whom his unit division is, independently, in general agreement). He points out that there is considerable agreement among commentators about the segmentation of various units (as indicated in Ellermeier, *Qohelet I/1*, 131–41), but there is no hierarchical organization of the whole. Instead, he proposes to analyze the book in terms of the two time-frame perspectives (*Qohelet*, 311–20), which provide a certain structure. The first frame is that of the narrator, the true author of the book (1:2–12:14), who transmits the teachings of Qoheleth, who is his persona. The second time frame is that of Qoheleth: as reporter (the narrating "I"), and as observer (the experiencing "I"). The narrator is the epilogist who praises Qoheleth (12:9–10), whose teaching he agrees with and which in effect he has composed. Qoheleth is a persona, a mask through which the author's voice is heard. In support of this view Fox adduces several examples from Egyptian wisdom literature, such as Ptah-hotep, Ankhsheshonq, and others.

D. Michel (*Qohelet*, 9–45) provides a survey of various proposals about structure, and regards the division urged by N. Lohfink (that the book has a systematic unity) as having the soundest basis (42). Michel's view of the structure of the book is unusual (see *Eigenart*, 245–47; *Qohelet*, 32–33). In 1:3–3:15, Qoheleth lays down his philosophy concerning human attempts to gain any profit from life. In the rest of the book he deals with individual cases that illustrate his philosophy. Indeed, they are sometimes so curtly presented that one cannot understand them without presupposing the doctrine of 1:3–3:15 (*Eigenart*, 133; 246–47). Sometimes Qoheleth will quote the opinions of others in order to provide his own comment on them (e.g., 7:1–10, 11–14). At other times he will pursue a theme, with the help of a quotation from some source (such as v 9 in the treatment of unfulfilled desire in 6:1–12). Even if one is inclined to agree in general that Qoheleth is "quoting" or at least is in dialogue with opinions that he does not really adhere to, the extensive list of quotations that Michel proposes must give one pause. His argument is that 1:3–3:15 enables one to determine the quotations; it provides a material criterion *(sachliches Kriterium)*. But the criterion is not all that clear. In particular, the many instances in which Qoheleth is allegedly quoting himself *(Selbstzitat)* seem tenuous (could he not be in dialogue with some tag of traditional wisdom?). Thus, 3:22 is alleged to be a "quotation" of the position expressed in 3:11–12. It is true that it repeats the idea in 3:11–12. There are many repetitions in the book, but little is gained by introducing the notion of "self-quotation" (cf. Michel, *Eigenart*, 248, 262).

W. Zimmerli (*VT* 24 [1974] 221–30) laid down the extreme choices for the structure of Qoheleth: is it a treatise, or a collection of sayings? His answer was that the truth is somewhere between these two: "The book of Qoheleth is not a treatise with clearly recognizable structure and with one definable theme. At the same time it is more than a loose collection of sayings, although in some places indications of a collection are not to be overlooked. . . . It follows that the exegete of Ecclesiastes must work on more levels than the exegete of Proverbs. He must first of all discover the primary form-critical units. Then . . . he must inquire after the possible combination of two or more of these primary units. There is still a further task. . . . He must ask how the content determines the sequence of the complex form-critical units. The element of uncertainty is the greatest precisely at this point, and the exegete must also have the courage to register a 'non-liquet'" (230). While form-critical considerations are an important stage in the determination of structure, they tend to an atomization of the text. As Zimmerli notes, one must go beyond them to consider sequence and unity. When this is done in a logical and conceptual way, different structural outlines invariably emerge despite efforts to be "objective." In recent times, two perceptive efforts have been made to treat the structure in a less subjective way. J. Loader has argued for the principle of polarity as the key to the structure, while A. Wright has pointed to the repetitions and refrains, as well as to numerological factors, as the means of establishing the structure.

J. Loader *(Polar Structures in the Book of Qohelet)* interprets the structure of the book in terms of thought patterns, which he calls "polar structures": "By 'polar structures' I mean patterns of tensions created by the counterposition of two elements to one another" (1). Obviously this zeroes in on a fundamental characteristic of the book: the tensions existing in Qoheleth's thought. Apart from the epilogue, Loader recognizes twelve structural units (111–16). At this point logical analysis takes over, as it must, with the result that some dubious structural claims are made. For example, 1:12–2:26 is termed the "worthlessness of wisdom." But it is difficult to see how the experiment with riches (2:1–12) can be seen as in polarity with the surrounding verses that deal with wisdom and folly, remembrance, death, and toil. A conceptual relationship can perhaps be established, but one seems to have departed from the principle of polarity. There *are* polar structures within the book. One need merely recall the remarkable example of "times" in 3:1–8. But the issue is structure, and not the general characteristics of Qoheleth's thought. It is difficult to claim an over-arching structure of polarities that holds the work together. Individual verses are in tension with each other at several points. In his commentary (*Ecclesiastes* [Grand Rapids: Eerdmans, 1986] 7–8), Loader recognizes the prologue; the "king's" investigation (1:12–2:26); seven poems about time and its manifestations (3:1–4:16); views on the worthlessness of riches (5:10–6:9); poems on human incompetence and worthlessness of wisdom (6:10–8:1); powerlessness (8:2–9; see Loader, 94–98); three separate sections (8:10–9:10; 9:11–10:11; 10:12–20); a final poem on joy and vanity (11:7–12:8).

A. G. Wright (*CBQ* 30 [1968] 313–34 = *SAIW*, 245–66) first approached the problem of structure from the point of view of the repetition of key phrases, seeking a norm more objective than logical connection. In later studies (*CBQ* 42 [1980] 38–51; cf. *CBQ* 45 [1983] 32–43) he confirmed his original outline of the work by the discovery of a numerological pattern in the structure. The key points in his analysis are as follows:

1. Recognition of a superscription and prologue (1:1–11) and an epilogue (12:9–14), along with most commentators.
2. Division of the book into two main parts, on the basis of key phrases.
   a. 1:12–6:9. This contains six sections (2:1–11; 2:12–17; 2:18–26; 3:1–4:6; 4:7–16; 4:17–6:9), each ending with the repetition of "vanity" and/or "chase after the wind." Two introductions (1:12–15, 16–18), each ending with the same key phrase plus a proverbial saying, precede the six sections.
   b. 6:10–11:6. This contains two parts:
      1) 6:10–8:17, composed of an introduction (6:10–12) and four sections (7:1–14; 7:15–24; 7:25–29; 8:1–17), which are separated by the phrase "not find out"/"who can find out." Note the triple repetition of "not find" in 8:17.
      2) 9:1–11:6 comprises four sections (9:1–12 [a problematic section]; 9:13–10:15; 10:16–11:2; 11:3–6), set off from each other by the phrase "do not know." Note the triple repetition of "not know" in 11:5–6.
3. A final poem about youth and old age appears in 11:7–12:8, followed by the epilogue (12:9–14).

The value of Wright's structural analysis is that it follows the lead of clear repetitions of key phrases within the book. Moreover, the subsections are strictly limited by these repetitions; they are not the result of conceptual or logical analysis, but neither do they sin against logic; as conceptual divisions they are at least adequate.

The confirmation of this general outline was achieved by the recognition of numerological patterns (*CBQ* 45 [1983] 32–43) controlling the book, as the following observations indicate.

1. The book has 222 verses, and the midpoint occurs at 6:9/6:10, as the Masoretes also noted. This observation is not simply to be dismissed by the statement that verse division did not exist in Qoheleth's day. There can be a sense of verse division without explicit stichometry.
2. The numerical value of the Hebrew letters in הבל הבלים הכל הבל, "Vanity of vanities! All is vanity!" in the inclusion (1:2; 12:8) is 216. And there are 216 verses in 1:1–12:8.
3. In 1:2 "vanity" (הבל *hebel* = 5+2+30 = 37) is repeated three times, yielding a numerical value of 3 x 37, or 111, which is the number of verses at midpoint (6:9).
4. The numerical significance of "vanity" (=37) is underscored by the fact that it occurs 37 times (if one eliminates the very doubtful second הבל *hebel* in 9:9, as many scholars have done, independently).

5. The numerical equivalent of דברי, "words of," in the title (1:1) is 216. This would be the title of a book of 216 verses: 1:1–12:8, exclusive of the epilogue.

6. In the epilogue 6 additional verses have been added to reach the number 222. A hint of this can be seen in ויתר in 12:9, 12, which can be understood to say "six additional"; ו = 6, and יתר = additional.

A. G. Wright has added some other details to strengthen his case, but the above considerations constitute the main bases supporting his outline. While numerical patterns are usually associated with arbitrary flights of fantasy, it should be noted that the above observations are relatively sober, and deal with key phrases and verses. Second, the likelihood that the verbal and numerical patterns are merely coincidental is minimal, since the observations reinforce each other. Third, the numerical patterns are in a different line of reasoning altogether from the literary analysis indicated by the repetition of key phrases in many instances, and yet they lend confirmation to it. Finally, this formal structural analysis, whatever imperfections it may have, is in general harmony with many logical analyses of the book.

J. S. M. Mulder (*Von Kanaan*, 341–65) adopted A. G. Wright's division except for minor changes. He argues that 3:11 (לא ימצא) and 8:7 איננו ידע demand more attention because they link 7:1–8:17 with 2:17–6:9, and with 9:1–11:6. He concludes with the claim that 3:1–4:6 and 8:1–17 constitute "the heart of all Qoheleth," which is that no one can understand God. In his presentation of Ecclesiastes (*The Old Testament: An Introduction* [Philadelphia: Fortress, 1986] 265), R. Rendtorff adopts "the illuminating suggestion" of Wright.

The commentary follows in the main structural pattern discovered by A. Wright, and pursued in his commentary in the *NJBC*, 66, pp. 489–95. The outline is as follows:

I. Prologue, 1:1–11.
   A. Superscription (1:1). This is an obvious heading for the book.
   B. Inclusion (1:2 and 12:8). This inclusion contains the author's basic judgment about life.
   C. Introductory poem of the prologue (1:3–11). The poem begins properly with the question in 1:3 about the profit of toil. This question is answered indirectly in the following verses; that there is no profit is illustrated by the examples of monotonous repetition (vv 4–7), which climax in the futility of human sight and hearing (v 8). The point is further secured by vv 9–11, which emphasize repetition (nothing new under the sun). A more explicit answer to v 3 is found in 2:11, 22 (cf. 3:9), which echo the futility of toil.

II. Part I, 1:12–6:9.
   Part I is divided not on the basis of content but by means of the occurrence of the term "vanity" and/or "chase after wind." There is not necessarily a conceptual unity to the division; several topics can be treated within one section (e.g., 4:17–6:9).
   A. Introduction (1:12–18). "I, Qoheleth" announces (vv 12–15) the wise search into events under the sun, and its failure, as the phrase "vanity and a chase after wind" indicates. This is followed by an appropriate saying (v 15). In a second phase (vv 16–18), stress is laid on the pursuit of wisdom, which also turns out to be "a chase after wind." Again an appropriate saying follows (v 18).
   B. The experiment with joy (2:1–11). Qoheleth announces the experiment and delivers judgment upon it (vv 1–2), before describing it in detail (vv 3–10). The judgment follows in v 11, "Vanity and a chase after wind." A kind of small inclusion with 1:3 occurs in v 11 (no *profit*).

C. What is the profit of wisdom? (2:12–17; cf. 1:17–18). V 12a announces the topics that will be pursued in vv 12–17: wisdom and its failure (hence the key phrase in v 17). V 12b (of uncertain meaning) seems to indicate the problem of succession that will be taken up in vv 18ff. Although wisdom is theoretically superior to folly, it fails because the same lot (מקרה) befalls both the wise and the foolish (vv 12–17).

D. In view of one's successor, toil is vanity (2:18–23). This is followed (vv 24–26) by one of Qoheleth's frequent conclusions about eating and drinking (cf. 3:13, 22; 5:17; 8:15; 9:7–10; 11:9–10), ending with the key phrase, "chase after the wind."

E. Time and toil (3:1–4:6). The famous poem on time (3:1–8) provides the background for a reflection on human toil and divine activity (vv 9–15). Vv 16–22 are a reflection upon judgment, both divine and human, against the backdrop of human mortality (מקרה, v 19; cf. 2:14). It culminates in another of Qoheleth's resigned conclusions (vv 21–22).

In 4:1 the theme of injustice is taken up from 3:16, with a decision in favor of the dead and unborn (vv 2–3). Qoheleth returns to the topic of toil (cf. 3:9) in the light of envy and diligence (vv 4–6). The section ends with the key phrase, "vanity and a chase after wind."

F. A reflection upon "two" (4:7–16). The disadvantages for one who toils alone (v 8; on toil, see 2:18–23; 3:10) are treated in vv 7–12. These are followed by an example story dealing with succession (cf. v 8 and also 2:12b) to the royal throne. The catchword "two" dominates this section (שׁנִי in vv 8–10, 15, and שׁנַיִם in vv 9, 11, 12). "Vanity and a chase after wind" ends the reflection (v 16).

G. Varia (4:17–6:9). Several different topics are treated in this section (in many English versions, e.g., NRSV, the enumeration of the verses in chap. 5 is one digit ahead of the Hebrew numbering followed here).

The first is speech, particularly speech before God (4:17–5:6). It is characterized by admonitions, culminating in the command "fear God."

The topic of oppression (cf. 4:1) returns briefly in an obscure admonition about officials, to which the advantage of kingship is added (5:7–8).

In 5:9–6:9 the theme of riches/possessions is taken up. They do not satisfy, and allow no rest (vv 9–11; cf. 2:12; 4:8). Qoheleth shows by an example story how they can be lost (vv 12–16); there is no profit from toiling for the wind (v 15). The only recompense for toil is "eating and drinking," provided God *gives* it (vv 17–19). The uncertainty of possessions is shown by another example of misfortune (רע, twice in 6:1–2); even the stillborn are better off than such a thwarted individual (vv 3–6).

The conclusion (6:7–9) returns to the topic of insatiable appetite (cf. 4:8; 5:9–11) that is fed by human toil (v 7).

The first half of the book ends here at 6:9, the midpoint of the number of verses in the book (111 of 222).

III. Part II, 6:10–11:6

As with Part I, the divisions within the second half of the book are determined by consistent repetitions. Chaps. 7–8 are divided by the phrase "[not] find out," yielding four sections: 7:1–14; 7:15–24; 7:25–29; 8:1–17. Chaps. 9:1–11:6 are divided by the phrase, "not know," also yielding four sections: 9:1–12; 9:13–10:15; 10:16–11:2; 11:3–6. The book ends with an address concerning youth and old age (11:7–12:7), the inclusion (12:8), and the epilogue (12:9–14).

A. Introduction to the second half of the book (6:10–12). Qoheleth states a thesis: whatever happens has been determined by God (cf. 1:9; 3:15), with whom humans cannot contend (cf. 1:15; 3:14; 7:13). This is so because there is no profit in human talk (v 11); hence they do not know what is good nor what will happen in the future (6:12).

B. Part IIa, 7:1–8:17.

1. Four confrontations with traditional wisdom concerning: a good name (7:1–4); the failure of a wisdom ideal (7:5–7); the caution of the sage, which orients him toward the past (7:8–10); wisdom's inability to find out what God is about (7:11–14).
2. A reflection (7:15–18) on the failure of retribution, and what one should do about it. Another confrontation with wisdom: her vaunted strength is undone by human sinfulness, i.e., folly (7:19–22). Qoheleth's avowal of his failure to attain wisdom (7:23–24).
3. A reflection of human righteousness (7:25–29).
4. Two confrontations with wisdom: the high calling of the sage is demeaned by opportunistic conduct before the king (8:1–4); the security of the wise comes to naught because of human ignorance and impotence (8:5–8). A reflection about injustice, despite wisdom's claims concerning divine retribution (8:9–14). A conclusion about "eating and drinking" (8:15). A reflection upon the mystery of "the work of God" (8:16–17).

C. Part IIb, 9:1–11:6.
1. A reflection, especially on one's "lot" that is not as fortunate as that of the dead (9:1–6). Another of Qoheleth's conclusions about the enjoyment of life (9:7–10). An observation about the evil time that "falls" upon humans (9:11–12).
2. An example story about the failure to recognize the wise man and his wisdom (9:13–17). Sayings about the power of a small thing to undo wisdom (9:18–10:1). A series of sayings concerning: the fool (10:2–3), the ruler (10:4). A reflection about the breakdown in order (10:5–7). A collection of sayings concerning: the unexpected (10:8–11), the fool (10:12–14a), and ignorance (10:14b–15).
3. A collection of sayings: 10:16–17, 18, 19, 20; 11:1–2.
4. A collection of two sayings (11:3–4), an address (11:5), and a command (11:6), all dealing with the theme of uncertainty.

IV. Poem on youth and old age, 11:7–12:7.
V. Inclusion, 12:8.
VI. Epilogue, 12:9–14.

Ancient Near Eastern Background

Bibliography

Braun, R. *Kohelet und die frühhellenistische Popularphilosophie.* BZAW 130. Berlin: de Gruyter, 1973. **Gammie, J.** "Stoicism and Anti-Stoicism in Qoheleth." *HAR* 9 (1985) 169–87. **Gemser, B.** "The Instructions of 'Onchsheshonqy and Biblical Wisdom Literature." In *Congress Volume, Oxford, 1959.* VTSup 7. Leiden: Brill, 1960. 102–28. **Gregg, J. A. F.** *The Wisdom of Solomon.* CBSC. Cambridge: UP, 1922. **Heinisch, P.** *Das Buch der Weisheit.* EHAT 24. Münster: Aschendorff, 1912. **Hengel, M.** *Judaism and Hellenism.* 2 vols. Philadelphia: Fortress, 1974. **Kaiser, O.** "Judentum und Hellenismus." *VF* 27 (1982) 69–73. **Lambert, W.** *Babylonian Wisdom Literature.* Oxford: Clarendon, 1960. **Larcher, C.** *Etudes sur le livre de la Sagesse.* EB. Paris: Gabalda, 1969. **Lichtheim, M.** *Ancient Egyptian Literature.* Vol. 3. Berkeley: University of California Press, 1980. [= *AEL*]. ———. "Observations on Papyrus Insinger." In *Studien zu altägyptischen Lebenslehren.* Ed. E. Hornung. OBO 28. Freiburg: Universitätsverlag, 1979. 284–305. ———. *Late Egyptian Wisdom Literature in the International Context.* OBO 52. Freiburg: Universitätsverlag, 1983. **Lohfink, N.** "Der Bibel Skeptische Hintertür." *SZ* 105 (1980) 17–31. **Loretz, O.** *Qohelet.* 45–134. **Michel, D.** *Qohelet.* 52–75. **Middendorp, T.** *Die Stellung Jesu Ben Siras zwischen Judentum und Hellenismus.* Leiden: Brill, 1973. **Pritchard, J.**

Ancient Near Eastern Texts. 3rd ed. Princeton: Princeton UP, 1978. [= *ANET*]. **Ranston, H.** *Ecclesiastes and the Early Greek Wisdom Literature.* London: Epworth, 1925. **Skehan, P. W.** "Wisdom and Ecclesiastes." In *Studies in Israelite Poetry and Wisdom.* CBQMS 1. Washington, DC: Catholic Biblical Association, 1971. 213–36. **Whitley, C. F.** *Koheleth.* 122–46, 152–81. **Williams, R. J.** "The Sages of Ancient Egypt in the Light of Recent Scholarship." *JAOS* 101 (1981) 1–19.

It goes without saying that Ecclesiastes is an intensely Jewish work. The commentary bears out his dependence upon the Hebrew Bible. But exaggerations are to be avoided, especially in the manner in which this influence is worked out. Thus, the claim of H. Hertzberg (230) that there is no doubt but that the book was written with Gen 1–4 open before *(vor den Augen)* Qoheleth is entirely too specific. It is true that Qoheleth draws on the biblical tradition, and especially is he the heir of the creation theology that is characteristic of the wisdom perspective. O. Loretz (*Qohelet,* 196–212) has provided an instructive list of seventy-one *topoi* treated by Qoheleth in common with other biblical (and nonbiblical) works. Among them are such themes as joy, life and death, time, the problem of retribution, riches and poverty, royalty, and fear of God. These indicate that Qoheleth stands firmly in the tradition of biblical wisdom.

At the same time the relationship of Ecclesiastes to the thought world of the ancient Near East has to be recognized. This relationship has been debated on three fronts especially: Mesopotamia, Egypt, and Greece (Hellenism). No firm consensus among scholars exists concerning the precise links that can be established to these areas. Nonetheless, the research has illustrated the teaching of Qoheleth against the background of the ancient world in which he lived. At this stage of the discussion it seems better to indicate the current state of the question and to describe the various contacts of Ecclesiastes with extrabiblical literature than to mount any claims of specific influence from a particular school of thought. This cautious attitude is suggested by two factors: the ambivalent nature of the arguments to prove literary or cultural dependence, and the existence of mutually contradictory claims for dependence that have been made in the past.

MESOPOTAMIA

There is hardly need to recall Israel's general indebtedness to ancient Sumer and Babylon. As regards wisdom, the achievements of Mesopotamia are considerable (see W. G. Lambert, *Babylonian Wisdom Literature* [Oxford: Clarendon, 1960]). Here also "problem" literature developed, in which the age-old enigma of human suffering appeared. In the *ludlul bel nēmeqi* ("I will praise the Lord of wisdom") there is the complaint that the wicked and the just receive the same treatment and that the decrees of the gods cannot be understood (2.10–38; *ANET,* 434–435; cf. Eccl 8:12–14 and 3:11; 8:17). The pessimism of the *ludlul* appears also in what has been called the "Babylonian Qoheleth," although it is also similar to Job: "A Dialogue about Human Misery" or "The Babylonian Theodicy." But Qoheleth does not blame human wickedness on the gods, as this work does (27.276–280; *ANET,* 440; cf. Eccl 7:29). The "Pessimistic Dialogue between Master and Servant" shares several themes with Ecclesiastes: woman as threatening to man (7.55–60; *ANET,* 438; cf. Eccl 7:26), the recommendation to eat (2.10–15; *ANET,* 438; cf. Eccl 2:24). The dexterity the slave displays in affirming both the positive and negative aspects of a situation is reminiscent of Qoheleth's own style (cf. Eccl 2:2 with his repeated statements about joy). The Hebrew work has in common with the Gilgamesh epic the theme of death and transient human life, and the concern for one's name and memory. Commentators do not fail to point out the similarities between the advice given Gilgamesh and that which is offered in Eccl 9:7ff.

EGYPT

The influence of Egypt upon Israel's wisdom is an acknowledged fact (R. Williams, *JAOS* 101 [1981] 1–19). Among the Egyptian works, the "Harper's Songs" (*ANET*, 467) have been compared to Ecclesiastes because of the *carpe diem* ("enjoy the day") motif. The dialogue between "The Man Who Was Tired of Life" and his soul shows a certain kinship to Ecclesiastes in its preoccupation with death (*ANET*, 405–7). These motifs, of course, are common to the Semitic as well as to the Egyptian world. A more fundamental similarity between Egyptian wisdom and Ecclesiastes was advanced by K. Galling (see his comment on 1:12) and seconded by G. von Rad and others: that the literary form of the book is the *Königstestament*, or "royal testament," such as is exemplified by the teaching of Merikare already in the twenty-second century B.C. (cf. *ANET*, 414–418). However, two facts tell against this view. Qoheleth does not write a legacy for his descendants, even if he lays claim to kingship. Besides, the royalty claim is a literary fiction that is dropped after chap. 2.

Comparisons have been made between Ecclesiastes and some late demotic Egyptian compositions, the Papyrus Insinger and the Instruction of Ankhsheshonq (texts in *AEL* 3:184–217, 159–84). The similarity is quite general. Ecclesiastes and Papyrus Insinger are both concerned with the mystery of God and the divine determination of human fate. But these resemblances are far from proving dependence of one upon another. Similarly, Ankhsheshonq has been compared to Qoheleth (B. Gemser, VTSup 7, 102–28), but M. Lichtheim has since shown that the comparison is rather with Sirach, and even here the question of dependence seems to be the wrong one to ask. Lichtheim emphasizes the "international currents" that influenced both Egypt and Palestine (M. Lichtheim, *Late Egyptian Wisdom Literature in the International Context*, 184, 195).

GREECE

The question of Hellenistic influence upon Qoheleth is still moot. The early history of this debate need not be summarized here (see H. Ranston, *Ecclesiastes and the Early Greek Wisdom Literature* [London: Epworth, 1925]). In more recent times O. Loretz (*Qohelet*, 45–134) weighed the arguments of Egyptian, Greek, and Mesopotamian influence and came down decidedly on the Semitic background, and hence Mesopotamian influence. He does not argue for *direct* dependence upon Mesopotamian works, although he finds the similarity of Ecclesiastes to certain parts of the Gilgamesh epic most striking (see below the *Comment* on 9:7–9). Rather, he is content to characterize Ecclesiastes as a work that is to be understood "against the background of the literature and world view of the Semites of the ancient Near East" (134). To this end he discusses the classical Mesopotamian counterparts (mentioned above) and focuses on notable features that are held in common: הבל *hebel*, "vanity," as an image for something transient and unsubstantial (Akkadian *šāru*, "wind, breath"), the importance of the name, memory, and reputation, and finally the problem of divine justice. It should be said that these are modest arguments. They point to Qoheleth's roots in the Semitic tradition, which are common to Mesopotamia and to Palestine. Indeed, these considerations can be readily granted, but they do not directly deal with the problem of Hellenism and Qoheleth's activity in a Hellenistic milieu.

Loretz meets the charge of Greek influence by pointing out how uncertain, if not false, are the alleged "Grecisms" (e.g., the correspondence between מקרה and τύχη). He also denies that there is any real evidence in favor of the various schools of thought to which Ecclesiastes has been compared (Epicurus, Stoics, Theognis). His argument is somewhat wide of the mark. Qoheleth could have been influenced by these schools without belonging to them. It is too easy to dismiss parallels by focusing on the specifics of the pertinent schools of thought. Loretz is impatient with even giving a role to the Hellenistic *Zeitgeist* which many scholars, such as M. Hengel (*Judaism and Hellenism*, 1:115–30, 126–27), see as influencing Qoheleth.

In response to O. Loretz is the study of R. Braun *(Kohelet)*, who argues that the Hellenistic hypothesis cannot be easily dismissed, since Qoheleth lived and wrote in the Hellenistic world. Braun surveys the Greek literature, early and late, that is pertinent to the mood of Qoheleth, especially the Sophists, Cynics, Stoics, and Skeptics. He discusses the "Grecisms" that have figured in the debate (הבל *hebel* and τυφος; יתרון *yitrôn* and ὄφελος, etc.), and he concludes that Qoheleth has been influenced by Hellenistic culture in the choice of such terms. The old argument that recognized ὑφ᾽ ἡλίῳ or ὑπὸ τον ἥλιον behind תחת השמש, "under the sun," does not prove literary dependence, but this can be explained as the *indirect* influence of Hellenistic culture (50). Braun also presents a detailed comparison of style and motifs common to Ecclesiastes and Hellenistic thought: the evaluation of wisdom, the lack of profit from human activity, the fate of humans, etc.

The nature of such evidence boils down to this: while there is no proof that Ecclesiastes is directly dependent upon Greek sources, the parallels between many facets of Qoheleth's thought and the common stock of Greek philosophical literature are sufficiently frequent and striking to suggest some relationship. Braun concludes "that Qoheleth was acquainted with the Greek reflection of his time, indeed even more, he took over its thoughts and teaching and put it into Hebrew form in his own didactic work" (170). It is easy to see that "acquaintance" can be justified on the basis of the many parallels adduced. It can hardly be a coincidence that Qoheleth wrote in the Hellenistic period and that his work echoes contemporary currents of thought. However, the main contention seems too specific; no evidence exists for such a sweeping judgment as transposing Greek thought into Hebrew. In a critique of R. Braun, O. Kaiser (*VF* 27 [1982] 69–73) found only one-third of the parallels cited by Braun to be convincing. The question is more subtle than lists of parallels.

N. Lohfink (7–15; see also *SZ* 105 [1980] 17–31) more or less takes for granted the Hellenistic character of the book, without arguing for it. The book may have been written between 190 and 180, just before Sirach and the Maccabean revolt. Third-century Judea clearly belongs to the Hellenistic world, and the leading Jewish families were smitten with Greek language and life style. Homer and Hesiod et al. vied with Proverbs and Torah. In this crisis of loyalty, Ecclesiastes emerged, a book that "can only be understood as an attempt to acquire as much as possible of the Greek view without letting Israelite wisdom lose its own character" (Lohfink, 9). According to Lohfink, Qoheleth probably taught in the open marketplace in the style of the Greek wandering philosophers, and he attracted a group of followers who gave him the name Qoheleth. He belonged to a priestly family that had social and religious clout. Lohfink further hypothesizes that the entry of the book into the canon was facilitated by its use as a school book in the Jerusalem Temple, which was the rival of the private Greek elementary school. The book was seen as "modern," but at the same time the superscription tied it to the Solomonic corpus. It was written in Hebrew, but "Greek syntax and stereotypes of Greek cultural language come through in the Hebrew just as we find today English elements in the cultural jargon of many intellectuals" (9). The mixture of prose with poetry of various meters is derived from the Cynic Menippos of Gadara, "a philosophical prose hitherto unknown in Israel: a series of observations, detailed and with gradual development of thought—abandoning motifs only to pick them up again, commenting on traditional sacred terms and coining new words but in such a fashion that they come out looking new while resembling the old" (9). This reconstruction of the historical background to Qoheleth and his book is exciting and even attractive. But the evidence for it remains thin. In the course of his commentary Lohfink refers to similarities between Qoheleth and several Greek thinkers (among them Menander, Euripides, Theognis, Pindar, and Homer). They illustrate the broad range of thought that Qoheleth shared with other writers. Moreover, this is to be expected in biblical wisdom literature, which is admittedly international in character. One must also bear in mind the similarities with Mesopotamian wisdom. Such "similarities" cancel each other out, as far as dependence is concerned. They witness to certain relatively common ideas of the ancient world.

By way of conclusion, one can easily admit a "Greek connection" for Ecclesiastes, but it is not at all clear how this Greek influence was mediated. The evidence suggests a certain *Zeitgeist* that influenced Qoheleth, but the borrowing of specific ideas is a delicate area to deal with. The view of M. V. Fox (*Qohelet*, 16) is both realistic and fair: "This is not to say that Qoheleth's thoughts and attitudes had a specific 'source' in Greek philosophy, but only that Qoheleth shared the concerns and attitudes of various philosophies known in the Hellenistic period, that focused on the achievement of happiness by an individual in an indifferent, if not inimical, universe."

INTERTESTAMENTAL LITERATURE

Ecclesiasticus and the Wisdom of Solomon, among the so-called Apocrypha, have been associated in varying ways with the book of Ecclesiastes. The question of the relationship between Qoheleth and Ben Sira has in a sense followed the fortunes of scholarly investigation of the book of Sirach. Prior to the discovery and publication of the Hebrew text of Ben Sira just before the turn of the century, there had been modest comparison between the Greek Sirach and Hebrew Ecclesiastes. The discussion then increased, with the majority favoring the view that Ben Sira was dependent, in whatever measure, upon Qoheleth (see E. Podechard, 55–56). With the relatively recent renascence of interest in Ben Sira, spurred on by the Hebrew manuscripts discovered at Qumran and Masada, the question has begun to resurface. T. Middendorp concluded that dependence in either direction cannot be shown (see *Die Stellung*, 85–90). On the other hand, C. Whitley (*Koheleth*, 122–31) concluded that Qoheleth shows dependence on Ben Sira. In this discussion the only certain date is approximately 180 B.C. for the writing of Ecclesiasticus and the activity of Ben Sira, whereas Ecclesiastes has been assigned to the fourth-second centuries. Hence the possibility of the dependence of Qoheleth upon Ben Sira cannot be discounted a priori. As far as ideas are concerned, there is no serious sign of dependency between Ben Sira and Qoheleth. Ben Sira spread his net rather wide and composed a true *vademecum* of Hebrew wisdom. As his translator noted in the preface to the Greek translation, he knew the Hebrew Bible well, "having devoted himself for a long time to the diligent study of the law, the prophets, and the rest of the books." *Style anthologique* or anthological composition (the use of earlier biblical phraseology) is charac-teristic of the Qumran writings and of later biblical literature, including Sirach. Not much is to be gained by highlighting the differences between Ecclesiastes and Sirach. These are fairly obvious and have their own inner logic. The mood of Sirach is clearly different from that of Qoheleth. Although both authors work within the typical OT perspective of Death and Sheol, Ben Sira reflects traditional resignation in the face of death (38:16–23; cf. 40:1–11; 41:1–13), and he gener-ally reflects the optimism of the wisdom movement. He has his own program of theodicy, which frequently provokes hymns of praise (16:24–28:14; 39:12–35; 42:15–43:33). He writes without any concern for the disturbing note introduced into the wisdom movement by Qoheleth. One might say that the epilogue in Eccl 12:9–14 (see the *Comment* on these verses) is an attempt to assimilate Qoheleth to Ben Sira or to the thinking that Ben Sira represents.

When one turns to consider verbal similarities between Ecclesiastes and Sirach (whether in the Hebrew or Greek form), several associations have been pointed out. Among these the following seem to be the most significant.

1. All is beautiful/good in time (כל ... יפה/טוב ... בעתו), Eccl 3:11; Sir 39:16.
2. The divinity (Lord/God) seeks (נרדף [בקש]/[שׁ]), Eccl 3:13; (נרדפים) Sir 5:3; see *Comment* below on 3:15.
3. An association between חכמה/לב ("wisdom") and a change of face (פנים שׁנא); Eccl 8:1; Sir 13:25, but cf. Prov 15:13; Job 14:20; Dan 3:19.
4. One in a thousand (אחדמעלף); Eccl 7:28; Sir 6:6; cf. Job 23:33.
5. The proper time (עת and זמן), Eccl 3:1; Sir 4:20 (emended text); cf. Sir 33:16b, 33b.
6. End of the matter (סוף/וקץ דבר), cf. Eccl 12:13; Sir 43:27; cf. Dan 7:28.
7. Either (for) good or (for) evil (אם [ל] טוב ואם [ל] רע), Eccl 12:14; Sir 13:25.
8. On snake-charming, Eccl 10:11; Sir 12:13.
9. Some verbal echoes can be found in the idea expressed in Sir 40:11 and Eccl 3:20; 12:7; both depend on Gen 3:19 (cf. Job 34:15).

On the strength of these and other associations it is not possible to prove de-pendence in either direction. The data are simply ambiguous, and some of the similarities could easily derive from a common source. The most intriguing is the relationship between Eccl 3:15 and Sir 5:3. The meaning of the former is quite obscure (see the *Comment* below).

Over the last two centuries there has been considerable discussion about the relationship of the Wisdom of Solomon (esp. chap. 2) to Ecclesiastes. Although there are nuances to various positions, it is widely claimed that Wisdom was directed in part against Ecclesiastes. As F. Delitzsch put it (212), the work has "the appearance of an anti-Ecclesiastes, a side-piece to the Book of Koheleth, which aims partly at confuting it, partly at going beyond it." Some see in the Wisdom of Solomon an attempt to straighten out the record in favor of Solomon, the reputed author of Ecclesiastes. Others speak of an attack on the misuse of the book by free-thinking Jews in Alexandria. It may be observed that commentators on Ecclesiastes are often prone to see that book under attack by the author of Wisdom (C. H. Wright, G. Barton; E. Podechard is a notable exception). On the other hand, many commentators on Wisdom represent the negative opinion (J. Gregg, P. Heinisch).

A careful examination of the data along with a survey of older discussion has been provided by P. W. Skehan (*Studies*, 213–36). The topic has not been pursued to any extent since then, but the latest explicit discussion by C. Larcher (*Etudes*, 93–103) accepted the conclusions of Skehan. The nature of the argumentation can be merely illustrated here. The general run of claims and counterclaims has the appearance of being more impressionistic than substantive. When the evidence is based upon ideas, rather than upon verbal echoes, one must face the serious objection that the alleged ideas are too broadly current in the Hellenistic world to be narrowed down to a particular book such as Ecclesiastes. Then there is the uncertainty whether the author of Wisdom knew Ecclesiastes in Hebrew and/or in Greek. Verbal contacts, individually and cumulatively, are the strongest evidence for some kind of relationship, but even here ambiguities appear. Thus the use of $\mu\epsilon\rho\iota\varsigma$ in Wis 2:9 *can* be an echo of חלק *ḥeleq*, a favorite word in Eccl (2:10, 21; 3:22; 5:17; 9:9). This type of argument however has to be governed by clearly pertinent usage. Thus, in the case of $\mu\epsilon\rho\iota\varsigma$ we discover that it is embedded in a typical biblical phrase on the lips of the impious: "this is our portion [$\mu\epsilon\rho\iota\varsigma$] and this is our lot [$\kappa\lambda\hat{\eta}\rho\sigma\varsigma$]," which reflect חלק וגורל or חלק ונחלה. They are claiming that *their* portion is the enjoyment of life, regardless of human rights. They are attacking not Qoheleth but rather the general biblical idea of the Lord as the giver and perfecter of one's lot (see Skehan, *Studies*, 228–29). Moreover, even if a word might echo an idea found also in Ecclesiastes, a broad base of instances is necessary. One needs far more than the examples, themselves inconclusive, of $\mu\iota\sigma\theta\acute{o}\varsigma$/שכר, "recompense," in Wis 2:22 and Eccl 9:5, and $\sigma\kappa\iota\alpha$/צל, "shadow," in Wis 2:5 and Eccl 6:12. A significant number of pertinent examples are not forthcoming to make a case for the dependence of Wisdom upon Ecclesiastes.

If one makes a general comparison of the two books, it may be said that Wisdom gives an "answer" to a question that appears in Eccl 2:16: how does the wise man die, just like the fool? The reply lies in the doctrine of a blessed immortality that is the lot of the just; they are truly in the (loving) "hand of God" (Wis 3:1; 7:16, contrast Eccl 9:1). But this answer is a general one to the OT perspective of Sheol—to the faith of Job (19:25ff.) as well as to the resignation of David (2 Sam 12:23). In particular, the question of the psalmist (in Sheol, who will praise you? Pss 6:6; 30:10; 88:11–13) is resolved, because the $\mu\iota\sigma\theta\acute{o}\varsigma$, "recompense," of the just is in the Lord who takes $\phi\rho\sigma\nu\tau\iota\varsigma$, "thought," of them (Wis 5:15). Thus the message of Wisdom may not be envisioned solely in terms of Ecclesiastes. There is simply no necessary connection; as P. Skehan (*Studies*, 232) puts it: "both derive some fundamental thoughts from the stock common to the Wisdom writers, but each then goes his own way, and it cannot be said that Wisdom is dependent on Ecclesiastes for the turn taken in the discourse."

The whole question receives some perspective if one examines the relationship of Wisdom to other sources, biblical, Jewish, and Hellenistic, as done by C. Larcher. When Wisdom is viewed in the light of its use of LXX, and its analogies to the literature about Enoch, to the writings of Qumran, Philo, and other intertestamental works, its supposed links to Ecclesiastes fade away. Speaking merely of the inner biblical echoes in Wisdom, Larcher (*Etudes*, 102) summarizes the situation: "Finally one will note the very variety of biblical books that are exploited . . . . Wis 1 (chaps 1–5) uses above all Gen 1–2 and Isa 40–56; then Isa 1–39, Prov, Sir and certain Psalms." The interest of the author of Wisdom seems clearly to have been in another direction than to be "anti-Ecclesiastes."

History of Interpretation

Bibliography

Most commentaries have at least short summaries of the history of interpretation, e.g., G. A. Barton, 18–31, and especially C. D. Ginsburg, 27–243. Note also the following:

Patristic and Medieval:

Holm-Nielsen, S. "On the Interpretation of Qoheleth in Early Christianity." *VT* 24 (1974) 168–77. ―――――. "The Book of Ecclesiastes and the Interpretation of It in Jewish and Christian Theology." *ASTI* 10 (1976) 40–55. **Jarick, J.** *Gregory Thaumaturgos' Paraphrase of Ecclesiastes.* SBLSCS 29. Atlanta: Scholars Press, 1990 (see also *Abr-Naharain* 27 [1989] 37–57). **Leanza, S.** "Sul *Commentario all'Ecclesiastes* di Girolamo." In *Jérôme entre l'occident et l'orient.* Ed. Y. M. Duval. Paris: Etudes Augustiniennes, 1988. 267–82. **Monti, D.** "Bonaventure's Interpretation of Scripture in His Exegetical Works." Diss., University of Chicago, 1979. **Murphy, R. E.** "Qoheleth Interpreted: The Bearing of the Past on the Present." *VT* 32 (1982) 331–37. **Rayez, A.** "Ecclésiaste: 3, Commentateurs." In *Dictionnaire de Spiritualité.* Ed. M. Viller et al. Paris: Beauchesne, 1932. 4:47–52. **Salters, R.** "Exegetical Problems in Qoheleth." *IBS* 10 (1988) 44–59. **Smalley, B.** *Medieval Exegesis of Wisdom Literature.* Ed. R. E. Murphy. Atlanta: Scholars Press, 1986.

Jewish:

Diez Merino, L., ed. *Targum de Qohelet.* BHB 13. Madrid: Consejo superior de Investigaciones Scientificas, 1987. **Flesher, P. V. M.** "The Wisdom of the Sages: Rabbinic Rewriting of Qohelet." In *AAR/SBL Abstracts.* Atlanta: Scholars Press, 1990. 390. **Levine, E.** *The Aramaic Version of Qohelet.* New York: Sepher-Hermon, 1981. **Saadia Gaon.** *The Book of Beliefs and Opinions.* Tr. S. Rosenblatt. New Haven: Yale UP, 1940. **Schiffer, S.** *Das Buch Kohelet nach der Auffassung der Weisen des Talmud und Midrasch und der Jüdischen Erklärer des*

Mittelalters. Frankfort A. M./Leipzig, 1884. Since this work does not reach beyond A.D. 500, the best general summary is in the commentary of C. D. Ginsburg, 27–99. See also **Vajda, G.** *Deux commentaries Karaïtes sur l'Ecclésiaste.* EJM 4. Leiden: Brill, 1971.

Reformation:

Brenz, J. *Der Prediger Salomo: Faksimile-Neudruck der ersten Ausgabe Hagenau 1528.* Stuttgart: Frommann, 1970. **Kallas, E.** "Ecclesiastes: *Traditum et Fides Evangelica.* The Ecclesiastes Commentaries of Martin Luther, Philip Melanchthon, and Johannes Brenz Considered within the History of Interpretation." Diss., Graduate Theological Union, Berkeley, 1979. **Luther, M.** "Notes on Ecclesiastes." In *Luther's Works.* Ed. J. Pelikan. St. Louis: Concordia, 1972. 15:3–187. **Melanchthon, P.** "Enarratio Brevis . . . Ecclesiastes." In *Corpus Reformatorum.* C. G. Bretschneider, ed. Halle: Schwetschke, 1847. 14:89–159. **Wölfel, E.** *Luther und die Skepsis: Eine Studie zur Kohelet-Exegese Luthers.* FGLP X,12. München: Kaiser, 1958.

Other Literature:

Barucq, A. "Qohéleth." *DBSup* 9. 609–74. **Bretón, S.** "Qoheleth Studies." *BTB* 3 (1973) 22–50, 276–99. **Crenshaw, J. L.** "Qoheleth in Current Research." *HAR* 7 (1983) 41–56. **Galling, K.** "Kohelet-Studien." *ZAW* 50 (1932) 276–99. ―――――. "Stand und Aufgabe der Kohelet-Forschung." *TRu* 6 (1934) 355–73. **Palm, A.** *Die Qoheleth-Literatur: Ein Beitrag zur Exegese des Alten Testaments.* Mannheim, 1886. **Pedersen, J.** *Scepticisme Israélite.* Cahiers de *RHPR.* Paris: Alcan, 1931.

A sketch of the history of the interpretation of Ecclesiastes is more rewarding than the corresponding history for most other biblical books (see R. E. Murphy, *VT* 32 [1982] 331–37). There is a remarkable homogeneity in the way in which the book was interpreted over the centuries because of certain clearly defined presuppositions, or directions, of exegesis. The term, presuppositions, is not meant pejoratively; it is just that certain factors emerged as primary in the interpretation of the book by the majority of both Christian and Jewish writers.

1. Solomonic authorship. The identity of Qoheleth with Solomon created a certain aura for the author; he could share in that monarch's piety and wisdom. Moreover, the work was seen as part of the Solomonic corpus, and this context created a way of looking at the book. Beryl Smalley (*Medieval Exegesis,* 40) comments on this: "The patristic tradition on 'the books of Solomon' derived from Origen; it was transmitted by St. Jerome, and reproduced in the *Gloss.* Solomon wrote his three books, Proverbs, Ecclesiastes and the Canticle, in order to instruct mankind in the three states of the spiritual life. Proverbs taught men how to live virtuously in the world and was meant for beginners. Ecclesiastes taught them to despise the things of the world as vain and fleeting and was meant for *proficientes* [those who are progressing]. The Canticle told initiates of the love of God."

2. The motto of the book, "vanity of vanities" (Eccl 1:2). This was interpreted against the perspective of a belief in immortality in the next life. Hence it lent support to asceticism and discipline. Coupled with 12:13 ("fear God and keep his commandments"), the motto actually worked against the harsh view of reality taken by Qoheleth.

3. The recognition of tensions within the book. Early on it was thought that "Solomon" was dialoguing with others, whether fools or knaves. This meant that

certain views of Qoheleth could be judged as out of harmony with "Solomon" and were to be attributed to someone else.

The above considerations do not exhaust all the directions taken over the course of centuries; other features of the work, such as the emphasis on שמחה śimhâ, "joy," also play a role. But these factors set the tone for interpretation, and keep reappearing throughout the history of exegesis.

CHRISTIAN INTERPRETATION

The works of Hippolytus of Rome and of Origen on Ecclesiastes have been preserved only in a few fragments (see S. Leanza, *L'esegesi di Origene al libro dell'Ecclesiaste* [Reggio Calabria: Edizioni Parallelo 38, 1975]). The earliest extant work is by Gregory Thaumaturgus ("Metaphrasis in Ecclesiasten," *PG* 10:987–1018; see J. Jarick, *Paraphrase*, 1–6, 309–16). His *Metaphrasis* is an extremely free paraphrase of Ecclesiastes, and he speaks in the first person, like Qoheleth. He readily brings out many of the difficulties of the human condition scored in the work. However, he generally gives a twist to the more refractory reflections that do not sit well with Christian orthodoxy. Thus, commenting on 2:16, he remarks, "There is nothing common to the wise and to the fool, whether it be human memory or God's reward. The end comes upon human things even when they seem to be just beginning. The wise person never participates in the same end as the fool" (10:993–94; J. Jarick, *Paraphrase*, 48–44). The sting is generally taken out of Qoheleth's statements, and at one point (on Eccl 9:1–3), Gregory asserts, "Now I think these are the thoughts and deceits and pretenses of fools" (10:1009–10; J. Jarick, *Paraphrase*, 226–28). This distinction between the thought of Qoheleth and the views of others whom he is refuting is continued in Gregory of Nyssa, and Gregory the Great, right on into modern times.

The principle of several opinions being represented in Ecclesiastes has also received classical expression in the Dialogues of Gregory the Great (see *Gregory the Great: Dialogues*, FC 39 [New York: Fathers of the Church, 1959] 193–94): "This book, then, is called 'the preacher' because in it Solomon makes the feelings of the disorganized people his own in order to search into and give expression to the thoughts that come to their untutored minds perhaps by way of temptation. For the sentiments he expresses in his search are as varied as the individuals he impersonates. But, like a true preacher, he stretches out his arms at the end of his address and calms the troubled spirits of the assembled people, calling them back to one way of thinking. This we see him do at the close of the book, where he says, 'Let us all hear together the conclusion of the discourse. Fear God and keep His commandments: for this is man's all.' If he did not impersonate many individuals in his manner of speaking, why did he urge all of them to listen together to the conclusion of his discourse? When at the end of the book he says, 'Let us all hear together,' he is his own witness that he was speaking for many persons and not for himself alone. Therefore, we find that some statements of this book are introduced as inquiries, while others are meant to give satisfaction by their logic. In some he reproduces the thoughts of one tempted and still given over to the pleasures of his life; in others he discusses matters that pertain to reason and tries to restrain the soul from pleasure" (Dialogue 4).

The preface that Jerome writes for his commentary in 338–389 tells us something of the setting (see "Commentarius in Ecclesiasten," 249–361). About five years before, in Rome, he had read and explained Ecclesiastes to a certain Blesilla, "to provoke her to contempt of the world." Her request for a "little commentary" was never honored, one reason being her sudden death. Now Jerome writes his commentary in Jerusalem, addressing Paula and Eustochium. He distinguishes assiduously between the literal *(haec juxta litteram)* and spiritual meaning *(secundum intellegentiam spiritalem)* as he proceeds with a verse-by-verse commentary. Many of his comments show him coming to grips with the literal meaning of the text. Of Eccl 1:12 he asks, "if God made everything very good, how is it vanity?" He answers that everything is good *per se*, but nothing compared to God. Jerome replies to the difficulty of 3:18–21 by denying that Ecclesiastes says that the soul perishes with the body, but in fact "before the coming of Christ all things were brought *ad inferos*." In commenting on 9:7–8 he recognizes a προσωποποιίαν, ("personification"; he uses the Greek word) at work: "in the style of orators and poets" the author says certain things (that are unacceptable from Jerome's view). Then, "as it were not from the person of another but from his own person," Ecclesiastes is reinterpreted from an orthodox point of view. As has already been remarked, this hermeneutical device is characteristic of the history of the exegesis of the book.

While noting the influence of Origen and the allegorical approach on Jerome, S. Leanza (*"Commentario,"* 269–81) correctly insists upon the fairly liberal interpretation found in Jerome's commentary: erudite philology, command of the ancient Greek versions, lessons from his Jewish tutor, Bar-Aqiba, etc. The statement in the comment on Eccl 1:14 is meaningful: "necessity compels us to discuss the Hebrew terms more frequently than we wish. But we cannot know the meaning, unless we learn it from the words." Leanza remarks a certain eclecticism in Jerome. Thus, he borrows from Gregory Thaumaturgus the idea of a fictitious dialogue that Solomon is having with atheists and Epicureans. While Jerome has recourse to allegory to get out of a difficulty (e.g., Eccl 8:15), he does not avoid the problems provided by 2:24–26 and 3:12–13. He first gives a literal treatment before going to any allegorical meaning. Leanza points to the comment on 12:1 and 12:6–8 to indicate that Jerome's general position is that Qoheleth maintains that all is vanity, but it is right to have licit enjoyment, even if this is ultimately also vain (261). The fact remains, however, that Jerome did not properly reckon with the OT understanding of Sheol (cf. Eccl 9:10).

The influence of Jerome's commentary was dominant in the rest of the patristic and medieval period. However, B. Smalley (*Medieval Exegesis*, 42–43) has called attention to the significance of the commentary by Bonaventure (d. 1274). This book gave Bonaventure "an opportunity to enlarge on his favorite theme: wisdom as a means to sanctification." As usual, the "contempt of the world" is discussed, and Bonaventure raises the problem of how the world can be despised as mere vanity. He has recourse to a simile, comparing the world to a wedding ring given to a bride by her husband. She can hardly love her ring more than her lover, and on the other hand she cannot despise it as worthless, since that would reflect upon the giver. Smalley summarized Bonaventure's solution: "She must regard it as nothing *relatively* to her love for her husband and this will be to his glory. In a relative, not in an absolute sense, therefore must we despise the world."

Bonaventure characterized the message of Ecclesiastes (D. Monti, *Bonaventure's Interpretation of Scripture in His Exegetical Works*, 85): "If a person wishes to be happy, he must love future goods and spurn those of the present." This view reflects the traditional *contemptus mundi*, which, however, is relativized by the eschatological perspective. Bonaventure was influenced by Jerome and accepted the characterization of Solomon's three books for beginners (Proverbs), for the proficient (Ecclesiastes), and for the initiates (Song). Great influence upon him seems to have been exercised by the *Homilies* of Hugh of St. Victor (*In Salomonis Ecclesiasten Homiliae, PL* 175:113–256, esp. 119), in particular, Hugh's conceptualization of the *triplex vanitas* or triple emptiness: the emptiness of the temporal world (*vanitas mutabilitatis*); the emptiness of those who seek only the goods of this world (*vanitas curiositatis vel cupiditatis*); and the emptiness of the misery that results (*vanitas mortalitatis*). This governs Bonaventure's outline of the book into three sections corresponding to the *triplex vanitas:* 1:3–3:15; 3:16–7:23; 7:24–12:7. In addition, Bonaventure's prologue carries an analysis of Ecclesiastes by means of the Aristotelian four causes: final, material, formal, and efficient. Under the formal cause he recognizes an old device: Solomon "acts like an orator, proposing various opinions, first of a sage, then of a fool, so that a single truth from various opinions becomes evident to his audience" (See "Commentarius in Ecclesiasten," in *Doctoris Seraphici S. Bonaventurae opera ommia* [Florence: Quaracchi, 1983] 6:6). In the commentary itself he clearly distinguishes between the literal interpretation and the spiritual sense (the latter is provided for only thirteen passages, and then placed at the end of the pericope). No less than eighty-three "questions," about a quarter of the commentary, deal with theological issues (ethics, science, etc.) that arise from text.

The last of the medieval commentators is also one of the first moderns, the Franciscan Nicholas of Lyra (d. circa 1349), whose *Postillae Perpetuae* was the first *printed* biblical commentary (Rome, 1471–72). He concludes that the fear of God (Eccl 12:13) is the true source of happiness, in contrast to wealth and other topics treated by Qoheleth.

The beginning of the Reformation was marked by no less than three commentaries on Ecclesiastes, authored by Johannes Brenz (1528), Martin Luther (1532), and Philip Melanchthon (1550) (See E. Kallas, *Ecclesiastes: Traditum et Fides Evangelica*). These three reformers unite in rejecting the influence of Jerome, and particularly the monastic appropriation of Ecclesiastes in the spirit of *contemptus mundi*. For Luther, what is condemned in the book is "the depraved affection and desire of us men." He writes: "The summary and aim of this book, then, is as follows: Solomon wants to put us at peace and to give us a quiet mind in the everyday affairs and business of this life, so that we may live contentedly in the present without care and yearning about the future" ("Notes on Ecclesiastes," in *Luther's Works*, 15:7–8). His "Notes on Ecclesiastes" are filled with many vital and sharp references to the contemporary situation. Ecclesiastes is seen as a book "against free will," which thus serves Luther in his dispute with Erasmus. Some problematic passages in the work are deprived of their bite, such as 3:19–20, where the similarity of man and beast is said to be only "in appearance." Of course, the theological concerns of the Reformation are frequently to the fore, as when Luther hails 9:6 as proof against "the invocation of the saints and the fiction of purgatory."

Melanchthon ("Enarratio Brevis . . . Ecclesiastes," 14:89–159), although he never mentions Luther's commentary nor joins the controversy over free will, likewise opposed his interpretation to "the ravings of monks (14:100)." He found a doctrine of providence in the book: God cares for his creation (14:95).

Brenz comments on Luther's German translation (completed 1524); he too is against the monastic interpretation and, with Luther, interprets 3:1–15 as militating against a doctrine of free will. In the preface to his commentary, he likens the book to an addition to the Mosaic Law. For the Law teaches that humans do not have the power to act virtuously, that their own works merely led to failure. Thus none can boast that they can achieve anything of virtue apart from God. The book also contains "what Paul says about righteousness: circumcision avails nothing" (J. Brenz, 2–3). It is clear that the theological concerns of the Reformation are perceptible in this reading.

Juan de Pineda, S.J. (d. 1637), wrote what C. D. Ginsburg (130) characterized as a "gigantic commentary" without equal on Ecclesiastes: 1079 pages in folio. It is a mine for patristic and medieval sources and reflects the pious interpretation of the vanity of the earthly compared with the heavenly, the theme in *Imitation of Christ* (Book I, Chap. 1) attributed to Thomas à Kempis (d. 1471). The commentary of Cornelius à Lapide, S.J. (d. 1639), a contemporary of Pineda, is in the same direction.

The remarkable polymath Hugo Grotius (d. 1645) has been acclaimed as the first of the moderns to deny that Solomon was the author of Ecclesiastes. In his *Annotationes in Vetus Testamentum* (ed. G. Vogel [Halae: I. Curt, 1875–76] 1:434), he writes that the book "was written later under the name of that king as one who was penitent." The motif of Solomon's "conversion" in the production of Ecclesiastes appeared early on, especially in Jewish interpretation (Targum, Rashi, et al.).

C. D. Ginsburg's summary of the interpretation of the seventeenth and eighteenth centuries indicates a relatively conservative and even traditional interpretation of Ecclesiastes, especially among English divines. The same trend is illustrated in the work of Augustin Calmet, O.S.B. (d. 1752), author of a twenty-six-volume commentary on the entire Bible. The remarks of Bishop Robert Lowth (*Lectures on the Sacred Poetry of the Hebrews,* Lecture 24 [Boston: Buckingham, 1815] 342) about Ecclesiastes are particularly true and appropriate today: "scarcely any two commentators have agreed concerning the plan of the work, and accurate division of it into parts or sections."

JEWISH INTERPRETATION

In the discussion of canonicity (in "Introductory Questions," xxiii) it was pointed out that early on there was some question about the canonicity of the Song of Songs and Ecclesiastes, as related in *Yadayim* 3.5. The subsequent history of the interpretation of the book shows that while difficulties were recognized, they were also resolved. The principle of Solomonic authorship was an important factor in Jewish understanding. This is shown by several moves in the Targum. Thus, in general, the Targum claims that Solomon foresaw Israel's later history, the division of the kingdom and the exile. The labor of Solomon had indeed been in vain, in the light of the work of such descendants as Rehoboam and Jeroboam (1:2). In 1:12–13 of the Targum is reflected the deposing of Solomon from the throne (cf. Eccl 1:12, הָיִיתִי, "I *was* king") as a result of his sins. Legend had it that he was deposed by Asmodeus, king of demons—a story related also in the Talmud (*b. Giṭ.* 68a, 68b) and elsewhere.

More important, however, is the influence of the Torah upon the interpretation of Qoheleth. Paul V. M. Flesher (*AAR/SBL Abstracts*, 1990, 390) has spoken correctly about the "rabbinic rewriting" of the book. He points out the difference between the sage of the Hebrew Bible, open to experience and to change, and the sage of rabbinic Judaism, open to the Torah. It is a striking fact that no midrashim were written about the biblical wisdom books in the rabbinic period (roughly A.D. 70 to A.D. 640). Qoheleth was made into a rabbinic sage who is governed by the Torah. The profit for a person is to have studied the word of God, the law (Eccl 1:3), and thus to be rewarded in the world to come by the ruler of the world. The strategy is similar to Christian interpreters who also interpreted Qoheleth in the light of (Christian) beliefs. For Judaism the primacy of the Torah and the belief in the world to come were two basic premises.

In addition, the epilogue (Eccl 12:9–14) also helped later readers, as can be illustrated by the following:

> Rab Judah son of R. Samuel b. Shilath said in Rab's name:
> The Sages wished to hide the Book of Ecclesiastes, because its words are self-contradictory, yet why did they not hide it? Because its beginning is religious teaching and its end is religious teaching, as it is written, *What profit had man of all his labour wherein he laboreth under the sun?* And the School of R. Jannai commented: Under the sun he has none, but he has it [*sc.* profit] before the sun. The end thereof is religious teaching, as it is written, *Let us hear the conclusion of the matter, fear God and keep his commandments: for this is the whole of man.* What is meant by, 'for this is the whole of man'?—Said R. Eleazar. The entire world was created only for the sake of this [type of] man. Simeon b. ʿAzzai— others state, Simeon b. Zoma—said: The entire world was created only to be a companion to this man (*b. Šabb.*, 30b; Epstein edition, *Seder Moʿed*, 1:135).

This kind of understanding is also reflected in Ibn Ezra's interpretation, which is summarized thus by C. D. Ginsburg (46): "the Lord inspired Solomon to explain these things, and to teach the right way, to show that all the devices of man are vanity, that the fear of God can alone make him happy, and that his fear can only be obtained by the study of wisdom."

According to G. Vajda (*Deux commentaires*, 1–2) Saadia Gaon never wrote a commentary on Ecclesiastes, although he quoted him several times. He never explicitly doubted the orthodoxy of this "Solomon," but he does interpret the book in a benign way. Thus, an old device (already among Christian interpreters as well; see above, p. 1) appears: certain opinions expressed were not held by Solomon but by fools (Eccl 9:3–6 seems to be against any belief in immortality).

At the end of Saadia's *Book of Beliefs and Opinions* (tr. S. Rosenblatt [New Haven: Yale UP, 1948] 404–7) there is a remarkably full use of Ecclesiastes to elucidate the Gaon's view of proper conduct. The Gaon also interpreted some statements like this: "these utterances did not represent his own [Solomon's] point of view but were a recounting quotation by him of the speech of the foolish and of the insane thoughts entertained by them in their hearts" (419; see also 275).

What once passed as a commentary of Saadia on Qoheleth has been shown to be a summary of a commentary by Salmon ben Jeruhim. G. Vajda has published a translation of the commentary by Salmon and also one by another Karaite, Yefet ben ꞌEli (both from the tenth century). Salmon's views can be summarized under five points: the vanity of this world, the emphasis on life beyond death, the pursuit of wisdom over folly, the importance of good works (cf. Eccl 12:13, fear God and keep the commandments), the punishment and reward of the next world (cf. Vajda, *Deux commentaires,* 12–13). Yefet shares many of the concerns of Salmon, such as observance of the Law and belief in the victory of justice in the world to come.

A wide diversity among modern Jewish commentators, from Moses Mendelssohn (d. 1786) to Samuel Luzzatto (d. 1865), is described in the summary given by C. D. Ginsburg (78–98).

CONCLUSION

It is appropriate to terminate this sketch of the history of interpretation at this point. The current views will be evident in the discussion found in the rest of the commentary. The purpose of this brief summary is to provide a handle for the reader on the more significant views of the past, but also thereby to raise questions about assumptions and preconceptions in the present.

If there is one feature that is common to *all* periods in the history of the interpretation of Ecclesiastes it is that of selective emphasis. In *Scepticisme Israélite* Johannes Pedersen concludes from his brief resume of history of exegesis (with particular attention to J. D. Michaelis and Ernest Renan) that "very different types have found their own image in Ecclesiastes, and it is remarkable that none of the interpretations mentioned is completely without some basis. There are many aspects in our book; different interpreters have highlighted what was most fitting for themselves and their age, and they understood it in their own way. But for all there was a difficulty, namely that there were also other aspects which could hardly be harmonized with their preferred view" (20). This observation is true of other ages and interpreters as well. If the trend of the patristic writers and most medievals was to find in the book a doctrine to abjure the world, later emphases were equally selective, such as fear of the Lord (Eccl 12:13), and enjoyment of life (שִׂמְחָה *śimḥâ*), the vanity of the world in the perspective of one who believes in a blessed immortality, or the issue of the greatest good *(summum bonum).* Or sometimes the book was interpreted in a pious vein as an expression of Solomon's "conversion." These directions appear over and over again, and they are the inevitable expression of the tensions that exist in the book itself and also within the interpreters.

It has been said that we must learn history so that we will not repeat the mistakes that have been made in the past. These few *windows* into the history of the interpretation of Ecclesiastes can be profitable to modern exegetes: (1) They enable one to understand the origin of various exegetical trends. (2) They serve, at least in a negative way, to help us examine and clarify our own presuppositions. If we do not accept Solomonic authorship, what is the concept of authorship that we are working with today. Is it Q^1 and Q^2 and Q^{inf}? Will a future generation find this position unsatisfactory, and center its attention on the book instead? How many far-fetched theories have been hazarded by modern writers who are locked up in their own crippling presuppositions? Even the vagaries and extravagances of ancient exegesis can have a sobering effect on current scholarship. We need not repeat the mistakes of the past, and we can be made more aware of our own presuppositions.

As David C. Steinmetz ("John Calvin on Isaiah 6," *Int* 36 [1982] 156–170, esp. 170) has remarked, "The principal value of precritical exegesis is that it is not modern exegesis; it is alien, strange, sometimes even, from our perspective, comic and fantastical. Precisely because it is strange, it provides a constant stimulus to modern interpreters, offering exegetical suggestions they would never think of themselves or find in any recent book, forcing them again and again to a rereading and re-evaluation of the text. Interpreters who immerse themselves, however, not only in the text but in these alien approaches to the text may find in time that they have learned to see, with eyes not their own, sights they could scarcely have imagined and to hear, with ears not their own, voices too soft for their own ears to detect."

The Message of Ecclesiastes

General Bibliography

Armstrong, J. F. "Ecclesiastes in Old Testament Theology." *PSB* 94 (1983) 16-25. **Barucq, A.** "Qohéleth." *DBSup* 10:609–74. **Beauchamp, P.** "Entendre Qohelet." *Christus* 16 (1969) 339–51. **Chapineau, J.** "L'image de Qohélet dans l'exégèse contemporaine." *RHPR* 59 (1979) 595–603. **Collins, J. J.** "Proverbial Wisdom and the Yahwist Vision." In *Gnomic Wisdom.* Ed. J. D. Crossan. Semeia 17. Chico: Scholars Press, 1980. 1–17. **Crenshaw, J. L.** "The Birth of Skepticism." In *The Divine Helmsman: Studies on God's Control of Human Events Presented to Lou H. Silberman.* Ed. J. L. Crenshaw and S. Sandmel. New York: KTAV, 1980. 1–19. **Crüsemann, F.** "Hiob und Kohelet." In *Werden und Wirken des Alten Testaments.* FS C. Westermann. Ed. R. Albertz et al. Göttingen: Vandenhoeck & Ruprecht, 1980. ————. "Die unveränderbare Welt: Überlegungen zur 'Krisis der Weisheit' beim Prediger (Kohelet)." In *Der Gott der kleiner Leute.* Ed. W. Schottroff et al. Sozialgeschichtliche Auslegungen, Altes Testament, Bd. I. München: Kaiser, 1979. 80–104 (ET: *God of the Lowly: Sociohistorical Interpretation of the Bible.* Ed. W. Schottroff. Maryknoll: Orbis, 1984. 57–77). **Duesberg, H.,** and **Fransen, I.** "La critique de la sagesse par le Qoheleth." In *Les Scribes Inspirés.* Maredsous: Editions de Maredsous, 1969. 537–92. **Festorazzi, F.** "Il Qohelet: un sapiente d'Israele alla ricerca di Dio. Ragione-fede in rapporto dialectico." In *Quaerere Deum.* Atti della XXV Settimana Biblica. Brescia: Paideia, 1980. 173–90. **Forman, C.** "The Pessimism of Ecclesiastes." *JSS* 3 (1958) 336–43. **Galling, K.** *Die Krise der Aufklärung in Israel.* MU 19. Mainz, 1952. **Gerleman, G.** "Adam und die alttestamentliche Anthropologie." In *Die Botschaft und die Boten.* FS H. W. Wolff. Ed. J. Jeremias et al. Neukirchen-Vluyn: Neukirchener, 1981. 319–33. **Gese, H.** *Lehre und Wirklichkeit in der alten Weisheit.* Tübingen: Mohr/Siebeck, 1958. ————. "Die Krise der Weisheit bei Kohelet." In *Les sagesses du proche-orient ancien: Colloque de Strasbourg, 1962.* Paris: Presses Universitaires, 1963. 139–51 (= "The Crisis of Wisdom in Koheleth." In *Theodicy in the Old Testament.* Ed. J. Crenshaw. Philadelphia: Westminster, 1983. 141–53). **Ginsberg, H. L.** "The Quintessence of Koheleth." In *Biblical and Other Studies.* Ed. A. Altman. Philip W. Lown Institute of Advanced Judaic Studies Brandeis University, Studies and Texts, 1. Cambridge: Harvard UP, 1963. 47–59. **Good, E. M.** "Qoheleth: The Limits of Wisdom." In *Irony in the Old Testament.* 2nd ed. Sheffield: Almond Press, 1981. 168–95. **Hengel, M.** *Judaism and Hellenism.* Philadelphia: Fortress,

1974. **Kaiser, O.** "Die Sinnkrise bei Kohelet." In *Der Mensch unter dem Schicksal.* BZAW 161. Berlin: de Gruyter, 1985. 91–109. **Klopfenstein, M. A.** "Die Skepsis des Qohelet." *TZ* 28 (1972) 97–109. **Lang, B.** "Ist der Mensch hilflos? Das biblische Buch Kohelet neu und kritisch gelesen." *TQ* 159 (1979) 109–24. **Lauha, A.** "Die Krise des religiösen Glaubens bei Kohelet." In *Wisdom in Israel and in the Ancient Near East.* Ed. M. Noth et al. VTSup 3. Leiden: Brill, 1953. 83–91. ————. "Kohelets Verhältnis zur Geschichte." In *Die Botschaft und die Boten.* FS H. W. Wolff. Ed. J. Jeremias et al. Neukirchen-Vluyn: Neukirchener, 1981. 393–401. **Lohfink, N.** "Gegenwart und Ewigkeit: die Zeit im Buch Kohelet." *GL* 60 (1987) 2–12 (ET: *TD* 34 [1987] 236–40). **Michel, D.** "Qohelet-Probleme: Überlegungen zu Qoh 8,2–9 und 7,11–14." *TV* 15 (1979/80) 81–103 (= Eigenart, 84–115). ————. *Qohelet.* EF 258. Darmstadt: Wissenschaftliche Buchgesellschaft, 1988. 87–107. **Müller, H.-P.** "Theonome Skepsis und Lebensfreude: Zu Koh 1,12–3,15." *BZ* 30 (1986) 1–19. ————. "Neige der althebräischen 'Weisheit': Zum Denken Qohäläts." *ZAW* 90 (1978) 238–64. ————. "Der unheimliche Gast." *ZTK* 84 (1987) 440–64. **Murphy, R. E.** "Koheleth, der Skeptiker." In *Leiden und christlicher Glaube.* Concilium 12/11 (1976) 567–70. ————. "Qohelet's 'Quarrel' with the Fathers." In *From Faith to Faith.* Ed. D. Y. Hadidian. PTMS 31. Pittsburgh: Pickwick Press, 1979. 235–45. ————. "Qoheleth and Theology?" *BTB* 21 (1991) 30–33. **Ochoa, J. M. R.** "Estudio de la dimensión temporal en Prov., Job y Qoh." *EstBib* 22 (1963) 33–67. **Pedersen, J.** *Scepticisme Israélite.* Cahiers de *RHPR.* Paris: Alcan, 1931. **Perdue, L.** *Wisdom and Cult.* SBLDS 30. Missoula: Scholars Press, 1977. **Pfeiffer, R.** "The Peculiar Skepticism of Ecclesiastes." *JBL* 53 (1934) 100–109. **Preuss, H. D.** "Der Prediger Salomo (Qohelet)." In *Einführung in die alttestamentliche Weisheitsliteratur.* Urban-Taschenbucher 383. Stuttgart: Kohlhammer, 1987. 114–36. **Priest, J.** "Humanism, Skepticism, and Pessimism in Israel." *JAAR* 36 (1968) 311–26. **Rudolph, W.** *Vom Buch Kohelet.* SGFWW 42. Münster: Aschendorf, 1959. **Schmitt, A.** "Zwischen Anfechtung, Kritik und Lebensbewältigung." *TTZ* 88 (1979) 114–31. **Stiglmaier, A.** "Weisheit und Jahweglaube im Buche Koheleth." *TTZ* 83 (1974) 257–83, 339–68. **Vogels, W.** "Performance vaine et performance saine chez Qohélet." *NRT* 113 (1991) 363–85. **Whybray, R. N.** *The Intellectual Tradition in the Old Testament.* BZAW 135. Berlin: de Gruyter, 1974. ————. "Conservatisme et radicalisme dans Qohelet." In *Sagesse et Religion, Colloque de Strasbourg, 1976.* Paris: Presses Universitaires, 1979. 65–81. ————. "The Identification and Use of Quotations in Ecclesiastes." In *Congress Volume, Vienna, 1980.* VTSup 32. Leiden: Brill, 1981. 435–51.

Special Bibliography

On הבל *hebel,* "vanity": **Fox, M. V.** *Qohelet.* 29–48. ————. "The Meaning of *Hebel* for Qohelet." *JBL* 105 (1986) 409–27. **Lauha, A.** "Omnia Vanitas: Die Bedeutung von *hbl* bei Kohelet." In *Glaube und Gerechtigkeit.* FS R. Gyllenberg. Ed. J. Kiilunen et al. SFEG 38. Helsinki, 1983. 19–25. **Loretz, O.** *Qohelet.* 218–34. **Michel, D.** *Eigenart.* 40–51. **Ogden, G.** *Qoheleth.* 17–22. **Polk, T.** "The Wisdom of Irony: A Study of *Hebel* and Its Relation to Joy and the Fear of God." *SBTh* 6 (1976) 3–17. **Staples, W. E.** "The 'Vanity' of Ecclesiastes." *JNES* 2 (1943) 110–12. ————. "Vanity of Vanities." *CJT* 1 (1955) 141–56.

On יתרון *yitrôn,* "profit": **Fox, M. V.** *Qohelet.* 60–62. **Michel, D.** *Eigenart.* 105–15. **Ogden, G.** *Qoheleth.* 22–26. **Staples, W. E.** "'Profit' in Ecclesiastes." *JNES* 4 (1945) 87–96. **Williams, J. G.** "What Does It Profit a Man? The Wisdom of Koheleth." *Judaism* 20 (1971) 179–93 (= *SAIW,* 375–89). **Zimmerli, W.** "Zur Struktur der alttestamentlichen Weisheit." *ZAW* 51 (1933) 177–204 (ET: *SAIW,* 175–207).

On חלק *ḥēleq,* "portion": **Fox, M. V.** *Qohelet.* 57–59. **Michel, D.** *Eigenart.* 118–25.

On עמל *ʿāmāl,* "toil": **Foresti, E.** "*ʿāmāl* in Koheleth: 'Toil' or 'Profit.'" *EphCarm* 31 (1980) 415–30. Fox, M. V. *Qohelet.* 54–57.

On שמחה *śimhâ*, "joy": **Fox, M. V.** *Qohelet.* 62–77. **Gordis, R.** 122–32. **Johnston, R. K.** "'Confessions of a Workaholic': A Reappraisal of Qoheleth." *CBQ* 38 (1976) 14–28. **Ogden, G.** *Qoheleth.* 14, 22. **Whybray, R. N.** "Qoheleth, Preacher of Joy." *JSOT* 41 (1982) 87–98.

On חכמה *hokmâ*, "wisdom": **Fox, M. V.** *Qohelet.* 79–120. **Müller, H.-P.** "Neige der althebräischen Weisheit: Zum Denken Qohäläts." *ZAW* 90 (1978) 238–64. **Murphy, R. E.** *The Tree of Life.* ABRL. New York: Doubleday, 1990. **Schmid, H. H.** *Wesen und Geschichte der Weisheit.* BZAW 101. Berlin: Töpelmann, 1966.

On fearing God: **Becker, J.** *Gottesfurcht im Alten Testament.* AnBib 25. Rome: Biblical Institute, 1965. **Nishimura, T.** "Quelques reflexions sémiologiques à propos de 'la crainte de dieu' de Qohelet." *AJBI* 5 (1979) 67–87. **Pfeiffer, E.** "Die Gottesfurcht im Buche Kohelet." In *Gottes Wort und Gottes Land.* Ed. H. Reventlow. Göttingen: Vandenhoeck & Ruprecht, 1965. 133–58.

On retribution: **Fox, M. V.** *Qohelet.* 121–50. **Koch, K.** "Gibt es ein Vergeltungsdogma im Alten Testament?" *ZTK* 52 (1955) 1–42 (ET: *SAIW,* 58–87). ———. *Um das Prinzip der Vergeltung in Religion und Recht des Alten Testaments.* WF 125. Darmstadt: Wissenschaftliche Buchgesellschaft, 1972. **Miller, P. D.** *Sin and Judgment in the Prophets.* SBLMS 27: Chico: Scholars Press, 1982. 121–39.

On death: **Crenshaw, J. L.** "The Shadow of Death in Qohelet." In *IW.* 205–16. **Lohfink, N.** "Man Face to Face with Death." In *The Christian Meaning of the Old Testament.* Milwaukee: Bruce, 1968. 139–69. **Schoors, A.** "Koheleth: A Perspective of Life after Death?" *ETL* 61 (1985) 295–303.

On God: **Barucq, A.** "Dieu chez les sages d'Israël." In *La notion biblique de Dieu.* Ed. J. Coppens. BETL 41. Gembloux: Duculot, 1976. 169–89. **Gorssen, L.** "La cohérence de la conception de Dieu dans l'Ecclésiaste." *ETL* 46 (1970) 282–324. **Luder, E.** "Gott und Welt nach dem Prediger Salomo." *SThU* 28 (1958) 105–14. **Michel, D.** "Vom Gott, der im Himmel ist (Reden von Gott bei Qohelet)." In *Eigenart.* 274–89 (= *TV* 12 [1975] 87–100). **Müller, H.-P.** "Wie sprach Qohälät von Gott?" *VT* 18 (1968) 507–21. **Murphy, R. E.** "The Faith of Qoheleth." *WW* 7 (1987) 253–60. **Zimmerli, W.** "'Unveränderbare Welt' oder 'Gott ist Gott': Ein Plädoyer für die Unaufgebbarkeit des Predigerbuches in der Bibel." In *Wenn nicht jetzt, wann dann?* Ed. H. G. Geyer et al. FS H. J. Kraus. Neukirchen-Vluyn: Neukirchener, 1983. 165–78.

The message of Ecclesiastes has suffered from excessive summarizing (e.g., "all is vanity" or "fear God and keep the commandments"). It is truly difficult to give an overall picture of the work. Qoheleth's thought is tortuous, and the danger of selectivity on the part of the interpreter is ever present. The following discussion of the message presupposes the translation and commentary in this book. There are only slight (even indifferent) textual changes from the MT, and the interpretation rests on the integrity of the whole book as discussed above ("Integrity and Structure," xxxii–xli). The following summary will deal with key terms and aspects of Qoheleth's thought.

1. הבל *hebel*, "vanity." The term occurs thirty-eight (or perhaps only thirty-seven) times in the book (slightly over half of the number of times it appears in the entire Bible). Because it is such a key word, it formed the inclusion in the motto, "vanity of vanities." The word has a basic meaning of breath or vapor. Deriving from this are such meanings as fleeting (human existence), vain and ineffectual, and even deceitful (idols that cannot satisfy a worshiper's desires).

In general, the meaning is negative—futile, worthless, etc. M. Fox (*Qohelet*, 38–44; see also Michel, *Eigenart*, 40–51) has catalogued the various uses of הבל in Ecclesiastes. The term is applied to toil and its products (e.g., 2:11; 6:2), joy (2:1; 6:9), wisdom (e.g., 2:15), speech (e.g., 6:11), human existence (e.g., 2:12), death ("days of darkness," 11:8), injustice in retribution (8:14). Both Fox and Michel are in agreement that the best equivalent is "absurd," the term which both note is characteristic of the late French writer, Albert Camus. But they do not seem to agree on the nuance. Fox claims that הבל designates "the manifestly irrational or meaningless" (34). This differs from "incomprehensible," in that it denies meaning, not merely knowability. It seems extreme to apply the category of rational/irrational to Qoheleth. Such a distinction is foreign to him. Instead, he uses the simple verbs, know/not know. For this reason I think "absurd" in the sense of incomprehensible is an adequate equivalent of the term (with A. Barucq, 55, and also B. Pennachini, *ED* 30 [1977] 491–510). Perhaps D. Michel would also agree. He defines הבל as "absurd" in the sense of meaningless (*sinnlos*, 44), and he would classify Qoheleth as a skeptic, but not a pessimist: "a sceptic with reference to the knowability of the world. For him the human will to know runs up against a world that does not let itself be seen through" (43). It should be noted that הבל is paired with רעות / רעין רוח (1:14; 2:11, 17, 26; 4:4, 16; 6:9), which probably means "a chase after wind," but this does not add anything significant to the more basic judgment of הבל. It is a colorful expression for achieving nothing. "Vanity" is certainly not the best rendering, but I am using it as a code word in the translation in order to call attention to הבל as it occurs in the book. A. Lauha ("Omnia Vanitas," 24–25) argues with some justification that since there is no one word to express all the nuances that Qoheleth could attach to הבל (ephemeral, futile, etc.) the traditional rendering as "vanity" (*Eitelkeit*, so also Luther) serves best.

The desperate claim of "vanity" is written up and down the entire book. There is not, Qoheleth avows, a single unspoiled value in this life. Riches, toil, wisdom, life itself—all these are examined and found wanting. His criteria are perhaps more extreme than those one might care to apply. Others might settle for less; he does not. The underlying and pervasive criterion for his judgment is the fact of death; it casts a fatal shadow over all human existence. The wise man dies as well as the fool (2:10)!

The book provides no basis for relativizing the fundamental perception of "vanity." One may agree with Qoheleth that one should seize the opportunities for pleasure (2:24; 3:12, 22; 8:15). But the situation is not ameliorated thereby; he is merely offering a possible and basic *modus vivendi* in an incredible world. One takes whatever one can get. The modern reader may desire a larger view of the situation and may conclude that humankind is not helpless (cf. B. Lang, *TQ* 159 [1979] 109–24). But this relativization is not Qoheleth's doing. It comes only from placing him in a broader context of biblical thought and theology.

2. יתרון *yitrôn*, "profit." W. Zimmerli (*SAIW*, 176) claimed that Eccl 1:3 put forward the "central question" of wisdom: what profit (יתרון)? The term designates what is left over, or surplus, and is used only by Qoheleth in the Hebrew Bible, and has synonyms in יותר (cf. 2:15; 7:16; 12:9, 12) and מותר (cf. 3:19). M. Fox (*Qohelet*, 61–62) distinguishes between "comparative advantage," where the nouns are used in a comparison, and "adequate gain" (e.g., 1:3), where there may be

some gain, but not sufficient. D. Michel (*Eigenart*, 105–15) rightly claims that much depends upon the exegesis of an individual passage. Is יתרון, twice in 2:13, meant in the traditional wisdom sense of profit, only to be rejected by the fact of death (2:15)? The point is well taken; each case has to be examined for itself. That no profit comes from toil (1:3; 3:9) does not deny that there may be an intrinsic pleasure in a given instance (this would be the חלק *ḥēleq*, "portion," that Qoheleth allows in 2:10). What seems clear is that יתרון is not bound up with an eternal dimension (contra Ogden, 24).

3. חלק *ḥēleq*, "portion." The term is best translated as "portion" and occurs in 2:10, 21; 3:22; 5:17–18; 9:6, 9; 11:2. By and large it has a positive meaning, although limited by the total perspective taken by Qoheleth. Thus it means riches in 2:21 and 11:2, and Qoheleth recognizes that there is an intrinsic pleasure in having such possessions (2:10; 3:22). However, there is no certainty that one will actually get to enjoy this portion, either to receive it (5:18[19]) or to keep it (2:21; cf. 6:2). It is clear from 9:9 (cf. 9:6) that any positive meaning of "portion" is limited strictly to this world.

4. עמל *ʿāmāl*, "toil." This term designates toil, or what one obtains by toiling, the fruits of toil. It generally has a negative tone, even extending to life itself (2:22, 24). M. Fox (*Qohelet*, 54) points out that toil and life are virtually equivalent (cf. 3:12 and 3:13; 2:24). The heavy mood of toil suffuses 2:18–24, which is introduced by "I hated all my עמל."

5. שמחה *śimḥâ*, "joy." The word means joy or pleasure. The noun or verb, or an equivalent expression (experience good, eating and drinking, etc.) is used in the many recommendations that are given to enjoy life: 2:10; 2:24; 3:12; 3:22; 5:17–18; 8:15; 9:7–9; 11:7–10. Four of these (2:24, slightly emended; 3:12; 3:22; 8:15) are in a "nothing better than" (eating, drinking, etc.) comparison. Qoheleth is not expressing a verdict about values in life, and expressions like these are not a positive recommendation. They are a concession to human nature. He grants that one must still live in this world, and what is one to do? Answer: "There is nothing better than . . ." The intense recommendation to "eat your bread with joy . . . do with all your power" (9:7–10) shows Qoheleth's zest for life (cf. 11:7–10), but it is significantly limited by the fact that one is going to Sheol (9:10) after "all the days of your vain life" (9:9). Moreover, joy is at best a precarious possibility since it is entirely the gift of a God (3:13; 5:18) who arbitrarily grants it to (and also withholds it from) human beings. Paradoxically, it is not a given, unless God "gives" (2:26) it as one's "portion" (חלק *ḥēleq*). Those who are dead have no "portion" (9:6). For those who are alive, joy can be a portion only if the inscrutable God gives it. As M. Fox remarks, "when Qohelet's frustration at human helplessness peaks, he advises pleasure" (*Qohelet*, 75).

This basic attitude about שמחה *śimḥâ* in this life is reflected in the texts about eating and drinking. This may be the "portion," and as such it is to be enjoyed, but it cannot be controlled. The grim perspective of death conditions the strong recommendation to "take joy" in all one's years—before old age and death set in (12:1–7). Nevertheless, many interpreters (R. Gordis, G. Ogden, R. N. Whybray, *JSOT* 41 [1982] 87–98) think that Qoheleth "had an affirmative rather than a negative view of human life" (Ogden, 22). With some Jewish religious authorities, Gordis regards שמחה, "the enjoyment of life," as "the basic theme of the book"

(131). Such an interpretation is too sweeping and selective, and fails to respect Qoheleth's complex views on life.

6. חכמה *ḥokmâ,* "wisdom." In its nominal or verbal form the term "wisdom" occurs fifty-two times in the book (only the root עשׂה *ʿśh* = "do" occurs more often). It is almost a matter of course among scholars (K. Galling, H. Gese, H. D. Preuss, H. H. Schmid, et al.) to speak of the "crisis" of wisdom because of the books of Job and Ecclesiastes. Indeed, this crisis looms almost as large in scholarly discussion as does the fall of Jerusalem in 587. That disaster produced relatively few reflections (explicitly in Ps 89 and also pervading the Deuteronomistic history). But OT wisdom is hardly ever discussed without the mention of its "crisis." The striking thing is that in the Bible itself the "crisis" was never interpreted to be that. There is no record that the book of Ecclesiastes was received with consternation. Some commentators have attempted to see a criticism of Qoheleth in 12:9–14. On the contrary, the laudatory tone of vv 9–11 is unmistakable. The warning of 12:13 is to be seen as an approval of "these"—namely the previous wisdom writings among which the book of Ecclesiastes is included. The incontrovertible fact is that the earliest witness (see *Comment* on 12:9–14) interpreted Qoheleth as working within the wisdom tradition. It is also clear that Qoheleth is in conflict with this tradition. But "crisis" or "bankruptcy" of wisdom is not the issue; that was left for later generations to discover. A more subtle investigation of this sage is called for.

There is a kind of scenario, or series of presuppositions, that undergirds the approach of many scholars to wisdom literature and to Ecclesiastes in particular. The views of H. D. Preuss (*Einführung,* 114–36 and passim) can be taken as an example of a widespread assessment of wisdom and Qoheleth. First of all, wisdom is judged to be marginal to Israel's faith, indeed a foreign import. Second, the God of wisdom is not יהוה *YHWH* who was revealed at Sinai and preached by the prophets, etc. This god is an *Urhebergott,* a god of origins, who has established an order of things for the wise person to try to discover. Wisdom concentrates on these orders in reality and then propounds sayings and admonitions in order to master life. One basic order, elaborated by K. Koch (*SAIW,* 58–87), is that of retribution: a good/wise action will inevitably produce a good/wise result; an evil action produces an evil result. This mechanical correspondence between action and consequence was the order that the sages (supposedly those whose wisdom is reflected in the Book of Proverbs) went about trying to discover, the order by which they lived and advised others to live. Such a view locked up the divinity tightly (after all, it was only an *Urhebergott*), for the god was bound by the order inherent in reality. At this point it is quite clear that retribution has become the issue in the wisdom enterprise. H. D. Preuss terms the deed-consequence viewpoint (*Tat-Ergehen Zusammenhang*) the "basic dogma of early wisdom" (*Einführung,* 124). We shall return to the issue of retribution later; but for now it is important to realize by the same token that there was a "basic dogma" operative in Deuteronomy and the entire Deuteronomic history of Israel that recognized a bond between a good/bad action and a corresponding reward/punishment. It avails little to single out the wisdom perspective as foreign to Israelite thinking, or to think that the sages were unaware of their own limitations vis-à-vis the Lord. The scenario that some scholars have drawn up for the wisdom movement is not sensitive to the subtleties of the Israelite sages.

Perhaps the most striking, not to say ominous, phrase used by an interpreter of Qoheleth is the "eerie guest" (*der unheimliche Gast,* the title of the article by H.-P. Müller in *ZTK* 84 [1987] 440–64). The phrase is taken immediately from M. Heidegger's description of the philosophy of Nietzsche, who used it to describe Nihilism. Müller raises the question: Has Qoheleth contributed in some way to Nihilism? (442). Like H. D. Preuss, he has also interpreted the God of Ecclesiastes as a distant "god of origins," but he now sees that Qoheleth has moved beyond this concept. The notion of "creator" in 12:1 reminds him of the intervention of the Lord in Job 38:1. He sees it as the only ray of hope in Ecclesiastes, and ties it in with the emphasis that Qoheleth placed on the enjoyment of life. But no clean answer is given to the question Müller raised at the outset. Qoheleth remains a problem. Then Müller shifts the question: "Is it finally *Wisdom,* in order to quote Nietzsche exactly now, that is the 'eerie guest' in the canon?" (458). So it appears to be, for it is Qoheleth's critical thought that has brought about the bankruptcy *(Scheitern)* of traditional wisdom. Thus while Qoheleth is somewhat exonerated, wisdom (as represented presumably in the Book of Proverbs, and in the speeches of Job's friends) is the culprit, not merely an unwelcome guest, but an eerie one!

The previous remarks are not meant to homogenize Ecclesiastes with the comfortable and consoling lessons of the sages. He is clearly in conflict with traditional wisdom (R. E. Murphy, "Quarrel," 235–45). Perhaps his views on wisdom are best synthesized in the following points.

a. Folly is never a viable option for Qoheleth. Although expressed negatively, this point establishes one pole of his thought. He is intent on finding the "profit" (1:3 and passim), to discover what is "good" for one to do (2:3; 6:10). Such is the task of wisdom: folly cannot even ask the question. It matters not that Qoheleth arrived at the verdict of vanity; he never ceased to reach for a true good, a more insightful wisdom.

b. Moreover, folly is explicitly condemned. This seems to be the sense of 10:2–3 concerning the right/left tendencies of the wise and the foolish. The context of 9:17–10:1 deals with what has been called the vulnerability of wisdom; she is a delicate treasure and is easily negated by even a little folly. The story in 9:12–16 is meant to exemplify how valuable, yet vulnerable, wisdom is. The issue of speech is discussed in 10:12–15. V 12 ascribes to wise speech the quality of חן, "favor," either as an attribute or, more likely, as an effect. In contrast stands the ruin brought on by foolish speech (cf. Prov. 14:3; 10:19, 32; 15:17; Sir 21:16–17). V 13 continues the description and a climax is reached in v 14a: הסכל, "the fool," talks on and on. In v 15 there is a shift from speech to conduct: the fool cannot even find his way to the city. Again, folly is portrayed as undesirable.

c. Qoheleth avowed that he himself failed in the quest for wisdom; she was too distant, too deep (7:23–24). That he failed is not unusual in the wisdom movement. One need only recall the poem in Job 28 ("where is wisdom to be found?"), and the words of Agur (Prov 30:1–4). It is useless to guess what lay behind this admission of failure. The very dialogue, the very conflict, that Qoheleth carried on with traditional wisdom was part of his search. Despite the failures he detected in traditional wisdom, he knew there was a wisdom, but it was always ahead of him.

d. A distinction between wisdom as teaching and wisdom as method should be made. Wisdom is a corpus of doctrine, such as that contained in the book of

Proverbs. But it is also a style, a methodology that implies an analytical approach to life's situations. This may be superficial (one thinks of the ultimate conclusion of the three friends of Job, despite their obvious learning) or subtle (in the way that was recognized in Eccl 12:11 where the *mĕšālîm*, or sayings, are described as "goads"). Qoheleth is often in conflict with wisdom teaching, but his methodology is nonetheless that of the sage. He frequently reminds the reader how he applied himself "with wisdom." In this manner he describes his investigation of events "under the heavens" (1:13) and also his testing of life's pleasures (2:3; cf. 2:9). Several times wisdom is held out as the goal of his efforts: to "see" wisdom as well as madness and folly (2:12, doubtless this is a critical seeing as Michel claims, *Eigenart*, 25–29). He "seeks" wisdom, and would have an answer (7:25), and desires to "know" wisdom, a sleepless task (8:17). True, the point of these instances is less methodology than correct conclusion, the proper understanding of what wisdom is. After soundings in several areas, in traditional wisdom, toil, riches, etc., he concludes that all is vanity. But he trusts in the methodology of wisdom, experience and observation, throughout his investigation. He develops it to a high art, with more subtlety than the sages before him.

e. Qoheleth's attitude toward traditional wisdom is ambivalent. He rejects traditional wisdom for the security it offers. Life is much more complicated than the sages made it out to be. They were not explicit enough, nor did they "test" reality in the way that Qoheleth envisioned. They were out to teach and persuade; Qoheleth was out to assess reality at a deeper level. Everything was הבל *hebel*, "vanity," and wisdom eluded him in his own search. But it would be shortsighted to sweep everything under הבל and fail to attend to the delicacy of his thought. We have already seen above some positive judgments he made about wisdom. Here we wish to delve more into the nature of the ongoing dialogue that he had with traditional wisdom. That it is a dialogue should be stressed, and the best examples of this depend upon the way in which the traditional and the new in the book are interpreted. There are various possibilities in dealing with this dialogue. One can say that the striking differences between the new and the traditional result from later hands, which touched up the book to make it safe for future readers. We have seen that this is ultimately too subjective a judgment and too easy a way out. Similarly, the claim that Qoheleth simply contradicts himself and remains in a never-never land of indecision does not do justice to his thought. One may grant a contradiction or two, but the book offers more than that if the dialogical nature of the work is recognized. The arguments for this rest upon exegesis of given texts, and not all will agree. More recent expositors (e.g., N. Lohfink, D. Michel, R. N. Whybray) may differ among themselves, but there is a growing recognition of dialogue in the book. This is not a novelty. The "yes, but" character of Qoheleth's thought was recognized by K. Galling ("broken sentences?") and by H. W. Hertzberg (*zwar-aber Aussage*). Moreover, we have seen that the idea of "voices" (other than Solomon's) within the book goes back to the patristic period. The recognition of dialogue is a basic construal of the meaning of the work, and not all will agree, or they will vary in their agreement. Some subjectivity is inescapable.

One example of dialogue, among the many discussed in the *Comment* below, is Eccl 2:13–17. This contains a clear statement of the superiority of wisdom over folly, as light over darkness, vision over a blinding darkness (2:13–14a).

This positive assessment of wisdom is severely modified in 2:14b–17: the foolish and the wise have the same מִקְרֶה, "lot"; they both die. So Qoheleth queries the value of wisdom at wisdom at a deeper level, and even utters his customary הֶבֶל *hebel* judgment. Some would explain 2:13–14a as a "quotation" from another source presumably more traditional than Qoheleth. The issue of "quotations" is hard to resolve, because of the difficulty of proof. But what seems unassailable is the tension or conflict posed by Qoheleth's reflection on 2:13–14a. He certainly puts the traditional superiority of wisdom in a new light, and raises a fundamental issue with which he struggles. There lies the dialogue. In these and other instances he does not simply cancel out the wisdom of his forebears. They had their uncertainties, although they did not develop them in the style of Qoheleth. M. Fox (*Qohelet*, 104) has wisely pointed out: "the conventional sages too taught that the future is hidden. It is hidden first of all from an individual whose plans violate the moral working of the world. The consequences of his behavior are different from what he expected. He falls into the pit he dug for another [a footnote refers to the well-known saying in Prov 26:27; Pss 7:16; 9:16; Sir 27:26, and elsewhere]. More fundamentally, the sages taught that there can never be certainty about the future in any specific case." This insight shows the continuity between the traditional wisdom and the thought of Qoheleth, without denying the edge, the counterpoint, that he provides. Ironically, the sages were also certain about death; they recognized its finality, but they did not use it in the argumentative style of Qoheleth. By and large, M. Fox is inclined to recognize "contradictions" in Qoheleth's thought, but he has well described the difference between the tradition and the new sage: "Qohelet believes that wisdom can grasp significant truths, but these do not include an understanding of the rationale of events, for an absurd world defies such insight. He believes that wisdom has great value, but that this value is often undermined by the accidents and injustices of an absurd world. Qohelet diverges from didactic Wisdom also in recognizing that knowledge—genuine knowledge, and not just opinion—could cause unhappiness. . . . He is certainly not directing a polemic against wisdom or Wisdom teachings. . . . he does not treasure wisdom less for recognizing—and complaining about—its vulnerability" (116–17).

To summarize Qoheleth's relationship to traditional wisdom: First, it is within this tradition that he thought and wrote; his work is intelligible only in this perspective. Second, even while he quarrels with views of traditional wisdom, his goal remains that of an Israelite sage: the discovery of what is good for humans to do (Eccl 2:3b). He does not simply jettison past teaching; he purifies and extends it. His grief against classical wisdom is its claim to security, not its methodology. Third, his argument is not theoretical; it is practical. Hence he bases his reasoning on the failure of a just retribution, on human ignorance, on the significance of death, on the mystery of God's work. It is in the best wisdom style to confront, as he did, the questions that existence puts to human beings. Like the classical sage, he too proclaimed "life," but at the same time he could "hate" it (2:17). His resigned conclusions about accepting whatever pleasures this life can afford, and as they come, testify to this concern. That was as far as he could go, out of fidelity to the wisdom ideal. "The fool walks in darkness" (2:14), and for Qoheleth the road of the wise led nowhere, but it was the only one he could walk.

7. *Fear of God.* Paradoxical as it may seem, the traditional wisdom association of fear and God appears frequently in Ecclesiastes, but only in the verbal form

(to fear): 3:13; 5:6; 7:18; 8:12; 12:13. The problem is the precise connotation that Qoheleth attaches to fearing God. The concept is elusive since it takes on several meanings in the Bible (J. Becker, *Gottesfurcht im Alten Testament*). The fundamental idea is reverence before the numinous, the *tremendum* (Exod 20:18–21). The meaning expands to designate those who are faithful to the covenant God (Deut 5:29; 6:2, 13, 24). In the psalter it is the pious worshipers who are "those who fear the Lord." A moral sensitivity is indicated in the wisdom books generally (cf. Job 1:1; 28:28). The correlation between the fear of God/Lord and observance of the Law (Eccl 12:13) is found in Pss 19:10; 112:1; 119:63, and especially in the book of Ecclesiasticus (e.g., Sir 1:11–30). In the wisdom tradition, fear of God/Lord is correlative to all that wisdom and knowledge stand for. It is the beginning of wisdom (Prov 1:7; cf. 9:10; 15:33; Ps 111:10; Job 28:28).

Perhaps the best-known example in Ecclesiastes is the recommendation in the epilogue, "Fear God and keep his commandments" (12:13). F. Delitzsch called this "the kernel and star of the whole book" (438). Obviously the epilogist (or editor, or whoever was responsible) would agree with him, since it is part of the interpretation given to the book in the epilogue. G. Sheppard (*Wisdom as a Hermeneutical Construct*, 120–29) has pointed out that the hermeneutical direction suggested by this verse is in harmony with Ben Sira's teaching on fear of God and Torah observance. But it is an oversimplification of the book's message (see the *Comment* on 12:13–14). Qoheleth never mentions "commandments" (מצות) and would not likely join them with fear of God in this facile manner.

In two instances Qoheleth understands fear of God in a sense that captures the quality of the numinous. In 3:14 we discover the sole purpose he ever ascribes to divine governance: "Thus has God done that they (human beings) may fear him." He is referring to the unchangeability, and ultimately the mystery (3:11), of divine activity, before which "fear" is the appropriate response (see the perceptive remarks of W. Zimmerli on 3:14).

The command to fear God appears in the "liturgical" context of 5:6. It is a conclusion from several admonitions that advise caution relative to speech and making vows before God. The temper of the advice is clear from 5:1—God is in heaven and you are on earth, so let your words be few. In short, God is dangerous for humans to deal with in a casual way.

The nuance of "the one who fears God" in 7:18 is difficult to determine. Such a person is said to "come through" or succeed (literally, "go out") with respect to the alternatives Qoheleth proposes—but any translation is uncertain and the sense is far from clear. The alternatives are excessive wickedness (= folly) and excessive wisdom (= virtue). Neither course of action is per se profitable, because God in Qoheleth's view is not bound to any kind of retributive justice. Both recommendations (7:16–17) illustrate the failure of human wisdom to understand what God is about. It is the God-fearer who will come out of it all in the best shape. Fear of God is more basic for living than doctrines about wisdom and moral conduct. The spirit of v 18 is close to 3:14 and 5:6.

In 8:12–13 the God-fearers are in contrast to the wicked in the style of the wise/foolish comparisons that abound in traditional wisdom. Hence many commentators claim that Ecclesiastes has been glossed here—not a satisfactory solution. Others claim (R. Gordis, 105; R. N. Whybray, VTSup 32 [1981] 435–51) that he is quoting something, which he proceeds to disagree with. This passage should be taken as an example of his dialoguing with the tradition, and is best explained by this paraphrase: "Sinners are not punished, although I am well aware of the teaching that there is a difference between the deserts of the God-fearers and the wicked." In context Qoheleth is denying the efficacy (a sense of religious security) that traditional wisdom attached to fearing God.

Qoheleth's understanding of what it means to fear God seems to flow from the mystery and incomprehensibility of God. If one cannot understand what God is doing (3:11; 8:17; 11:6), and indeed if one does not perceive either divine love or hatred (9:1), reverential fear is in order (cf. 3:14; 5:6).

8. *Retribution*. It is clear that Qoheleth denies that there is any intelligible retribution or justice in this life. "There are just who are treated as if they had acted wickedly, and there are wicked who are treated as if they had acted justly" (8:14). This succinct statement can stand for many others (7:15; 8:11–12a; 9:11–12). Qoheleth could find no distinction in the treatment meted out to the good and the wicked. He does not contradict himself by the statements in 3:17; 5:5b [6b]; 8:5, 12b–13; 11:9b (see the *Comment* below). It is important to recognize that Qoheleth attributes judgment to God (3:17; 8:5), but its working out is a mystery because the work of God is beyond human ken.

As indicated above, many interpreters regard Qoheleth (and Job) as responsible for the breakdown of the mechanical correspondence between (good/evil) action and (good/evil) result, a mentality that derives from a god of origins *(Urhebergott)* who set up the world to run along that line. It is questionable if this "deed-consequence" mindset is as universal and important as claimed. True, it was considered right ("poetic justice," as we say) that the (unjust) person who dug a pit for another should be the one to fall into it (Eccl. 10:8). But the sages were aware of God's surprises. Moreover, there is another understanding that is even more widespread: everything happens because of the Lord's action. The figure of a midwife (K. Koch) supervising mechanical correspondence between action and result is not an image of God in the OT; rather, God is portrayed as intimately involved in all that occurs. The dilemmas of Job and Qoheleth are nothing new. The psalms of lament and the "confessions" of Jeremiah are as radical as anything in the wisdom literature. The responsibility rests with God—everyone knew of divine responsibility. Job singles out God ("if it is not he, who then is it?" 9:24), and Qoheleth asks, "who can make straight what he has made crooked?" (7:13). What is alleged to be a crisis for wisdom is no less a crisis for the rest of the Bible. The optimism of Proverbs is matched by the optimism of Deuteronomy and the promises to the fathers. The crisis did not consist in a breakdown of an order of deed-consequence; the crisis is no less than the mysterious ways of the Lord.

In this connection words like determinism and fatalism are used to describe Qoheleth's thought. Much depends on the way these terms are defined, and thus how much of ancient and modern philosophy is mixed in with them. If determinism means the sovereign disposition of all things by the divinity, then Qoheleth affirms this with the rest of the biblical writers. This is "determinism," not fatalism. But it is a determinism of an unusual kind because it does not exempt human beings from responsibility. Israel never engaged in any theoretical discussion concerning the reconciliation of these contraries. This has been pursued, without much success, by postbiblical thought. The OT affirms equally determinism and human responsibility (or in other words, freedom of the will; cf. Sir 15:11–20). That is the "determinism" out of which Qoheleth operates.

Neither are the terms "fate" or "fatalism" appropriate. There is nothing truly "fatal" in the book of Ecclesiastes; there is a מקרה, "happening" or "lot," that catches human beings (usually it is death) and there is also a "falling time" or a time of calamity (9:11–12; see *Comment*) that oppresses human beings. But this is all God's doing, which humans do not understand (F. Nötscher, "Schicksal und Freiheit," *Bib* 40 [1959] 446–62).

Seven times the word מקרה, literally, "happening," is to be found in Ecclesiastes: 2:14–15; 3:19 (thrice); 9:2–3; this is more than it occurs anywhere else in the Bible. Qoheleth uses it clearly to indicate the "happening" that is death. This is not "fate" (*Schicksal;* against Preuss, *Einführung,* 129), which carries with it too much philosophical baggage. The word is better translated as "lot," for death is the human lot.

9. *Death.* Qoheleth's views on death are in some respects startlingly different from the standard biblical view. By and large, there was a remarkable resignation to death on the part of the ancient Israelites. And they found some solace in the fact that the "memory" of the just lived on as a blessing (Prov 10:7). But of course, Qoheleth denied there was any "memory" (Eccl 1:11; 2:16). Immortality rested in the continuity of one's posterity, but Qoheleth asks whether the one to come after him will be wise or foolish (2:18–19). The sages had a problem with death, if it occurred soon in contrast to a long life, or if it was marked with adversity. The death of the wicked had to be a sad one, a "day of wrath" (Prov 11:4). Those who rely on riches instead of God could not "take it with them" (Ps 49:16–17); their death would leave them desolate without any comfort or strength to rely on. Qoheleth's view of death is conditioned by his particular interests.

In a given situation, death might be preferable to life. Thus Qoheleth considered the dead as more fortunate than the living who are suffering; or better, the unborn who can never experience human evil (4:2–3). In 6:1–6 he regards the misfortunes of a given person as so great that even the aborted one is better off. Obviously these are very narrow cases, but nonetheless sincere. And in these instances, death or Sheol is seen as a respite from suffering. This motif is found several times in Job (3:3–26; 10:18–22). Outside of these extenuating circumstances, death is totally unwelcome. The lugubrious tone of 12:1–7 illustrates his view of the "days of darkness," or old age, followed by death and the "everlasting home" (see the *Comment* on 12:5). The most bitter complaint to escape his lips is that the wise person dies as well as the fool (2:16). Death was the complete opposite of the life of pleasure that he proclaimed to be the best humans might hope for: "Enjoy life with a wife whom you love. . . . All that your hand finds to do, do with might because there is no action, or answer, or knowledge, or wisdom in Sheol where you are going." After death there was nothing, in his view. It may be going too far to say that he held a view of "total extinction" (A. Schoors, *ETL* 61 [1985] 295–303; C. F. Whitley, *Koheleth,* 151). Such a conclusion rests on the Western notion of the human composite, which was far from Qoheleth's mind. His words may suggest a resolution of the human being into nothingness, even annihilation, only because he is using the images of Gen 2:7—the breath of life returns to God who gave it, and the body obviously corrupts in the dust. One should not read (Greek) philosophical concepts into such a phenomenological description.

It is abundantly clear that Qoheleth does not hold out any hope for life after death. Basically humans do not differ from beasts (3:18–19). The only time he explicitly attributes בטחון, "hope," to human beings is in 9:4, where he quotes what was doubtless an old saw about a living dog being better off than a dead lion. The difference between the living and the dead is knowledge—and the living know . . . that they must die! (for the irony here, see *Comment* on 9:4–5).

10. *Who is the God of Qoheleth?* Is that divinity an *Urhebergott*, a god of origins, or truly the God of Israel? The sacred name יהוה *YHWH* is never used by Qoheleth. The generic name, "god," is found twenty-six times with the definite article, האלהים, and seven times without the article. This is a very active God—the subject of the verbs נתן, "give," and עשה, "do," no less than eighteen times (H.-P. Müller, *VT* 18 [1968] 507–21). While the "gift" of God is often the joy of eating and drinking as one's "portion" (2:24, 26; 5:17), it is also correlated with the "task" (ענין; 1:3; 3:10) that God gives to humans—the worst being that they cannot figure out what God is doing (3:10–11). The "doing" of God is even more mysterious than the giving. Human beings cannot know (3:11); they cannot "find out what is done under the sun" (8:17). If something is made crooked, no one can straighten it out (7:13; cf. 1:15). The mystery of divine activity is comparable to the mystery of human gestation (11:5).

On this basis one may agree with the summary characterization of L. Gorssen (*ETL* 46 [1970] 313) that the God of Qoheleth is "un Dieu souverain à l'extrême." All that happens is his doing, and it is unintelligible. Gorssen goes on to point out that this notion is not new in Israel. The failure to comprehend the Lord is implied by Israel's celebration of the events of the saving history as "marvels" (נפלאות; פלא) and as "works" (the same word that Qoheleth uses for the "work of God," מעשה; cf. Pss 62:3; 92:6; 118:17). Qoheleth radicalizes this basic datum in Israel's faith. He does not allow it to become a reason or source of consolation and security. Since one cannot know what God is doing, fear and reverence are in order. There seems to be no room for the personal relationship with God to which the rest of the Bible testifies. This is not to say that Qoheleth is unbiblical. There is plenty of biblical precedent for the mystery of God; the difficulty is that Qoheleth does not say anything else. Precisely at this point one must be careful not to read into him what he does not say. We have no evidence of what he thought about the traditional salvation history, and it is useless to try to interpret his mind on this. One may be justified in asserting that in his own time he sees no evidence for an ongoing history of salvation. God's revelation in history seems to have ceased, although Qoheleth is not explicit on the point. It should be remembered that wisdom bracketed out the sacred traditions; neither Job nor Qoheleth have recourse to them. But this does not give one the right to play off the God of Qoheleth against the Yahweh of Israel, or an *Urheberreligion* rooted in creation and "natural" philosophy, against Yahwism (H.-P. Müller, *ZAW* 90 [1978] 238–64). Qoheleth did not have two heads. The God he was dealing with was the God he knew from his tradition, whom he worshiped in the Temple. In short, it was יהוה *YHWH*. But some would claim that his was "not the God of Abraham, nor of Isaac, nor of Jacob, nor the God in Jesus Christus" (so D. Michel, *Eigenart*, 289: cf. R. E. Murphy, *BTB* 21 [1991] 30–33).

L. Gorssen has caught the dialectic in Qoheleth's thought: "God is utterly present and at the same time utterly absent. God is 'present' in each event and yet no event is a 'place of encounter' with God, since humans do not understand what his will is. . . . Events do not speak any longer the language of a saving God. They are there, simply" (*ETL*, 46 [1970] 314–15). Qoheleth demonstrates that there is more to religion than salvation. The very fact that he sees that everything done under the sun is vanity (1:14) is a sign, paradoxical though it be, of the reverence he had for a God who created a history in which Israelites could encounter him.

H. Hertzberg concluded his commentary (238) with these words: "The book of Qoheleth, standing at the end of the Old Testament, is the most staggering messianic prophecy to appear in the Old Testament." This is meant to be understood in the sense that the "Old Testament was here on the point of running itself to death. Behind this total nothing from a human point of view, the only possible help was the 'new creature' of the New Testament" (237). One can sympathize with what Hertzberg is trying to say, but a fellow countryman, Dietrich Bonhoeffer (*Letters and Papers from Prison*, ed. E. Bethge, tr. R. H. Fuller [New York: Macmillan, 1971] 157), put it better, "It is only when one loves life and the world so much that without them everything would be gone, that one can believe in the resurrection and a new world." Qoheleth loved life: "All that your hand finds to do, do with might, because there is no action, or answer, or knowledge, or wisdom in Sheol where you are going" (9:10). It was because of his appreciation of life and wisdom that he perceived the awfulness of death and the vanity of life itself. One may fail to appreciate Qoheleth and his faith in God, if one makes comparisons too easily. Whatever their personal beliefs, readers do themselves and him a disservice by approaching the book with a "superior" attitude. The work of Qoheleth can be seen as a veritable purification of the ongoing wisdom movement, a blow in favor of divine freedom. It can also serve to purify the faith and convictions of the modern reader, whose eschatological hopes can sometimes distort the proper relationship of human beings to God (R. E. Murphy, Concilium 12 [1976] 567–70).

It is unwise to isolate an "essential" religion within the Bible and to discount the role of Ecclesiastes within the totality of biblical religion. N. Lohfink remarks that God's action in history, unmentioned in Ecclesiastes, should not be allowed to become a mythological datum; it needs theological explication. "When one characterizes Ecclesiastes—as has become fashionable among exegetes—in comparison with the rest of the Bible as 'no personal God,' 'denial of human freedom,' 'a falling way from *heilsgeschichtlich* thought,' 'a lost of trust in life,' one flees the challenge which this book puts to the mind; one exposes oneself to the danger of even understanding wrongly what one was intending to defend" (Lohfink, 15–16).

Ecclesiastes

In the translation that follows and also in the translations in the body of the commentary, words in parentheses have been supplied for the sake of the reader's understanding. Words in brackets are changes from the Masoretic Text based on other ancient sources. Chapter and verse references at the right of the translation refer to other occurrences of similar words or ideas elsewhere in Ecclesiastes.

^{1:1} *The words of Qoheleth, son of David, king in Jerusalem.*   1:12

² *Vanity of vanities! says Qoheleth,*   12:8
  Vanity of vanities! All is vanity!

³ *What profit does one have for all the toil*   1:4; 2:11, 22; 3:9; 5:15; 8:9
  with which one toils under the sun?
⁴ *One generation goes and another comes,*
  while the earth stands forever.
⁵ *The sun rises and the sun sets;*
  to its place it hastens, there to rise.
⁶ *Going to the south,*
    and turning to the north—
  Turning, turning goes the wind,
    and upon its rounds the wind comes back.
⁷ *All the streams go to the sea,*
    but the sea is never filled;
  To the place that they go,
    there the streams keep going.
⁸ *All words are wearisome;*
    there is nothing one can say.
  The eye is not satisfied by seeing,   4:8; 5:9–11; 6:3
    nor the ear filled by hearing.
⁹ *What has been is what will be, and what has been done*   3:15; 6:10
is what will be done; there is nothing new under the sun! ¹⁰ *If there is*
something about which one says, "Look, this is new," it existed already
in ages that have gone before us. ¹¹ *There is no memory of those in the*
past; of those in the future there will be no memory among those who will
come afterwards.   2:16; 9:5

¹² *I, Qoheleth, was king over Israel in Jerusalem.* ¹³ *I applied my mind*   1:1
to investigating and exploring with wisdom all that is done under the
heavens. This is an evil task that God has given to humankind   3:10
to be occupied with. ¹⁴ *I saw all the deeds that were done under the sun;*
and the result: all is vanity and a chase after wind!   1:3; 2:11; 3:9; 5:15; 8:9

¹⁵ *The crooked cannot be made straight,*   3:11; 7:13; 8:17; 11:5
   and what is missing cannot be made up.

¹⁶*I said to myself: "I have become greater and increased*   2:7, 9
in wisdom beyond all those who were over Jerusalem before me.
My mind has carefully observed wisdom and knowledge." ¹⁷*So I*
applied my mind to know wisdom and knowledge, madness and folly,
(and) I realized that this also was a chase after wind.   2:12; 7:25; 8:16
¹⁸ *For, the more wisdom, the more trouble;*   12:12
   whoever increases wisdom, increases pain.

^{2:1}*I said to myself: "Come, try out joy and partake of*
good things!" Ah, that is also vanity. ²*Of laughter, I said:*
madness! and of joy: what can this achieve? ³*I explored in my*
mind how to refresh my body with wine—my mind always leading
on with wisdom—and how to get hold of folly till I could see what
is good for humans to do in the limited number of days they
live under the heavens. ⁴*I did great things: I built*
houses for myself, I planted my vineyards. ⁵*I made gardens*
and parks for myself, and I planted in them fruit trees of every
kind. ⁶*I made reservoirs of water with which to irrigate a*
forest of flourishing trees. ⁷*I acquired slaves, male and female,*
and I had servants who were born to the house. I also had a flock
of cattle and sheep, more than all who were before me in Jerusalem.   1:16; 2:9
⁸*I gathered for myself silver and gold, the wealth of kings and*
provinces. I had for myself singers, male and female, and the
delights of mankind, many women. ⁹*I became great and I*   1:16; 2:7
flourished more than all who were before me in Jerusalem—my
wisdom also stayed with me. ¹⁰*Nothing that my eyes*
desired did I keep from them. I did not refuse my heart
any joy; rather, my heart took joy from all my toil. That
was my portion from all my toil. ¹¹*Then I turned to all*
my handiwork, and to what I had so actively toiled for. Ah,
all is vanity and a chase after wind; there is no profit
under the sun.   1:3, 14; 2:22; 3:9; 5:15; 8:9

¹²*I turned to consider wisdom and madness and folly, for*   1:7; 7:25; 8:16
what can the man do who comes after the king? What they have
already done! ¹³*I saw that wisdom has an advantage over*
folly—the advantage of light over darkness: 6:8
¹⁴ *The wise have eyes in their head,*   8:1; 10:2
   but fools walk in darkness.
But I knew also that the same lot comes to them both. ¹⁵*So*   3:19; 9:2-3
I said to myself: the lot of the fool also comes to me,

so why should I be so very wise? Then I said to myself
that this also is vanity. [16]*For there is no remembrance*
ever of the wise as well as the fools; in the days to come   1:11; 9:5
both will have been forgotten. How can the wise die just like
the fools? [17]*So I hated life, because whatever happens under*
the sun was evil for me. All is vanity and a chase after wind.

[18]*I hated the fruit of all the toil for which I toiled*   4:8
under the sun because I have to leave it to the one who will
come after me. [19]*But who knows whether he will be wise or*   2:21; 4:8; 6:2
foolish? Yet he will control all the fruit of the toil for
which I toiled under the sun, and for which I became wise.
This also is vanity. [20]*I turned to heartfelt despair over all*   2:19; 4:8;
the toil with which I toiled under the sun. [21]*For though a*   5:9–11; 6:2
person toils with wisdom and knowledge and skill, he has to give
the portion over to someone who did not toil for it. This also is
vanity and a great evil. [22]*For what does one get for all the*
toil, and the striving of the heart, with which   1:3, 14; 2:11; 3:9;
one toils under the sun? [23]*All his days are painful, and*   5:15; 8:9; 5:16
grievous, his task. Even at night his mind is not at rest.
This also is vanity. [24]*There is nothing [better] for a person*   3:12–13, 22;
[than] to eat and drink and provide pleasure for himself in his   5:17–18;
toil—this also I saw is from the hand of God. [25]*For who can*   8:15; 9:7–9
eat or rejoice, if not I? [26]*To whomever he pleases God gives*
wisdom and knowledge, but to the errant one he gives the trouble   7:26
of collecting and gathering, only to give to whomever God pleases.
This also is vanity and a chase after wind.

[3:1] *For everything there is a moment,*   3:17; 8:5–6; 9:11–12;
      and there is a time for every affair under the heavens: 11:9; 12:14
[2]   *A time to give birth and a time to die,*
      a time to plant and a time to uproot what is planted;
[3]   *A time to kill and a time to heal,*
      a time to tear down and a time to build up;
[4]   *A time to weep and a time to rejoice,*
      a time for lament and a time for dancing;
[5]   *A time to cast stones and a time to gather stones,*
      a time to embrace and a time to be far from embraces;
[6]   *A time to search and a time to lose,*
      a time to keep and a time to cast away;
[7]   *A time to tear up and a time to sew,*
      a time to be silent and a time to speak;
[8]   *A time to love and a time to hate,*
      a time for war and a time for peace.

⁹What profit does the worker have from his toil?   1:3, 14; 2:11, 22; 5:15; 8:9
¹⁰I have seen the task that God has given to humankind to be   1:13
occupied with: ¹¹He has made everything appropriate in its time, and
he has also placed a sense of duration in their hearts, so that   7:13; 8:17; 11:5
they cannot find out, from beginning to end, the work which
God has done. ¹²I know that there is nothing better for them   2:24–26; 3:22;
than to rejoice and do well in life. ¹³And also, if   5:17–18; 8:15; 9:7–9
anyone eats and drinks and prospers for all his toil—that
is a gift of God. ¹⁴I know that all God does will be
forever. To it nothing can be added, and from it nothing can
subtracted; for God has done so that they may stand in awe   5:6; 7:18;
of him. ¹⁵What is already has been, and what is to be   8:12; 12:13
already is. And God seeks out what has been pursued.   1:9; 6:10

¹⁶I observed continually under the sun: in the place for
judgment, wrongdoing! and in the place for justice, wrongdoing!   4:1; 5:7
¹⁷I said to myself: both the just and the wrongdoers God   3:1; 8:5–6;
will judge, for there is a time for every affair, and upon every   9:11–12;
deed there. ¹⁸I said to myself concerning human beings: God   11:9; 12:14
is testing them, and [showing] that they are really animals.
¹⁹For the lot [of] humans and the lot [of] animals is [   ] the
same lot. As one dies, so does the other; both have the same   2:14–15; 9:2–3
life-breath. So humans have no advantage over animals; all is
vanity. ²⁰Both go to the same place; both are from the dust   6:6; 12:7
and both return to the dust. ²¹Who knows [if] the life-breath
of humans goes upwards, and [if] the life-breath of animals goes
down into the earth? ²²I saw that there was nothing better for   2:24; 3:12–13;
humans than to rejoice in their works, for that is their portion.   5:17; 8:15; 9:7
For who can bring them to see what will come after them?   6:12; 8:7; 10:14

⁴:¹Again I saw all the oppressions that were done under   3:16; 5:7
the sun. Ah, the tears of the oppressed! But there was no
one to give them comfort. On the side of their oppressors was
power! But there was no one to give them comfort. ²So I
praised the dead who had long since died, more than the living
who must still live. ³But better than both: the one who has never
lived, who has never seen the evil work that is done
under the sun.   6:3–5

⁴I saw that all toil and all skillful activity are (a matter
of) rivalry between one person and another. This also is vanity
and a chase after wind.
⁵   "The fool folds his hands and destroys himself."
⁶   "Better is one handful with rest
*   than two handfuls with toil and a chase after wind."*

⁷*Again I saw a vanity under the sun:* ⁸*There was a single
person, without any companion, either son or brother. There was
no end to all his toil, nor did his desire for riches ever cease:
"For whom am I toiling and depriving myself of good things?"*
This also is vanity and an evil task.

     1:8; 5:9–11;
     2:19, 21; 6:2

⁹*Two are better than one because they have a good payment for
their toil.* ¹⁰*For if they fall, one can help the other up.
But [woe to] a single person who falls, for there is no one to help
him up.* ¹¹*Also, if two people lie together they keep warm, but
how can a single person keep warm?* ¹²*A single person may be
overcome, but two together can resist. A three-ply cord cannot be
easily broken.*

¹³*Better is a youth poor but wise, than a king old but foolish,
who can no longer heed a warning.* ¹⁴*For out of a prison he came
forth to reign, although in his kingdom he was born poor.* ¹⁵*I saw
all the living, who move about under the sun, on the side of the second
youth who will succeed him.* ¹⁶*There was no end to all the people,
all whom he led. But those to come have no joy in him. This also is a
vanity and a chase after wind.*

^{17(5:1)}*Watch your step when you enter the house of God. The approach
of one who listens is better than the sacrifice fools offer, for they
have no knowledge of doing evil.* ^{5:1(2)}*Do not be quick with your tongue,
and let not your heart hasten to speak before God, for God is in heaven
and you are on earth. Therefore let your words be few.*
²⁽³⁾ *For as dreams come from many tasks,
     so the speech of fools from many words.*

     5:6; 6:11; 10:12–14

³⁽⁴⁾ *When you make a vow to God, do not be slow to fulfill it,
for he has no pleasure in fools. Fulfill what you vow!* ⁴⁽⁵⁾*It
is better for you not to vow, than to vow and not fulfill it.* ⁵⁽⁶⁾
*Do not allow your mouth to bring you to sin, and do not say before
the representative, "it was a mistake," lest God be angry at
your words and destroy the work of your hands.*
⁶⁽⁷⁾ *For in many dreams—
     also many vanities and words.
     But fear God!*

     3:14; 7:18; 8:12; 12:13

⁷⁽⁸⁾ *If you see in a province the oppression of the poor, the
violation of right and justice, do not be surprised by the affair,
for over one official, another official keeps watch, and (still)
over them are officials.* ⁸⁽⁹⁾*An advantage for a country in every
way is this: a king for the tilled land.*

     3:16; 4:1

9(10) *Whoever loves money never has enough of it,*   1:8; 4:8; 5:11; 6:7
    nor the lover of wealth, enough income.
    This too is vanity.
10(11) *When goods increase,*
    those who consume them increase.
    What gain has the owner,
    except something for his eyes to look upon?
11(12) *Sweet is the sleep of the laborer,*
    whether he eats little or much,
    But the abundance of the rich   1:8; 4:8; 5:9; 6:7
    allows no sleep.

12(13) *There is a grievous evil I have seen under the sun: riches kept by their owner to his own hurt.* 13(14) *Namely, the riches are lost by an evil turn; then he begets a son when there is nothing to hand!* 14(15) *Just as he came forth from his mother's womb, naked will he again go as he came; and nothing for his toil will he have in hand to take with him.* 15(16) *This is a grievous evil: as he came, so must he go—then what profit does he have from his toiling for the wind?* 16(17) *Even all his days he eats in darkness, and in much [vexation], and sickness [   ] and spite.*   1:3, 14; 2:11, 22; 3:9; 8:9

17(18) *This is what I have seen as good, as beautiful: to eat and to drink and to prosper for all the toil that one must toil at under the sun in the limited life that God gives, for that is one's portion.* 18(19) *Also, anyone to whom God gives riches and possessions and the power to partake of them, to have his portion and to rejoice in his toil—this is a gift of God.* 19(20) *Indeed, he will hardly be concerned with the days of his life, because God keeps (him) occupied with the joy of his heart.*   2:24; 3:12–13; 8:15; 9:7–9 2:19, 21; 3:13; 6:2

6:1 *There is an evil I have seen under the sun and it is grievous for humans:* 2 *One to whom God has given riches, possessions, and glory so that he lacks nothing of what he desires—but God has not given him the power to partake of them! Instead, a stranger consumes them. This is a vanity and a grievous sickness.*   2:19, 21; 4:8

3 *If a man beget a hundred children and live many years— though many be the days of his years—if his desire for good things is not met, then even without a burial, I say the stillborn is better off than he.* 4 *Though in vain it comes and in darkness it goes, and with darkness its name is covered;* 5 *though it sees*   4:2–3

not the sun nor knows anything, it has more rest than he. [6]*If
one were to live twice a thousand years, but without experiencing
good, do not all go to the same place?*   3:20; 12:7
[7] *All human toil is for the mouth,
    but the appetite is never satisfied.*   1:8; 4:8; 5:9, 11
[8] *What advantage have the wise over the foolish?*   2:13
    what advantage has [a] poor person who knows how to cope with life?
[9] *Better is it that the eyes see,
    than that the appetite wanders;
    this too is vanity and a chase after wind.*

[10]*That which is has already been given its name; one knows*   1:9; 3:15
*what human beings are, and that they cannot contend with one who
is stronger.* [11]*For where there are many words, vanity is*   5:2, 6; 10:12-14
increased. What profit is there for humankind? [12]*For who
knows what is good for human beings during life, the few days
of their vain lives that they pass through like a shadow? For
who will tell them what will come after them under the sun?*   3:22; 8:7; 10:14

[7:1] *Better is a good name than good ointment;
    and the day of death, than the day of one's birth.*
[2] *Better to go to a house of mourning
    than to a house of feasting,
For that is the end of every person,
    and let the living take it to heart.*
[3] *Better is vexation than laughter,
    for despite a sad face the heart can be joyful.*
[4] *The heart of the wise is in a house of mourning,
    but the heart of fools is in a house of joy.*
[5] *Better to heed the reproof of the wise
    than to hear the song of fools.*
[6] *For like the sound of thistles under a pot
    is the laughter of fools.
This also is vanity,*
[7] *for oppression can make fools of the wise
    and a bribe corrupt the heart.*
[8] *Better is the end of a thing than its beginning;
    better is a patient spirit than a proud spirit.*
[9] *Do not be hasty in spirit to get angry,
    for anger lodges in a fool's bosom.*
[10] *Do not say, "How is it that the former days are better than these?"
    for it is not out of wisdom that you ask about this.*
[11] *Wisdom is as good as an inheritance,
    and profitable to those who live.*

¹² *For the protection of wisdom is (as) the protection of money,*
     and the advantage of knowledge is that wisdom keeps its owner alive.
¹³ *Consider the work of God. For who can make straight*   1:15; 3:11; 8:17; 11:5
what he has made crooked? ¹⁴ *On a good day enjoy the good, and*
on an evil day, consider: God made them both so that no one may
find fault with him.

¹⁵ *I have seen everything in my vain days: a just person*   8:14
who perishes despite his justice, and an evil person who lives
long despite his evil. ¹⁶ *Do not be overly just or be wise to*
excess! Why should you be ruined? ¹⁷ *Do not be*
overly evil and do not be a fool! Why should you die before
your time? ¹⁸ *It is good for you to hold to this, and not let*
go of that. But the one who fears God will come through with
respect to both.   3:14; 5:6; 12:13

¹⁹ *Wisdom is stronger for the wise,*   9:16
     than ten officials who are in a city.
²⁰ *Still, no one on earth is so just*
     as to do good and never sin.
²¹ *To all the words that are spoken,*
     pay no attention,
     lest you hear your servant cursing you.
²² *For you know in your heart*
     that many times you also have cursed others.

²³ *All this I tested with wisdom. I said, "I will become wise." But*
it was beyond me. ²⁴ *What happens is distant and very deep.*
Who can find it out?

²⁵ *I turned my mind to know, by investigation and search,*   1:17; 2:12; 8:16
wisdom and (its) answer, and to know that wickedness is foolishness
and folly is madness. ²⁶ *And I found more bitter than death*
the woman who is a snare, whose heart is a net, whose hands are
bonds. By God's pleasure, one will escape from her, but the   2:26
errant one will be caught by her. ²⁷ *Indeed, this I have*
found—says [   ] Qoheleth, (adding) one thing to another to find an
*answer—*²⁸ *what my soul has always sought without finding*
(is this): One man in a thousand I have found, but a woman among
all of these I have not found. ²⁹ *See, only this have I found:*
God made humans upright, but they have sought out many devices.

⁸:¹ *Who is like the wise man,*
     and who knows the meaning of a thing?

Wisdom makes one's face shine,
and hardness of face is changed.

2 [   ] Observe the command of the king,
because of the oath of God.

3 Do not hasten to leave his presence;   10:4
do not persist in a bad situation,
for all that he wishes he can do.

4 Because the word of a king is powerful,
and who can say to him, "what are you doing?"

5 Whoever observes a command will not experience a bad turn,
for a wise heart knows the time and judgment;

6 Indeed, there is a time and judgment for everything.   3:1, 17; 9:11–12;
But misfortune lies heavy upon a person,   11:9; 12:14

7 In that no one knows what will happen,
because how it will turn out—who can tell him?   3:22; 6:12; 10:14

8 There is no one who has power over the breath of life
so as to retain it, and there is no one who has power over the   12:7
day of death, or dismissal in war; but neither does wickedness
save those who practice it.

9 All this I have seen and I have given my attention to   1:3, 14; 2:11, 22;
every deed that is done under the sun when one person   3:9; 5:15
has power over another so as to harm him. 10 Then I saw the
wicked buried. They used to come and go from the holy place!
But those were forgotten in the city who had acted justly. This
also is vanity. 11 Because sentence against an evil deed is
not quickly executed, therefore the human heart is set on doing
evil. 12 For the sinner does evil a hundred times, and yet
prolongs his life—although I know that those who fear God will
be well off because they fear him, 13 and that the wicked person
will not be well off, and will not prolong his shadowy days
because he does not fear God. 14 There is a vanity that is done
on the earth: there are just who are treated as if they had   7:15
acted wickedly, and there are wicked who are treated as if they
had acted justly. I said, this also is vanity. 15 So I praised
joy because there is nothing better for a human under the sun than
to eat and drink and to be joyous. This can be his part for the   2:24;
toil during the days of his life which God gives him under the sun.   3:12–13, 22;
    5:17–18; 9:7–9

16 When I put my mind to know wisdom and to contemplate   1:17; 2:12; 7:25
the task that is carried out on earth—even though neither
by day nor by night do one's eyes have sleep—17 I looked
at all the work of God: no one can find out what is done

under the sun. Therefore humans search hard, but no one   3:11; 7:13;
can find out; and even if the wise man says he knows,   8:17; 11:5
he cannot find out.

⁹⁺¹*Indeed, all this I took to heart, and all this I*
examined: the just and the wise and their actions are in the
hand of God. Love from hatred human beings cannot tell;
both are before them. ²*Everything is the same for everybody:*
the same lot for the just and the wicked, the good, the clean
and the unclean, the one who offers sacrifice and the one who
does not. As it is for the good, so it is for the sinners; as
it is for the one who takes an oath, so it is for the one who
fears to take an oath. ³*This is an evil in all that is done*
under the sun: there is the same lot for all, and also the heart   2:14–15;
of human beings is set on evil, and folly is in their hearts   3:19; 8:11
during their lives. Then afterwards—to the dead! ⁴*Indeed,*
who can be set apart? For all the living there is hope, because
"a live dog is better off than a dead lion." ⁵*For the*
living know that they will die, but the dead know nothing! There
is no longer any recompense for them because the memory of them   1:11; 2:16
has disappeared. ⁶*Their love, their hate, their jealousy, are*
long gone, and they have no portion ever again in all that is done
under the sun.

⁷*Go, eat your bread with joy and drink your wine with a merry*   2:24;
heart because God has already accepted your deeds. ⁸*At all*   3:12–13, 22;
times let your clothing be white, and let no oil for your head be   5:17–18;
lacking. ⁹*Enjoy life with a wife whom you love all the days of*   8:15
the vain life that are given you under the sun [   ], for that is
your portion in life, and for the toil with which you toil under
the sun. ¹⁰*All that your hands find to do, do with might,*
because there is no action, or answer, or knowledge, or wisdom in
Sheol where you are going.

¹¹*Again, I observed under the sun that the swift do not win*   3:1, 17; 8:5–6;
the race, nor the strong the battle, nor do the wise have bread,   11:9; 12:14
nor the clever have riches, nor do those who know find favor;
but a time of calamity happens to them all. ¹²*For no one*
knows even his own time; like fish taken in a fatal snare or
like birds taken in a trap, so people are caught at a bad time
when it suddenly falls upon them.

¹³*This also I observed under the sun: (an example of) wisdom*
which seemed great to me: ¹⁴*There was a small town with few men*

in it, to which a great king came. He surrounded it and invested
it with great siegeworks. ¹⁵ In it was to be found a poor wise
man who saved the town by his wisdom, but no one had
any thought for that poor man. ¹⁶ So I said, "better is wisdom
than strength," but the wisdom of a poor man is despised and his
words are not heeded.

7:19; 9:18

¹⁷ The calm words of the wise are better heeded
than the cry of a ruler among fools.
¹⁸ Wisdom is better than weapons of war,
but one bungler can destroy a lot of good.

7:16; 9:16

¹⁰:¹ Dead flies corrupt and ferment the perfumer's oil;
a little folly counts more than much wisdom.

² The heart of the wise tends to the right,
the heart of the fool to the left.

2:14

³ Also, when the fool goes on his way,
he lacks any sense and he tells everyone that he is a fool.

⁴ If a ruler's wrath rises against you,
do not yield your place,
for calmness makes up for great mistakes.

8:3

⁵ There is an evil I have seen under the sun,
the kind of error made by one who wields power:
⁶ The fool is placed among the exalted;
the great and the rich dwell at the bottom.
⁷ I have seen slaves on horseback,
and princes walking on foot like slaves.

⁸ Whoever digs a pit may fall into it;
whoever tears down a wall a serpent may bite.
⁹ Whoever quarries stones can be hurt by them;
whoever chops wood can be endangered by it.

¹⁰ If the iron is dull
and the blade has not been sharpened,
one must exercise more strength;
but the advantage of skill is (a matter of) wisdom.
¹¹ If the serpent bites without being charmed,
then there is no advantage in being a charmer.

¹² Words from the mouth of the wise win favor,
but the lips of a fool destroy him.
¹³ The words of his mouth start with folly;
his talk ends in dangerous nonsense—

5:2, 6; 6:11

¹⁴   *for the fool never stops talking.*
       No one knows what is going to happen,   3:22; 6:12; 8:7
           for, what will happen after him—who can tell him?
¹⁵ *The toil of a fool wears him out,*
       for he does not even know the way to town.

¹⁶ *Woe to you, O land, whose king is a (mere) youth,*
       whose princes dine in the morning.
¹⁷ *Happy the land whose king is noble,*
       whose princes eat at the proper time,
       with discipline, not in debauchery.

¹⁸ *Because of laziness the roof sinks in,*
       and because of slack hands the house leaks.

¹⁹ *For enjoyment one prepares a meal,*
       and wine makes life happy,
       and money answers for everything.

²⁰ *Even in your thought do not curse the king,*
       and in your bedroom do not curse a rich person,
       for a bird in the sky can carry the news,
       a winged creature can report what is said.

¹¹:¹ *Send forth your bread upon the waters—*
       after many days you may have it back!
²   *Divide what you have in seven or even eight ways—*
       you do not know what misfortune may befall the land!

³   *When the clouds become full,*
       they pour rain on the land.
       Whether a tree falls to the south or to the north,
       wherever it falls, there it will remain.
⁴   *Whoever observes the wind will not sow,*
       and whoever looks at the clouds will not reap.
⁵   *Just as you do not know the way of the life-breath*   3:11; 7:13; 8:17
       [in] the limbs within a mother's womb,
       so you do not know the work of God
       who does everything.
⁶   *In the morning sow your seed,*
       and in the evening let not your hands be idle,
       For you do not know which will be profitable,
       or if both will be equally good.

⁷   *Sweet is the light,*
       and pleasant it is for the eyes to see the sun!

⁸ *However many years one lives,*
   one should rejoice in them all,
but remember
   that the days of darkness will be many;
   all that is coming is vanity.
⁹ *Rejoice, O youth,*
   while you are young.
Let your heart be merry
   in the days of your youth.
Walk where your heart leads you,
   and where your eyes look,
but know that on all these (counts)
   God will bring you to judgment.   3:1, 17; 8:5–6; 9:11–12; 12:14
¹⁰ *Banish trouble from your heart*
   and remove suffering from your body,
   for youthfulness and black hair are fleeting.
^{12:1} *Remember your creator in the days of your youth,*
   before the days of misfortune come
and the years arrive, of which you will say,
   "I have no pleasure in them";
² *Before the darkening of sun and light,*
   and moon and stars,
and the return of clouds
   after the rain;
³ *When the guardians of the house tremble,*
   and strong men are bent over,
and the women at the mill cease because they are few,
   and the ladies who look out of the windows are darkened;
⁴ *When the doors in the street are closed,*
   and the noise of the grinding mill is low,
and one arises at the sound of a bird,
   and all the daughters of song are quiet;
⁵ *When one has fear of heights,*
   and terrors are in the road;
And the almond tree blossoms,
   and the locust is heavy,
   and the caperberry is opened.
When humans go to their everlasting home,
   and mourners go about the street;
⁶ *Before the silver cord is [torn],*
   and the golden bowl is shattered,
And the jar by the fountain is broken,
   and the pulley is [shattered] on the cistern,
⁷ *And the dust returns*

> to the earth as it was,   3:20; 6:6
> And the life-breath returns   8:8
>   to God who gave it.

⁸ *Vanity of vanities! says Qoheleth,*   1:2
>   *all is vanity!*

⁹*Besides being a sage, Qoheleth continued to teach
the people knowledge; he weighed and examined and corrected
many sayings.* ¹⁰*Qoheleth sought to find out pleasing words and he
[wrote] true words carefully.* ¹¹*The words of the wise are like
oxgoads, like fixed nails are the collected sayings; they are given
by one shepherd.* ¹²*As for more than these, my son, beware; there
is no end to the writing of many books, and much study wearies
the flesh.* ¹³*The end of the matter, when all is heard: fear*   3:14; 5:6;
God and keep his commandments, for this is (the duty of) everyone.   7:18; 8:12
¹⁴*For God will bring every deed to judgment, over all
that is hidden, whether good or evil.*   3:1, 17; 8:5–6; 11:9

Superscription (1:1)

Bibliography

Albright, W. F. "Some Canaanite-Phoenician Sources of Hebrew Wisdom." In *Wisdom in Israel and in the Ancient Near East.* Ed. M. Noth and D. W. Thomas. VTSup 3. Leiden: Brill, 1955. 1–15. **Ginsberg, H. L.** *Studies in Koheleth.* New York: Jewish Theological Seminary, 1952. 12–14. **Joüon, P.** "Sur le nom de *Qoheleth.*" *Bib* 2 (1921) 53–54. **Kamenetzky, A. S.** "Der Rätselname Koheleth." *ZAW* 34 (1914) 225–28. ———. "Der ürsprunglich beabsichtigte Aussprache des Pseudonyms קהלת." *OLZ* 24 (1921) 11–15. **Ullendorff, E.** "The Meaning of *qhlt.*" *VT* 12 (1962) 215.

Translation

[1] *The words of Qoheleth, son David, king* [a][b] *in Jerusalem.*

Notes

1.a. The Greek and Latin have added "of Israel" at this point, probably on the basis of 1:12. As Jerome remarks in his commentary, it is quite superfluous.

1.b. The efforts of H. L. Ginsberg (*Studies,* 12–14) and W. F. Albright ("Sources," 15, n. 2) to interpret מלך as "property-holder" and "counselor," respectively, have not gained support.

Form/Structure/Setting

The superscription is a characteristic feature of biblical books, doubtless added when they were edited for public consumption. The purpose of the title is to ascribe the following work to a son of David, presumably Solomon, who was the only son of David to rule in Jerusalem (cf. 1:12). Such an ascription implies that Ecclesiastes is another "wisdom" book in the tradition of Solomon, Israel's premier sage.

Comment

"The words of Qoheleth" are to be taken in the sense of the "words" in the titles of Prov 30:1, 31:1 (and see the widely adopted emendation of Prov 22:17, "the words of the wise"). The phrase does not have the same nuance as "the words of Jeremiah" in Jer 1:1, or "the words of Solomon" (his acts) in 1 Kgs 11:41. It is rather a typical wisdom title, comparable to the משלי שלמה in Prov 1:1; 10:1.

As indicated in the Introduction ("Author, Date, and Canonicity"), the meaning of קהלת (*qōhelet*) remains a mystery. In the broadest sense it indicates that the author has something to do with a קהל, or congregation. In form the word is the qal feminine singular active participle of the root קהל, although the designee is clearly masculine. For all intents and purposes it is used as a proper name, despite the presence of the definite article in 7:7 and 12:8.

As "Son of David," the author receives the aura of Solomon, Israel's sage par excellence (1 Kgs 5:9–14[4:29–34]), to whom Jewish tradition attributed the Book of Proverbs, the Song of Songs, and the apocryphal Wisdom of Solomon.

Explanation

This innocent looking superscription raises more questions than can be answered. One can "explain" it along the lines of the traditional ascription of wisdom writings to Solomon, but the name "Solomon" never occurs explicitly as it does in the Song of Songs and in Proverbs. Moreover, a king fiction seems like a weak justification of the admittedly royal pretense that never goes beyond chap. 2. It was not necessary for the writer to describe himself (or be described) as a king for the sake of that chapter. By contrast, one can understand better the ascription of the Song of Songs to Solomon. In the Song of Songs, a Solomonic air breathes through the work. There seems to be a hidden reference to that king in the שׁלמית and the שׁלום that occur in Cant 7:1 [6:13] and 8:10, and there are several explicit references to him elsewhere in the eight chapters. But in the case of Qoheleth there is no compelling reason for royal identity. It is easy enough to say, after the fact, that the Solomonic authorship facilitated the canonization of the work. But we are in the realm of hypothesis; the identity remains a puzzle. From this point of view, it is interesting to compare the work with the Wisdom of Solomon. Although Solomon is never mentioned by name in that work, it is crystal clear that the writer implicitly identifies himself with the famous king (e.g., chaps. 7–9). The author is a king addressing other "kings" (Wis 1:1; 6:1). But Qoheleth makes little use of royal identity. From the very first, our author is wrapped in mystery.

The appearance of this superscription raises the question of editor(s). While it is theoretically possible for an author to have edited his own work and furnished it with a title, it is more likely that the title is a later addition, in the case of the biblical books. Since Qoheleth was a teacher (12:9), perhaps one of his students or followers was the editor. Scholars commonly identify this editor as R(edactor), and then hypotheses begin to multiply. Many commentators (e.g., A. Lauha) detect two redactors, R^1 and R^2, particularly in the epilogue (12:9–14). It is a delicate procedure to assign verses to an editor, or to another hand, and we have seen in the Introduction (p. xxxii) that this practice has been exaggerated in the case of Ecclesiastes. Perhaps the most convincing indication of another hand in this work is the reference to the author in the *third person* (12:9), when elsewhere Qoheleth writes in the first person. On this basis, one may legitimately suspect 12:9–14 of being a later addition, and perhaps the writer of the superscription is the same as the writer of the epilogue in 12:9–14. As for the existence of several redactors, see the *Comment* on 12:9–14.

A Motto   (1:2)

Bibliography

See the special bibliography on הבל *hebel,* "vanity," in the Introduction (p. lvii), to which the following can be added: **Ellermeier, F.** *Qohelet I/1.* 36–38. **Lohfink, N.** "Koh 1,2 'alles ist Windhauch'—universale oder anthropologische Aussage?" In *Der Weg zum Menschen: Für Alfons Deissler.* Ed. R. Mosis and L. Ruppert. Freiburg: Herder, 1989. 201–16. **Loretz, O.** *Qohelet.* 218–34.

Translation

2   Vanity[a] of vanities![b] says[c] Qoheleth,
    Vanity of vanities! All[d] is vanity!

Notes

2.a. הבל properly means "breath" (rendered as ἀτμίς/ἀτμός in Aq, Sym, Theod), or "vapor," and hence can designate what is lacking in substance, ephemeral, without any result (as when paired with "chase after wind" in 1:14). It was rendered as vanity in the LXX (ματαιότης) and Vg *(vanitas).* The vocalization of the construct as הֲבֵל is unusual, occurring only here and in 12:8. Joüon (§96Ae) explains it as derived from הֲבֵל *hĕbel**, another form of הֶבֶל. It might also be an Aramaizing vocalization (cf. עֲבַד in Dan 6:21).

2.b. The repetition is an idiomatic expression for the superlative (cf. Joüon §141). There are many examples: "king of kings" is the supreme king.

2.c. The perfect tense (אָמַר, "says") can be rendered by the past, as though the writer looked back, while placing one of Qoheleth's *logia* here. But the present tense, expressing a summary of his teaching, is preferable.

2.d. Thus far there is no subject, only exclamations. Now the subject appears, and in an emphatic position.

Form/Structure/Setting

By their very nature these exclamations stand out. The function of the sentence as a motto, or *Leitwort,* for the entire work derives from the frequency of the word הבל (*hebel;* thirty-eight times) and also from the deliberate placing of this verse here and at the end, in 12:8, forming an *inclusio.* Thus many assign this inclusio to the editor of the work, and hypothesize further that it is not from Qoheleth because he never uses the superlative form elsewhere. It may be editorial, but the superlative is surely not foreign to Qoheleth's thought; one should recall that הבל occurs thirty-eight times in the book. The superlative could very well be his own making and, if so, the *inclusio* as well.

Comment

Let it suffice to recall here that הבל can be rendered in many different ways, as futile, absurd, useless, etc. (see above, pp. lviii–lix). It is obviously used in a pejorative sense. Qoheleth makes the term into a value judgment that he applies to various things and situations throughout his work.

What does it mean to say that *everything* (הכל) is הבל? A general tendency of exegetes is to take it as the world and all that is in it: "in a word what we would call the world and life" (Podechard); "the whole (of the things namely, which present themselves to us here below for our consideration and use) is vanity" (Delitzsch).

N. Lohfink ("Koh 1,2") calls attention to the quotation of Monimos the cynic, which Y. Amir first pointed out as similar to 1:2: τὸ γὰρ ὑποληφθὲν τῦφον εἶναι πάντ᾽ ἔφη ("for he said that what was accepted [as existing] was all delusion"). Lohfink then raises the question whether הכל in 1:2 has a cosmic or anthropological meaning. He argues that the biblical use of הכל is not universal but specific to things that are mentioned in context. In the case of Qoh 1:2–3, הכל is an anticipation of כל עמלו in v 3 (so also C. D. Ginsburg): all the toil with which he toiled under the sun. In this case, "all" is not cosmic, but designates the worldly realities with which humans must deal. It is instructive to note the objects that הבל *hebel* is applied to in the book (see Lohfink, "Koh 1,2," 213–14; Fox, *Qohelet*, 37–46): joy, human actions, wisdom, labor, riches. It is clear that God is excepted, and so is the cosmos. Qoheleth uses no Hebrew equivalent for the cosmos (despite the availability of the merism, "heaven and earth"). In the poem to follow (1:4–7), the world will be indicated by the elements of the sun, wind, and rivers. The reasoning of Fox is in the same line with Lohfink: "The scope of 'everything' can be restricted further, for Qoheleth is actually concerned only with what happens in human life. . . . *Hakkol* in 1:2 and 12:8 is therefore synonymous . . . with (all that happens under the sun), in 1:9, 13, 14; 2:17; 8:17; 9:3, 6" (*Qohelet*, 44–45).

Explanation

Time has dulled the edge of this fundamental judgment made by Qoheleth. He was of the firm conviction that there was *nothing* in this world that was an unqualified good. It was all "vanity," without exception. The grim reality of his verdict has to be seen in and for itself before it is absorbed into an interpretive context. Readers who supply the dimension of eternal life with God can, by comparison, reduce all other values to zero. This fits well with an ascetic interpretation, but not with Qoheleth's expressed thought. Others would modify or seek exceptions from Qoheleth's drastic judgment on the basis of those passages that seem to express a positive enjoyment of life (symbolized, e.g., in 3:12–13 and 5:17–18 by "eating and drinking"). In either case, it is important to realize that the reader is placing Qoheleth in a specific context (the reader's context?), which he did not envision. No matter the eventual reinterpretation of the word, one should avoid using the term הבל ("vanity") *casually* as it were, without even an inkling of the depth of meaning that Qoheleth attached to it.

A Poem about Human Toil   (1:3–11)

Bibliography

Alonso Schökel, L. *A Manual of Hebrew Poetics.* SubBib 11. Rome: Pontifical Biblical Institute, 1988. **Eliade, M.** *Cosmos and History.* Tr. W. R. Trask. TB 50. New York: Harper, 1950. **Ellermeier, F.** *Qohelet I/1.* 186–211. **Fox, M. V.** "Qoheleth 1.4." *JSOT* 40 (1988) 109. **Good, E. M.** "The Unfilled Sea: Style and Meaning in Ecclesiastes 1:2–11." *IW.* 59–73. **Lohfink, N.** "Die Wiederkehr des immer Gleichen: Eine frühe Synthese zwischen griechischem and jüdischem Weltgefühl in Kohelet 1,4–11." *AF* 53 (1985) 125–49. **Loretz, O.** *Qohelet.* 193–96. **Michel, D.** *Eigenart.* 2–8. **Rousseau, F.** "Structure de Qohélet I 4–11 et plan du livre." *VT* 31 (1981) 200–209. **Whybray, R. N.** "Ecclesiastes 1.4–7 and the Wonders of Nature." *JSOT* 41 (1988) 105–12. **Wright, A. G.** "Structure." *CBQ* 30 (1968) 313–34.

Translation

3 *What profit[a] does one[b] have for[c] all the toil[d]*
    with which[e] one toils under the sun[f]?
4 *One generation goes and another comes,*
    while[a] the earth stands forever.
5 *The sun rises[a] and the sun sets;*
    to its place[b] it hastens, there to rise.
6 *Going[a] to the south,*
    and turning to the north—
    Turning, turning goes the wind,
    and upon its rounds[b] the wind comes back.
7 *All the streams go to the sea,*
    but the sea is never filled;
    To the place that they go,
    there the streams keep going.[a]
8 *All words[a] are wearisome;[b]*
    there is nothing one can say.
    The eye is not satisfied by seeing,
    nor the ear filled by hearing.
9 *What[a] has been is what will be, and what has been done is what will be done; there is nothing new under the sun!* 10 *If there is[a] something about which one says, "Look, this is new,"[b] it existed already[c] in ages[d] that have gone before us.* 11 *There is no memory[a] of those in the past;[b] of those in the future there will be no memory among those who will come afterwards.*

Notes

3.a. יתרון occurs only in Ecclesiastes (and fourteen times, if one includes its cognate forms, מותר and יותר), usually in the sense of "profit." It is rendered literally in LXX: περισσεία, "surplus." R. Braun (*Kohelet*, 47–48) argues for the influence of the Greek ὄφελος, "advantage," which occurs in Hellenistic writers (gnomic literature).

3.b. Both אדם and בני אדם, which serves as a plural for the collective אדם, occur frequently in Ecclesiastes to designate human beings, regardless of gender. Qoheleth's observations are essentially universal in thrust, although we know nothing about the "people" (12:9) whom he taught.

3.c. The *beth pretii* (Joüon §133c) occurs in בכל (cf. also 5:14).

3.d. עמל is another favorite term of the author, occurring thirty-eight times either as noun or as verb; it comes to have, especially in later Hebrew, a nuance of pain and trouble, and this note is sounded throughout the work.

3.e. "It is estimated that -שׁ is used as the relative particle sixty-eight times in Koheleth, while אשׁר is used eighty-nine times" (Whitley, *Koheleth*, 7). It appears more frequently in later books, but also in early ones as well (Judg 5:7).

3.f. תחת השׁמשׁ, "under the sun," is also a favorite phrase, occurring twenty-nine times. It seems to be sufficiently established in Semitic culture, as shown by the Eshmunazzar and Tabnit inscriptions and it even occurs in Elamite. Hence the old allegations of a "Grecism" (ὑφ᾽ ἡλίῳ) can hardly be sustained (so Loretz, *Qohelet*, 46–47). However, R. Braun argues that Greek influence is at work here "indirectly" (Braun, *Kohelet*, 49–51).

4.a. "While" (literally, "and") is preferable to "but." No contrast seems to be intended between the succession of generations and the relative permanence of the earth, which is merely the backdrop for the succession. The stability itself of the earth suggests monotony.

5.a. The *waw* before זרח is unusual in that none of the lines in vv 4–8 begin with "and." Besides, the participial form dominates the style, as indicated by the participle of זרח itself at the end of v 5. One can explain the *waw* by metathesis for זורח; in any case זרח is to be vocalized as participle.

5.b. מקומו, "its place," is really the starting point. The punctuation in MT ties this phrase to the previous words, but it is to be construed with "hastens" (literally, שׁואף, "pants").

6.a. This translation is certain, despite the fact that some ancient versions (LXX, Vg) referred the opening words to the sun (v 5).

6.b. "Rounds" is literally "turnings," a word that climaxes the repetition of the root סבב.

7.a. Other translations are possible. K. Galling, following Sym and Vg proposes: "to the place from whence they flow, there the streams return, in order to flow again." See the discussion in Ellermeier, *Qohelet I/1*, 197–99. Such a rendering makes a tight little comparison with the action of the wind and sun in vv 5–6, but it over-interprets v 7. Rather, the point is that the streams do the same thing over and over again (without the sea being filled), not that they go in circles.

8.a. "Things" is a possible translation (so RSV, NEB), but דברים can be interpreted by the use of the verb דבר, "can say," in v 8b; the reference to the faculties of speech and hearing in 8b suggests that the faculty of speech is meant in 8a. See the discussion in Ellermeier, *Qohelet I/1*, 201–8.

8.b. The meaning of יגעים, "wearisome," is not assured (cf. Whybray, 39, 43). It has been taken in both an active ("tiring") and passive ("faded, tired") sense. Elsewhere (only Deut 25:18; 2 Sam 17:2) it seems to have a passive meaning.

9.a. מה־שׁ occurs eight times, to indicate indefinite "what (ever)"; normal Hebrew would have אשׁר or כל אשׁר (in Aramaic מה די). The phrase seems to belong to late Hebrew (cf. Whitley, *Koheleth*, 10–11). The stylistic expression is noteworthy: הוא . . . מה־שׁ.

10.a. שׁ is used frequently to introduce a case for discussion (2:21, 4:8, etc.; see Michel, *Eigenart*, 185–86). A conditional rendering (not interrogative as in Sym and Jerome's commentary) is appropriate here (cf. GKC §159dd).

10.b. The accentuation in MT indicates the translation: "look at this—it is new."

10.c. כבר, "already," is found only in Ecclesiastes in the Hebrew Bible, and nine times. It is frequent in Mishnaic Hebrew, and may be an Aramaism (cf. Wagner §126).

10.d. The plural, "ages," can be considered a plural of extension (GKC §124b). It is construed with the singular verb, היה, but the fluctuation in agreement between subject and verb occurs elsewhere; cf. 1:16; 2:7; 10:1, 15. For further discussion of this phenomenon in connection with an alleged original text in Phoenician writing, cf. Whitley, *Koheleth*, 11.

11.a. For the construct (זכרון) before the preposition *lamedh*, cf. GKC §130a.

11.b. Both "past" and "future" are masculine in the MT, and hence can properly designate human beings rather than phenomena. But it is also possible to refer these terms to עלמים, "ages," in v 10. אחרנים, "the future," is a kind of *casus pendens* (E. Podechard), which begins the second part of the statement; it is taken up by להם.

Form/Structure/Setting

There are differing opinions whether v 3 is to be separated from v 2. K. Galling, E. Podechard, and R. Kroeber unite them as a kind of introduction to the book. But two reasons would suggest that v 3 begins a new section: (1) v 2, as has been indicated, is tied in with the inclusion in 12:8; (2) v 3 proposes the context (so A. Wright, *CBQ* 30 [1968] 333) for the following lines in which repetition symbolizes the monotony of toil.

Vv 4–8 form a compact unit, with an inclusion (הלך, "goes") in vv 4–6 and another in vv 7–8 (מלא/תמלא, "fill"). Moreover, the participial structure remains through vv 4–7 and bonds these lines together. The description of nature then leads into the application to human activity in v 8.

Vv 9–11, printed here somewhat hesitantly in prose, appear to be a kind of commentary or reflection on the poem about toil: the constant repetition means that there is nothing ever really new.

Comment

3 The rhetorical (but nonetheless genuine) question is a typical feature in wisdom literature, and is employed many times in Ecclesiastes. It often tends, as here, to suggest a negation (cf. 2:11; 3:9): there is no profit from one's hard lot, the toil inherent in human existence. Thus the answer has been anticipated by the exclamations in v 2 (perhaps "all" is a catch word in vv 2–3).

"Under the sun" is a phrase peculiar to Ecclesiastes in the OT (see note 3.f.): the expression is varied in 1:13; 2:3; 3:1, as "under the heavens." This has more than the pale meaning of "on the earth" (against A. Lauha). It suggests the troubled life of humanity in this world against the background of inevitable death ("the accent of oppressive constriction and incarceration," Zimmerli; "death-limit," Galling).

4 This verse affirms the ephemeral character of humankind, against the background of the ever-standing earth. One should not press the "eternity of the world" here, since as Zimmerli remarks, "the permanence of the earth is merely the foil against which the restless coming and going of human beings is outlined." It is the "dance of the dead" with which Qoheleth is concerned. The constant repetition, the coming and going, is brought out in the metaphors of vv 4–7. The image of generation stands for repetition, ongoing and relentless, always monotonous, and this is reinforced by the succeeding examples. The comparison of human generations to tree leaves is found in Sir 14:18 and, as pointed out by R. Braun (*Kohelet*, 57–58), seems to go back to Homer (*Iliad*, 6.146ff.). Podechard remarks that v 4 has nothing to do with the supposed immobility of the earth, as alleged in the case against Galileo.

Fox denies that there is any contrast here between the transience of generations and the permanence of the earth. To this end he interprets "earth" as meaning humanity (see also *JSOT* 40 [1988] 109). It is true that the remaining images do not underscore ephemerality (vv 4–7), but it is hard to eliminate the note of impermanence and transience here when they appear with such frequency throughout the book; cf., e.g., 2:16.

5 The description of the sun's "journey" is in lively contrast with Ps 19, where it is compared to a warrior. Here it is presented as a creature that simply does what has to be done. In the context this is another symbol for ineluctable repetition. One can only speculate whether Israel shared the common belief that the sun went "under the earth" and around to its place of rising.

6 Again, the participial style is very effective, and two verbs are repeated: הלך, "go" (twice), and סבב, "turn" (four times). The position of רוח, "wind," in v 6b is deliberate and striking. Podechard points out that the movement is not circular: rather the wind sweeps the area in two contrary directions, north and south, only to begin again. As in the previous examples, the direct meaning of the image is constant repetition; the wind (which is mentioned in another context in 11:4) returns to its starting point in order to begin again.

7 The sense of the verse is that the streams keep pouring into the sea, not that they return to their source and resume their rounds (see note 7.a.). Hence, מקום, "place," is to be taken in the sense of goal, not origin, and it is useless to speculate about an "eternal return," or that the waters return under the earth (so K. Galling, Jerome). The image of the sea never being filled (cf. Aristophanes, *Clouds*, l. 1294) expresses exactly the futility of the action of the streams (so also H. Hertzberg, R. Gordis, F. Nötscher, A. Lauha). W. Zimmerli remarks that the sea that is never filled is the counterpart to human effort that never comes to fulfillment.

8 After surveying instances of the constant repetition of an action in nature, the author now turns to the activity of humans (the primary interest in the work) and finds the same phenomenon there: they are part of that world, always active and yet never satisfied. The inadequacy of words is not merely the inability of humans to find words that fit (the ideal of the sage was the right word at the right time; cf. Prov 15:23, 25:11). Rather, the point is that human words never achieve their purpose.

This verse closes the short poem in vv 4–8. The poem is not merely a *māšāl* about nature, as O. Loretz (*Qohelet*, 193–94) terms it, which underscores marvels in nature that humankind is unable to understand (see also Lohfink; R. N. Whybray, *JSOT* 41 [1988] 105–12). Rather, all the events are example of fruitless repetition. This central idea blends into the following vv 9–11. There is "nothing new," because there has been futile repetition going on in past generations, and in natural phenomena.

9 The author denies any distinction between the past and the future. They are really the same; the future repeats the past. The sameness of yesterday and today is stressed in an Akkadian proverb: "The life of last night (is the same as) every day" (W. Lambert, *BWL*, 249). But here the emphasis on sameness is much greater than general boredom. In v 9a there seems to be no difference between the verbs "be" and "do"; they serve to embrace all reality (against Podechard and others who refer "be" to the phenomena of vv 4–8 and "do" to human activities). Nor can one speak properly of cyclical thought here. Rather, there is simple repetition, as shown by the examples in vv 4–8. The idea will be taken up again in 3:15 in slightly altered form.

"Under the sun" may form an inclusio with v 3, thus linking this passage with the question of toil. H. Hertzberg rightly points out that the denial of anything new is unusual in biblical thought. The OT refers frequently to "new" things (e.g., song, Ps 96:1; covenant, Jer 31:31; see Isa 43:19). How rigidly did Qoheleth understand "nothing new under the sun"?

10 This verse is a flat denial that there is anything really new, in answer to an objection that the author anticipates. H. Odeberg interpreted the lack of remembrance (v 11) as the absence of an "active memory" whereby one learns something new and profitable from the past. But Qoheleth seems to mean something more than this subjective, faulty memory. M. Fox (*Qohelet*, 172) adopts the view of Augustine (*City of God*, 12.13) that "Qoheleth is speaking of recurrence of *types* of being and events." Particular events derive their reality by their conformity to the archetype. Thus, neither the *City of God* nor Ecclesiastes are really new; they belong to the archetype, book. Does the thought of Qoheleth reach that degree of abstraction? Perhaps one can say that his meaning is that at least there is nothing new that is profitable or that is not vanity. In short, there is nothing of value that pierces the monotony of life: "the eye is not satisfied by seeing"; nothing new or out of the ordinary emerges to satisfy it.

11   One reason for the denial in v 10 is now given: there is no (active, as Odeberg would put it) memory of the past, nor in turn, of the future. It makes little difference whether the reference of past and future is to persons or events; if people are forgotten, so are events. O. Loretz (*Qohelet*, 225–30) narrows the perspective to deeds and events that create a name and reputation. But Qoheleth seems to have in mind more than that basic concern. Memory is as flat as the experience described in vv 3–8, and it does not serve to liberate humans from the monotony of life.

Explanation

The understanding of this passage depends in large part on the general construal placed upon verses and groups of verses within it, and indeed on the construal of the entire book. We have indicated that v 3 is to be separated from v 2 because the latter forms an inclusion with 12:8. Then the question concerning toil in v 3 is understood to dominate the rest of the section. Vv 4–7 are not a simple "nature" poem (against O. Loretz, N. Lohfink, R. N. Whybray, and also *JSOT* 41 [1988] 105–12). They epitomize the fruitless nature of human activity that is expressed in v 8 and is reflected upon in vv 9–11, which describe the tiresome sameness of experience when there is no memory of the past.

Not all would agree with this somber beginning. N. Lohfink and many others speak of an *ewiger Wiederkehr*, or eternal return, in these verses. For him, vv 4–11 are written in praise of the cosmos as majestic and eternal. In this view the "new" (v 10) would be something bad, in the sense that the times were becoming worse. However, an introductory poem in *praise* of the world is hardly consonant with Qoheleth's thought; the world here seems merely to serve as a foil for his conclusions about humans and their useless activity. It is not helpful to speak of the myth of the eternal return in connection with this passage. Is one designating the Greek myth, Nietzsche's interpretation of it, or Eliade's interpretation (see M. Eliade, *Cosmos and History*)? The myth of the eternal return can be interpreted as a positive thing, the means by which time is wiped out and a kind of contemporary relationship with a past event is established: "In a certain sense, it is even possible to say that nothing new happens in the world, for everything is but the repetition of the same primordial archetypes" (*Cosmos*, 89–90). Nothing of this appears in vv 4–11. The four examples of generation, sun, air, and sea can be seen to correspond to the four elements (earth, fire or sun, air, and water). The point is their constant repetition, which serves as an analogue to aimless and futile human experience. The thrust of vv 9–11 is to blame the lack of remembrance on the failure to recognize the sameness of things. There is nothing of the "optimism" that Eliade (*Cosmos*, 87–88) attributed to this world view. If one is going to have recourse to the classical world for an image of this section, the myth of Sisyphus (suggested as long ago as E. Podechard) is more apt: that stone never gets up the hill. There is a treadmill to life's experiences. The mood has been well expressed by L. Alonso Schökel: "In what another might see as the rich, limitless variety of creation, he contemplates the monotony of existence. The result is that the theme reveals his attitude, and the technique he uses is synonymy. He wants us to focus on what is the same and overcomes his readers with the fatigue of monotony" (*A Manual of Hebrew Poetics*, 71).

Introduction (1:12–18)

Bibliography

Bons, E. "Zur Gliederung und Kohärenz von Koh 1, 12–21." *BN* 24 (1984) 73–93. **Loader, J. A.** *Polar Structures.* 35–39. **Loretz, O.** *Qohelet.* 57–65, 148–54. **Lux, R.** "'Ich, Köhelet bin König . . . ': Die Fiktion als Schlüssel zur Wirklichkeit in Kohelet 1, 12–2, 26." *EvT* 50 (1990) 331–42. **Michel, D.** *Eigenart.* 8–14.

Translation

[12] *I, Qoheleth, was[a] king over Israel in Jerusalem.* [13] *I applied my mind[a] to investigating and exploring with wisdom[b] all that is done[c] under the heavens. This is an evil task[d] that God has given to humankind to be occupied with.* [14] *I saw all the deeds that were done under the sun; and the result: all is vanity and a chase after wind![a]*
[15] *The crooked[a] cannot be made straight,[b]*
  and what is missing cannot be made up.[c]

[16] *I said to myself: "I have become greater and increased[a] in wisdom beyond all those who were over Jerusalem before me. My mind has carefully[b] observed wisdom and knowledge."* [17] *So I applied[a] my mind to know wisdom and knowledge,[b] madness[c] and folly,[d] (and) I realized that this also was a chase after wind.*
[18] *For, the more wisdom, the more trouble;*
  whoever increases wisdom, increases pain.

Notes

12.a. From a grammatical point of view היית can be an aorist ("was") or present perfect ("I still am king"). For the considerable discussion among commentators, see Loretz, *Qohelet*, 57–65.

13.a. נתתי את־לבי, "I applied my mind," is repeated in almost identical phraseology in 1:17; 8:9, 16, and see also 2:3 and 7:25. The formula serves to introduce a reflection.

13.b. The interpretation of the preposition *beth* varies. It is usually interpreted as instrumental *beth* (E. Podechard, R. Gordis, et al.). This view is supported by the references to wisdom in 2:3, 9. However, others (A. Lauha, N. Lohfink) construe בחכמה as the object of דרש, "investigate." Then the second verb, "explore," would introduce another object, "all that is done." It makes little sense to construe על as introducing a reason, as Ellermeier (*Qohelet I/1*, 179) does. Podechard points out that על is used after דרש to indicate the object in 2 Chr 31:9.

13.c. Qoheleth varies the phrase many times; see the cognate nouns and verbs in v 14, and cf. 1:9a; 2:17; 4:3; 8:9, 17; 9:3, 6. The reference is to "all that *happens* in life" (so Fox, *Qohelet*, 175), not to everything that human beings do.

13.d. ענין, "task," is peculiar to Ecclesiastes, occurring eight times as a noun and twice in the verbal form. Although the general meaning is "task, occupation," the nuance is that the work is disagreeable (and it is characterized as "evil" here). The word may be an Aramaism (Wagner §222). The grouping of words (לענות/עניו) is repeated in 3:10.

14.a. Only in Ecclesiastes do the words רעות (1:14; 2:11, 17, 26; 4:4, 6; 6:9) and רעיון (1:17; 2:22; 4:16) appear, and they are practically synonymous (cf. 1:17; 4:16). The root seems to be רעה, but the nuance is unclear. Some insist on "pasture" (cf. Hos 12:2), but there is enough basis for the meaning, "be occupied with" (LXX προαίρεσις). Wagner (§§285, 286) lists both words as Aramaisms. The difficulty with the word goes back to Jerome, and he has an interesting disquisition on it: "Necessity forces us to discuss Hebrew words more often than we wish, but we cannot know the meaning except through words. Aquila and Theodotion rendered *routh* by νομήν [law]; Symmachus by βόσκησιν. The Septuagint translators used an Aramaic, not a Hebrew word: προαίρεσιν. Therefore, whether the word is νομή, or βόσκησις from pasturing, προαίρεσις better expresses will than *praesumptio*. This refers to the fact that each person does what he wishes, and as seems right; humans are carried by free choice to diverse things, and all under the sun is vain while we by turns are unhappy with good and evil intent. A Jewish person, by whose instruction I read the Scriptures, says that the above written routh in this place means affliction and evil rather than feeding or will. Evil is meant not in the sense of contrary to good, but in the sense that is contained in the Gospel: 'the evil of the day suffices.' The Greeks have a better word for this: κακουχίαν, and the sense is: I considered all that is done in the world and I observed nothing but vanity and evils, i.e., miseries of the spirit by which the soul is afflicted by various thoughts" (CChrSL, 72:259–60).

15.a. מעות, "crooked," is masculine, but in context it must stand for the neuter (cf. נרדף in 3:15).

15.b. The verb תקן is peculiar to Ecclesiastes (7:13; 12:9) and also is found in the Aramaic of Dan 4:13. One can understand the form as intransitive qal infinitive construct, "to be or become straight." The sense is passive; emendation to nipal or pual is not necessary.

15.c. המנות, "made up," is literally "counted (as present)"; there is no reason to change to המלות, "filled up."

16.a. One could also translate, "I greatly increased" (cf. GKC §120d). Qoheleth has a predilection for more or less synonymous verbs (cf. 1:13; 2:26).

16.b. ראה חכמה, literally, "saw wisdom," is another characteristic phrase; cf. 2:12, 9:13. D. Michel (*Eigenart*, 21, 25–29, 35–38 and passim) emphasizes strongly that ראה in Qoheleth's usage is not a passive observation but a critical consideration.

17.a. ואתנה is one of the few examples of *waw* consecutive in the book (cf. 4:1,7).

17.b. The Masoretic punctuation suggests that דעת is the verbal infinitive, "to know." But it appears that the phrase, "wisdom and knowledge," is being repeated from v 16, forming a contrast with "madness and folly." This is also the understanding of LXX, Syr, and Vg. See also 2:12 and 7:25.

17.c. הוללות, "madness," can be explained as an abstract plural; it appears also in 2:12; 7:25; 9:3. A singular abstract form, with ות ending appears in 10:13, and also in many MSS at 1:17. In any case, the general meaning remains the same.

17.d. שכלות is found only in Eccl (2:3, 12, 13; 7:25; 10:1, 13), and usually written with *samekh*.

Form/Structure/Setting

Despite all the variations in structure put forth by commentators, there is general agreement that a new unit begins at 1:12. The way in which Qoheleth speaks of himself in the first person and his implication that he is a Jerusalemite king make clear that this is an introduction. The first-person address is used throughout the rest of the work.

The king fiction, which it is generally agreed does not extend beyond chap. 2, fits in with the traditional associations of wisdom with kingship in the ancient Near East. One need only recall the Egyptian *sebayit* ("Instructions") given by kings and viziers (e.g., Merikare, Amenemhet in *ANET*, 414–19; cf. R. E. Murphy, *The Tree of Life*, ABRL [New York: Doubleday, 1990] 160–68). It would be an exaggeration, however, to speak of the work, or even this particular section, as a "royal testament" (against G. von Rad, *Wisdom in Israel*, 226). R. Braun, too, overestimates the resemblance of this king fiction to the Hellenistic model of king and wise man (Braun, *Kohelet*, 78–79, 162–63).

Indeed one is left with the question (cf. R. Lux, *EvT* 50 [1990] 331–42) why *did* Qoheleth adopt this royal identity when he uses it so sparingly and almost without need, since the experiment with riches in chap. 2 does not *demand* a king as the actor. Perhaps it lent some authenticity, so that he could make the boast he presents in 1:16.

The self-introduction is followed by a statement, in the broadest terms, of the author's project: a search for wisdom—followed immediately by the verdict: הבל *hebel!* This is stated twice (vv 14, 17), and each time it is supported by sayings that emphasize how problematic wisdom is. There is an unmistakable symmetry to 1:12–15 and 1:16–18, whether or not they are viewed as two introductions or reflections (see R. E. Murphy, *Wisdom Literature*, 134). N. Lohfink would include 2:1–2 as part of this unit, which he entitles "Drei Überblicke," or three summary views. It is true that the symmetry with 1:12–18 persists because in 2:1–2 Qoheleth gives an anticipatory (unfavorable) judgment about his project and follows it with what may be interpreted as sayings (v 2). However, the opening verses of chap. 2 seem inextricably tied with what follows, and the project is not the general one of wisdom as in 1:13, 16.

The separate introductory character of 1:12–18 is also implicitly admitted by commentators who recognize the verses as really belonging to larger units, such as 1:3–3:15 (D. Michel, *Eigenart,* 1–83) or 1:12–2:26 (A. Lauha, who regards 1:3–11 as a redactional insertion preceding Qoheleth's own self-introduction in 1:12).

Comment

12 This verse has all the marks of an introduction, and has been regarded by many as the true beginning of Qoheleth's book. It is worth noting that the association with David (1:1) is absent from this verse. The impact of "was king" has been variously interpreted. In a straight aorist sense, it could mean that he is no longer king. This gave rise to the Talmudic legend (*Sanh.* 2.6b; *Git.* 68b) that Solomon was deposed toward the end of his life. It is better to understand the verb as present perfect ("I have been and still am"). Hence Qoheleth is well able to carry out the projects that he will speak of.

13 He states his purpose somewhat redundantly in v 13a ("explore" is used of the scouting party in Num 13:2). His emphasis on wisdom as a guiding principle (see the *Notes*) is found also in 2:3, 9 and 7:23. As W. Zimmerli remarks, this is the "principle of questioning," the approach of a tough-minded thinker who is not satisfied with the view of his optimistic ancestors. He immediately characterizes this God-given task as an evil or unfortunate imposition (cf. 4:8; 5:13; 8:16). This phrase is a suggestive one, and the mood is reflected in 3:10. The transition to v 14 is all the easier. The mention of God (for the first time) in v 13 and God's "giving" are important for understanding some basic presuppositions of this book. It is to be interpreted within Qoheleth's own religious traditions: God controls everything and grants "gifts," even if arbitrarily. This is all part of the inscrutable divine action, which defies understanding.

14 The "deeds" are the events that make up the fabric of human life, and they are inseparable from the "work of God" that will be explicitly mentioned later (7:13; 8:17). The metaphor of chasing the wind is self-explanatory, since the wind, changeable and invisible, yields nothing, even were it to be caught. This is the first single occurrence of הבל, "vanity," the favorite term.

15 This proverbial saying is partially echoed in 7:13 (cf. 12:9). It serves here as a justification for the observation in v 14. The reference should be interpreted broadly: the physically and spiritually crooked. The meaning of v 15b (cf. 3:14) is somewhat obscure: if a thing is absent, one simply cannot claim that it is present. Whether this saying was coined by Qoheleth or by another can be only a matter of speculation; it suits his purpose here and may have been broadened in application at this point. K. Galling thinks that originally it referred to the twisted back of an old man (15a), and the "missing" (15b) refers to the ensuing lack of height. Although God is not mentioned in the saying, the presence is felt: a stark submission to the divine decrees appears throughout the book. No education and training can neglect this reality.

16 Again, the Solomonic aura appears; as H. Hertzberg remarks, the passage "begins like a royal edict." The claim to have surpassed his predecessors need not be taken to refer to Jebusite royalty; the renown of Solomon's wisdom is the issue. The meaning of wisdom should be taken broadly as the judicial, experiential, and nature wisdom associated with Solomon (1 Kgs 3–10). The passage really presupposes a long history of wisdom before the speaker, who thus relaxes somewhat his fictitious identity with Solomon and allows the reader into his own present work (Hertzberg).

17 After the royal posturing in v 16, Qoheleth admits that an even more intense involvement with wisdom ended in vanity (cf. 7:23–25; 8:16). It is the more intense by reason of dealing with *both* folly and wisdom. On this Jerome comments appropriately: *contraria contrariis intelliguntur,* "contraries are understood by means of their opposites." A similar resolve is found in 2:12 (cf. 7:25; 8:16). The fivefold repetition of the root ידע, "know," in vv 16–18 is doubtless deliberate.

18 A wisdom saying is quoted in support of the contention that the pursuit of wisdom is vanity. One can imagine (with K. Galling and W. Zimmerli) that the original setting of such a saying (in school) may have suggested a more positive meaning; the teacher would have encouraged the student: wisdom is not to be gotten without work or pain (even corporal punishment), but one can obtain it. But now the point is quite different: wisdom only brings trouble ("trouble" and "pain" will occur again; see 2:23; 5:16). The saying can be explained both as process and end result. One has to reckon with difficulties: the failures and trials that the pursuit of wisdom entails. Moreover, the end result is not satisfactory: the more you know, the less you know. Qoheleth himself confessed that wisdom eluded him (7:23–24).

The function of the saying in v 18 finds an analogue in v 15, and both sayings introduce us to the supple way in which Qoheleth will use proverbial sayings in his book. Generally speaking, he will radicalize them, applying them in the sharpest ways to the futilities of life. If v 15 originally referred to those who are unteachable and indocile, it now applies to every human being who strives after wisdom. If v 18 was originally meant as encouragement, now it is a warning (see D. Michel, *Eigenart,* 11–14).

Explanation

As an introduction to the book, these verses are central to Qoheleth's purpose. They tell us of his object and the means to it. The object is "wisdom and knowledge" (three times in vv 16–18, although separated in v 18). This is far from theoretical wisdom; it deals with the things that happen under the sun (vv 13–14). But it is not mindless; it is by means of wisdom (v 12) that his search will proceed. This distinction between style and content is an important observation for judging Qoheleth's views on wisdom. He is not "anti-wisdom" (see R. E. Murphy, *The Tree of Life,* 55). He recognizes the pain associated with the task (v

18), as well as its futility. He coolly places wisdom and folly together (v 17); in the balance wisdom will somehow come off better if one recognizes its vulnerability (10:1), even its unattainability (7:23–24; 8:17). He begins with underscoring the futility of wisdom at the outset, but he never gives up the struggle.

A Reflection upon Pleasure   (2:1–11)

Bibliography

Bons, E. "*šiddā w-šiddōt:* Überlegungen zum Verständnis eines Hapaxlegomenons." *BN* 36 (1987) 12–16. **Ellermeier, F.** *Qohelet I/1.* 166–71. **Lohfink, N.** "Technik und Tod nach Koheleth." In *Strukturen christlichen Existenz: Beiträge zur Erneuerung des geistlichen Lebens.* FS F. Wulf. Ed. H. Schlier et al. Würzburg: Echter-Verlag, 1989. 27–35. **Loretz, O.** *Qohelet.* 154–61. **Michel, D.** *Eigenart.* 15–20.

Translation

[1] *I said to myself: "Come try out joy and partake of good things!"*[a] *Ah, that is also vanity.* [2] *Of*[a] *laughter, I said: madness! and of joy: what can this*[b] *achieve?* [3] *I explored in my mind how to refresh*[a] *my body with wine—my mind always leading on with wisdom*[b]*— and how to get hold of folly till I could see what*[c] *is good for humans to do in the limited number of days they live under the heavens.* [4] *I did great things: I built houses for myself, and I planted my vineyards.* [5] *I made gardens and parks*[a] *for myself, and I planted in them fruit trees of every kind.* [6] *I made reservoirs of water with which*[a] *to irrigate a forest of flourishing trees.* [7] *I acquired slaves, male and female, and I had servants who were born to the house.*[a] *I also had a flock of cattle and sheep, more than all who were before me in Jerusalem.* [8] *I gathered for myself silver and gold, the wealth of kings*[a] *and provinces. I had for myself singers, male and female, and the delights of mankind, many women.*[b] [9] *I became great and I flourished more than all who were before me in Jerusalem—my wisdom also stayed with me.* [10] *Nothing that my eyes desired did I keep from them. I did not refuse my heart any joy; rather, my heart took joy from all my toil. That was my portion*[a] *from all my toil.* [11] *Then I turned to all my handiwork, and to what I had so actively toiled for. Ah, all is vanity and a chase after wind; there is no profit under the sun.*

Notes

1.a. The Hebrew reads, literally, "Come let me test you with joy; and look upon good." The second imperative continues the volitive mood contained in the opening words. רָאָה (בְ) טוֹב has the nuance of "experience, partake of"; cf. 2:24, 3:13, 9:9; Job 9:25; Ps 34:9. שָׂמַח, "joy," is another favorite term of Qoheleth, occurring seventeen times as noun or verb.

2.a. *lamedh* before "laughter/joy" can be understood as the dative of reference (Joüon §133d).

2.b. זֹאת is the normal feminine form for "this," but it never appears in Ecclesiastes; זֶה is used instead (cf. Mishnaic זוֹ).

3.a. מָשַׁךְ means to "draw, pull," and it is supported by the ancient versions. But to "draw my flesh with wine" is a difficult phrase that has never been satisfactorily explained. It is usually rendered by paraphrase as "tempt" (NJV), "cheer" (RSV), "beguile" (NAB), "stimulate" (NEB); cf. Whitley, *Koheleth*, 19, for further discussion.

3.b. ולבי נהג בחכמה is usually understood as a kind of parenthetical remark, drawing attention to the spirit in which Qoheleth conducted his experiment; this would be a circumstantial clause (GKC §116o). Whitley (*Koheleth*, 19–20) argues for the Mishnaic sense of נהג, "to behave"; so also A. McNeile and C. H. Wright.

3.c. אֵי־זֶה introduces an indirect question with the meaning of "which, what," as in 11:6. NJV translates, "which of the two" (folly and wisdom).

5.a. פַּרְדֵּס, "park," occurs also in Cant 4:13 and Neh 2:8, in the singular; it seems to be derived from the Persian, *pairidaeza*, "forest enclosure."

6.a. The masculine pronominal suffix in מהם refers to a feminine antecedent. Such irregularities occur elsewhere in Ecclesiastes (2:10; 10:9; 11:8; 12:1); cf. GKC §135.

7.a. A house-born slave (cf. בן ביתי in Gen 15:3) is distinguished from one who is purchased (Gen 17:12).

8.a. סגלה normally means property and is applied to Israel as chosen by God (Exod 19:5; Deut 7:6), but it is used in 1 Chr 29:3 in the sense of treasure. The use of the definite article before "kings" is curious; yet cf. 7:25 for another example of fluctuating usage.

8.b. שדה ושדות, "many ladies," is *hap. leg.* and has never been satisfactorily explained. The context (delights of men; cf. Cant 7:7) suggests that the reference is to women. An idiomatic repetition to indicate a group (GKC §123c) is rare; cf. רחם רחמתים, "a damsel or two," Judg 5:30). LXX and Syr rendered the phrase as "a cupbearer and female cupbearers"; Vg has "cups and water-pots." Modern scholars usually refer to the phrase as women of the harem. An etymological basis has been sought in Akkadian *šaditum*, Ugaritic *št* (for *šdt;* cf. Arabic *sitt*), meaning "mistress" or "lady" (see the discussion in Whitley, *Koheleth,* 21–22; E. Bons, *BN* 36 [1987] 12–16).

10.a. There is a striking repetition of key words and phrases within this verse. חלק *(hēleq,* "portion"), is another favorite term and usually has a positive connotation (see the discussion above, p. lx), with some potential for joy, as here.

Form/Structure/Setting

Chap. 2 is dominated by the fiction of "king" Qoheleth, the guise adopted for the opening of the book (1:1; 1:12). Perhaps any king might have served, but Solomon's reputation for wisdom and riches was outstanding. Hence the achievements recorded in 2:4–11 are freely modeled on the Solomonic tradition. There follows a detailed description of an experiment with joy or pleasure in the many forms that a king could indulge, along with a verdict concerning the experiment. The rather solemn introduction (2:1) marks this off from the traditional saying in 1:18. The conclusion is clearly presented in v 11, and a new thought begins in v 12. This section is recognized as a unit even by those who incorporate it into a larger complex, such as Michel, *Eigenart,* 15–20. The repetition of "I turned" (anaphora—the repetition of the same word[s] at the beginning of successive verses or sentences) at the beginning of vv 11–12 also suggests a break there. Within the unit, vv 1–2 seem to be an anticipatory verdict passed on the experiment that is presented with some prolixity in the following verses.

The *Gattung* or form is usually described as royal fiction (see J. Loader, *Polar Structures,* 19–20), but the extent is disputed; does the fiction end at 2:11 (so J. Loader, with K. Galling and others) or 2:26 (so A. Lauha; much depends on the reading in 2:25)? This uncertainty is not so important, since Qoheleth clearly passes from king to sage in his considerations in vv 12–24.

The sequence of thought is as follows: an announcement of an experiment and a preliminary judgment about the value it yielded (vv 1–2); a description of the experiment (vv 3–9); an immediate judgment that the toil yielded pleasure as its "portion" (v 10); and an ultimate judgment in v 11. An inclusion may be indicated by הבל . . . . הנה, "Ah . . . vanity," in 2:1b, 11b.

Comment

1 Qohelet relates his determination to carry out an experiment with שמחה *(simḥâh,* "joy" or "pleasure"; see the discussion above, p. lx). He immediately anticipates the judgment to be rendered: vanity. One can judge from what follows that שמחה is to be understood as the good life, not the mindless joy of Prov 21:17

("the one who loves pleasure . . .") or something superficial.

2   Another adverse verdict concerning joy is given (cf. Prov 14:13), and thus vv 1–2 seem to sum up the results of the experiment that is about to be described.

3   This is not a second experiment as though the first had been described in vv 1–2 (contra R. Kroeber). The thought of v 3 is expressed obscurely. The parallelism between refreshment with wine (see note 3.a.) and laying hold of folly is not to be misunderstood. His experiment is neither artificial, as though he did not put his heart into it, nor mindless, as though he simply gave himself to dissipation and a dissolute life. He seriously wishes to discover if joy is the answer to human desires. The mention of folly may be an anticipation of the ultimate verdict (cf. v 2), but it is also meant to contrast with the role that wisdom has to play. Wisdom is what W. Zimmerli has called the "critical principle" in the analysis of a life given to joy. The guidance of wisdom is directed to the purpose, "till I could see what was good." One is reminded of Micah's famous statement that "what is good" has been shown to humans: "to do justice, and to love kindness, and to walk humbly with your God" (Mic 6:8). Qoheleth's perspective is quite different. He is taking the measure of a life of pleasure. Pleasant living, riches, and imposing surroundings are the symbols of his quest.

4–8   Qoheleth describes his achievements, which reflect the power and riches of royalty. The redundancy of "for myself" stresses the personal investment he made in the experiment. The "houses" seem to be a reflection of the famous buildings by Solomon (1 Kgs 6–9); 1 Chr 27:27 refers to his vines (cf. Cant 8:11). There is no clear distinction between garden and park, although in Cant 4:13 fruits are given particular mention. The reservoirs served to irrigate the young trees that grew in the forest; later tradition pointed out the "pools of Solomon" near Bethlehem. Further evidence of opulence is the retinue of servants. The implication of a servant "born in the house" is that the children of the servant were also indentured. The references to the flock can be illustrated from the description of Solomon in 1 Kgs 5:3(4:23). Similarly, precious metals are not lacking from the traditional assessment of his riches in 1 Kgs 10:10–11.

9   Qoheleth has completed his listing and puts forth a claim to have surpassed any of his predecessors in Jerusalem. All this is in the pursuit of his experiment, as the repetition of "wisdom" (cf. v 3) indicates.

10   This is a clear statement that the experiment was successful in that it yielded pleasure (שמחה *śimḥâh*). The joy inherent in his "toil" is simply undeniable, and he has no wish to deny it. That is in fact the "portion" for all his toil. "Portion" (חלק *ḥēleq*) is another key term (see note 10.a.). Qoheleth does not yet say if this was a "good" (v 3). The mention of "toil" (עמל *ʿāmāl*) is ominous, since it often connotes the heavy price that must be paid for any goal (cf. v 11).

· **11**   The "handiwork" refers to the experiment that has been described; in v 3 Qoheleth had indicated the purpose: "to see what was good for human beings to *do.*" The affirmation of v 10 is limited to the intrinsic result of the experiment; now it is evaluated as vanity. He does not give any reasons for the verdict; at the very least, death is one of them (cf. 2:15–16; 3:18–21). In 1:14 the same verdict was passed on "all deeds" done under the sun. "Profit" has not been mentioned since 1:3, but it is obvious that it has not been far from the author's mind. Merely different phraseology (e.g., 2:3) has been used.

·

Explanation

This Solomonic experiment is particularly important in view of the typical welcome that the OT gives to the good life, and also in view of the several conclusions that Qoheleth will draw concerning eating and drinking (e.g., 2:24). The best that can be offered to humankind in this line (typified by Solomon) is הבל (*hebel*, "vanity"). It is important to note that he recognizes the difference between the inherent pleasure that activities might produce (2:10), and the value that is to be assigned to them (2:11). He is not a killjoy; he is a realist. He refuses to be satisfied with anything less than his standards call for.

A Reflection upon the Merits of Wisdom and Folly (2:12–17)

Bibliography

Fox, M. V. *Qohelet*. 79–120, 182–84. **Ginsberg, H. L.** "The Structure and Contents of the Book of Koheleth." In *Wisdom in Israel and in the Ancient Near East*. Ed. M. Noth and D. W. Thomas. VTSup 3. Leiden: Brill, 1955. 138–49. **Michel, D.** *Eigenart*. 20–31. **Ogden, G.** "Qoheleth's Use of the 'Nothing is Better' Form." *JBL* 9 (1979) 339–50. **Wright, A. G.** "Numerical Patterns." *CBQ* 42 (1980) 38–51.

Translation

[12] *I turned[a] to consider wisdom and madness and folly,[b] for what can the man do who comes after the king? What they have already done![c]* [13] *I saw that wisdom has an advantage over folly—the advantage of light over darkness:*
[14]   *The wise have eyes in their head,*
        but fools walk in darkness.
But I knew also that the same lot comes to them both.[a] [15] *So I said to myself: the lot of the fool also comes to me,[a] so[b] why should I be so very[c] wise? Then I said to myself that this also is vanity.* [16] *For there is no remembrance ever of the wise as well as[a] the fools; in the days to come[b] both will have been forgotten. How can the wise die just like[a] the fools?* [17] *So I hated life, because whatever happens under the sun was evil[a] for me. All is vanity and a chase after wind.*

Notes

12.a. The figure of anaphora (see *Form/Setting/Structure* on vv 11–12) is employed in vv 11–12 and again in vv 17–18.

12.b. The threefold enumeration has bothered some commentators such as R. Gordis, who attempts to justify "that wisdom is both madness and folly." Others (M. Fox, *Qohelet*, 183) see here a hendiadys, for "inane folly."

12.c. The translation of v 12b is very uncertain. The Hebrew text is ambiguous and apparently corrupt; it has given rise to various translations, along these lines: "what (will be? will do?) the man who will come after the king?—what they have already done (or perhaps: the king whom they made a long time before?)." This calls for understanding "will do" from עשׂוהו at the end of the verse (aposiopesis; cf. GKC §167a). Then the answer to the question is the את אשׁר clause. The final "they" is an indefinite reference to royal predecessors. The ancient versions also had difficulty with this verse. LXX makes little sense, primarily because it understands המלך to mean "advice" (Aramaic מלך). Syr and Vg interpret the last four words as referring to God as "maker," which suggests עשׂהו. The adverb, כבר, is not reflected in any of those versions. The text was as obscure for the ancient versions as it is to us. Our translation indicates that the meaning of the question deals with the king's successor, who will simply continue old and foolish ways. In the context of the king fiction, this would refer to Rehoboam, the successor of Solomon.

Many translations (NAB, NJV, TEV) and commentators shift the sequence within the verse and read 12b before 12a. This supposedly gives a desirable conclusion to v 11, and a more intelligible transition to v 13. NEB reads v 12b after v 18. There is no textual evidence for these rearrangements.

14.a. כל is used frequently in a context that in fact refers to two; hence the rendering "both"; cf. v 16.

15.a. אני גם is emphatic, and an accusative in apposition to the pronominal suffix in יקרני; cf. GKC §135e.

15.b. The evidence for אז, "then," "so," is shaky; it is lacking in Syr, in Vg, and in Jerome's commentary, and in some MSS of LXX (in the Greek tradition it is attached with יותר to the following phrase). Hence it has been proposed to read אז as אי זה and render the line "where is the profit" (see the discussion in Whitley, *Koheleth*, 24–25). It seems better to retain the MT.

15.c. יותר, "very," is to be understood as an adverb, as in 7:16 (cf. 12:9, 12).

16.a. עם is used as a particle of comparison; cf. 7:11, Gen 18:23, etc. (Williams §§333–34).

16.b. בשכבר is equivalent to באשר כבר, "for already," and is followed by the accusative of time ("in the days to come").

17.a. The use of על in רע עלי seems to be a sign of late Hebrew; cf. the discussion in Podechard and in Whitley, *Koheleth*, 26.

Form/Structure/Setting

The careful reader will have noticed how often the units in this book seem to be governed by what A. Wright (*CBQ* 42 [1980] 50) has called "section enders," the statement of הבל (*hebel*, "vanity"). Thus we may regard 2:12 as beginning a new section, which ends with the judgment of vanity (v 17). That this is not an arbitrary view is indicated by the relatively simple topic: a reflection on wisdom and folly. The recognition of at least vv 12–17 as a subsection is apparent in the analysis of those who favor a larger complex, such as A. Lauha who regards vv 18–24 as a "continuation" of the thought of vv 12–17. Similarly J. Loader, *Polar Structures*, 41.

The topic is straightforward. Does wisdom have an advantage over folly? Such an explicit comparison between the two is unusual in the book. More often, Qoheleth is addressing the inadequacy of wisdom in view of its failure to handle the situations he contemplates (there is not even a hint that folly can accomplish anything in such situations). The topic itself suggests that this unit is clearly distinct from the experiment described in 2:1–11. And it will be seen that 2:18–26 leaves the theoretical discussion in order to bring up concrete issues.

Again there is a הבל "ender" in 2:11. Although the meaning of v 12 remains unclear, the following verses obviously deal with the failure of wisdom to satisfy Qoheleth. After the experiment with pleasure, he turns to wisdom itself. Its superiority to folly is effectively cancelled by the identical lot (death) shared by both the wise and the foolish. The value of wisdom is thus severely relativized by this reflection, which ends with the customary phrase, "vanity and a chase after wind" (v 17, another "ender").

Comment

12 This verse is notoriously difficult (see the *Notes*). In v 12a Qoheleth takes up the proposal of 1:17 to consider wisdom and folly, and this topic is pursued in 2:13–17. But v 12b is a question that seems to reflect on the action of the successor to the king: the successor will fall in line with the routine established by his predecessors. As the text stands, v 12 announces the topics that will be taken up in the verses to follow: 12a, wisdom and folly (vv 13–17); 12b, the theme of the successor (vv 18–23). There is not much to be gained by shuffling 12a and 12b around, or shifting v 12b to another position.

13–14 The wise/foolish contrast is a stereotype in wisdom literature; for the association of wisdom with light, cf. Ps 119:105; Prov 6:23, and of folly with darkness, cf. Job 12:25. What credence does Qoheleth give to the "advantage" (יִתְרוֹן *yitrôn*) of wisdom? He ranks it over folly (cf. 2:3, 9), which is never a viable option for him. But it is clear that v 14b modifies the saying in v 14a about the superiority of wisdom. Qoheleth is not to be described as "anti-wisdom," but he is its severest critic; after all, he tried to attain wisdom, and he acknowledged failure in 7:23–24.

This is the first example of the strong tensions that abound in the book (see above, pp. lxiii–lxiv). How is one to understand the train of thought of the author? R. Gordis (and also D. Michel, *Eigenart*, 28–29) has recourse to the device of quotations: Qoheleth is quoting someone else's view in vv 13–14a and then introduces an emphatic "but I know" in 14b, which contains his own view. M. Fox is unwilling to recognize quotations without more evidence (cf. *ZAW* 92 [1980] 416–31). Fox emphasizes the polarity between light and darkness, and he argues that 2:13–14a "is a superlative affirmation of the advantage of wisdom over folly" (*Qohelet*, 183; cf. 113). It is true that Qoheleth does not simply dismiss wisdom, but Fox seems to overstate the profit of wisdom, unless he wishes to claim that Qoheleth simply contradicts himself here. It will be seen that vv 14–16 introduce the great equalizer: death.

German scholarship recognizes in these verses a *zwar-aber Tatsache* ("yes, but"). So H. W. Hertzberg, W. Zimmerli, and A. Lauha, but F. Ellermeier (*Qohelet I/1*, 125–28) rejects this as a *Zauberwort* or magic, at least for 3:17 and 8:12–13. The movement of thought is conceived as follows: Qoheleth will put forth a judgment, only to follow it with a serious qualification: "yes . . . but." This eliminates the "contradiction" and also the need that older commentators such as C. Siegfried felt to attribute several statements to a glossator. In this view, v 14b relativizes vv 13–14a without denying all value to wisdom. It is because v 13 enunciates a real truth, that one can feel the poignancy of the cry in v 16 ("how can the wise die just like the fools").

מִקְרֶה, "lot," is a favorite and key word (rendered in LXX by συνάντημα, "meeting," not τύχη, "chance," "fate"). It designates what happens to a person. The "happening" may refer to events in life for which there is no palpable explanation (9:1–3, 11–12), but particularly to one's final lot or death, as here and 2:15, 3:19, and 9:2–3. The import of the argument is that wisdom counts for nothing because both the fool and the wise have the same מִקְרֶה; they both have to die. The superiority of wisdom therefore is seen to be quite theoretical.

15 Qoheleth applies his reasoning to himself and to the futility of his attempting to be wise. The repetition of "I said to myself" is striking and suggests a certain emphasis.

16 Another thing that the wise and the foolish have in common is that they are forgotten. There is an echo here of 1:11. The lack of remembrance of things past includes humans as well. This is another argument that relativizes the superiority of wisdom. Even the hope of an immortality of name (see Prov 10:7) is rejected (Eccl 1:11; 9:5). But one should not think that Qoheleth would have been satisfied with a remembrance that would never die. It is death itself, the great leveller, that he feels most deeply, as the question in v 16b indicates and as is also shown by the outburst in v 17.

17 Qoheleth picks up on the words for action (עָשָׂה, מַעֲשֶׂה) that occurred earlier. In 1:13–14 he regarded all that happens under the heavens as vanity, as an evil (עִנְיַן רָע) imposed by God. A similar judgment was passed in 2:11 upon his own achievements. The context of v 17 indicates that he has particularly in mind the reality of death and lack of remembrance as part of the מעשה, or deed, that is grievous for him. The events of life do not make sense, so he loathes life. As commentators have remarked, this is an unheard of statement in the context of OT wisdom, which always aimed at life (Prov 8:35; see R. E. Murphy, *Int* 20 [1966] 3–14). All that happens will come to be explicitly termed the מעשה האלהים, God's doing, which is beyond human ken (7:13; 8:17; 11:5; cf. 3:11).

Explanation

This section calls for a fundamental decision about the thought of Qoheleth. Is he really "anti-chokmatic," as J. Loader (*Polar Structures*, 39) characterizes him? Our analysis would preserve the reputation of Qoheleth as a sage (cf. 12:9–11). But he is a sage who goes beyond the traditional figure, the one who would make wholesale comparisons (as in vv 13–14) about the superiority of wisdom. The sticking point for Qoheleth is death, inescapable and final.

In the rest of the Bible, the sting of death is somewhat assuaged by the thought that one lives on through one's good name (Deut 25:5–6), and this consolation perdures down to the days of Ben Sira (Sir 38:9–11):

> The human body is a fleeting thing,
> but a virtuous name will never be blotted out.
> Have regard for your name, since it will outlive you
> longer than a thousand hoards of gold.
> The days of a good life are numbered,
> but a good name lasts forever. (Sir 41:11–13, NRSV)

By the same token, the wicked are threatened with the loss of their name:

> May his posterity be cut off;
> may his name be blotted out in the second generation. (Ps 109:13, NRSV)

For Qoheleth, however, an impenetrable curtain was drawn over the dead: there is no remembrance (Eccl 1:11; 2:16), and the inertia of Sheol remains (Eccl 9:10). Job could welcome Sheol as a place of respite, of surcease from his sufferings (3:16–22; 10:20–22). But Qoheleth's attitude toward death is implacable—how can the wise die like the fools!

A Reflection upon Human Toil   (2:18–26)

Bibliography

Ellermeier, F. *Qohelet, I/1.* 277–83. ———. "Das Verbum חוש in Koh. 2,25: Eine exegetische, auslegungsgeschichtliche und semasiologische Untersuchung." *ZAW* 75 (1963) 197–217. **Fox, M. V.** *Qohelet.* 39–40, 57–59, 185–90. **Johnston, R.** "'Confessions of a Workaholic': A Reappraisal of Qoheleth." *CBQ* 38 (1976) 14–28. **Michel, D.** *Eigenart.* 31–51. **Seligmann, I.** "Voraussetzungen der Midraschexegese." In *Congress Volume, Copenhagen, 1953.* VTSup 1 (1953) 150–81. **Smend, R.** "Essen und Trinken—Ein Stück Weltlichkeit des Alten Testaments." In *Beiträge zur alttestamentlichen Theologie.* FS W. Zimmerli. Ed. R. Hanhard and R. Smend. Göttingen: Vandenhoeck & Ruprecht, 1977. 446–59. **Waard, J. de.** "The Translator and Textual Criticism (with Particular Reference to Eccl 2,25)." *Bib* 60 (1979) 509–29.

Translation

[18] *I hated the fruit of all the toil* [a] *for which I toiled* [b] *under the sun because I have to leave it to the one who will come after me.* [19] *But who knows whether he will be wise or foolish? Yet he will control all the fruit of the toil for which I toiled under the sun, and for which I became wise. This also is vanity.* [20] *I turned to heartfelt despair over all the toil with which I toiled under the sun.* [21] *For though* [a] *a person toils with wisdom and knowledge and skill,* [b] *he has to give the portion over to someone who did not toil for it. This also is vanity and a great evil.* [22] *For what does one get* [a] *for all the toil, and the striving of the heart, with which one toils under the sun?* [23] *All his days are painful, and grievous, his task.* [a] *Even at night his mind is not at rest. This also is vanity.* [24] *There is nothing [better] for a person [than] to eat* [a] *and drink and provide pleasure for himself in his toil—this also I saw is from the hand of God.* [25] *For who can eat or rejoice,* [a] *if not I?* [b] [26] *To whomever he pleases God gives wisdom and knowledge, but to the errant one he gives the trouble of collecting and gathering, only to give to whomever God pleases. This also is vanity and a chase after wind.*

Notes

18.a. עמלי can be understood as what is achieved by toil, as well as the process itself (cf. v 20); cf. Whitley, *Koheleth*, 23 on 2:11.

18.b. עָמֵל is the verbal adjective; cf. 2:22; 9:9; elsewhere a finite form of the verb occurs, as in 2:11, 19, 20; 5:17.

21.a. As in 1:10, שׁ can be understood as providing a particular instance, and can be translated as conditional.

21.b. כשׁר (cf. Ugaritic *ktr*, "skilled") is found twice as a verb (10:10; 11:6) and three times as a noun (2:21; 4:4; 5:10); only in Ecclesiastes is the basic meaning "skill, success."

22.a. הוה, "to fall, to be," used here in the participle, is relatively rare in the Hebrew Bible, but common in Aramaic and in later Hebrew.

23.a. Another translation is possible, but less likely: "during all his days, pain and vexation are his occupation." There is an air of a proverb about v 23a.

24.a. The MT seems to say, "it is not good for man that he eat. . . ." This might mean that eating and drinking are not an ultimate good, or that they are not part of man's טוב, "happiness," without God's giving. But on the analogy of similar statements in 3:12, 22 and 8:15 it is better to read the comparative מן before שׁיאכל. This is a case of haplography, in view of the final *mem* in באדם; cf. מאשר in 3:22. The emendation is supported by Syr, Vg, Tg, and has some MSS of LXX. It is not necessary to correct באדם to לאדם; cf. 3:12.

25.a. The meaning of חוּשׁ is "hasten," but this does not fit the context. LXX, Syr, and Theod rendered "drink"; Vg has "abound in delights"; Aq and Sym (φείσεται) and Jerome *(parcet)* seem to have read יָחוּשׁ, "pity, spare" (for יָחוּס). Many verbs from cognate languages have been proposed to solve the problem: Akkadian *ḥāšu*, Arabic *ḥass*, in the sense of "be worried"; Akkadian *ḥasāšu* (and perhaps Ugaritic *ḥšt?*) in the sense of "rejoice," but there is no consensus on the meaning. See F. Ellermeier, *ZAW* 75 (1963) 197–217.

25.b. חוּץ מִן is unique in the Bible, but frequent in the Mishnah in the sense of "without, apart from." MT can be translated "(who) but I," and this is supported by Vg and Tg. LXX, Syr, and Jerome read: "who apart from him." Either reading fits the context. MT can be understood as a kind of parenthetical remark as the author (continuing the fiction of King Solomon) reflects back upon the gifts he had from God. If מִמֶּנּוּ is read, the verse underscores the divine generosity (v 24) and divine control (cf. 3:13; 5:18). On the textual problems of v 25, see J. de Waard, *Bib* 60 (1979) 510–27.

Form/Structure/Setting

Vv 18–23 provide reflection about toil, but from a new point of view: the quality of the heir(s). It takes up the theme of the successor that was obscurely alluded to in v 12. The issue of inheritance is used here to demonstrate the futility of personal toil (עמל *ʿāmāl*, "trouble," as noun or verb, occurs eleven times in this section). גַּם זֶה הֶבֶל, "this too is vanity," appears in vv 19, 21, and 23 and finally in the "ender" in v 26. The whole argument creates an air of repetitiousness, and K. Galling labels vv 20–23 "explanatory repetitions."

Vv 24–26 terminate this unit, just as similar passages do elsewhere (see, e.g., 3:22; 5:18–19). They are Qoheleth's often repeated conclusions concerning the only good that may be available for a person: enjoyment of life, if possible.

Comment

18 In the context of his great experiment Qoheleth had already judged toil to be unprofitable (2:11). Now he repeats his judgment from a different perspective: inheritance. The problem is that one must leave the fruit of one's toil to another who has never toiled for it. The repetition of "I hated" (v 17; anaphora and a catch word) continues the intense expression of feeling. Inheritance is a recognized theme in the wisdom tradition (Pss 37:18, 25; 49:15; Sir 11:19; 14:15). It was regarded in a positive fashion. Yet all acknowledged that "you cannot take it with you" (Ps 49), and a certain resignation softened this law of reality. Qoheleth, however, exploits the theme in bitter fashion.

19 Two reasons exacerbate the problem of inheritance: (1) the inheritor may be a fool; (2) the inheritor has made no personal investment in the acquisition of the inheritance. The first reason implies a value judgment in favor of wisdom, but even if the inheritor were wise, the second reason would count against such a person. The issue of succession reflects back on the thought expressed in v 12b concerning the conduct of royal successors. "This too is vanity" serves as a divider from vv 20–23, but the theme remains the same.

20 This is another emotional expression on the part of Qoheleth, comparable to vv 17, 18. He is despairing not only about his personal experience but about what he sees as the common experience of all, as the following verse indicates.

21 He expands on the considerations that he advanced in vv 18–19, stressing the irrelevant role that toil and wisdom play in the matter of inheritance, and hence the basic injustice that takes place. E. Podechard aptly quotes the comment of Jerome: "one has the fruit of another's labor, and the sweat of the dead is the ease of the one who lives" (*alter labore alterius perfruatur et sudor mortui, deliciae sint viventis;* see CChrSL, 72:271). Qoheleth never takes the optimistic attitude that at least the one to whom possessions are left is fortunate (perhaps because he thought that such an individual will not be able to take it with him, but must leave it to someone else?). The biblical sense of values certainly had a greater appreciation of common good, but he is quite individualistic in this matter (contrast 4:10ff.). He seems insensitive to the considerations of family.

22   This rhetorical question underscores the verdict of vanity uttered in v 20 (and cf. 1:3). The "striving of the heart" (רעיון; cf. 1:17) connotes all the human effort and hope involved in toil. Frustration, rather than injustice, is the point.

23   K. Galling and A. Lauha regard v 23a as a proverbial saying derived from merchant life (cf. 4:6; 5:11), but the observation is not to be limited to one area of life. Qoheleth continues to stress the restlessness and frustration that accompany toil.

24   This verse introduces a typical conclusion which Qoheleth frequently offers to terminate a discussion. As indicated in note 24.a., the MT can be interpreted to say that life's pleasures are not an ultimate good, or that they can be considered good only by reason of divine generosity. Instead, the present translation interprets v 24 in line with the many resigned conclusions found in the work (e.g., 3:12–13; 5:17–18).

The phrase "eat and drink" is symbolic of the good life and its pleasures (see R. Smend, *"Essen und Trinken,"* 446–59). There is no basis here for the charge of hedonism since the biblical emphasis on the good life simply cannot be viewed in those terms. Moreover, such a charge is denied by 2:2, that pleasure is folly. The accent in v 24 differs from 2:2, which envisioned a deliberate striving after pleasure as a goal. Now it is a question of the טוב, "pleasure," God *may* provide in the ordinary course of life. When Qoheleth looks at pleasure as an absolute, as something that really answers to human happiness, he finds it wanting (2:1–11). But in v 24 he sees it as a God-given reality that can compensate for the inevitable toil (בעמלו). There is no judgment about what is good *per se;* pleasure is a gift of God (v 24b) but arbitrary at that (9:1–2).

25   This verse is to be understood in the light of the king fiction ("if not I," i.e., the king). It reinforces the recommendation made about accepting the pleasures of life. The man who surpassed all before him in Jerusalem can speak with authority about pleasures. If the MT is changed (see note 25.b.) to "apart from him," then the verse underlines the primacy of God in human affairs. Such a view is basic to biblical understanding and in harmony with Qoheleth's thoughts on divine causality. TOB translates the MT but understands the question as spoken by God; it seems better to attribute it to "king" Qoheleth.

26   No moral connotation is to be given to the terms טוב, "good," and חוטא, "one who misses the mark," "sinner." Elsewhere Qoheleth clearly denies any distinction in the lot of the good and the evil (4:1–3; 7:15; 8:10–14; 9:1–3), and there is no reason to interpret v 26 in contradiction to this position. E. Podechard (and others who attribute a moral evaluation to these terms) is forced to recognize a gloss in v 26a, and it is assigned to a חסיד who would have toned down the message. H. L. Ginsberg is right when he remarks that these terms "mean respectively (as is today generally recognized) 'pleasing to God' and 'displeasing,' or 'lucky' and 'unlucky'—not 'righteous' and 'wicked.' This applies not only in ii 26, but also e.g. in vii 26" (see H. L. Ginsberg, "Structure and Contents," 139). This point of view is also adopted by H. Hertzberg, W. Zimmerli, R. Kroeber, and others.

The import of the verse is to claim sovereign freedom for God in imparting gifts. There is a sardonic note in v 26b, which underscores the futility of human effort. A person may "collect and gather," but God disposes even of this very personal achievement; it is merely to be given to someone else to whom God pleases to give it. This is in vivid contrast to Prov 13:22, where the riches of the wicked are stored up for the just: "The good leave an inheritance to their children's children, but the wealth of the sinner is stored up for the just." I. Seligmann has pointed out that not only are the meanings of טוב and חוטא "emptied," but also there is a transposition of motif (see "Voraussetzungen," 156). Prov 13:22, 28:8, and Job 27:16–17 speak of ill-gotten goods finally being gathered for the just: in v 26b this motif is transposed in order to emphasize divine liberty.

The final verdict of "vanity" refers to the arbitrary (from the human standpoint) action of God who does as he pleases. The traditional considerations about divine retribution fall short. Qoheleth's views on joy and pleasure are summarized above, p. lx.

Explanation

This passage is built around the notion of עמל (ʿāmāl), understood both as the fruit of one's toil and as the toiling itself. As a noun or as a verb, it occurs no less than eleven times in this short section. The vanity of toil is manifold. In itself it merely brings on pain (v 23). The traditional view that the children of the just fared well (e.g., Ps 37:25) made no impression on Qoheleth. Even after the penalty of death one could not rely on one's descendants! There was no way of ensuring inheritance; it could be used properly or squandered foolishly. As already indicated, this is a very narrow notion of family and inheritance that is taken by Qoheleth. One feels that he is straining his argument here. There is an unremitting note of "vanity" that fills the passage.

In view of this situation, how is one to live? There is only pain for one's toil, and uncertainty about the way its fruits will be employed. Qoheleth places here one of the seven conclusions of his book that give positive advice on living and enjoying it ("eat and drink" is the preferred phrase; see 3:18; 5:17). Such passages as these have given rise to the charge of hedonism and Epicureanism, a characterization that is simply off the mark. More pertinent are the views of R. Gordis, R. N. Whybray, and others (see the summary by R. Johnston, *CBQ* 38 [1976] 14–28) that these passages constitute the true message, a message of solid joy in God's creation, that Qoheleth advocates. But it is difficult to find more than the mood of a resigned conclusion in such passages. There are not recommendations that Qoheleth truly finds joy in. He can only offer them in a mysterious and incalculable world: What else can one do? So take whatever joy one can find. But even here, there is a wild card. One never knows the way things will turn out with this God (see *Comment* on v 26), who disposes of things according to an inscrutable divine will.

A Reflection upon Time and Toil   (3:1–4:6)

Bibliography

Crenshaw, J. L. "The Eternal Gospel (Eccl. 3:11)." In *Essays in Old Testament Ethics.* Ed. J. Crenshaw and J. T. Willis. New York: KTAV, 1974. 23–55. **Eissfeldt, O.** "Alles Ding währt seine Zeit." In *Kleine Schriften.* Ed. R. Sellheim and F. Maass. Tübingen: Mohr/Siebeck, 1973. 5:174–78. **Ellermeier, F.** *Qohelet I/1.* 284–87, 309–22. **Fonzo, L. di.** "Ecclesiastes 3,21." *VD* 19 (1939) 257–68, 289–99; 20 (1940) 421–37. **Fox, M. V.** "The Identification of Quotations in Biblical Literature." *ZAW* 92 (1980) 416–31. **Galling, K.** "Das Rätsel der Zeit im Urteil Kohelets (Koh 3,1–15)." *ZTK* 58 (1961) 1–15. **Günther, J.** "Der Zusammenhang in Koh 3,11–15." *ZAW* 51 (1933) 79–80. **Herman, W.** "Zu Kohelet 3,14." *WZLGS* 3 (1953/54) 293–95. **Horton, E.** "Koheleth's Concept of Opposites as Compared to Samples of Greek Philosophy and Near and Far Eastern Wisdom." *Numen* 19 (1972) 1–21. **Irwin, W.** "Ecclesiastes 3,18." *AJSL* 56 (1939) 298–99. **Jenni, E.** "Das Wort ʿōlām im Alten Testament." *ZAW* 64 (1952) 197–248; 65 (1953) 1–35. **Johnston, R.** "'Confessions of a Workaholic': A Reappraisal of Qoheleth." *CBQ* 38 (1976) 14–28. **Kugel, J. L.** "Qohelet and Money." *CBQ* 51 (1989) 32–49. **Loader, J. A.** "Qohelet 3,2–8: A 'Sonnet' in the Old Testament." *ZAW* 81 (1969) 240–42. ———. *Polar Structures.* 29–33, 88–90, 105. **Lohfink, N.** "Gegenwart und Ewigkeit: Die Zeit im Buch Kohelet." *GL* 60 (1987) 2–12 (see *TD* 34/3 [1987] 236–40). **Maltby, A.** "The Book of Ecclesiastes and the After-Life." *EvQ* 35 (1963) 34–44. **Michel, D.** *Eigenart.* 52–83. **Salters, R. B.** "A Note on the Exegesis of Ecclesiastes 3,15b." *ZAW* 88 (1976) 419–21. **Savignac, J. de.** "La Sagesse du Qôhéléth et l'épopée de Gilgamesh." *VT* 28 (1978) 318–23. **Staples, W. E.** "The meaning of *ḥepeṣ* in Ecclesiastes." *JNES* 24 (1965) 110–12. **Whybray, R. N.** "The Identification and Use of Quotations in Ecclesiastes." In *Congress Volume, Vienna, 1980.* VTSup 32. Leiden: Brill, 1982. 435–51. **Wright, A. G.** "'For Everything There Is a Season': The Structure and Meaning of the Fourteen Opposites (Ecclesiastes 3,2–8)." In *De la Tôrah au Messie: Mélanges Henri Cazelles.* Ed. J. Dore et al. Paris: Desclée, 1981. 321–28.

Translation

1 *For everything there is a moment,*
   and there is a time[a] *for every*[b] *affair under the heavens:*
2 *A time to give birth*[a] *and a time to die,*
   a time to plant and a time to uproot what is planted;
3 *A time to kill and a time to heal,*
   a time to tear down and a time to build up;
4 *A time to weep and a time to rejoice,*
   a time for[a] *lament and a time for*[a] *dancing;*
5 *A time to cast stones and a time to gather stones,*
   a time to embrace and a time to be far from embraces;
6 *A time to search and a time to lose,*[a]
   a time to keep and a time to cast away;
7 *A time to tear up and a time to sew,*
   a time to be silent and a time to speak;
8 *A time to love and a time to hate,*
   a time for war and a time for peace.

⁹*What profit*ᵃ *does the worker have from his toil?* ¹⁰*I have seen the task that God has given to humankind to be occupied with:* ¹¹*He has made everything appropriate in its time, and he has also placed a sense of duration*ᵃ *in their*ᵇ *hearts, so that*ᶜ *they cannot find out, from beginning to end,*ᵈ *the work which God has done.* ¹²*I know that there is nothing better for them*ᵃ *than to rejoice and do well*ᵇ *in life.* ¹³*And also, if any*ᵃ *one eats and drinks and prospers for all his toil—that is a gift of God.* ¹⁴*I know that all God does will be forever. To it nothing can be added, and from it nothing can be subtracted; for God has done so that*ᵃ *they may stand in awe of him.* ¹⁵*What is already has been, and what is to be already is. And God seeks out what has been pursued.*ᵃ

¹⁶*I observed continually under the sun: in the place*ᵃ *for judgment, wrongdoing! and in the place for justice, wrongdoing!*ᵇ ¹⁷*I said to myself: both the just and the wrongdoers God will judge, for there is a time for every affair, and upon every deed there.*ᵃ ¹⁸*I said to myself concerning*ᵃ *human beings: God is testing*ᵇ *them, and [showing]*ᶜ *that they are really animals.*ᵈ ¹⁹*For the lot [of] humans and the lot [of] animals is [ ] the same lot.*ᵃ *As one dies, so does the other; both have the same life-breath. So humans have no advantage*ᵇ *over animals; all is vanity.* ²⁰*Both go to the same place; both are from the dust and both return to the dust.* ²¹*Who knows [if]*ᵃ *the life-breath of humans goes upwards, and [if] the life-breath of animals goes down into the earth?* ²²*I saw that there was nothing better for humans than to rejoice in their works, for that is their portion. For who can bring them to see what will come after them?*

⁴:¹*Again I saw*ᵃ *all the oppressions that were done under the sun. Ah, the tears of the oppressed! But there was no one to give them comfort. On the side of their oppressors was power! But there was no one to give them comfort.* ²*So I praised*ᵃ *the dead who had long since died, more than the living who must still*ᵇ *live.* ³*But better than both: the one who*ᵃ *has never lived, who has never seen the evil work that is done under the sun.*

⁴*I saw that all toil and all skillful activity are (a matter of) rivalry between one person and another. This also is vanity and a chase after wind.*
⁵   *"The fool folds his hands and destroys himself."*ᵃ
⁶   *"Better is one handful with rest than*
        *two handfuls with toil and a chase after wind."*ᵃ

Notes

1.a. The words for "moment" and "time" are זמן (καιρός) and עת (χρόνος). The former is late and appears to be a borrowing from Aramaic; cf. Wagner §§77–78. There is no appreciable difference in meaning; both indicate a point of time as opposed to duration (עלם, v 11).

1.b. חפץ means "affair" in 3:1, 17; 5:7; 8:6, but it designates "desire" in 5:3; 12:1, 10. See W. Staples, *JNES* 24 (1965) 110–12.

2.a. לדת means "to give birth," in contrast to הולד, "to be born," which occurs in 7:1. This meaning can also be seen in parallelism with "to plant." However, many translations (NRSV, NEB, NAB) and commentators render לדת as "to be born," in opposition to מות, "to die. The ancient versions, except Vg (*tempus nascendi*) have "to give birth." The fourteen antitheses that follow have to do with actions that are fixed for certain times, and which mutually exclude each other.

4.a. Only in v 4b and before כנוש in v 5 is the preposition *lamedh* omitted before the infinitive; see also the genitival use in v 8b.

6.a. Literally, אבד means "to be lost, go astray," and in the piel it can be declarative, "count as lost."

9.a. This is the second of the three מה יתרון questions; cf. 1:3; 5:15.

11.a. The meaning of העלם is disputed. It can mean "duration," "eternity," or "world"; the latter is reflected in LXX and Vg. Whitley (*Koheleth*, 31–33) reviews the solutions proposed by various scholars, and favors the meaning "darkness," or "ignorance." Such a meaning can be justified philologically, but the contrast between עלם and עת in the context suggests a temporal meaning, like "duration."

11.b. The suffix in לבם refers back to the plural בני האדם in v 10, not to הכל (as Lauha thinks); an emendation is not necessary, and the alliteration with מבלי seems intentional.

11.c. מבלי אשר לא is a unique phrase. It can be rendered as negative purpose (LXX, ὅπως μή; Vg, ut non); then העלם is an obstacle to knowledge. Or it can be rendered "without," and העלם need not be viewed as an obstacle. See the discussion in Podechard and Whitley, Koheleth, 33.

11.d. סוף (instead of קץ for "end") seems to be a late word, and relatively rare; it may be an Aramaism, cf. Wagner §199.

12.a. The plural suffix in בם can be explained as referring back to the collective האדם in v 11; the difficulty is that it is resumed by the third person singular suffix in בחייו at the end of the verse. The use of the preposition beth with טוב is unusual, but is found also in 2:24.

12.b. לעצות טוב, "do well," has been associated with the Greek εὖ πραττεῖν, but R. Braun points out that it does not have a reflexive meaning, and he proposes instead, εὖ δρᾶν ("do well," Kohelet, 53–54). In 7:20 the phrase means "to do good," but in v 12 it is reflexive, as עשה רע seems to be in 2 Sam 12:18. The phrase is close in meaning to ראה (ב) טוב, which is used frequently by Qoheleth (2:1, 24; 3:13).

13.a. The translation preserves the anacoluthon: כל האדם is a casus pendens, and is not to be translated, "the whole of man is to. . . ."

14.a. Like אשר, ש can introduce a purpose clause (GKC §165b).

15.a. The phrase את־נרדף (literally, "the one pursued") is problematical; את is not normally used with the undefined accusative (but cf. 4:4; 7:7; GKC §117e). The masculine gender would normally indicate a person, and the masculine is reflected in the interpretation of the ancient versions, except Vg, which has the neuter. The sense would be that God seeks out the pursued, presumably in order to help him. But this idea is not relevant to the context, which deals with events (v 15a), not persons. Even the neuter rendering is obscure: "what has been chased away" (Podechard), or "flown away" (Zimmerli). A similar reading in Sir 5:3 is invoked with reference to Eccl 3:15, but it sheds no light on the situation. It seems best to recognize the similarity of 3:15a to 1:9, and the context of the phrase must be time. נרדף can be understood to designate what is rushed after, or even caught up with, such as time. The reference then is to the past or the events of the past, which God will call back into existence, in line with the thought of v 15a.

16.a. ועוד can suggest a reference back to ראיתי in v 10; hence "furthermore." But with K. Galling it can be taken adverbially in the sense of "everywhere I saw."

16.b. מקום can be construed as an anacoluthon, rather than as the object of ראיתי (cf. the athnach under השמש). שמה is the equivalent of שם, "there," but also may have a locative meaning, "(to) there." The repetition of רשע is surprising; but cf. מנחה in 4:1. There is no reason to emend the text.

17.a. שם, "there," can be referred back to the שמה of v 16 or to the judgment of God within v 17 itself; in either case the meaning is obscure. The adverb is taken to indicate the time (Vg, tunc) of judgment, or the place (with God?). Syr and Vg did not read a different text; LXX construes ἐκεῖ with the next verse. G. Barton, R. Scott, and many others propose reading שם, "put," with God presupposed as subject, even though it is at the end of the verse. NAB reads משפט, taking its cue from 8:5 (cf. 9:11); see the discussion in E. Podechard and A. Williams. MT is problematical (e.g., the difference between the prepositions ל and על), but the proposed solutions (surveyed in Whitley, Koheleth, 34–36) leave much to be desired. The text seems to be corrupt.

18.a. Another difficult text. על דברת occurs again in 7:14 in the sense of "so that (not)." Here and in 8:2 it is analogous to על דבר, "because of," "concerning" (Exod 8:8, 2 Sam 18:5, etc.).

18.b. A copula is to be understood before לברם, the qal infinitive of ברר (cf. Joüon, §82l); God is the subject, and ם֗ is the object (cf. GKC §115h–k). The meaning is "separate" (LXX, διακρινεῖ; Jerome, separat), or "select," but Vg and Tg interpret it to mean "test," and this is widely accepted by modern commentators.

18.c. MT reads לראות, "to see," but the presumed subject of this infinitive qal is not obvious ("sons of men"? "I"?). It is better to read לראות (hipil, for להראות), as reflected in LXX, Syr, and Vg.

18.d. The alliteration in the final clause is striking, and there may be some dittography: שהם בהמה המה להם. However, one can construe המה as the copula, with להם as dativus commodi (GKC §119s).

19.a. The vocalization of MT suggests: "humans are a lot, and animals are a lot, and one lot (is) to them." It is better to understand the consonantal text with the ancient versions by reading the construct, מקרה, instead of the absolute, and deleting the waw before the third מקרה. The Masoretes may have vocalized as they did in order to avoid the implications of Qoheleth's statement.

19.b. מותר (Prov 14:23; 21:3) means "advantage"; elsewhere יתרון and יתר, all from the same root, are used in Ecclesiastes.

21.a. Perhaps out of consideration for orthodox belief, the Masoretes vocalized the interrogative ־ה as the definite article, so that the translation would be: "the life-breath of humans that goes upwards, and the life-breath of animals that goes downwards." The ancient versions correctly recognized that ה is the interrogative particle. The question, "who knows," implies a negation; cf. 1:3; 2:2, and the final question in v 22.

4:1.a. Both vv 1 and 7 (not an *inclusio*) are introduced by the same three words: ואראה is one of the few instances of *waw consecutivum* in the book (cf. 1:17, 4:7).

2.a. There is no reason to emend the text; on the use of the infinitive absolute (שבח), see GKC §113gg.

2.b. עדנה, "still," like עדן in v 3, is a *hap. leg.;* they are probably contractions of עד הנה. See the discussion in Whitley, *Koheleth*, 41–42.

3.a. It is possible to interpret את אשר as the object of שבח in v 2, or a verb of judging can be understood (GKC §117l).

5.a. The phrase "eats his own flesh" is usually taken to mean that he destroys himself by a laziness that is so great he will not even provide himself with food. However, as R. Whybray observes (VTSup 32 [1982] 440, n. 9), there is no true parallel for this meaning. Mic 3:3 and Ps 27:2 refer to eating the flesh of others, not one's own; neither is Isa 49:26 pertinent. Hence the translation in Eü may be correct: "and he still has his meat to eat." If so, the saying expresses a paradox: despite everything, even the lazy person can have enough to eat.

6.a. In both half-lines, "with" translates an adverbial accusative. The last phrase, "and a chase after wind," hardly belongs with the saying, but it appears to be a deliberate insertion, and hence not to be deleted.

Form/Structure/Setting

This section is as long as it is because the typical "vanity" ender does not appear until 4:4 ("vanity") and 4:6 ("chase after wind"). But the content is fairly compact; a new item, "time," is introduced, and an old one, "toil," receives more treatment. From the point of view of content, the following units are usually identified by commentators: 3:1–15; 3:16–22; 4:1–3; 4:4–6. This division follows in part the fourfold occurrence of the verb ראה, "see": v 10 (followed by ידע, "know," twice); v 16 (followed by אמר, "say," twice); 4:1; and finally 4:4. The observation in 3:10–15 seems to be a clear development of the initial poem on time. In 3:1–15 there are several repetitions that bind the ideas together. The poem on time is dominated by עת, "time," which is significantly contrasted with העלם, "duration," in v 11, a word that is also used to characterize the divine activity in v 14. There are three "gifts" of God: ענין, "task" (v 10), העלם, "duration" (v 11), and "eating and drinking" (v 13). Two verses begin with a strong affirmation, "I know" (vv 12, 14).

The question in v 9 about the profit of toil is the clue to the fate of time-bound human beings. It harks back to the question of 1:3, just as v 10 also recalls 1:13. It is not surprising, then, to see the topic of "toil" (cf. 2:18–22) reappear and receive further development in chap. 4. In other parts of the book, there is a curious redoubling on previous topics, as here.

The poem on time may very well be a separate poem with its own meaning (so A. Wright, "'For Everything . . . ,'" 321–28). In context it can be summarized thus: the key activities of life serve as examples of how all times are *fixed* by God, and over them humans have no control. Hence the futility, the absence of "profit" (v 9). Most serious of all, humans not only lack a free disposition of such events in the face of the determinism of vv 1–9, they also fail to comprehend what God is about (v 11). The temporal side of things is just another aspect of the basic activity at work in the world (עשׂה, "do," as verb or noun in vv 12, 14 occurs five times)—an activity that is לְעֹלָם, "forever" (v 14).

Vv 16–22 may seem only loosely connected with vv 1–15 (but compare 3:17 with 3:1). They deal with human injustice (vv 16–17) and the similarity of humans and beasts (vv 18–21), followed by another of Qoheleth's patented conclusions (v 22; perhaps רָאִיתִי forms an inclusion with v 16). The topic of injustice can be seen as a prelude to the treatment of the similarity of humans with beasts.

This section picks up ideas that appeared earlier in the work: the constant repetition of events (vv 14–15; cf. 1:9–11); death (vv 19–21; cf. 2:14–17). In 4:1–3 the theme of injustice is picked up from 3:16–17, and it ends with a comparison between the living and the dead, in favor of the latter. An observation about human toil and rivalry (4:4) is balanced by two sayings, neither of which in itself is an infallible principle of human conduct (4:5–6).

Comment

3:1 Qoheleth lays down a principle that will be illustrated by the fourteen antitheses of vv 2–8. Both terms in v 1 indicate a specific point of time, as opposed to duration. He is not interested in affirming that everything is ephemeral, or that there is a rhythm to time as there is to movement (1:4–8). The events in vv 2–8 are presented as simply elements of human experience, some of them peak experiences (birth and death).

The fourteen antitheses present actions that are mutually exclusive; they cannot be done at the same time. J. Loader (*Polar Structures*, 11–13) has pointed out the intricate chiastic structure of vv 2–8, in such wise that not only are vv 2–3, 4–5, 6–7 in chiastic opposition, but v 2 is in chiasm with v 4 and v 3 with v 5. The antithesis is between "desirable" (D), and "undesirable" (U). When a stichos begins with what is desirable, the following hemistichos is "undesirable," and vice versa. This yields the following pattern: v 2: D/U, D/U; v 3: U/D, U/D; v 4: U/ D/, U/D; v 5: D/U, D/U; v 6: D/U/, D/U; v 7: U/D, U/D; v 8: D/U, U/D. This can best be illustrated in his cross-projection:

2	DD	3	UU
	UU		DD
4	UU	5	DD
	DD		UU

"The third quatrain (v. 6–7) then follows the pattern of the first, viz. two stichoi of the DU-form and two of the UD-form. V. 8 is a simple chiasmus ordered DUUD" (11).

A. G. Wright (see "'For Everything . . . ,'" 321–28) has further refined this structure by pointing out that vv 4 and 7 both deal with mourning and can be conceived to be the ending of two stanzas, each of them expressing separate ideas: vv 2/3 show constructive/destructive actions, and vv 5/6 show union/separation. "The meaning of the poem as a self-contained unit appears to be that the joys and sorrows of life come from constructive/destructive actions and from separations and unions caused by love and hate on the individual and social levels" (NJBC, 492).

This could have been a separate, independent poem, but in its present context its purpose is to underscore that all events are determined by God and are beyond human control (cf. 6:10; Sir 33:13–15). Everything happens at the time determined for it by God. This determinism is characteristically biblical (Amos 3:6; Isa 45:7). Time is filled by event, and hence the psalmist (31:16) can say, "my times are in your hand." This determination extends to every חֵפֶץ, "affair," particularly to human activities, as the following examples show. Alonso Schökel points out the significance of the poem's beginning at v 2; these are the limits of human existence, a significant fact since they are limits over which human beings have no say. They stand out from the succeeding times, which are within the limits of life and death.

Time is a common *topos* in wisdom writings: the right word at the right time was the ideal (Prov 15:23; 25:11). Ben Sira discusses the subject at great length (Sir 3:2–8; 39:16, 21, 34; καιρός occurs about sixty times in the Greek text). Qoheleth comes back again to the question of time in 3:17; 8:5–6, 9, and especially the "falling time" in 9:11–12. The antitheses in vv 2–8 deliberately exclude one another, and every activity is tied to a specific time (K. Galling, *ZTK* 58 [1961] 1–15).

W. Zimmerli understands 3:1ff. as continuing a theme already present in 2:24–26 (the propitious time). However, the mood and emphasis of 3:1ff. are quite different; time is something determined by God and a mystery to humans who are involved in it.

2 The first antitheses (birth/death; plant/uproot) are uneven in importance. The activities of the farmer are not a central issue for Qoheleth, but life, and especially death (2:16; 9:5–6), weigh upon him. Indeed, the planting and uprooting can be viewed almost as metaphors for life/death. Hertzberg remarks that attention is centered on the child and the plant, not the mother and the gardener. Humans have no control over birth and death, and even such relatively less important details as planting and uprooting are beyond their measure. The "right time" is not within human disposition.

3 Although killing and healing (of and by humans presumably) are not perfect opposites, they are parallel to the operations in the second pair, which have to do with destruction/construction.

4 The pairs are closely paralleled, and the rhyme of lament/dance (סְפוֹד, רְקוֹד) is noteworthy. The terms refer to universal human experiences and are not to be limited to particular contexts, such as cult.

5 The meaning of v 5a remains obscure. Many interpretations of casting and collecting stones have been offered, but none of them is totally convincing. On the basis of 2 Kgs 3:19, 25, the line has been understood as referring to the sterilization of a field of an enemy. Or in virtue of Isa 5:2, it could mean the removal of stones from a field before a planting. Many commentators propose the view found in *Midrash Rabbah* that interprets the actions as sexual intercourse; thus a certain parallelism with v 5b is obtained. But the peculiar nature of the metaphor remains unexplained. K. Galling, who points out that metaphor is otherwise absent in vv 2–8, suggests that these are stones for counting, used in commercial transaction. H. Hertzberg refers to the actions of a farmer working his field. The embracing of v 5b can be understood in the narrow sense of intercourse or more broadly for any sign of affection.

6 There is a certain parallelism between the contrasts: the sense of the searching is actually to acquire something (cf. Jerome, *tempus acquirendi*), and its opposite is losing something, whatever be its value, and whether intentional or not (*contra* A. Lauha). The unnamed objects of the verbs can be presumed to be personal possessions. Both K. Galling and A. Lauha favor the context of a housewife (cf. also v 7a) in the home, but why should such experiences be thus limited?

7 The actions in v 7a seem to be independent of v 7b; the context changes from the domestic use of clothes to speech (Galling, Hertzberg). Some commentators follow *Midrash Rabbah* and correlate the tearing and silence in the context of grief. One can also understand speaking and silence in the broad sense of the wisdom tradition—the appropriate time for these actions (Sir 20:6–7). The line from the *Odyssey* (11:379) is then appropriate: "There is a time for the telling of tales, time also for slumber."

8 The chiastic structure is obvious. Qoheleth moves from general feeling of love/hatred to definite social events of war/peace.

9 The rhetorical question (cf. 1:3) passes judgment on human activity as being without profit. One is locked into a world of events that one cannot shape. Such is the direction given to the litany of times in vv 1–8. The conclusion leaps ahead of the data and is to be explained by the reasoning in vv 10–15, where Qoheleth will also emphasize that humans do not know the right time. In v 9 he is applying the poem on time to human toil; no amount of effort can change the time that God has determined.

10 Qoheleth begins a reflection (רָאִיתִי; cf. 3:16; 4:1, 4, 7; 6:11; 7:15; 8:10; 9:11, 13) that grows out of the poem on time. Already in 1:13 he has spoken of the harsh task (עִנְיָן) with which God has afflicted humans; there it referred to the attempt to make sense out of what is done in the world; here it is applied to the problem of determinate times.

11 Qoheleth says that God has put הָעֹלָם, "duration," into the human heart. Whether this action is seen as positive or negative (see the interpretation of מִבְּלִי in note 11.a.), the result is the same: humans have not been helped because they cannot understand what God is about. The interpretation of הָעֹלָם has been a *crux interpretum*. LXX (αἰῶνα) and Vg (*mundum*) understood it to mean "world." This could be taken as a desire for knowledge of the world in a good sense, or as a kind of secularism or worldliness (1 John 2:16). However, עֹלָם in the sense of world is not found in biblical Hebrew, and Qoheleth elsewhere (e.g., 3:14) uses the word in a temporal sense. A traditional view understands the word to mean "eternity" (so the RSV and many commentators such as W. Zimmerli and H. Hertzberg; but NRSV, "a sense of past and future"). F. Delitzsch understood it to be the *desiderium aeternitatis,* or "the desire of eternity." F. Ellermeier (*Qohelet I/1,* 320) argued for *Unaufhörlichkeit,* "incessability." N. Lohfink interprets the "eternity" of Eù to mean "ever new repetition" (cf. 3:15), through which the events described in 1:4–11 are now rooted in God's activity.

Here עֹלָם has the meaning of duration (see E. Jenni, *ZAW* 65 [1953] 24–27), as opposed to עֵת, which means a definite period of time; this antithesis should be preserved in v 11. E. Podechard describes it well: "עֹלָם means the whole, of which עֵת designates each part; it is the whole of duration or the totality of the particular times that were mentioned in the preceding vv 1–8." Moreover, since according to v 14 God's action is לְעֹלָם, עֹלָם seems to be a divine, not a human, category. But so also is עֵת in the sense that it stands for the specific times fixed by God (vv 1–8). The divine timing of human events is good (v 11, יָפֶה, "beautiful"—perhaps a reminiscence of טוֹב, "good," in Gen 1). Both of these aspects of time impinge upon human existence, but no one is able to comprehend their effects.

12–13 The opening "I know" lends emphasis and is balanced by the "I know" that begins a new thought in v 14. The verses are typical of the resigned conclusions found elsewhere, esp. 2:24 (see *Comment* there). Although this concession to pleasure as a "gift of God" for human toil seems grudging, it is evaluated positively by R. Johnston (*CBQ* 38 [1976] 14–28), who argues from the "intentionality" or underlying consciousness of Qoheleth. In this view positive value is given to joy in this life; it is the gift of God.

14 Another "I know" forms an emphatic introduction to certain data about God that underlie what has been previously said: God's actions are in the category of עֹלָם (‛ōlām). They are unchangeable, and the divine intention in this is "fear" of God. In contrast to v 12, where הָעֹלָם (hā ‛ōlām) was put in the human heart, Qoheleth states here that the divine actions are לְעוֹלָם (le ‛ōlām); they belong to the realm of the permanent and unchangeable. The meaning of this "forever" category is further explained by the following formula about permanence.

The formula in 14b has interesting antecedents in Deut 4:1–2 and 13:1, where it is used relative to the commandments of the Law, God's words (Prov 30:6 is only distantly similar): "You must neither add anything to what I command you nor take away anything from it, but keep the commandments of the Lord your God with which I am charging you" (Deut 4:2). The ultimate source of the formula is disputed. Some Egyptologists have claimed that it occurs in the teaching of Ptah-hotep (ll. 608–9), but such an understanding of these lines has been challenged by other experts, and the truth of the situation is unclear, as can be seen by contrasting translations (*AEL* 1:75; and see the discussion in Loretz, *Qohelet*, 66–69). In any case, it is worth noting that Qoheleth is speaking of the immutability of the divine *deed*, not word.

The purpose assigned to the divine action is fear of God. This is one of the most elusive concepts in the OT, even if it is a truism within the wisdom literature. See the discussion above, pp. lxv–lxvi. The fact that a verbal form with preposition is used here suggests that Qoheleth is placing greater emphasis upon the action of fearing, on the proper attitude which God wants to evoke in creatures by means of his mysterious action. Elsewhere he claims that the work of God is incomprehensible (7:13; 8:17; 11:5). In giving it a "purpose" here, he is not conceding anything; the purpose turns out to be rather modest. The notion of fear lacks the consoling aspects that are usually associated with "fear of the Lord" among the sages. According to Qoheleth, one is caught between the nearness of a God who fixes times and the mystery of a God whose work is unintelligible; in this situation fear of that God is the proper response.

15 Qoheleth has just characterized the divine action as belonging to the category of עֹלָם, and as unchangeable. To support this he takes up the thought of 1:9, the constant repetition of events. There the emphasis was on vanity, the fruitless repetition of events. Here the context is different: the mysterious unchangeability of divine action. He underscores this by backward/forward characterization in v 15a; the past and the present are open before God and are at the sovereign disposition of the divinity.

The obscurity of v 15b (see note 15.a.) remains a problem, but the words seem to be complementary to v 15a: nothing escapes the dominion of God, who has everything within the divine purview. God will seek out "what is pursued," i.e., the events of the past. There is a certain similarity of structure with v 14b. Both parts speak of divine action in the face of unchangeability (v 14) and repetition (v 15).

16–17 Qoheleth maintains that the justice exercised by humans is corrupt: wickedness prevails, and precisely where it should not—in the realm of public justice. This is doubtless a general observation; at any rate it cannot support any conclusion about a particular historical period. In v 16 he observes the fact. In v 17, despite the uncertainty in the translation (see note 17.a.), he clearly asserts that, nonetheless, this iniquity will not escape the judgment of God. As the text of v 17b stands ("and upon every deed there"), judgment is affirmed, but it is referred to a time or place that is left hanging in the air ("there" = ?). The thought of v 17b is similar to 8:6a; in any case, judgment by God is clearly stated.

As K. Galling remarks, in v 16 Qoheleth does not attack the system; he simply notes miscarriages of justice. Is his clear and calm assertion that God will exercise judgment upon both the just and the wicked inconsistent with his teaching? Many commentators think so, and hence claim that v 17a must be an editorial addition (E. Podechard, K. Galling, A. Lauha, et al.). It is true that he denies that there is any just retribution in this life—the righteous are treated as if they were wicked and vice versa (7:15; 8:14). This is part of his general lament that one cannot understand what God is doing. But he never denies that God is a judge (on the contrary, cf. 5:5[6]; 11:9), even though Qoheleth is unable to see any evidence of it in this world. It can be said that he clings to the biblical belief that God is somehow just and that God does judge, however contrary the evidence may appear to be. Judgment belongs to God's time, not to human time. In v 17b he seems to take up the theme of the determined times of 3:1ff. God's judgment is among these. Indeed, v 17b is introduced by "because," and the determination of time (עת לכל־חפץ, "for every affair," as in 3:1) is the reason for v 17a. Some commentators have tried to determine the nature of the judgment, but without much success. H. Hertzberg understands it to be death. O. Loretz (*Qohelet*, 294–97) describes it as God's "exercise of his absolute power over human life"—i.e., God determines death and life, good fortune and bad, according to his own will, and has laid down the law of death for all indiscriminately (3:18–21).

18 "I said to myself" is a reprise of the opening words of v 17, but the connection between vv 16–17 and v 18 is not easy to see. Perhaps Qoheleth is saying that human injustice, despite the divine "judgment," shows that humans are beasts (v 18). Then he goes on in vv 19–21 to develop this similarity in another way: they both have the same מקרה, "lot." Certainly the theme of similarity is introduced in v 18. The precise nuance of the divine purpose remains ambiguous: לברם, "separate," "select," "test" (see note 18.b.). If it is taken to mean testing, this could consist in the manifest injustice in human affairs (v 16), which shows whether human beings will throw off moral restraint since there is no principle of justice at work in their experience (cf. 8:11). Or the testing might be to provoke another response: will they accept God's mysterious ways and so fear him as in 3:14 (so W. Zimmerli)? Or is death itself the test, since both humans and animals die (vv 19–21; so H. Hertzberg)? If ברר is taken to mean "separate," then Qoheleth may be referring to the distinction between humans and beasts, which he will deny in the following verses. The separation could be ironic (K. Galling), since there is no distinction. If separation is effected by human death, the sense is the same as testing them by death. It would seem that death is the key factor in the divine plan. It comes now as a climax to the considerations about the incomprehensibility of God's actions in the world (vv 10–15) and the observation of injustice: humans die the same as the beasts.

19–20 These verses supply the reason for equating humans and animals. Both have the one מקרה, "happening" or "lot": death. Both have the same רוח, "spirit," or "life-breath," which is from God (Ps 104:29–30). The passage illustrates how disparate are the Greek and Hebrew categories translated by spirit, soul, immortality, etc. Qoheleth is expressing himself in terms of Gen 2:7, where God breathes the נשמת חיים, "life-breath," and of Ps 104:29–30, where life is dependent upon the presence of the רוח, "spirit," of God in living beings. Everything lives because of the divine breathing. There is no logical consistency within the OT as regards the terms used to convey the make-up of the human individual.

V 20 reflects Gen 3:19 as background. The "one place" to which all go is specified by the "dust" (cf. 6:6), although Qoheleth readily acknowledges the existence of Sheol (9:10). The theme of return to the dust is frequent (Job 10:9; 34:15; Pss 104:29; 146:4, Sir 40:11).

21 Qoheleth is apparently replying to a contemporary view that affirmed some kind of distinction in the ultimate fate of humans and animals. His question, "who knows?" is equivalent to a denial. We cannot determine what precise philosophy he is arguing against, and perhaps he has described it only in general terms. N. Lohfink refers to the idea in Euripides that what comes from the earth returns to it in death, but what comes from the αἰθήρ, "the heavenly vault," ascends to it. He remarks, "This may have been a popular expression of Platonizing belief in the immortality of the soul, at least in Qoheleth's milieu." It is quite clear that Qoheleth rejects any view that claimed some kind of differentiation in treatment, as the "upwards" and "downwards" imply. It is useless to try to determine from this denial his specific views on Sheol and the next life. He is clear about Sheol in 9:10, and in 12:7 he recognizes that the רוח, "spirit," returns to God, but this is obviously not the same claim that he rejects in this verse.

22 Another "I saw" (cf. 2:24; 3:10, 16) introduces a concluding thought which is an echo of 2:24 and 3:12 (אין טוב, "nothing better"), and makes use of one of his key theological terms: חלק, the "portion" or "fate" that is dealt out to a person in this life (cf. 2:10). The portion (God-given, according to 3:13) is described as enjoyment in human activities. Qoheleth recognizes nothing better for humans who cannot see any real future for themselves. His emphasis on human ignorance concerning "what will come after" is striking (2:18; 6:12; 8:7; 10:14), and also ambiguous. "After him" means after his death (cf. 2:12, 18; 9:3), but here in 3:22 "what will come" refers to this world (not to the next; cf. 6:12, "under the sun").

4:1 The subject of Qoheleth's observation is human oppression (the root עשק, "oppress," occurs three times). He simply registers the fact without condemnation. This is not to deny that he feels deeply about it; the repetition concerning the absence of consolation suggests the contrary. The point of view is broader than 3:16, which focused on the administration of justice. The repetition ("no one to give comfort") is deliberate and not to be deleted; it foreshadows the description of the plight of the solitary person in vv 7–12.

2–3 Qoheleth does not simply conclude "better off dead than alive." But death is preferable to oppression; it frees one from trouble:

> O death, how welcome is your sentence
>   to one who is needy and failing in strength,
> worn down by age and anxious about everything;
>   to one who is contrary, and has lost all patience! (Sir 41:2, NRSV)

His judgment is at odds with the typical wisdom emphasis on life, but it is in agreement with one who "loathes life" (2:17). Paradoxically, this judgment is rooted in a high appreciation of life. Because life is not what it should be—in the face of human oppression, he can praise the dead and the unborn. In this case "praise" has an ironic edge, since death is not normally preferable. Similar irony is apparent in 9:4–5 (see the *Comment* and cf. also 11:7–8), where he pursues a different tack: it seems better to be alive. From one point of view it is better not to experience the evil turns of life (4:3); on the other hand, it is better to know something (9:5) even if this is (ironically) only that one must die! The thought of 4:2–3 is close in spirit to Job 3 and Jer 20:14–18.

4 One can infer from this verse (cf. also 2:10b) that Qoheleth recognizes that prosperity and success can be achieved by toil. Some people succeed. But at what price? Behind it all he sees envy at work. This is the dark side of human activity (cf. Prov 14:30). Not only the feeling of jealousy, but the competitiveness that sparks the desire to outdo the other, is meant (*homo homini lupus*, "human rivalry is wolf-like"). The rivalry is seen as part of the המעשה הרע, "evil work," of v 3; המעשה is repeated in v 4.

5 This verse seems to be a traditional saying in favor of diligence over laziness (but see note 5.a.). Prov 6:10 and 24:33 are similar ("folding of hands"), and warnings against laziness are frequent in wisdom teaching (Prov 10:4; 13:4; 19:15; 20:13; 21:25). The saying therefore goes in a direction contrary to v 4, which scored the futile rivalry in human activity. But it is not to be deleted as a corrective editorial gloss (C. Siegfried, A. Lauha, and others). It is to be viewed in tandem with v 6.

6 The topic of rivalry (v 4) underlies v 6, another saying that points out the loss that a work-centered life can suffer. The thought is similar to ideas expressed in Prov 15:16; 16:8; 17:1. The addition, "and a chase after wind," is appended to the saying (by Qoheleth?), and it qualifies "toil" (cf. 2:18–23). It also echoes and reinforces the phrase in v 4, bringing this section to an end.

What is Qoheleth's position on the two sayings that he presents in vv 5–6? First of all, it is important to note the scathing remark in v 4 about skills and rivalry between individuals. This certainly deflates the advantages of diligence, which, as we have seen, finds many counterparts in traditional wisdom. In the context of v 4, the typical saying of the fool's laziness (v 5) loses much of its sting; at least the fool is not harming others in the way skillful and diligent rivals manage to do. It is not adequate to say that at least v 4 shows that one has to be diligent enough to a make a living. In v 6 the work that was seen to be an occasion of rivalry in v 4 is approved so long as it functions without the עמל (*ʿāmāl*, "toil") that Qoheleth has been excoriating all along. This is faint praise indeed for the busy, unfolded, hand of the worker. Anything that smacks of "toil" is ultimately vanity, but the absence of toil does not beatify its opposite—as though diligence "with rest" were an ideal. These considerations lead one to think that Qoheleth is balancing off two sayings of traditional wisdom, *neither* of which is foolproof, despite their support in the tradition. There is a general tendency among commentators to adopt the solution of R. Gordis, that Qoheleth comes down in favor of the saying in v 6 over v 5. But this seems to be a flat observation after the words about rivalry. M. Fox calls the proverbs complementary, not contradictory. Could it be that Qoheleth sees little value in either of them? His purpose, as so often, may be to balance two sayings against each other, almost as a warning to a careless reader.

Explanation

The poem on time is perhaps the most famous passage in Ecclesiastes (one may recall the popular song of years ago, "Turn, Turn") and perhaps the least understood. Once a questioner begins to ask about the precise significance of these fourteen antinomies, even where they seem to be clearly understood, as in to be born and to die, certain unpleasant conclusions surface. We may readily grant ignorance and lack of control over our births and deaths, but the religious person lets this rest in the beneficent Providence of God. Qoheleth will have none of this. He seizes upon this poem on time in order to underscore the sad human condition. These are *God's* times, not our times. They happen to us; they are under divine control. Very few recognize the strong theological note of divine determinism that pervades 3:1–8. Then it culminates with a devastating claim: in the toil that marks these time limits there is no profit for a human being. These are all God's times, and Qoheleth has no quarrel with them in themselves: they are all "appropriate" in the divine plan. But the divinity has played a desperate trick upon humanity, placing that mysterious הָעֹלָם, "duration," "world," in human hearts so that they can make no sense out of God's work. That is a fantastic statement of divine sabotage.

There can be no pleasant connection between the gift of הָעֹלָם in the human heart and the other divine "gift"—eating and drinking. That meager pleasure—symbolic of the best that humans can enjoy—seems to be a compensation for the העלם. In what appears to be a play on the word, the divine activity is characterized as לעלם, "eternal." This sets the stage for the proper response of humans to God: numinous, reverential fear (v 14).

Two other important themes occur in this section: injustice and death. Qoheleth was quite aware of the reality of injustice (cf. also 4:1–4), and nowhere did he see it adequately handled in human affairs. And what is the divine role? He did not deny that God is just, but he saw no evidence for it. The divine judgment, so often affirmed in his biblical tradition, was something he could not deny, but it appeared useless in reality. This situation (3:17–18) was compounded by the lack of a distinction between animals and humans. The same divine life-breath sustained them all, and both then returned to the dust, as the text of Genesis assured him. The austerity of his description of the human condition renders all the more piteous his resigned conclusion about the pleasures at which human beings can only grasp.

A Reflection concerning "Two" (4:7-16)

Bibliography

Ellermeier, F. *Qohelet I/1.* 217–32. **Irwin, W. A.** "Eccles. 4:13–16." *JNES* 3 (1944) 255–57. **Loretz, O.** *Qohelet.* 69–72. **Ogden, G. S.** "Historical Allusion in Qoheleth IV 13–16?" *VT* 30 (1980) 309–15. **Schaffer, A.** "The Mesopotamian Background of Qohelet 4:9–12." *EI* 8 (1967) 246–50. ————. "New Light on the 'Three Ply Cord.'" *EI* 9 (1969) 159–60, 138–39. **Schunck, K. D.** "Drei Seleukiden im Buche Kohelet?" *VT* 9 (1959) 192–201. **Torrey, C. C.** "The Problem of Ecclesiastes IV, 13–16." *VT* 2 (1952) 175–77. **Wright, A. G.** *CBQ* 30 (1968) 313–34.

Translation

[7]*Again I saw a vanity under the sun:* [8]*There was a single person, without any companion,*[a] *either son or brother. There was no end to all his toil, nor did his desire*[b] *for riches ever cease: "For whom am I*[c] *toiling and depriving myself of good things?" This also is vanity and an evil task.*

[9]*Two are better than one because they have a good payment for their toil.* [10]*For if they fall,*[a] *one can help the other up. But [woe*[b] *to] a single person who falls, for there is no one to help him up.* [11]*Also, if two people lie together they keep warm, but how can a single person keep warm?* [12]*A single person may be overcome,*[a] *but two together can resist. A three-ply cord cannot be easily broken.*

[13]*Better is a youth poor but wise, than a king old but foolish, who can no longer heed a warning.* [14]*For out of a prison*[d] *he*[a] *came forth to reign, although*[c] *in his*[b] *kingdom he*[a] *was born poor.* [15]*I saw all the living, who move about under the sun, on the side of the second*[a] *youth who will succeed him.* [16]*There was no end to all*[a] *the people, all*[a] *whom he led.*[b] *But those to come have no joy in him. This*[c] *also is a vanity and a chase after wind.*

Notes

8.a. Literally, "without a companion" is "and not a second"; notice the key word שֵׁנִי.

8.b. It makes no difference whether one reads "his eyes" (ketib), or "his eye" (qere); the organ of vision expresses desire (cf. 2:10).

8.c. The quotation marks are added in v 8b to show that this is a direct statement of the person ("I").

10.a. Although יִפֹּלוּ is plural and is attested in most of the ancient versions, it is used distributively. The sense must be that only one of two falls (cf. Gen 11:3; Judg 6:29).

10.b. אִילוֹ (cf. 10:16) can be read as the conditional "if," as the Tg has done (cf. Eccl 6:6). But it is better to understand אִי as a later form of אוֹי, "woe" (cf. Isa 6:5). So also LXX, Syr, Vg, and many Hebrew MSS.

12.a. There are some irregularities in this verse. The subject can hardly be הָאֶחָד; hence it must be indefinite, with הָאֶחָד the object. The verb has an unusual third person pronominal suffix: יִתְקְפוֹ instead of יִתְקְפֶהוּ (cf. GKC §60d). Moreover, the suffix anticipates the object; such a construction can be verified elsewhere, as in Exod 2:6; Eccl 2:21 (cf. GKC §131m). The ancient versions (LXX, Syr, Tg, for example) do not reflect the presence of the suffix, but this may be because of the way in which they interpreted the text. The verb is probably an Aramaism, and it means "overpower" (cf. Wagner §329). It is found in Job 14:20; 15:24; cf. also Eccl 6:10.

14.a.b. The translation of vv 14–16 is uncertain in many respects (see the commentaries). In v 14 the references are vague: the subject of the two verbs, and the person indicated by the suffix in מלכותו. This translation understands the youth as the subject of the verbs, while the suffix pronoun refers back to the old king.

14.c. Another problem is כי גם. This is said to be equivalent to גם כי, "although" (GKC §160b), and is adopted by many translations. The two phrases introduced by כי are merely coordinated in LXX, Syr, and Vg. In Eccl 8:12 כי גם occurs again and can be rendered concessively, but primarily because of the context (cf. D. Michel, *Eigenart*, 211).

14.d. הסורים is to be understood as האסורים, "prisoners"; for the omission of the *aleph*, compare 2 Kgs 8:28 and 2 Chr 22:5 (הרמים), and cf. GKC §35d. This is supported by all the ancient versions except the Tg which understands הסורים as idol-worshipers. It is the youth, not the king, who comes out of the prison and is born poor.

15.a. The text is supported by all the versions. השני, "the second," is omitted by many as a gloss, but it seems to be a catch word with what precedes (see A. G. Wright, *NJBC* 31:20, p. 492). The second youth is obviously different from the youth mentioned at the beginning in v 13. In fact, he is his successor: תחתיו, to "stand in the place of," means "to follow in office" (cf. Dan 8:22–23).

16.a. The text is ambiguous. The second לכל is in apposition to the first.

16.b. The subject of היה could be the people (so LXX, Vg, and most of the ancient versions) or the successor(s) to the throne. Similarly לפניהם can be construed as referring to the rulers, but more likely it refers to the people. Hence either translation is possible: "(the people) who lived before them (kings)," or "(the people) whom he led." See the helpful discussion in Gordis.

16.c. The introductory כי is affirmative; cf. GKC §155ee.

Form/Structure/Setting

This section has been aptly characterized as "the problem of the 'second'" by A. Wright (*CBQ* 30 [1968] 328). The key word is "two," occurring in six verses (שני, 8, 10, 15; שנים, 9, 11, 12). The reflection about the "second" covers three situations: the absence of an heir (vv 7–8), the advantage of a companion (vv 9–12), and the presence of a successor (vv 13–16). The plight of a single person is described in vv 7–8, and this is followed by four examples (salary, accident, warmth, and attack) in vv 9–12. The saying about the three-ply cord rounds off the unit. There follows in vv 13–16 an example story that is only loosely united to the theme by the appearance of "the second" in v 15. The story itself relates how even a wise king is ultimately the victim of human fickleness. In this case, a "second," or successor, provides an occasion for the change in loyalty of the subjects. The case is typical and need not refer to any specific historical incident such as during the Seleucid reign (*contra* K. D. Schunck, *VT* 9 [1959] 192–201). This is another defeat for wisdom (the youth "poor but wise"). In effect, the observation of v 13 has been controverted by the story in vv 14–16.

Comment

7–8 Qoheleth turns his attention to the situation of a person who is totally alone, without companion or progeny. With endless toil (cf. 4:4) he achieves riches, but these merely leave him wanting more (his "eyes" never satisfied; cf. 1:8). And then the inevitable question (cf. Sir 14:3–5), vividly expressed in a direct quotation: for whom all this toil? This stands in only slight contradiction to 2:18–22, where Qoheleth lamented the possibility of his inheritance being handed down to a fool (who might consume it). Now he scores the futility of the laborer who has no inheritor to share with him. There is little sense in toiling for merely personal gain. It should be noted that עמל, "toil," figures in both passages.

9–12   These verses are in support of the claim in vv 7–8 and consist of a series of examples and a traditional saying. The first case deals with labor: two will achieve for each other more than one worker can attain. The point is less the actual wages that are granted for the labor than the circumstances of the toil—two people can complement each other by working together. V 10 illustrates the idea of mutual support: if one fails, the other can help. The next case does not necessarily refer to a married couple but is a practical instance of how two people can combine for the purpose of warmth (1 Kgs 1:1–2; Luke 17:34). Presumably, their outer garments provide two "blankets" that keep them both warm. The final example (v 12) envisions a physical attack, as from a robber; two are better than one. The examples are topped off by what has the ring of a proverb concerning the three-ply cord (see A. Schaffer, *EI* 9 [1969] 159–60). The number three has no particular significance as opposed to two; the point is plurality.

In these verses we see Qoheleth plying his trade as a sage, providing homely examples and wisdom to prove his point. The whole argument seems quite straightforward and leaves no room for Gordis' view that vv 10–12 are an ironic comment on v 9. Commentators point to the *Iliad*, 10:224–26 as a parallel to the cases in vv 10–12.

13   Any translation, and hence interpretation, of vv 13–16 is uncertain, because of the vagueness of the text (see the *Notes*). It seems clear that this is an "example story," a kind of parable, which illustrates the uncertainty of royal popularity and, hence, the vanity of (royal) wisdom. Commentators have sought, in vain, to identify the historical characters behind the story: Joseph and the Pharaoh, Saul and David, Astyages and Cyrus, and others. None of these identifications has won acceptance. It may be that the story is prompted by some historical event, even if this is not recoverable. But the story presents the typical rather than a specific event or historical characters. The occurrence of "the second" in v 15 serves as a catch word that ties vv 13–16 with vv 9–12, in which "two" occurs so frequently.

The story begins with a "better" saying, echoing the form utilized in vv 6, 9. The saying itself can be illustrated by the traditional wisdom emphasis on the role of royal counselors (Prov 24:5–6); it is precisely the mark of the wise man to take counsel (Prov 13:10). The contrast between the youth and the king is in line with the contrast between the intelligent servant and the worthless son in Prov 17:2. Qoheleth's own assent to the saying is to be judged as limited. It has its truth, but the later events in the life of the wise youth indicate that the whole story is oriented to a judgment of vanity.

14   This verse has caused many commentators to see a reference to Joseph (Gen 39–41), or even to Joseph and David (G. Ogden, *VT* 30 [1980] 309–15). But it is better understood as merely one trait in a "rags to riches" story.

15   Qoheleth begins to consider the aftermath of the youth's success, in such a way as to lead into his final verdict of vanity. He observed the popular support given to a second youth, the successor of the first one. If one were to delete הַשֵּׁנִי, "the second," the reference would be to the youth mentioned in vv 13–14. The story would be simpler in that case, for it would portray the case of a wise underprivileged youth who rose to power in place of a foolish king and then, after the wave of popularity among the fickle people (v 16), ends up in the same situation as the foolish king. But as the text stands, "the second" seems to indicate another youth who succeeds to the first one; it cannot be taken to mean merely that the first youth was the second king after the foolish one.

16 The text is ambiguous and translations differ (see the *Notes*). But it is at least clear that Qoheleth is underscoring that a king falls out of favor with succeeding generations. Such is the fickleness of the populace and the fate of royal power: vanity! Since the point of the story is the ephemeral character of popularity, it makes no difference who is identified as the subject of v 16 (the original youth, or the second who succeeded him).

Explanation

The most tantalizing aspect of 4:7–16 is the contrast between 2:18–22 and the complaint in 4:7–8. One can distinguish two emphases: the possibility that a fool inherits the fruit of one's toil, and the futility of having no heir or anyone else who might profit from one's toil. There is no real contradiction; both are instances of vanity. The complaint in 4:7–8 seems to have given cause to report several instances of the advantage that comes from plurality in community (vv 9–12). The example story in vv 13–16 is only distantly related to the topic of vv 7–12.

Varia: Worship, Officials, Wealth and Its Uncertainties (4:17[5:1]–6:9)

Bibliography

Ackroyd, P. R. "Two Hebrew Notes." *ASTI* 5 (1966/67) 82–86 (cf. M. Dahood, *Bib* 49 [1968] 368). **Barton, G. A.** "The Text and Interpretation of Ecclesiastes 5,19." *JBL* 27 (1908) 65–66. **Ellermeier, F.** "Die Entmachtung der Weisheit im Denken Qohelets: Zu Text und Auslegung von Qoh. 6,7–9." *ZTK* 60 (1963) 1–20. **Fredericks, D. C.** "Chiasm and Parallel Structure in Qoheleth 5:6–6:9." *JBL* 108 (1989) 17–35. **Kugel, J.** "Qohelet and Money." *CBQ* 51 (1989) 32–49. **Lohfink, N.** "Warum ist der Tor unfähig, böse zu handeln? (Koh 4,17)." In *Ausgewählte Vorträge*. Ed. F. Steppat. ZDMGSup 5. Deutscher Orientalistentag. Wiesbaden: Steiner, 1983. 113–20. ———. "Kohelet und die Banken: zur Übersetzung von Kohelet v 12–16." *VT* 39 (1989) 488–95. ———. "Qoheleth 5:17–19: Revelation by Joy." *CBQ* 52 (1990) 625–35. **Perdue, L.** *Wisdom and Cult.* SBLDS 30. Missoula, MT: Scholars Press, 1977. **Salters, R. B.** "Notes on the History of the Interpretation of Koh 5,5." *ZAW* 90 (1978) 95–101. ———. "Notes on the Interpretation of Qoh 6,2." *ZAW* 91 (1979) 282–89. **Schmidt, J.** "Koh 4,17." *ZAW* 58 (1940/41) 279–80. **Schulte, A.** "Zu Koh. 5,7 u. 8." *BZ* 8 (1910) 4. **Varela, A.** "A New Approach to Eccl 5:8–9." *BT* 27 (1976) 240–41. **Whitley, C. F.** *Koheleth.* 48–60.

Translation

17(5:1) *Watch your step[a] when you enter the house of God. The approach[b] of one who listens is better than the sacrifice fools offer,[c] for they have no knowledge of doing evil.[d]* 5:1(2) *Do not be quick with your tongue,[a] and let not your heart hasten[b] to speak before God, for God is in heaven and you are on earth. Therefore let your words be few.* 2(3) *For as dreams come from many tasks,*
so the speech of fools from many words.[a]
3(4) *When you make a vow to God, do not be slow to fulfill it,[a] for he has no pleasure in fools. Fulfill what you vow!* 4(5) *It is better for you not to vow, than to vow and not fulfill it.* 5(6) *Do not allow your mouth to bring you to sin,[a] and do not say before the representative,[b] "it was a mistake,"[c] lest God be angry at your words and destroy[d] the work of your hands.*
6(7) *For in many dreams—*
also many vanities and words.[a]
But fear God!

7(8) *If you see in a province[a] the oppression of the poor, the violation of right and justice, do not be surprised by the affair, for over one official another official keeps watch, and (still) over them are officials.[b]* 8(9) *An advantage for a country in every way is this: a king for the tilled land.[a]*

9(10) *Whoever loves money never has enough of it,*
nor the lover of wealth,[a] enough income.
This too is vanity.
10(11) *When goods increase,*
those who consume them increase.

What gain has the owner,[a]
  except something for his eyes to look upon?[b]
11(12) Sweet is the sleep of the laborer,
  whether he eats little or much.
  But the abundance[a] of the rich
  allows no sleep.

12(13) There is a grievous evil[a] I have seen under the sun: riches kept by[b] their owner[c] to his own hurt.[d] 13(14) Namely,[a] the riches are lost by an evil turn;[b] then he begets a son when there is nothing to hand![c] 14(15) Just as he came forth from his mother's womb, naked will he again go as he came; and nothing for his toil will he have in hand to take with him.[a] 15(16) This is a grievous evil: as[a] he came, so must he go[b]—then what profit does he have from his toiling for the wind? 16(17) Even all his days he eats in darkness,[a] and in much [vexation], and sickness [   ] and spite.[b]

17(18) This is what I have seen as good, as beautiful:[a] to eat and to drink and to prosper for all the toil that one must toil at under the sun in the limited life that God gives, for that is one's portion. 18(19) Also,[a] anyone to whom[b] God gives riches and possessions and the power to partake of them, to have his portion and to rejoice in his toil—this is a gift of God. 19(20) Indeed,[a] he will hardly be concerned with the days of his life, because God keeps (him) occupied[b] with the joy of his heart.

6:1 There is an evil I have seen under the sun and it is grievous for humans: 2 One to whom God has given riches, possessions and glory[a] so that he lacks nothing of what he desires—but God has not given him the power to partake of them! Instead,[b] a stranger consumes them. This is a vanity and a grievous sickness.[c]

3 If[a] a man beget a hundred children and live many years—though[b] many be the days of his years—if his desire for good things is not met, then even without a burial,[c] I say the stillborn is better off than he. 4 Though in vain it comes and in darkness it goes, and with darkness its name is covered;[5] though it sees not the sun[a] nor knows anything, it has more rest than he. 6 If[a] one were to live twice a thousand[b] years, but without experiencing good, do not all go to the same place?
7   All human toil is for the mouth,[a]
  but the appetite is never satisfied.
8   What[a] advantage have the wise over the foolish?
  what advantage has [a] poor person[b] who knows how to cope with life?[c]
9   Better is it that the eyes see,
  than that the appetite wanders;[a]
  this too is vanity and a chase after wind.

Notes

17.a. The ancient versions read the qere ("your foot," in the singular), as opposed to the ketib; cf. Prov 1:15.

17.b. קרוב is the qal infinitive absolute and is understood here in a nominal meaning ("approach"). But it is also possible to interpret it as an imperative ("enter"; cf. GKC §113a) parallel to "watch," as most of the ancient versions and many commentators (e.g., Lohfink) have done.

17.c. מתת הכסילים זבח can be translated "better than a fool's offering sacrifice"; for the ellipsis of טוב before the comparative מן, cf. GKC §133e. Although the use of נתן with זבח is singular, this is preferable to the variations in the ancient versions: Aq, Theod, and Jerome read מתת as a noun, "gift"; similarly LXX, "better than the gift of fools is your sacrifice."

17.d. רע לעשות יודעים אינם is ambiguous. "They have no knowledge of doing evil" can find support in 5:5, where the excuse of inadvertence is alleged. It is also possible to translate "they do not know how to do evil"; this could be considered as a sarcastic comment of Qoheleth. The ancient versions do not appear to have read a text different from the MT. Many commentators prefer to modify the text to read: "they know nothing but wrongdoing"—either by inserting אם כי on the analogy of 3:12, 8:15, or by reading *mem*, omitted by haplography, before לעשות.

5:1.a. For the phrase, על פיך, "with your tongue," compare Ps 50:16.

1.b. בהל has the meaning "dismay" (nipal and piel), but also "hasten" in late Hebrew; cf. 7:9, Esth 2:9; 2 Chr 35:21.

2.a. "Words" and "fools" are catch words with 4:17; 5:1. The two lines of the saying are joined by "and" (*waw adaequationis;* cf. GKC §161a), which can be rendered as "so."

3.a. The text resembles Deut 23:22 rather closely.

5.a. The MT reads, literally, "make your flesh sin"; חטא is written with the *he* elided (GKC §53q), the "flesh" stands for the person (cf. 11:10).

5.b. There is not sufficient reason to change מלאך to אלהים on the basis of LXX and Syr: the reference is to one of the temple personnel, such as a priest.

5.c. שגגה is used frequently in the Priestly tradition for sins of inadvertence; cf. Lev 4.

5.d. וחבל is a consecutive perfect. The evidence of the ancient versions is almost unanimously against the singular מעשה, but the meaning remains unchanged.

6.a. MT reads in v 6a: "For in a multitude of dreams (there are?) also vanities and words very many." This is probably corrupt, but the ancient versions do not reflect a better *Vorlage.* LXX renders the line literally; Vg translates freely: "where dreams are many, many are the vanities and words without number." C. H. Wright offers another possible translation: "for in the multitude of dreams are also vanities, and in many words also," although he recognizes that the ellipsis of *beth* before דברים is harsh. None of the emendations that have been proposed are convincing; see the discussion in Whitley, *Koheleth,* 49–50.

7.a. מדינה occurs also in 2:8; it is an Aramaic word (cf. Wagner §152) designating a province or section of the administrative division of the Persian empire.

7.b. גבהים, "officials," can also be understood as a plural of majesty referring to one person who is over all.

8.a. The translation is uncertain, especially for the last three words. In v 8a the ketib, היא, can be retained and understood as a neuter, "this"; LXX appears to have understood the qere (ἐστι). בכל means "in every respect"; cf. Gen 24:1.

The major problem is whether נעבד should be construed with שדה or with מלך, and opinions vary. LXX, Syr, Theod, and Jerome construe it with שדה, "a tilled field" (cf. the use of the nipal of עבד in Ezek 36:9, 34). If it is construed with מלך, one can translate "a king served by (or subject to) the field." This is perhaps reflected in Tg and Vg, which are quite free. It seems better to go with the first option: a king for a land that is tilled. In *BT* 27 (1976) 240–41, Alfredo Varela associates vv 7–8 in such a way that the complicity of officials (v 7) is commented on sarcastically in v 8: All of this means progress for the country . . . the king is the servant of the land!

9.a. *beth* before המון is unusual, and it may be the result of dittography after אהב. The entire phrase is generally considered to be the subject of the verb ישבע, which is supplied from the previous line. But one can also understand the relationship as juxtaposition: "whoever loves abundance—no income."

10.a. בעליה should be understood as the plural of excellence (GKC §124i); cf. 5:12; 7:12; 8:8.

10.b. ראות (qere) is literally the "seeing" (of his eyes). In vv 9–16 a characteristic trait of Qoheleth's style appears: a series of interlocking repetitions: אהב "love," כסף "silver," רבה "great," אכל "eat," עשר "riches," רע "bad," מאומה "anything," בוא "come," הלך "go," עמל "toil," רעה חולה "grievous evil," בידו "in his hand."

11.a. השבע, "abundance," is interpreted by some as satiety: Gordis, "a full stomach" (cf. Prov 25:16); Eũ, *voller Bauch;* and Jerome, *saturitas,* which he further elaborates: *redundante crapula, et incocto cibo in stomachi angustiis aestuante* ("in full drunkenness, while the undigested food rages in the narrow confines of the stomach").

12.a. The MT is to be kept, despite the variations among the versions (LXX omits רעה; Vg renders חולה as a substantive). חולה can be parsed as the feminine participle of חלה, or as a substantive in apposition to רעה (an evil, namely a sickness; Michel remarks that this is perhaps better since there can be no opposition between a sick and a healthy evil; *Eigenart,* 189).

12.b. The *lamedh* is to be translated as "by" (cf. Joüon §132f.); R. Gordis and several others prefer "for."

12.c. בעליו is the plural of excellence or majesty (cf. GKC §124i); see v 10.

12.d. The suffix in לרעתו is usually referred back to the man; hence, "his hurt." It is grammatically possible with Lohfink (*VT* 39 [1989] 491) to refer it to עשר, "riches." This would depend on the general construal of the meaning of vv 12–16, especially בידו in v 13.

13.a. The conjunction, "and," that begins the verse is best translated as "namely"; for the explicative *waw*, cf. GKC §154a, note b.

13.b. ענין רע refers to something disagreeable; cf. 1:13; 4:8. How specifically this "evil turn" is to be understood is not clear.

13.c. בידו refers more likely to the hand of the father, not the son. But does it have an idiomatic nuance? N. Lohfink has adopted the view of B. J. Capper (*RQ* 12/46 [1986] 223–36) that ביד followed by a personal name means "to the account of" so and so. Hence vv 13–14 refer to a bankruptcy, or some financial loss suffered by the father. He begets a child when he no longer has solid financial investment; cf. *VT* 39 (1989) 490–91. Lohfink has given an English translation of 5:12–16 in *CBQ* 52 (1990) 629, n. 29: "[12]Sometimes there is a grave evil which I have examined under the sun: existing riches, kept by a bank for its owner, only to end up in failure. [13]Through an unfortunate business transaction, these riches were lost. The owner has begotten a son, but now there is nothing in his account. [14]As he came from his mother's womb, he shall start his life anew, naked as he came, and he cannot withdraw any amount from a deposit which he would have set to work through his account. [15]Therefore, this too is a grave evil. Exactly as he came, so shall he start his life anew, and what profit will he have? Only that he toils for the wind. [16]Through the rest of his life, too, he will eat in darkness. Anger and illness are his, and wrath."

14.a. Our translation, with many others, understands the subject to be the father, who dies as empty-handed as when he came into the world, with nothing to pass on to his son. In the construal of Lohfink, several words take on nuances from the financial context that he presupposes: "(naked) must he begin anew his way of life—exactly as he came." Then ללכת does not imply death but a new life style. The father derives no profit from the riches he had paid to his bank account (so may one paraphrase v 14b). The suffix in this second בידו refers again to the father rather than to the son (*contra* Michel, *Eigenart*, 189).

15.a. The compound Hebrew expression, כל־עמת ש, can be taken as "in the very manner that." Since עמת is generally joined to *lamedh*, there may be a misreading; many of the ancient versions understood the expression as כי לעמת (LXX, ὥσπερ γάρ; Vg, *quia sicut*).

15.b. In keeping with his construal of vv 13–14, Lohfink would translate this "so must he begin anew."

16.a. It is possible, but less likely, to render: "He spends (eats) all his days" (cf. Amos 7:12). LXX (καὶ πένθει, "and [in] sadness") read אבל for אכל.

16.b. The MT has literally: "and he is vexed much, and his sickness, and wrath." It is better to understand three of the last four words as nouns, construed with the *beth* in the first part of the verse. The evidence of the ancient versions is in favor of this for וכעס; similarly וחליו was read by them without the suffix, a case of dittography (חלי, "sickness," is to be read as the versions suggest).

17.a. The MT is difficult to translate; perhaps it can be rendered: "this I have seen: (it is) good which (because?) (is) beautiful." Contrary to the Masoretic accent, טוב is to be joined to אני; "what I have seen as good." The second אשר can be understood as a conjunction instead of a relative: "(is) that it is beautiful to. . . ."

The venerable claim that a Grecism, καλὸς καγαθός, underlies the difficult phrase טוב אשר יפה is hardly urged any more. But R. Braun (*Kohelet*, 54–55) suggests "some probability" for a Hebraicisation of τὸ καλὸν φίλον; this seems even less likely.

18.a. גם, "also," introduces a second observation as "good."

18.b. For the construction, cf. כל האדם ש in 3:13; the translation has preserved the anacoluthon that is in the text.

19.a. It is possible to interpret the first כי as "indeed," rather than as causal.

19.b. מענה is generally considered to be the hipil participle of ענה (II), "occupy"; there is no undisputed use of ענה (I), "answer," in the hipil. Moreover, Qoheleth alone in the Hebrew Bible employs ענה (II); cf. 1:13 and 3:10. The matter would seem settled. Such was also the understanding of the LXX, περισπᾷ and the Vg, *occupet*. The absence of the objective pronoun, "him," is not a great problem; it can be understood, or vocalized defectively, מְעַנֶה, or one can read מענהו (cf. LXX, *auton*). The sense would be that God keeps a person busy with the little joy (שמחה) that is doled out (so many modern translations: NAB, NEB, NIV, NJV, NJB). Nonetheless, objections have been made over the years (cf. A. McNeile, 71–72). F. Delitzsch gave a spirited defense in favor of "answer," and recently this meaning has been urged by N. Lohfink (*CBQ* 52 [1990] 625–35). The grammatical argument is that in verbs with a first guttural, there can be in the hipil a form analogous to the qal. In the Hebrew Bible there are only two unmistakable hipil forms of ענה: מענה in Prov 29:19 and אענה in Job 32:17. Both of them can be understood to mean "answer." Hence, one may argue that the hipil form was used with the same meaning as the qal.

6:2.a. The phrase describing the riches is reproduced in 2 Chr 1:12, referring to the divine gifts to Solomon. The construction of v 2 is anacoluthon.

2.b. כי, "instead," is to be interpreted as an adversative conjunction (GKC §163a).

2.c. חלי, "sickness," is better understood metaphorically (cf. 5:12, 15). Although LXX translates literally, ἀρρωστία, physical sickness (alleged by Galling) is not necessarily the reason for failing to enjoy the riches.

3.a. The conjunction אם governs all the clauses down to the main verb, אמרתי.

3.b. ורב, "though many be . . . ," is parenthetical, a concessive clause modifying the previous words.

3.c. וגם קבורה לא היתה לו causes difficulty. C. D. Ginsburg lists seven different interpretations, and he understands it to mean "even if the grave did not wait for him" (i.e., he lived a very long life). Others (Zimmerli) move it to v 5 where it is associated with the stillborn. The same effect can be achieved without dislocation by recognizing that the וגם clause is anticipatory, with לו referring to the stillborn. So the NJV, "though it was not even accorded a burial," and it notes that "stillbirths were cast into pits or hidden in the ground in no recognizable grave; cf. v 4 end." See also D. Michel (Eigenart, 144–47).

5.a. For the phrase "to see the sun" (to live), see 7:11 and the Comment on 11:7.

6.a. אלו stands for אם and לו.

6.b. "A thousand years twice" is irregular Hebrew; one would normally expect אלפים שנה.

7.a. The suffix in פיהו need not be expressed if the reference is to the man who has just been described. However, if the suffix is referred to the "place" in v 6, it is possible to conceive of Sheol having a mouth, as in Isa 5:14, Hab 2:5. Then the line would mean "all human toil is for its (Sheol's) mouth" (see P. Ackroyd, ASTI 5 [1966/67] 82–86; and M. Dahood, Bib 49 [1968] 243). This is favored by A. Lauha and N. Lohfink (commenting on Eü). Then נפש, "throat," is interpreted to mean "maw." Although all this is possible philologically, the idea of Sheol consuming human toil is peculiar. The verse seems to return to the theme of v 3, and it is to be understood in the light of Prov 16:26, "the toiler's appetite toils for him, for his mouth urges him on." נפש means "appetite" rather than "throat" in this verse (pace Ellermeier, ZTK 60 [1963] 2, n. 4).

8.a. The opening כי can be taken as causal or as asseverative; it introduces a question that is equivalent to a denial.

8.b. לעני יודע is vocalized by the Masoretes in such a way that they do not go together: לֶעָנִי, "to the poor one," is pointed with the definite article. It seems better to read לְעָנִי. But the meaning of v 8b is obscure. C. D. Ginsburg carried over the mem from v 8a and rendered: "what [advantage hath] the poor man over him who knoweth . . . ?" He surveyed the ancient versions and rightly concluded that they are loose paraphrases that do not presuppose a different Vorlage. Many emendations have been proposed, but none is convincing. Whitley (Koheleth, 59) proposes reading ענו, "poor," as "the intelligent man" (who knows how to conduct himself before his fellows). Michel (Eigenart, 153–54) implicitly assumes the definite article: "what advantage has the poor one who knows . . ."

8.c. להלך נגד החיים is an ambiguous phrase. C. D. Ginsburg understood it in the sense of leading the public life of a leader. But הלך may merely mean "to conduct oneself," and the reference could be to the model conduct of the poor who rely upon God (K. Galling, A. Lauha). W. Zimmerli emphasizes נגד as "in opposition to," and sees here the hostile meeting with life that is the lot of the poor. All things considered, v 8 has resisted an exact translation and hence interpretation. D. Michel (Eigenart, 150–59) interprets it from v 9 to mean that Qoheleth is attacking one of the ענוים (the "poor" of the psalms), who places the fulfillment of personal desire (cf. vv 7 and 9) in the future, not in the present. M. Fox (Qohelet, 221–22) thinks v 8 interrupts vv 7 and 9 and "may be displaced." As it stands, it means that "since the wise man has no advantage over the fool, there is no reason for a poor man to know how to get along with the living" (222; cf. 9:16, which speaks of how the wisdom of the poor person is ineffectual).

9.a. This verse is usually translated so as to favor the action of (or object seen by) the eye (seeing) over the action (going, wandering) of appetite or desire. See NAB, RSV, NJB, TOB. The NJV is similar, but remarks in a note that the first half of the verse is uncertain. The Eü renders it in proverbial style: "Better to have something before one's eyes / than a hungry gullet" (Besser, etwas vor Augen haben, als ein hungriger Rachen). But then N. Lohfink notes its vagueness: (1) it could be the same as "a bird in the hand is better than a dove on the roof" (or in the American idiom, "than two in the bush"); or (2) it is better alive than dead (this is because of the way v 7 is translated—and rejected above in note

7.a.); or (3) since 5:10 took a dim view of the "seeing of the eye," perhaps the implication here is that when the eye sees the prosperity of others, this is better off than being dead (recall that in vv 6–7 the hungry "gullet" of Sheol is ready to devour human beings). The verdict of vanity in v 9b would cancel out this rather ironic observation as well as the sentiments in vv 6–8.

The key to the meaning of v 9a is the word מראה, which can denote either the action of seeing or the object seen. Our translation opts for the straightforward action of seeing (the meaning it seems to have in 11:9). Sight at least has something in its possession compared to the futility of desire's unfulfilled yearning.

Form/Structure/Setting

This section can be divided into an instruction concerning cultic conduct, with particular emphasis on sacrifice, prayer, and vows (4:17–5:6[7]), followed by a short instruction concerning officials (5:7–8[8–9]) and a reflection about possessions (5:9[10]–6:9).

Admonitions make their first appearance in the book, and Qoheleth warns particularly against the conduct of fools (כסיל, a catch word in 4:17, 5:2–3[3–4]; cf. the use of כסל/כסל in 10:1–3, 6, 12–14). The admonition about speech ends in 5:2(3) with what appears to be a traditional saying. There follows a treatment concerning vows, which ends with a text that seems somewhat garbled (5:6[7]). However, the imperative, "fear God!" at the conclusion is the key attitude that he wants to inculcate. This basic reverence for the numinous, the distance from the Wholly Other (5:1[2]), informs the entire instruction.

The admonition concerning officials (5:7–8[8–9], a rather obscure text), serves as a transition to the topic of riches, the subject of a lengthy reflection in 5:9(10)–6:9. Possessions are seen as deceitful because of the insatiable appetite that humans have (5:9–11[10–12]), or because they can be lost (5:12–16[13–17], a kind of story), or simply because they fail to bring happiness. Although they are a gift of God, they are inadequate compensation for human existence, serving only as a distraction from life's difficulties (5:17–19[18–20]). Moreover, riches are uncertain: God can give them to another to enjoy (6:1–2, perhaps another example story). Finally, even the stillborn is better off than the one whose desire for possessions is unfulfilled (6:3–6). The conclusion (6:7–9) returns to the topic of the human appetite (5:9–11[10–12]; cf. 4:8). The verdict of "vanity and a chase after wind" closes off the section and makes its final appearance in the book.

This final section (5:9[10]–6:9) has been subjected to a careful structural analysis by D. C. Fredericks. He has rightly remarked (*JBL* 108 [1989] 17–35) that its unity "is seen by many commentators, who with different titles distinguish it clearly from the surrounding materials" (18). He pursues his point (see the outline on p. 29 of his article) by indicating the parallel structure of 5:9–18(10–19) and 6:1–9 (to simplify this exposition only the Hebrew verse numbering will be used). While the parallelism is not perfect (5:9–11 is separated out as an introduction), the structural parallelism is quite clear: (1) the evil of having and losing riches (5:12b–13a and 6:1–2b); (2) begetting when one has nothing, along with the theme of coming and going (5:13b–15a and 6:3a–6); (3) what advantage from toil? none, but there is some contentment (5:15b–19 and 6:7a–9). I think that the parallelism breaks down at the point of contentment, which is claimed for 6:9, but for the rest the parallelism is remarkable. Furthermore he notes that the four main concerns of 5:9–6:9 can be detected: "(1) wealth or poverty (5:9, 10, 11, 12, 13, 14, 18; 6:2); (2) satisfaction, rest, or enjoyment—or not (5:9, 10, 11,

12, 16, 17, 18; 6:2, 3, 5, 6, 7, 9); (3) breath, transience (5:9, 13; 6:2, 3, 6, 9); (4) What advantage? (5:10, 15; 6:8)" (20). One may not agree on the chiastic precision which is presupposed (see Fredericks' diagram on p. 19), but the structure of 5:9–6:9 has been laid bare by his analysis.

Comment

17(5:1) Qoheleth's admonition (surprisingly?) fits well into traditional Israelite wisdom (Prov 15:8; 21:3, 27). The stance of the wise man more or less comes down to that of the prophet: obedience is better than sacrifice (1 Sam 15:22; see L. Perdue, *Wisdom and Cult*, 182). The linguistic expression is characteristic of the sage: "listen." This has been interpreted narrowly in the sense of hearing a specific temple teaching (E. Podechard, H. Hertzberg). In the light of 5:2, W. Zimmerli prefers to understand listening in opposition to talking (James 1:19), and he goes on to see a preference for passive acceptance of the word over the life-securing activity of the cult. This seems like over-interpretation. Qoheleth manifests in 4:17–5:6(5:1–7) a cautious but reverent attitude to the cult that is not essentially different from the usual critique of cultic abuses.

The translation of v 17b is uncertain (see the *Notes*), and the line is given various interpretations. Our translation leaves open the possibility that this is a sarcastic remark, or else that it gives a reason for the ineptitude of fools, who count on ritual excuses (5:5[6]) to cover their irreverence. According to N. Lohfink (ZDMGSup 5 [1983] 113–20), the fool makes sin out to be a harmless violation by offering a שגגה sacrifice that is for involuntary wrongdoing (Eccl 5:5[6]). This is tantamount to "being unable to sin," since they are without guilt.

1(2) Precipitate action is warned against in traditional wisdom (Prov 19:2b). When applied to speech, as here, the usual result of thoughtless activity will be just words, and often too many of them (see Eccl 10:14a). The wise person exercises restraint in speech (Prov 10:19). But the motivation provided by Qoheleth is unique: the difference between God and humans. As Ps 115:3 (and cf. Ps 115:16) says, "Our God is in heaven; whatever he wills, he does." The emphasis is upon the supremacy of God, not upon his indifference. It is a mistake to characterize Qoheleth's God as a "distant despot" (A. Lauha); rather, this God cannot be manipulated (5:5[6]). See Matt 6:7. The conclusion is in the form of an admonition.

2(3) This verse has the air of a wisdom saying. Loquacity stultifies the speech of the fool, just as weighty concerns cause dreams. In context it serves as another motivation for v 1(2). See also 10:12–14.

3–4(4–5) The transition from verbosity to rash vows is an easy one, and here Qoheleth restates the law of Deut 23:22–24. A. Lauha points out a subtle difference between Deuteronomy and Ecclesiastes. In the former the emphasis is on making vows, rather than in not making them; while in Ecclesiastes it is the other way around: the preference is not to make them lest they be unfulfilled. The same concern for the fulfillment of vows is evidenced in Prov 20:25 and Sir 18:21–23. The perspective would seem to be that of the wisdom teacher rather than of the priest. But the end result is the same. The prohibition is reformulated in typical wisdom style by the "better" saying in v 4.

5(6) The background for this verse is Num 15:22–31 (cf. Lev 4:2ff.), which legislates about sins of inadvertence (שגגה). Qoheleth speaks out against alleging inadvertence as an excuse before the מלאך or priest (certainly not God, as LXX inferred). The precise wrongdoing is not clear, except that it is a sin of the tongue. This could be understood in context as continuing the topic of vows. H. Hertzberg argues that the שגגה cannot be understood as a vow; it refers to commission of a sin, and in this case, a sin in which the tongue is involved. In any case Qoheleth warns against wrongdoing, under the threat of divine wrath and ensuing punishment (v 5b[6b]). The presumption behind vv 4–5(5–6) is that God hears what humans say, and that God reacts. There is no sign of the "deed-consequence" mentality here. In short, God judges and even punishes. Qoheleth never denies that there is divine judgment, even if it remains a mystery to him (cf. 11:5, 9b). It is not a satisfactory answer to claim (with Michel, *Eigenart,* 257) that 5:5(6) is not from Qoheleth but is a later orthodox insertion.

6(7) The text of v 6a seems to be corrupt (see note 6.a.), and perhaps the original reading was similar to 5:2 (NAB deletes these words as a dittography of 5:2). In any translation the line seems flat and repetitious, and it hardly leads into the imperious command in v 6b(7b).

The imperative, "fear God!" comes as a conclusion to Qoheleth's observations about ritual practice (4:17ff.). It is at the heart of his religious attitude (see the discussion above, pp. lxv–lxvi).

7(8) This admonition has no relationship to the previous lines. Qoheleth sees no cause for wonder at injustice, because of the hierarchy of officials, one over another. In itself, this reason is ambiguous. The hierarchy of powers could provide reassurance that one need not be concerned. After all, there is some supervision. The verb, תמה, can be understood in two senses: either "wonder" or "fear." On the other hand, Qoheleth is more probably making an ironic observation about dishonest bureaucracy—that one should not expect anything better from such operators. They look out (שמר, "keep watch") for each other.

It is not likely that this statement should be seen as a defense of Providence, as though the גבהים, "powerful," were a plural of majesty referring to God, who would be able to correct the injustice. Nowhere does Qoheleth narrate an actual divine intervention that would correct injustice, although God remains a judge (3:17; 5:4–5[5–6]).

8(9) Any interpretation of this verse hinges on the translation, on which there is no consensus (see note 8.a.). Hence commentators diverge widely. Our translation may be interpreted thus: in the context of v 7, the mention of the king seems to be a kind of corrective to the situation of villainous officials. His rule is seen as somehow an advantage for the farmers. How this is achieved, whether through stability or a better tax system, etc., is simply not stated (cf. N. Lohfink, *Bib* 62 [1982] 535–43 for an attempt to spell out the situation in the Ptolemaic period).

9(10) A series of reflections on the topic of riches begins at this point. The meaning of v 9a(10a) is clear: the person who is greedy for money will never be satisfied. The more one has, the more one wants. Qoheleth has already anticipated this notion in 1:8 (eyes not satisfied with seeing) and in 4:8 (eyes not satisfied by riches). This is not the same as the frequent warning against the deceitfulness of riches (Prov 11:28; Job 31:24; Ps 49:7). The saying stresses the subjective element, the self-destroying and self-defeating nature of greed. It seems best to understand v 9b(10b) as strictly parallel to v 9a(10a), but see the *Notes.*

E. Podechard prefers to tie this verse with v 10(11) in such a way that the lack of income is caused by those dependents, or others, who will consume it. In any case, there is no moral reproof about insatiable greed in v 10(11); it is an insight into a basic human trait: money will not answer (but see also 10:19).

10(11) Qoheleth now turns to the specific troubles that riches give rise to. They involve the care of several persons dependent on the master. The relation is symbiotic; the master will be dependent upon them also for his riches, since the workers labor for his profit. In addition there is the inevitable attempt on the part of others to partake of these riches (cf. Prov 14:20; 19:4, 6). V 10b(11b) points out that since the actual use of the riches is limited, they are no more than a sop to one's greed, something merely for the eyes to feast on, without any other profit. Just as wisdom begets trouble (1:18), so also do riches, and the next verse continues this theme.

11(12) Qoheleth contrasts favorably the laborer with the rich insomniac. The concerns occasioned by riches (rather than by a full stomach; see note 11.a.), do not allow one to sleep. It is as if the riches that the eyes contemplated so avidly (v 10b[11b]) now keep them from being closed in sleep. Qoheleth had already pointed out a similar result as stemming from one's toil (2:23; cf. 5:2[3]; 8:16). The theme appears also in Sir 31:1–2 (an uncertain text).

12(13) V 12 initiates the discussion of a particular case (יֵשׁ, "there is"), which extends down to v 16(17). Vv 12–15(13–16) are bound together by the repetition of "grievous evil." What is this evil? It is not only that riches have to be guarded by a person and thus give trouble (vv 9–11[10–12]), but the loss of these riches (vv 12b–13a[13b–14a], with the repetition of עֹשֶׁר, "riches," and רָע, "evil") is also a possibility. Qoheleth has just described a bad effect of wealth; it allows the possessor no sleep (v 11[12]). His hoarding, his concerned watching over possessions (v 12[13]), is to his own hurt. When the mainstay of his life disappears, the evil is compounded. The wealthy man is suddenly poor, indeed naked (v 14[15]).

13(14) The loss of riches is further aggravated by the motif of the birth of a son (contrast 2:18–23). A child is born, and the unfortunate man has "nothing to hand" (v 13[14]; note the repetition of מְאוּמָה בְּיָדוֹ in v 14[15]).

14(15) This verse appears to be a description of the destitution of the rich person in terms of the nakedness of a babe (cf. Job 1:21). In this case the subject of the verbs (יָצָא, יָשׁוּב, בָּא) would be the adult; at the end of his life he is as poor as the day he was born, with nothing to show for it all. "Naked" (עָרוֹם, which appears only once) dominates the preceding and the following words, and the final "as he came" resumes the initial "as he came forth from the womb of his mother." One is naked at both birth and death, and the earth is seen to be a mother. The parallelism of womb and earth appears elsewhere: Job 1:21; Ps 139:15; Sir 40:1cd. The theme that "you can't take it with you" is prominent in Ps 49.

R. Gordis argues that the child is the subject in v 14(15). There may be a deliberate ambiguity in v 14a(15a), but it disappears in v 14b(15b) where the subject must be the adult since "toil" is mentioned.

15(16) This verse repeats the formula of v 12(13) ("grievous evil") and also the theme of coming and going of v 14(15). There is no profit for all one's toil (עָמָל ʿāmāl; cf. also v 14b[15b]).

16(17) Although v 16 is textually uncertain (see the *Notes*), the general idea concerning the unhappy life of the rich person is clear. The vaunted possessions are now darkness, sickness, and wrath.

17(18) Vv 17–19(18–20) are reminiscent of the resigned conclusion already drawn in 2:24–26 and 3:12–13, 22. However, in the present context the case of the unfortunate rich person (vv 12–16[13–17]) serves as a contrast with vv 17–19(18–20), in which God enables a person actually to enjoy (ראה טובה, "see good"; cf. 2:1, 24) riches and not to lose them. That this can happen is solely God's doing.

Qoheleth introduces his conclusion rather solemnly (see the *Notes*): good and beautiful appear together. In 3:11 God is said to have made everything beautiful in its time; now what is beautiful is the "portion" (חלק *ḥēleq*, 2:10; 3:22) that comes to a person as a divine gift.

18(19) The key words of v 17(18) (give, portion, toil) are repeated in this affirmation of the divine (although arbitrary) gift.

19(20) The usual explanation of the verse (see note 19.b.) is that the gift of joy keeps a person from thinking much about life and its brevity (cf. v 17[18]). It could be merely an accurate summary of what the divine gift achieves, at least for some people. Obviously this was not true for Qoheleth, whatever his personal "portion" may have been, since he never ceases to think about "the days of his life." Rather than being a "consoling conclusion" (L. di Fonzo), this verse sounds a sardonic note. The implication can be drawn that the God-given joys ultimately distract humans (rather than satisfy them) from the misery of their short lives that must end in death; they fail to keep their minds on the weighty problems that occupy Qoheleth.

But if one translates by "answer" instead of "occupy" (see note 19.b.), then joy is affirmed as a divine gift (as in Eccl 3:13), and a more benign and positive interpretation is possible (so Lohfink, *CBQ* 52 [1990] 625–35, but not D. Michel, *Eigenart*, 190–91). Now humans will not brood (the meaning of זכר in the context?) over the shortness of life, since God "answers" a human being by revealing joy.

6:1 The formula (יש, "there is"; see D. Michel, *Eigenart*, 190–93—how riches can be an evil) that introduces another instance of vanity is reminiscent of 5:12(13), 15(16); cf. also 8:6. While this is a different case, it can be seen as having some continuity with the "evil" described in 5:12–16(13–17). See also 2:18 and 4:8.

2 The first complaint (vv 1–2) is about a rich person who has all his desires fulfilled but is prevented by God from enjoying his riches (the contrast with 5:18[19] is deliberate; "the power to partake of"). No detail is given on how this happens (perhaps sickness or some hindrance). The point would seem to be that it would have been better not to have had the riches rather than to have them and yield them to a stranger without ever partaking of them. The "stranger" cannot be identified; it does not necessarily mean a non-Jew (K. Galling claims that this is a Ptolemaic official in Jerusalem). Whereas in 2:18 Qoheleth complained about inheritance within the family, this verse envisions a harsher situation: the rich person failed to enjoy the wealth, and now a stranger takes over!

3 It is not clear whether vv 3–6 are meant to be taken with the previous case that concluded in v 2 with "evil" (רע), echoing the "evil" (רעה) of v 1. They can be considered an extension or an intensification of vv 1–2 in that the failure to enjoy one's possessions and to fulfill one's desires (cf. נפש in vv 2–3) remains the problem. A large progeny and a long life are typical ideals of divine blessing

(Gen 25:8; 35:9; Job 42:17). But they cannot offset the absence of good things (echoed by "good" in v 6) in this life. Qoheleth's verdict is not simply negative; it is sharpened by a comparison with the stillborn (cf. also 4:3). Even though the stillborn receives no burial (see note 3.c.), it is better off than the long-lived person whose desires remain unsatisfied. The importance of proper burial is obvious from such passages as 2 Kgs 9:33–37; Isa 14:19; Jer 22:18–19.

4–5 Qoheleth heightens his conclusion by elaborating on the awful fate of the stillborn (cf. Job 3:16), but favoring it over that of the long-lived person. He gives no explicit reason why the fate of the stillborn is superior, but one may infer that its affliction is negative in that it is in darkness (contrast 5:16[17]) without vision or knowledge, whereas the affliction of the rich is positive in that they have been thwarted. They have no enjoyment in life, only futile desire. Covering the name with darkness (v 4) is idiomatic for non-existence or death; the name is the person. In 6:10 giving the name means to call into existence, to create (cf. the opening lines of *Enuma Elish*: "Lahmu and Lahamu were brought forth, by name they were called" [*ANET*, 50–51]; see also Isa 40:26; Ps 47:4).

6 The theme of long life is taken up from v 3, and with heightened emphasis; not even the patriarchs before the flood attained such an age. But what good is extension in time "without experiencing good," if one cannot escape the dark "place" to which all must go (cf. the "going" in 3:20; 5:14[15]); 9:10)? The concrete examples of misfortune discussed since 5:12(13) come to an end here, to be followed by some loosely associated sayings.

7 Vv 7–9 seem to have little connection with the preceding, but D. Michel (*Eigenart*, 137) has pointed out that four of the seven occurrences of נפש, "soul," "appetite," in the book are to be found in 6:1–12. The two occurrences in vv 7 and 9 may serve as catch words to give a certain unity. This verse has the ring of a proverbial saying (cf. 1:8). The thought is that the appetite (נפש), although at the root of human activity, is never really satisfied. This saying does not reflect upon the immediate context (but see note 7.a.). It can be taken as loosely connected with v 3 (נפשו, "his desire"; cf. also 6:2b).

8 The first half of the verse repeats a favorite idea: the wise man has no advantage over the fool (cf. 2:14–16). The meaning of v 8b is uncertain (see note 8.b–c.). The parallelism of wise and poor (v 8b) is striking despite the fact that the terms occur (in contrast) in 4:13 and 9:15. The Bible does not usually associate wisdom and poverty. The second half of the verse seems to say that the poor man has no advantage either, despite being able to cope with life. According to the biblical ideal, the poor should be favored by God on whom they rely. But their situation is also futile.

9 Strictly speaking, the comparison in this "better" saying is not between objects but between actions. The object seen/desired is not the issue. Seeing is superior to desire because it implies some kind of possession. Vision is a kind of possession (cf. 11:9), a state of rest in contrast to insatiable desire (cf. 5:9–11[10–12]; 6:3, 7). In 5:10(11) Qoheleth scored the vanity of feasting one's eyes on riches (which also permit no sleep!). Now the point has shifted. The saying concentrates on what is available, what can be "seen." The one who sees something has an object in view, whereas the one who is locked into desire, by definition, has not attained the desired.

As the succeeding comment ("vanity") shows, Qoheleth rejects this "better" saying. He gives no reason, but one may infer that such traditional wisdom fails to take into account the voracious appetite of human beings, already expressed in 1:8 (eye, ear). The full vanity formula (v 9b) appears here for the last time in the book. It is justified by the cases discussed earlier and is applicable to the sayings in vv 7–9.

Explanation

It has already been indicated that several topics are to be found in this section, and most commentators treat them separately. Following the lead of "vanity and chase after wind" (6:9) as a section divider, all have been included here under the term "varia." Division is of relatively little import, provided that the course of Qoheleth's thought is correctly indicated: words before God (Temple presence; 4:17–5:6[5:1–7]), observations on government (5:7–8[8–9]), considerations about wealth (5:9–11[10–12]), a case of a rich person who loses possessions (5:12–16[13–17]), another of Qoheleth's frequent conclusions about enjoyment of life (5:17–19[18–20]). Finally, the uncertainty of riches and the futility of desires (6:1–9) close off the narrative.

This sequence seems reasonable enough but many questions remain. The ending of 4:17(5:1) is not clear. N. Lohfink has proposed that it be taken with 5:5(6), in which Qoheleth condemns a false excuse; it is only by such a ruse that it can be said that fools have no knowledge of doing evil (cf. ZDMGSup 5 [1983] 113–20). D. Michel (*Eigenart*, 254) prefers to see here a lack of knowledge that stems from not knowing the one to whom the sacrifice is offered: the God who cannot be influenced by sacrifice. Fools are therefore ignorant. Their sacrifices are "bad" in that they are senseless. Michel (258) refuses to acknowledge that 4:17(5:1)–5:5(6) reflects typical OT tradition. In any case, the command to fear God 5:6(7) is to be considered as a final comment on the liturgical instructions that have just been given.

The social conditions behind the seemingly cynical observations in 5:6–7(7–8) are not exactly known. Oppression (cf. 4:1–2) has never been lacking in human existence. Although we do not know the details of Qoheleth's period, there must have been many opportunities for exploitation (by way of taxes; see N. Lohfink for details). D. Michel interprets the passage as thoroughly pessimistic. He claims that "profit" is never used in a positive sense through the book, much less in v 7(8). He construes these lines as a quotation that suggests a changed political situation would be an improvement—and this is answered by v 9, denying such a possibility because of the destructive factor of human greed (*Eigenart*, 110).

The ambiguity, if not the harm, of riches (5:9–11[10–12]) is sharpened by the events related in vv 12–16(13–17). D. Michel (*Eigenart*, 187–90) recognizes here a "limit situation" or *Grenzfall*, introduced by שׁ, "there is"; it shows that wealth of itself is no guarantee of happiness. A bad business venture leads to a pauper's death. As indicated in the notes above, N. Lohfink (*VT* 39 [1989] 488–93) builds upon the "evil turn" suffered by the rich person. Many recognize it as some kind of business venture that turned out badly. Lohfink, on the strength of an idiomatic usage of בְּיָד ("in the hand," or "charged to one's account"—see note 13.c.) interprets it of a bank failure of some kind. In that case, v 14(15) does not speak of death. Rather, it compares the change in life style to the helplessness (and lack of possessions) of a newborn babe. Instead of enjoying the riches that had been saved up, that person has to begin again; vv 16–17(17–18) describe the dim prospects for the future. This interpretation is in harmony with the general understanding that commentators have reached about the passage, but it makes the "evil turn" very specific—an unsuccessful bank deal. This specification is possible, but not compelling.

More important is the interpretation of 5:17–19(18–20) proposed by N. Lohfink (*CBQ* 52 [1990] 625–35), following the lead of L. Levy. The first two verses are typical of the conclusions that Qoheleth puts forth many times in the book: eating and drinking are a joyous portion of life, the gift of God. Then v 19(20) reflects upon this divine "generosity." Everything hinges on the meaning of ענה ("to occupy, keep busy"—or "to answer, reveal"; see note 19.b.). Lohfink claims that God reveals self in a positive way by the joys of the heart that are provided to humans. There are three objections to this view. First, a "revelation" of God is an unusual idea for Qoheleth, and especially a revelation through "joy." While this joy is a divine gift, it remains arbitrary and given at divine pleasure. Hence one is to enjoy while one can. Second, "revelation" is a strained extension of the root meaning, "answer." L. Levy proposed this (99, *offenbart*) and referred to Gen 41:16; 1 Sam 9:17, and especially Job 33:12–13 (in 33:13 "speak" seems to mean "reveal," but the word is דבר). Not every response is revelation. Third, the tone of v 19a(20a) suggests that a divine strategy is at work: God uses "joy" to distract humans from the awful reality of their short lives. Of this verse M. Fox remarks, perhaps too strongly: "Pleasure is an anodyne to the pain of consciousness" (*Qohelet*, 73).

A Reflection upon Divine Knowledge and Human Impotence (6:10–12)

Bibliography

Fox, M. V. *Qohelet*. 223–25. **Michel, D.** *Eigenart*. 159–65. **Whitley, C. F.** *Koheleth*. 60–61. **Wright, A. G.** *NJBC*. 31:23, p. 493. ————. *CBQ* 30 (1968) 313–34.

Translation

[10] *That which is has already been given its name; one knows what human beings are,*[a] *and that they cannot contend with one who is stronger.*[b] [11]*For where there are many words, vanity is increased.*[a] *What profit is there for humankind?* [12] *For who knows what is good for human beings during life, the few days of their vain lives that they pass*[a] *through like*[b] *a shadow? For who will tell them what will come after them under the sun?*

Notes

10.a. The text is ambiguous, and uncertainty is reflected in many translations. Contrast NJV ("Whatever happens, it was designated long ago and it was known that it would happen; as for man, he cannot contend with what is stronger than he") with Eü ("Whatever anyone once was, he has previously received his name [i.e., been created; cf. 6:4]; it was known that he will be merely mortal, and that he cannot contend with one who is stronger than he"). Our translation of v 10a is reflected in LXX and Vg. The NJV (see also NEB) divides the verse after הוא, contrary to the punctuation of MT, and understands האדם as a *casus pendens* construed with the final clause. Since the verse has already begun with a *casus pendens* (מה־שהיה), this construal of האדם seems less likely. It is possible to translate with R. Gordis and others: "It is known that man cannot argue . . ."

10.b. תקיף, "strong," is a *hap. leg.*, but the verb תקף occurs in 4:12 (see *Notes* there). According to the qere (cf. also 10:3), this is a predicate adjective. The ketib (שהתקיף) can be read as the definite article with תקיף, or possibly a hipil form of the verb. The qere is to preferred. For further discussion of the entire verse, see Whitley, *Koheleth*, 60–61; Michel, *Eigenart*, 161–63.

11.a. Rendered literally, the MT reads "because there are many words that increase vanity."

12.a. ויעשם is in effect equivalent to a relative clause. In NAB God is understood to be the subject, making the days go by like a shadow that passes swiftly. If a mortal is the subject (as unsubstantial as a shadow), the meaning of the verb is "spend, pass" (so NRSV; cf. M. Fox; Whitley, *Kohelet*, 61). The verb עשה is "probably" used in Ruth 2:19 with this meaning (R. Gordis), and it occurs in post-biblical Hebrew. It has a Greek equivalent in ποιεῖν; cf. Acts 15:33; 20:3; Tob 10:7. One can also compare *facere dies* in classical Latin (cf. E. Podechard, 51).

12.b. כצל is to be retained against LXX, which has "in" instead of "as." H. Hertzberg and A. Bea favor the LXX, finding a contrast between "shadow" and "under the sun" in v 12b. See 8:13.

Form/Structure/Setting

Most commentators recognize this section as a unit, and that there is a natural break after the verdict of "vanity" in 6:9. In fact, the Masoretes recognized 6:10 as the beginning of the second half of the book. D. Michel (*Eigenart*, 158–65) admits that most recognize 6:10–12 as a unit (against O. Loretz, *Qohelet*, 230–31, n. 63), but he attempts to show that it belongs with 6:1–9. Thus, Qoheleth's firm conviction is that we do not know what human beings are, in opposition to the view that claims this will be known after death (v 10). Qoheleth characterizes such hopeful thinking as mere words (v 11) and dismisses the issue (v 12) with the statement about human ignorance concerning the (eschatological) future. Michel's interpretation is very subtle, because of his precarious identification of Qoheleth's opponents as apocalypticists who argue for a future life. The book does not offer enough evidence about such a confrontation concerning the next life (not even in 3:21).

A. G. Wright (*NJBC* 31:3, p. 489; *CBQ* 30 [1968] 313–34) has pointed out that the 111 verses (1:1–6:9) are the sum of 3x37 (37 is the numerical equivalent of הבל, "vanity"). This signal was already given in the *threefold* repetition of הבל in the inclusions (1:2 and 12:8). Therefore one may regard 6:10 as the beginning of a new section, the second half of the book. Since 7:1 clearly begins a series of sayings, 6:10–12 should be considered as the introduction to the second half. He also points out the *inclusio* in vv 10, 12 (נודע/יודע); see *CBQ* 30 [1968] 329–30.

Comment

10 According to our translation (see the *Notes*), Qoheleth reaches back to an earlier idea (1:9–10; 3:15), the determination of events that keep repeating themselves. To "give the name" to a thing is to make it exist (see *Comment* on 6:4), and hence dependent. God gave the name "sky" to the firmament he created to separate the waters one from another (Gen 1:8, 10). The emphasis is on the divine sovereignty over all that has been created.

L. Alonso Schökel and G. Wildeboer recognize a deliberate ambiguity in the mention of אדם, "man." Man's name is Adam, which means "of the earth." By this name he is known and understood; hence he is unable to contend with the God who created (or named) him, as v 10b asserts. One catches the ambiguity by a slightly different translation: "what has existed has a name, and we know it: it is Adam, and he cannot contend with one who is mightier than he."

Qoheleth moves on to assert the impotence of human beings before God. Many commentators (e.g., K. Galling, A. Lauha) see a possible reference to Job's stormy contention with the Almighty. This may also be suggested by the reference to wordiness in v 11.

11 The striking alliteration (*dĕbārîm harbeh marbîm hebel*) underlines the vanity of mere words (cf. 1:8; 5:2, 6; 10:12–14). In the present context the words refer to questioning the divine work. Whether or not this is an allusion to Job's wordy harangue with the Almighty, the futility is clear; there is no profit (יתרון *yitrôn*; cf. 1:3; 3:9). This conclusion flows from the determinism of events and from the human impotence mentioned in v 10.

12 The rhetorical question ("who knows?") expresses an issue that crisscrosses through the book (2:3; cf. the "nothing better" sayings of 2:24; 3:12, 22; etc.). It is also an introduction to the futile attempt to find out what is good (chaps. 7–8) or to know what lies ahead (chaps. 9–10). The failure of such an effort is rooted in human weakness (v 10), but also in the transient character of human existence, which is compared to a mere shadow (cf. Pss 39:7; 102:12; Job 8:9; 14:2) and qualified as "limited" or "numbered" (cf. 2:3; 5:17). Both the opaqueness and the transient character of the shadow are the point of comparison.

Human ignorance of the future has already been mentioned in 3:22 and will be raised again (10:14). Qoheleth does not have in mind the mystery of "life after death," but rather how things will turn out while one still lives on earth. He is speaking of what will come "under the sun." The uncertainty of life tomorrow is as bad, if not worse, than the uncertainty of "life" after death (cf. 3:21–22), which is better described as lifeless (cf. 9:10).

Explanation

As an introduction, these verses announce themes that are to come. The reflection begins with the determinism that has already been affirmed in 1:9, 15; 3:15. V 12 moves into the basic inability of humans to find out what is good for them (7:1–8:17) and to know the future (9:1–11:5). Key phrases are repeated in each of these two sections: "not find out/who can find out?" (7:14, 24, 29; 8:17) and "do not know/no knowledge" (9:5, 10, 12; 10:15; 11:6). Like the phrase "vanity and a chase after wind" in the first half of the book, these serve to indicate section endings (A. Wright, *CBQ* 30 [1968] 323–24).

M. Fox has pointed out the repetition of words and ideas in vv 10a and 12b. Whatever happens is a result of God's agency. Humans cannot even know what this is, much less change it. Humans in a particular way are the subject of his reflection; they are determined in their existence by God, and they cannot contend with the divinity. That is why their efforts amount only to words—words that are, as usual, ineffectual (see 5:2, 6; 10:12–13).

V 12 repeats a key affirmation of Qoheleth. Humans do not know what is good (this will be repeated in various ways several times) because they do not know how things will turn out (v 11b; also 3:22b). It will be recalled that the search for what is good was indicated already in 2:3. Now the "good" serves as a bridge to what follows in chap. 7.

Past and Present Wisdom   (7:1–14)

Bibliography

Ellermeier, F. *Qohelet I/1.* 73–75, 104–11, 137. **Fox, M. V.** *Qohelet.* 101–17. **Gelio, R.** "Osservazioni critiche sul *māšāl* di Qoh. 7, 5–7." *Lat* 54 (1988) 1–15. **Kugel, J. L.** "Qohelet and Money." *CBQ* 51 (1989) 32–49. **Michel, D.** *Eigenart.* 126–37, 101–5. ————. "Qoheletprobleme: Überlegungen zu Qoh 8:2–9 und 7:11–14." *TV* 15 (1979/80) 81–103 (revised in *Eigenart.* 84–105). **Murphy, R. E.** "A Form-critical Consideration of Ecclesiastes VII." SBLASP 1. Ed. G. MacRae. Missoula, MT: Scholars Press, 1974. 77–85. ————. "On Translating Ecclesiastes." *CBQ* 53 (1991) 571–79. **Osborn, N. D.** "A Guide for Balanced Living: An Exegetical Study of Ecclesiastes 7:1–14." *BT* 21 (1970) 185–96. **Piotti, F.** "Osservazioni su alcuni problemi esegetici nel libro dell'Ecclesiaste (studio II): il canto degli stolti (Qoh. 7,5)." *BeO* 21 (1979) 129–40.

Translation

1. *Better is a good name than good ointment;*
   and the day of death, than the day of one's birth.[a]
2. *Better to go to a house of mourning*
   than to a house of feasting,
   For that is the end of every person,
   and let the living take it to heart.
3. *Better is vexation than laughter,*
   for despite a sad face the heart can be joyful.[a]
4. *The heart of the wise is in a house of mourning,*
   but the heart of fools is in a house of joy.
5. *Better to heed the reproof of the wise*
   than to hear the song of fools.
6. *For like the sound of thistles under a pot*
   is the laughter of fools.[a]
   This also is vanity,[b]
7.   *for oppression can make fools of the wise*
   and a bribe[a] *corrupt*[b] *the heart.*[c]
8. *Better is the end of a thing*[a] *than its beginning;*
   better is a patient spirit than a proud spirit.
9. *Do not be hasty in spirit to get angry,*
   for anger lodges in a fool's bosom.
10. *Do not say, "How is it that the former days are better than these?"*
    for it is not out of wisdom that you ask about this.
11. *Wisdom is as good as an inheritance,*[a]
    and profitable[b] *to those who live.*
12. *For the protection of wisdom is (as) the protection of money,*[a]
    and the advantage of knowledge[b] *is that wisdom keeps its owner*[c] *alive.*
13. *Consider the work*[a] *of God. For who can make straight what he has made crooked?*
14a. *On a good day enjoy the good, and on an evil day, consider: God made them both so that*[b] *no one may find fault with him.*[c]

Notes

1.a. The pronominal suffix in הוֹלְדוֹ is to be understood in an indefinite sense; there is no obvious antecedent.

3.a. MT has, literally, "in evil of face, the heart is (may be) good." Translations, and hence interpretations (see the *Comment*), vary. רַע with פָּנִים means sadness or discomfort in Gen 40:7 and see Neh 2:2–3. יִיטַב לֵב connotes joy and contentment in Ruth 3:7; Judg 19:6, 9; 1 Kgs 21:7. Note the alliteration in v 3a: כַּעַס/שֹׂחַק.

6.a. There is a striking alliteration in the comparison to thorns, כְּקוֹל הַסִּירִים תַּחַת הַסִּיר, which continues the שִׁיר, "song," of fools in v 5.

6.b. According to J. Muilenburg (*BASOR* 135 [1954] 26–27) the fragment from Qumran (4QQoh[a]) has a lacuna at this point (after הֶבֶל). If this is not an erasure ("the safest assumption" declares Muilenburg), it could possibly indicate an omission of several words. The transition from v 6 to v 7 has long been considered a problem. F. Delitzsch called it a hiatus and filled it in with Prov 16:8, "Better a little with justice than a large income with injustice." For further discussion see D. Michel, *Eigenart*, 130–32.

7.a. The Greek tradition (Aq, Theod) and Vg interpreted מַתָּנָה as "strength" (εὐτονία; *robur*); the sense would be that oppression destroys the strength of the heart (favored by C. Whitley, *Koheleth*, 62–63). It is preferable to retain the Masoretic "gift," or "bribe."

7.b. There is no reason to modify the וִיאַבֵּד of MT in the direction of וִיעַוֶּה, "twist," of 4QQoh[a] (*BASOR* 135 [1954] 27).

7.c. There are grammatical irregularities in v 7b: אֵת before the indefinite לֵב; cf. GKC §117C and note אֶת־נִרְדָּף in 3:15; the feminine subject with a masculine verb is not unknown (GKC §145o).

8.a. Since דָּבָר can mean either "word" or "thing," translations will vary. The broader meaning seems more appropriate here (pace A. Lauha, who prefers "word" and sees this as referring to the thought of 6:10–11, that it is better to keep quiet before God than criticize the divine plan).

11.a. The preposition עִם can be understood in a comparative sense, "as good as"; cf. 2:16; Job 9:26. An alternative translation would be "wisdom with an inheritance is good" (reflected in LXX, Vg, NAB).

11.b. It is possible that וְיֹתֵר (cf. 12:12) conveys a comparative sense, "and even better" (NJV, EÜ).

12.a. The MT can perhaps be explained by the idiomatic *beth essentiae* (GKC §119i): wisdom is protection, money is protection. NJV supplies "to be": "to be in the shelter of wisdom is to be also in the shelter of money." The ancient versions (Sym, Syr, Vg) make explicit this comparison between wisdom and money, and may have read כְּצֵל . . . כְּצֵל. However, LXX read "in the shadow" for the first instance. Although the textual evidence is ambiguous, some kind of comparison between wisdom and money seems to be intended. For various construals of vv 11–12, see J. L. Kugel, *CBQ* 51 (1989) 40–44.

12.b. The accentuation of MT correctly separates "knowledge" (דַּעַת, without the article) from "wisdom" (with the article), although LXX, Syr, and Vg join them.

12.c. בְּעָלֶיהָ is plural (cf. 5:10), but the meaning is singular (GKC §124i).

13.a. LXX, Sym, Vg, and Jerome have the plural for the singular, מַעֲשֵׂה; the singular appears also in 3:11, 8:17, and 11:5.

14.a. There is striking alliteration in v 14a.

14.b. עַל דִּבְרַת שֶׁ is a *hap. leg.* here, as a conjunction (GKC §165b); cf. 3:8, 8:2, where עַל דִּבְרַת is a preposition.

14.c. Although most translations render the final words of v 14 in the style of the RSV, "may not find out anything that will be after him," it is possible to recognize an idiom in "find after." In Syriac *ʾeškaḥ bātar* means "to find an occasion of complaint against," and this meaning is reflected in Sym and Vg, as well as in NAB, NJV, NEB (alternate reading). See the discussion in Whitley, *Koheleth*, 66, with credit to Burkitt and Driver.

Form/Structure/Setting

This chapter, along with the later ones that feature disparate sayings, are a test case for commentators and their construal of this book. Suddenly a host of sayings appears, in contrast to the closely knit reflections and experiences that have characterized the work thus far. Are these relatively disparate sayings, more or less loosely united in the style of many sayings in the Book of Proverbs (e.g., chaps. 10–14), or are they to be grouped in units? Even in the case of Proverbs several connections can be forged on the level of catch words. Recent studies (O. Plöger, *Sprüche Salomos (Proverbia)*, BKAT 17 [Neukirchen-Vluyn: Neukirchener, 1984]; R. C. van Leeuwen, *Context and Meaning in Proverbs 25–27*, SBLDS 96 [Atlanta: Scholars Press, 1988]) have established contexts within chapters that illustrate subtle connections. It is clear that Prov 1–9 contain lengthy unified poems, but the general view of chaps. 10ff. is that there is little consecutive development of thought from one chapter to another, and even from one verse to another. Chaps. 7 and 10 of Ecclesiastes present a similar challenge. It will be quite apparent that the sayings are more tightly unified than the aphorisms in Proverbs. But the basic question remains: what is the nature of the relationship between the various sayings in these chapters?

The question in 6:12, "who knows what is good?" is a perfect preparation for the succession of sayings in 7:1–14, which are concerned with the "good." These display an intricate network of repetitions, catch words, and word plays. The most prominent catch word is טוב, "good"/"better," which appears fifteen times in the chapter, eight times in vv 1–12. But there are also other significant repetitions: כעס, "vexation," vv 3, 9; לב, "heart," vv 2, 3, 4 twice, 7; בית אבל, "house of mourning," vv 2, 4; כסיל, "fool," vv 4–6; חכם, "wise," vv 4, 5, 7, 10–12; רוח, "spirit," vv 8–9, with a rhymed ending in יְנוּחַ. There may be an inclusion with the appearance of יום, "day," and טוב, "good," in both vv 1 and 14. The most famous play on words is שׁם/שׁמן in v 1. Another instance is in v 6a: הסירים, "thorns," הסיר, "pot," and הכסיל, "fool." All this suggests that we are not dealing with a haphazard collection but with a sophisticated style that has worked over several sayings and tied them together. However, there is little agreement on the interpretation of this collection.

Older commentators (C. Siegfried, E. Podechard) were prone to regard many of the sayings as interpolations from various hands. Others have treated them as more or less disparate (a "rather random assortment of sayings," so Whybray, 118 on v 13). Surveys of several commentators have been arranged in a table by F. Ellermeier (*Qohelet* I/1, 137). He gives his own analysis with results on pp. 73–75: four sayings, two admonitions, two "broken" reflections, in 7:1–14, with reflections in 7:14–8:1. More recent studies display little agreement. M. Fox writes concerning 7:1–12 that Qoheleth "now may be speaking somewhat tongue-in-cheek, but he is still serious about the advice itself" (*Qohelet*, 226–27). A. Wright (NJBC 31:25, p. 493) judges that vv 1–6 portray a "grim" view of life, the validity of which is cancelled by the "vanity" verdict in v 6b. Moreover the sayings in vv 7–12 challenge the contents of vv 1–6. In similar fashion, D. Michel (*Eigenart*, 126–37) considers the pessimism of 7:1–6a as the object of Qoheleth's criticism in vv 7–10.

The approach taken here is derived mainly from the analysis of N. Lohfink: that Qoheleth is dialoguing with traditional wisdom, and modifying it. The dialogue with wisdom continues through chaps. 7–8. The recognition of this fact is generally in harmony with the division into units marked by the endings ("not find out/who can find out?") seen by A. Wright at 7:14, 24, 29 and 8:17 (*CBQ* 30 [1968] 330–31).

The movement within chap. 7 can be indicated as follows:

1. 7:1a, a good name—7:1b–4, but only after one has died!
2. 7:5–6, listen to the wise, not to the foolish—7:7, but this is vanity, since the wise also fail.
3. 7:8–9, the wisdom ideal is one of self-control and caution—7:10, but this leads to an (unwise) conservative praise of the past.
4. 7:11–12, the great value of wisdom—7:13, 14, but to the bewilderment of all, God's sovereign will is behind good and evil, and thus human beings are kept off balance.
5. Qoheleth makes an observation about the failure of the traditional theory of retribution (v 15). Ironically, this leads to conflicting advice (vv 16–17)—in the face of which one's attitude can only be the fear of God (v 18).
6. 7:19, the power of wisdom—7:20–22, but there is no one who is just (=wise), as is illustrated by the admonition in 21–22 (do not heed others who curse you, for you do the same).
7. 7:23–24, wisdom is unattainable. Here Qoheleth admits that he has failed to find wisdom.
8. 7:25–29, at least Qoheleth has "found" something: a conclusion about human beings (v 29).

Comment

1 The chiastic alliteration in v 1a is striking: טוב שם משמן טוב. A good name, or reputation, is treasured in biblical mentality (Prov 10:7; 22:1), even though Qoheleth does not find it viable, since no one remembers (1:11; 2:16). The point of the comparison to the precious ointment is not immediately obvious; how is reputation comparable to perfume? The שמן, "ointment," could have been chosen mainly for the play on the word שם, "name." Yet it can stand for something positive. In Cant 1:3, the comparison of the name to perfume indicates the delights of the person: "your name spoken is a spreading perfume" (without paronomasia). V 1 does not define but compares: a good reputation is better even than precious ointment. The alliteration and play on words suggest that v 1a was, or became, a popular saying. This proverb may have been originally directed to console a person who could not afford expensive perfume and ointments for burial but possessed a greater treasure in his reputation.

How does v 1b relate to v 1a? A. Lauha thinks that this is another instance of Qoheleth's pessimistic preference for death over life (4:2; 6:3). Similarly F. Delitzsch. But the parallelism between the two lines is deceptive; 1b is intended to moderate the meaning of 1a: only with death does the reality of a good reputation exist (cf. Sir 11:28, "Call no one happy before death; by how he ends a person is known"). At birth one has a whole life ahead, which may or may not yield a good reputation. As always with Qoheleth, life must be looked at from the point of view of death. Both A. Barucq and N. Lohfink recognize v 1b as Qoheleth's own thought, in contrast to v 1a. The satirical edge is thus preserved: it is all very well to speak of a good reputation, but not before death! As Lohfink remarks, the pleasant proverb of v 1a is pushed *ad absurdum* by the ironic comments that follow in vv 1b–4.

2 The dour and ironic note continues. The "house of mourning" is one that has experienced a death. The "house of feasting" suggests a joyous occasion, such as birth or marriage. Again, death remains the horizon of human existence and is never to be left out of human calculation, especially where a good reputation (v 1) is concerned.

3 An obscure verse in itself and in context. In 1:18 כעס, "vexation," "sorrow," was associated with wisdom, and laughter was termed madness in 2:2. One can see that v 3a suits Qoheleth's thought. The present context deals with the grimness of life (cf. the "house of mourning" in v 2a). But v 3b is difficult: how does the sad face relate to the joyful heart? In itself it might mean that appearances are deceiving (R. N. Whybray; cf. Prov 14:13, "Even in laughter the heart may be sad, and the end of joy may be sorrow"). Or paradoxically sorrow and its experience can bring some benefit; one can be better off because of misfortune. A sad face can conceal true joy. Sorrow is certainly better than laughter, which could be merely mindless frivolity (as in the house of feasting in v 2). Like v 2 this verse appears to temper the optimism of v 1a, for it points out the vexations that affect human life. W. Zimmerli interprets the line to mean that vexation is a state more honest to the real-life situation. R. Gordis thinks it is an observation that "a sad face reflects a wise mind." Others (cf. M. Fox) correlate this verse with v 5, in the sense that a rebuke is better than hollow joy. Interpretation of this verse and others depends on the construal of the entire chapter.

4 The "better" saying of v 2a is now expressed in the wise/foolish contrast. "Heart" is a catch word uniting vv 3–4. The two "houses" symbolize the deadly serious and the flippant sides of human purpose.

5 In the tradition, reproof is honored as a source of wisdom (Prov 12:1, "Whoever loves correction loves knowledge; but the one who hates reproof is stupid"; see also 13:1, 18; 17:10). But v 5 does not exalt the value of reproof as much as it ridicules the "song of fools." Thus it picks up the theme of frivolity expressed in v 4a ("house of joy").

6 The reason given for the "better" saying of v 5 also concentrates on fools. Their "song" (שיר *šîr,* v 5) is like the crackling of thistles (סירים *sîrîm*) under a pot (סיר *sîr*). Like thorns used for fuel, they generate more noise than heat. The "laughter of fools" matches their "heart" or character (v 4). (See F. Piotti, *BeO* 21 [1979] 129–40).

Vv 5–6 express the traditional view of the superiority of wisdom over folly. But just as he cited a similar opinion in 2:13–14, only to modify it in 2:15–17, so now Qoheleth tags these verses as vanity, because he can point to the weakness of the wise in v 7: even the wisdom of the wise can be perverted. This understanding of the text is also reflected in NJV, which associated the הבל, "vanity," phrase (v 6b) with v 7 and makes sense of the כי with which it begins: "But that too is illusory; for cheating may rob the wise man of reason. . . ." This seems to be the correct understanding of vv 5–7, and one is spared the dislocations of the text proposed by commentators.

7 The MT is to be followed here (see note 7.a.). "Oppression" can be understood as an abuse of power by the wise, but it refers rather to a situation in which they are victims of extortion. The general sense is that even the wise person can fail—through personal oppression or by means of a bribe. Bribery is a phenomenon both acknowledged (Prov 17:8) and warned against (Prov 15:27) in the wisdom tradition, and condemned in the Law (Exod 23:8; Deut 16:19). Here it is a temptation that can overcome even the wise. This is to be seen as balancing against the previous two verses, which placed the wise above the foolish; one should not always be optimistic about the effects of wisdom.

8 Many commentators (e.g., W. Zimmerli, R. Gordis) consider vv 8–10 as a unit in which Qoheleth offers advice that is very much like traditional wisdom. It is certainly true that vv 8–9 reflect such wisdom.

Taken independently, v 8a could be understood as a comment on vv 1–2. But paired with v 8b, it suggests a venerable wisdom ideal. The sage is better off for being at the end than at the beginning. He is not subject to overconfidence or pride (v 8b); he *knows*, for experience has taught him. The patient spirit is the opposite of the "short of spirit" (Prov 14:20), who lacks self-control (cf. Prov 25:28). The impatient and proud cannot wait for the final result; they act precipitously; cf. 1 Kgs 20:11. Instead, the wise are careful and cautious. The metaphors with רוּחַ, "spirit," are determined by extension in space. If רוּחַ is stretched out, it is patient; if stretched high, it is proud (cf. Prov 14:29, "short of spirit"; 16:5, "high of heart").

9 The "better" saying of v 8 fits with the admonition against anger in v 9, which has its counterparts in Prov 14:27 and 18:18. The nuance of כעס, "anger," is that of Prov 12:16 and 27:3 (wrath), whereas in 7:3 the parallelism suggests sorrow (also in 1:18; 2:23).

10 Is Qoheleth merely dispensing advice here—an admonition against anyone being a *laudator temporis acti* ("a praiser of times past," as Horace described it in *De Arte Poetica*, 173)? Accordingly, one might recognize that there are good and bad in every age (cf. 7:14), and live in the present, not the past. But it is better to see here, with N. Lohfink, a criticism of the traditional wisdom of vv 8–9. Qoheleth seems to be criticizing the ideal of the patient sage, who indeed cultivated the teaching of the past.

That ideal had a significant weakness. The tradition of the past, however valuable, could be a dead weight for a sage. Should a sage hold up the past over the present then (as v 8a puts it) better the end than the beginning. If the lessons of the past are fixed forever, there is no reason even to think, and Qoheleth would be dialoguing with the past in vain. V 8a corresponds to what is rejected in v 10a. One who is satisfied with the end of a thing is not one who is ready to begin; at the end of life the patient and cautious look back at the "good old days" as better (the risks are over). But it is not from *true* wisdom (v 10b) that one champions the past over the present. In fact, times are not getting worse. This idea is in harmony with what has been said about nothing new under the sun (1:9–11; 3:15 6:10); the past and present merge.

11–12 The sayings reflect traditional wisdom values. The point is not to set wisdom on the same plane with material possessions. These riches (vv 11a, 12a) are used to enhance the value of wisdom. Wisdom is consistently pegged higher than gold or silver in the tradition (Prov 3:14; 8:19; 16:16). The profit (יתר *yōtēr*, יתרון *yitrôn*, vv 11b, 12b) is *life*. Both wisdom (Prov 31:10–31) and money (Prov 13:8) keep their owner alive, although no one can escape death. This view might justify the translation "wisdom is good with an inheritance" in 11a; see note 11.a.

The thrust of the sayings is to praise wisdom rather than allow the *double entendre* suggested by Zimmerli: that ultimately wisdom is as undependable as money (v 12a).

13 Qoheleth is not merely repeating an old saw similar to 1:15 or 3:11–14 about the divine work. He is demolishing the security that was claimed for wisdom in vv 11–12. He invites the reader to "consider" (vv 13, 14), and he poses the problem of the incalculable work of God (מעשה, v 13; עשׂה אלהים, v 14). It can even be said that the main point of the book concerns "the work of God" (3:11; 8:17; 11:5)—so totally different that humans cannot understand or affect it (v 13b; 1:15).

14 Qoheleth shares the biblical belief that both good and evil are God's doing. One is to enjoy the good when it comes (when God "gives it"; cf., e.g., 2:24–26). The uncertain alternation between good and bad days is an issue for human reflection ("consider"). If everything were good or everything bad, there would be no room for the consideration that is offered. The connection between the experience of good and evil and human ignorance of the future (so the usual translation; see the *Notes*) is not clear. God has made both the good and the evil day to keep humans from finding out the future? That has little, if any, meaning. Ignorance of the future was already recognized in 3:22 and 6:12 as belonging to the human condition. Perhaps in v 14 it means that humans know not whether their portion will be good or bad, but the point is expressed very obscurely. The alternative translation ("so that no one can find fault with him"; see note 14.c.) yields better sense. It suits the style of Qoheleth's understanding of a God who is beyond human calculation. It is close to the biblical thought underlying Job 2:10 (if good, why not evil?). This understanding of God takes the existence of evil as well as good for granted. There may be a certain implicit irony here: as if God were keeping human beings off balance by an erratic performance.

Explanation

Chap. 7 is perhaps the most difficult chapter in a difficult book. Among other reasons, it is difficult because the words and sayings seems to be clear—but the way Qoheleth is using them is another matter. As indicated earlier (in *Form/Structure/Setting*), the fundamental decision is whether one should group these sayings as absolutes or construe them as a form of dialogue that Qoheleth has mounted. It is remarkable that most commentaries recognize 7:1–14 as a unit. But within these verses many explanations vie with one another. Not even those who find "dialogue" in the chapter agree. Thus, D. Michel argues that Qoheleth cannot be proposing the pessimism of 7:1–6 as something "good" for humans. These verses would be in contradiction with the several other passages concerning eating and drinking and joy. Therefore they must be quotations of views that Qoheleth rejects with the verdict of "vanity" in v 6b. His genuine opinion is to be gathered from vv 7–10, in which he is arguing against vv 1–6. According to Michel, Qoheleth is taking issue with a wisdom allied to the rising apocalypticism of his era, which exalted the past over the present time (7:10).

Commentators have made more of 7:14a than of 7:14b. H. Ranston (*Ecclesiastes and the Early Greek Wisdom Literature* [London: 1925] 18) compares 7:14 with some passages of Theognis, but he fails to note the most pertinent lines (355–360) pointed out by R. Braun (*Kohelet*, 120): "Be courageous in distress, O Kyrnos, after the good fortune you have enjoyed, since fate (μοῖρα) is giving you a share also in this. You have received the bad after the good, so try not to get out of this with prayer to the gods for help. Do not make a show of your trouble, O Kyrnos, or you will find few people to help you in your distress." (See the text and translation in J. Carrière, *Théognis* [Paris: Société d'édition "les belles lettres," 1975] 78–79.) However, the words of Theognis, and of others cited by R. Braun, do not have the nuance of 7:14; they tend to stoicism rather than to mystery. For a critique of Ranston, see K. Galling, "Stand und Aufgabe der Kohelet-Forschung," *TRu* 6 (1934) 355–73, esp. 361–66.

Wisdom Relative to Justice and Wickedness (7:15–24)

Bibliography

Brindle, W. A. "Righteousness and Wickedness in Ecclesiastes 7:15–18." *AUSS* 23 (1955) 243–57. **Fox, M. V.** *Qohelet.* 233–38. ———— and **Porten, B.** "Unsought Discoveries: Qohelet 7:23–8:1a." *HS* 19 (1978) 26–38. **Michel, D.** *Eigenart.* 260–61. **Loader, J. A.** *Polar Structures in the Book of Qohelet.* BZAW 152. Berlin: de Gruyter, 1979. 46–50. **Strange, M.** "The Question of Moderation in Ecclesiastes 7:15–18." Diss., Catholic University, 1969. **Whybray, R. N.** "Qoheleth the Immoralist? (Qoh 7:16–17)." In *IW.* 191–204.

Translation

[15]*I have seen everything*[a] *in my vain days: a just person who perishes despite*[b] *his justice, and an evil person who lives long despite his evil.* [16]*Do not be overly just or be wise*[a] *to excess! Why should you be ruined?*[b] [17]*Do not be overly evil and do not be a fool! Why should you die before your time?* [18]*It is good for you to hold on to this, and not let go of that. But the one who fears God will come through with respect to both.*[a]

[19] *Wisdom is stronger*[a] *for*[b] *the wise,*
      than ten officials who are in a city.
[20] *Still,*[a] *no one on earth is so just*
      as to do good and never sin.
[21] *To all the words that are spoken,*[a]
      pay no attention,
      lest[b] *you hear your servant cursing you.*
[22] *For you know*[a] *in your heart*
      that many times you also have cursed others.

[23]*All this*[a] *I tested with wisdom. I said, "I will become wise." But it was beyond me.* [24]*What happens*[a] *is distant and very deep.*[b] *Who can find it out?*

Notes

15.a. Literally "all"; כל can indicate "both" when the context calls for it; cf., e.g., 2:14; 3:19–20.

15.b. Literally, *beth* would mean "in," but it is also used in the sense of "in spite of" (cf. Deut 1:32).

16.a. תתחכם is sometimes given the nuance of falsity ("play the wise man"), as in Ezek 13:17 the hitpael of נבא means "to play the prophet." But the context seems to call for honest exertion in wisdom as in justice. The alternatives in v 17 are to be taken as serious efforts, and not just pretense.

16.b. The root of the verb is שׁמם, and the *taw* of the hitpolel has been assimilated into the first letter (GKC §54c). The root meaning seems to be "desolate," but the precise nuance here is difficult to determine. The LXX, Syr, and Jerome suggest a reaction to desolation: "be numb, shocked." Modern versions translate "destroy" (NRSV, NIV), "ruin" (NAB), but also in a subjective sense "dumbfounded" (NJV and M. V. Fox). See the discussion by Whybray, *IW*, 197–99.

18.a. The translations of the final three words are varied and all of them uncertain. Literally, it seems to say that the God-fearer "will go out with respect to all of them" (יצא את כלם), but this has no meaning. את can be explained as designating an accusative of specification (Joüon §125j), and "all" can be understood as "both," as in v 15. The meaning of יצא is the stumbling block. "Go out" has been interpreted as "escape" (e.g., Hertzberg, Zimmerli, Michel, *Qohelet*, 151), "win through" (so NAB, and REV is similar: "succeed"). Gordis has recourse to a Mishnaic idiom, יצא ידי חובה, meaning "fulfill one's duty" (cf. NJV, "will do his duty"; similarly M. V. Fox). For further discussion, see Whitley, *Koheleth*, 66–67; Whybray, *IW*, 200–201.

19.a. There is question as to how עזז is used here, transitively or intransitively. Both are possible (contra Whitley, *Koheleth*, 67). 4QQoh[a] reads תעזור, "help," and this is supported by LXX (βοηθήσει), but MT has the *lectio difficilor*.

19.b. The *lamedh* before חכם can be taken as a dative of respect.

20.a. The translation of כי depends upon the relationship of vv 20–22 to v 19. It is probably deictic; cf. D. Michel, *Eigenart*, 289–89. The phraseology at the beginning of the verse recalls 1 Kgs 8:46.

21.a. גם serves to join v 21 to the preceding; cf. also v 22, כי גם.

21.b. אשר לא is equivalent to פן (GKC §65b), and this is adopted by most translations. However, Eü takes it as causal *(denn niemals)*.

22.a. ידע of MT is to be preferred to ירע, "treat badly," reflected in the ancient versions.

23.a. זו refers back to the wisdom sayings in 7:1–22. It is joined with בחכמה; cf. GKC §119l.

24.a. The MT is to be preferred to משהיה, "than what is," which is reflected in several ancient versions.

24.b. The repetition of עמק is in effect a superlative; cf. GKC §133k.

Form/Structure/Setting

This short section is delimited by the recurrent phrase in v 24, "who can find." The form is not easy to determine, because of the various questions and admonitions. Ellermeier (*Qohelet I*, 74) regards vv 15–22 as a reflection that is composed of several individual pieces: observation, rhetorical questions that are joined to admonitions (vv 16–17), and advice (v 18). The bond between vv 15–18 and 19–22 is very loose, and v 19 has been judged by many (e.g., M. Fox) to be out of place and to be read after 7:12. V 19 is a wisdom saying that is followed by a contrast (v 20) and an admonition with the motive provided (vv 21–22).

The section has a natural closure in Qoheleth's failure to attain wisdom (vv 21–22). Most commentaries recognize as units either 7:15–24 or 7:15–22. It will be seen that vv 23–24 can easily be considered a transition to the search for wisdom mentioned in v 25. A. Lauha regards these verses as an individual, separate unit. Many others include them with vv 25ff.; thus M. Fox, who claims that "the close continuity of thought and the pattern formed by the BQŠ-MSʾ word-pair exclude a division at v 24 or 25" (*HS* 19 [1978] 26). However, the word-pair appears in vv 25ff., not in vv 23–24; only at the end of v 24 does מצא appear, where it serves as a transition to what follows.

Comment

15 The "evil day" of v 14 is reflected in the flat statement that the just perish while the wicked live heartily. This is a fact and indeed an example of what God has made crooked (7:13). The contradiction of the traditional theory of retribution provides the context for the advice that follows in vv 16–18: what is one to do?

16 The intent of the admonitions in vv 16–17 is elusive, and differing interpretations have been given. The concepts of being overly just or overly wicked are not clearly defined in themselves. One may begin with the premise that Qoheleth could hardly warn against being overly just in the sense of true virtue or justice. Excessive justice cannot be meant in a sinful way. That would be contrary to the general biblical tradition (e.g., Deut 16:20), and to his own thought in 7:20 where he states that justice is an unattainable ideal. Moreover, he joins justice and wisdom—a common equation in the wisdom tradition since the wise person is the just person. Just as wisdom is unattainable (7:23–24), so also is justice; both are impossible ideals. Since no one is truly just (v 20), and since the just derive no profit from their justice, v 16 must be a bitter and ironic admonition, to which Qoheleth appends the threat of ruin (שׁמם, possibly a state of numbness; see note 16.b.). This threat is simply following the facts of life that he has recorded in v 15: the just perish despite their justice. And if one is "overly" just, his ironic comment implies that that one is put at risk. R. N. Whybray (*IW*, 191–204) interprets the admonitions concerning excessive justice and excessive wisdom as a warning against hypocrisy (a pretention to these virtues). The hitpael could have this meaning (see note 16.b.), and Sirach warns against being a poseur in justice and wisdom (Sir 7:5[6]; cf. also 10:26; 32:4). Warnings against thinking that one is wise are also frequent in the tradition (Prov 3:7; 26:12). But the whole context of chap. 7 is against the notion that Qoheleth is simply defending traditional wisdom and warning against pretense.

17   On the other hand, Qoheleth now warns, wickedness and folly are not viable: neither vigorous evil-doing nor folly achieve anything. They are under the threat of an early death according to traditional wisdom ("why should you die before your time?" v 17b). Qoheleth is quite aware of the uncertainty of this threat (cf. v 15), but he invokes it with the same irony that he invoked the threat of ruin in v 16. He is simply utilitarian here; early death *also* occurs and can be used to support the admonition (the ironic touch): neither is this the way to go.

Vv 16–17, cast in the form of admonitions with motivating questions, are really typical wisdom conclusions. V 16 is a conclusion from observable fact (v 15); v 17 is a conclusion from traditional teaching (folly and injustice lead to death; e.g., Prov 10:2). Neither bit of advice is adequate! What is one to do? Qoheleth answers the question in v 18.

At first sight v 17 seems to say that a little injustice is all right (so G. Barton and others). But Qoheleth's point does not lie here; he is not setting down a moral principle. He is attempting to show that there are no privileged claims on life on the side of either wisdom or folly, of either justice or wickedness. Neither of them allows a person to be secure. He is even sarcastic in his expression of this: an excess of either profits nothing. The contradictory experiences of life (contradictory to the tradition) testify to the failure of human efforts (cf. 7:13).

18   The basic uncertainty of life emerges again in this conclusion, which urges that attention be given to *both* admonitions (זה . . . זה, "this . . . that"). This is not as pointless as it may at first sound. The recommendation is in line with the mystery of divine activity (vv 13–14) and the "vanity" of life. He has pointed out the limitations of both virtue and vice. Neither path of itself leads to a satisfactory result, despite the blessing and threats with which they are accompanied in the tradition. They have to be balanced against each other, even while they yield no satisfactory results. The only course that Qoheleth can recommend is to fear God (see the discussion of fear of God above, pp. lxiv–lxvi). This is the bottom line on which one must live. It cannot be called security nor can it ensure security. It is simply a basic attitude that one must have, no matter one's fate.

19 This verse seems to have no connection with v 18, which brought to an end the reflection that began in 7:15. It is a typical wisdom saying that compares wisdom favorably with administrative authority and power (cf. Prov 21:22; 24:5). Moreover its connection with the following verses seems tenuous. F. Delitzsch made a valiant attempt to unite vv 19–22: "The exhortation to strive after wisdom, contained in v 19, which affords protection against the evil effects of the failures which run through the life of the righteous, is followed by the exhortation, that one conscious that he himself is not free from transgression, should take heed to avoid that tale-bearing which finds pleasure in exposing to view the shortcomings of others." But the sequence is not as smooth as Delitzsch makes out. One may grant with several commentators (Zimmerli, Kroeber) that vv 21–22 provide an "example" of how awareness of one's sinfulness (v 20) creates a certain forgiving indulgence toward others who harm one by cursing (v 21–22; note גם כי ... גם). The problem of the connection between vv 19 and 20 remains. There can be no doubt that v 19 exalts wisdom over might in a traditional way. Then perhaps vv 20–22 are in dialogue with it in order to modify it. The modification is done by pointing out how little justice (=wisdom) is available to anyone; all are sinners. This anticipates, in a sense, vv 23–24, which clearly indicate that wisdom is unattainable for Qoheleth. Hence v 19 is relativized by v 20 (and 21–22), and further by vv 23–24.

There is no way of ascertaining the precise significance of the "ten officials." Many commentators understand this as a reference to the *deka protoi* who, according to Josephus (*Ant.* 20.8, 11), were even in Jerusalem as well as in Hellenistic cities.

20 See the discussion on v 19. The topic of moral weakness is genuinely biblical; cf. 1 Kgs 8:46; Ps 142:2; Prov 20:9; Job 4:17; Sir 19:16. This verse may reflect back upon v 16: even the effort to be totally just is foredoomed.

21–22 With many commentators (H. Hertzberg, K. Galling, L. Alonso Schökel) one can understand this admonition as an illustration of the truth contained in v 20. No one is free from sin, and this should have an effect on the way one responds to reports. There is much more than a mere prohibition against eavesdropping in v 21. If one hears rumors and discovers a curse that has been uttered, one should not respond foolishly; rather, one should look at one's own failings. Qoheleth seems to be urging a generous spirit of forgiveness or, at least, of indifference to vexing reports. There is no apparent connection with Prov 30:10, which also speaks of a servant who curses.

23–24 There is little consensus on whether these verses are to be related forward (K. Galling), or backward (R. Gordis), or treated as an independent unit (A. Lauha). They seem to be a transition to what follows (מצא, "find," the catch word), while they also look back on Qoheleth's experiment with wisdom (v 23). The immediate reference ("all this") is to the wisdom dialogue that has been going on in 7:1–22, but v 23 recalls 1:13, where Qoheleth announced his determination to explore "in wisdom" all that is done under the heavens. M. Fox has pointed out the ambiguity, indeed a contradiction, in the statements concerning wisdom (*HS* 19 [1978] 27). On the one hand Qoheleth claims to be employing wisdom (1:13 and passim) in his examination of reality. On the other hand, he affirms in v 23 that his quest for wisdom ended in failure. As Fox remarks, "it does seem that Qohelet is using HKM in two different ways here, and in so doing is presenting a semantic paradox: He used wisdom in investigating the world yet could not become wise. He was a wise-man who did not have wisdom" (28). The paradox does not seem to be all this formidable. Obviously Qoheleth was a sage in the traditional sense; the entire book testifies to his deep roots in the wisdom tradition. But the tests he put to it made him realize that he was not truly wise or did not possess the wisdom he sought for. Because he could not understand what God was doing in the world (3:11; 8:17), his affirmation of failure in v 23 is quite in order. He does not distinguish between degrees of wisdom, but it is clear that he set his sights higher than the tradition, and he is all the more strict in his judgment (e.g., 8:17b).

The "distance" of wisdom recalls the theme of Job 28 and the words of Agur (Prov 30:1–4), where "wisdom" is something beyond the practical wisdom that is the heritage of the sage. It is mysterious and unattainable; it belongs with God alone. However, Qoheleth is dealing with human wisdom, how to cope with the world. "The work of God" (3:11; 8:17) escapes human cognizance. Qoheleth has proved this by his thorough relativizing of traditional wisdom. His avowal of defeat is in line with the mysterious largesse of God who gives wisdom to whomever he pleases (2:26).

Explanation

Qoheleth continues his dialogue with tradition, somewhat in the style of 7:1–14. He takes up the theme of retribution and denies that in fact good or evil conduct has anything to do with it (v 15). He further compounds the problem by pointing out the conflicting advice that is given on this matter—by the traditionalists and those who disagree with the traditionalists. Wisdom is unable to provide a solution. One can only hold to the two sides of the dilemma and fear God. In certain respects one is reminded of Job 28. Wisdom, the true answer, cannot be found (no matter where mortals, especially Job, look); one can only fear God (Job 28:28). The admonitions in vv 16–17 have an ironic touch, and they underscore the mystery of the divine action to which Qoheleth so frequently refers.

Vv 19–22 revert to the dialogue pattern, perhaps less clearly than in vv 1–14. Wisdom is praised (v 19), but there is no one who is truly just, i.e., wise (v 20). The weakness of the wise/just person seems to be illustrated by the admonition that underscores the failure in concern for another (vv 21–22).

The final verses, 23–24, are Qoheleth's personal reflection on his vocation as a חכם (ḥākām) or wise person. They reflect particularly back on the mysterious ironic admonitions of 7:15–18.

It is hard to be satisfied with any commentary on this section; it is very difficult to understand. But at least one red herring should be eliminated. Qoheleth is not advocating in vv 16–18 a "middle way." The view that he has adopted the Greek notion of avoiding excess, that virtue stands in the middle (μηδὲν ἄγαν; ne quid nimis) is a common misreading of these verses. The formula "nothing in excess" does not have a univocal meaning or usage. When the medieval scholastics echo Aristotle (Nicomachean Ethics, 70–115) that virtue stands in the middle, this is a middle path between two extremes. Thus temperance (σωφροσύνη) is the mean between licentiousness (ἀκολασία), which is an excess of pleasure, and insensitivity (ἀναισθησία), which is a deficiency of pleasure. Virtue in this sense lies between two extremes. This kind of reason is simply not applicable to 7:16–17, which presents two points of view, not two extremes in moral activity.

The use of μηδὲν ἄγαν in Theognis (ll. 219, 335, 401) does not fit the situation of Eccl 7:16–18. In ll. 219–20 Theognis warns Kyrnos against being too excited about troubles in the city; in 335, 401, he is counseled not to be frantic about life (μηδὲν ἄγαν σπεύδειν).

Qoheleth's view is that neither virtue nor folly achieves desirable results in life, and one does well to attend to the failure of zealots in both areas. His alleged *via media* is in reality advice that amounts to mockery concerning any retribution for moral action. The traditional wisdom view of retribution is undercut by the facts of life. Neither claim, whether of the wise/virtuous or of the unjust/wicked, is true and absolute. This situation allows him to make his conclusion in v 18.

The uncertainty of life emerges in the conclusion that calls attention to both of these (basically inadequate) admonitions. One should hold on to both in the present state of affairs; such is the contradiction in life. This recommendation is not consoling; it is in line with the mystery of the divine activity (7:13–14). Qoheleth has pointed out the limitations of both virtue and vice. Neither path of itself leads to a satisfactory result, despite the blessings and threats with which they are accompanied in the tradition.

The only course he can recommend is to fear God. This is the bottom line on which one can achieve the only "security" possible. This is not security in the normal sense (see *Comment* on 3:14). He simply regards fear of God to be a basic attitude that one should have, no matter one's fate (which is beyond control).

A Reflection upon Humankind   (7:25–29)

Bibliography

Baltzer, K. "Women and War in Qohelet 7,23–8,1a." *HTR* 80 (1987) 127–32. **Ceresko, A. R.** "The Function of Antanaclasis (*mṣ'* 'to find'// *mṣ'* 'to reach, overtake, grasp') in Hebrew Poetry, Especially in the Book of Qoheleth." *CBQ* 44 (1982) 551–69. **Fox, M. V.** *Qohelet.* 236–44. ——— and **Porten, B.** "Unsought Discoveries: Qohelet 7:23–8:1a." *HS* 19 (1978) 26–38. **Lohfink, N.** "War Kohelet ein Frauenfeind? Ein Versuch, die Logik und den Gegenstand von Koh. 7:23–8:1a herauszufinden." In *SagAT.* 259–87, 417–20. **Michel, D.** *Eigenart.* 225–38.

Translation

[25] *I turned my mind to know,[a] by investigation and search, wisdom and (its) answer,[b] and to know that wickedness is foolishness and folly is madness.[c]* [26] *And I found[a] more bitter[b] than death the woman who is[c] a snare, whose heart is a net, whose hands are bonds. By God's pleasure, one will escape from her, but the errant one will be caught by her.* [27] *Indeed, this I have found,[a]—says [   ] Qoheleth,[b] (adding) one thing to another[c] to find an answer—* [28] *what[a] my soul has always sought without finding (is this): One man in a thousand I have found, but a woman among all of these I have not found.* [29] *See, only this have I found: God made humans upright, but they have sought out many devices.[a]*

Notes

25.a. MT reads, literally, "I turned, and my heart, to know." The construction is harsh, but it is supported by LXX and Syr, and the continuation of סבותי by לדעת can be justified (GKC §114p). Some MSS, Sym, Tg, and Vg have "in my heart."

25.b. חשבון "calculation," "conclusion," "sum," is peculiar to Ecclesiastes in the Hebrew Bible, but is found in Sirach and later Hebrew; cf. also vv 27, 29 (a catch word).

25.c. The sequence of the four nouns in v 25b is problematical: they may be merely an enumeration (e.g., NJV), or two double accusatives depending on לדעת. Moreover the use of the definite article is puzzling (found only with סכלות, "folly"). GKC §117ii would allow a second object with ידע: "*to know* something *to be* something." See also 1:17.

26.a. מוצא is clearly the qal participle of מצא, treated as if it were a ל"ה verb; מצא is used no less than seven times in vv 26–29. See A. Ceresko, *CBQ* 44 (1982) 551–69.

26.b. מר ממות, "more bitter than death," can be translated also "stronger than death." Eü and Lohfink adopt this understanding of מר on the basis of its meaning in cognate languages. In the only other occurrence of the two words together, the meaning of "bitter" is assured (1 Sam. 15:32; see also Prov 5:4; Sir 41:1).

26.c. אשר היא is usually understood as the relative particle with the pronoun serving as copula. Eü and Lohfink interpret אשר as causal and as introducing a saying about woman (היא the subject). On the use of אשר in Ecclesiastes, see Michel, *Eigenart*, 213–44, esp. 225–38, and also Lohfink, *SagAT*, pp. 264–65, n. 26.

27.a. מצאתי זה occurs here and in v 29; both times the "this" refers forward, not backward, and to the discovery that Qoheleth has made.

27.b. Read with LXX: אמר הקהלת, as in 12:8 (cf. GKC §122r); in 1:12 and 12:8, 10 קהלת appears with a masculine verb.

27.c. אחת לאחת is an adverbial accusative of manner (GKC §118q), and it is well rendered in NJV, "item by item."

28.a. Most translations understand אֲשֶׁר, at the beginning of the verse, as referring back to חֶשְׁבּוֹן, immediately preceding it. But it is also possible to interpret אֲשֶׁר as introducing a new statement that further defines the זֶה מָצָאתִי of v 27: "what my soul has always sought without finding is: . . ." Then Qoheleth would be denying the truth of the proposition that distinguished between man ("one in a thousand") and woman. This grammatical interpretation goes back at least as far as L. Levy (1912), and a minority of scholars have agreed: A. Bea, E. Glasser, R. Kroeber, O. Loretz (*Qohelet*, 268), D. Michel (*Eigenart*, 225–38), A. Strobel, A. Vaccari. This "minority" opinion simplifies the complicated style in vv 27–28a. Moreover, it is in agreement with the opinion expressed in v 29 that God made human beings (without distinction of gender) upright, but they have had recourse to their own devices.

29.a. חִשְּׁבֹנוֹת, "devices," occurs only here and in 2 Chr 26:15 (where it designates a kind of fortifications, hence also "devices" for this purpose). It is obviously a reflection on the חֶשְׁבּוֹן, and in v 29 he finds that human beings have marred the divine handiwork by seeking (בקש) חִשְּׁבֹנוֹת. הָאָדָם certainly means humankind in this verse; there is a contrast between what God did and what human beings have done.

Form/Structure/Setting

This unit is dominated by the sevenfold repetition of מצא, "find," the three-fold repetition of חֶשְׁבּוֹן, "sum," or the like (vv 25, 27, 29), and of בקש, "seek" (28, 29). The genre can be classified as reflection—about woman especially, but also man. The sequence of thought can be summarized as follows:

In v 25 Qoheleth states his unremitting, indefatigable search to know wisdom and folly (cf. 1:17; 2:12). In v 26 he introduces the theme of the adulterous woman, against whom the sages (Proverbs, passim) warned. He does not warn against this; he merely remarks that it is up to the divine will (as in 2:26) as to who will be her partner. In vv 27–28, he reacts unfavorably (he has not "found" it so) to another saying: one man out of a thousand (presumably, is good), but no woman. This saying he does not find verified (the translation of v 28 is problematical; see note 28.a.). In v 29 he states what he thinks is the case: God made both (man and woman) upright, but it is they who are responsible for moral troubles. Throughout chap. 7 Qoheleth has been in dialogue with traditional wisdom beliefs, and this continues in the complex structure of vv 25–29.

There is no unanimity on the extent of this section. Many commentators see the ending in 7:29, with 8:1 beginning a new unit (so Gordis, Crenshaw, Alonso Schökel, Michel, *Eigenart*, 262). Others end with 8:1, either in part (v 1a), or in whole. The arguments for incorporating 8:1 or 8:1a depend upon the overall construal. Thus 8:1a (the text is somewhat uncertain; see below) could be an echo of the previous verses (23, 25) about Qoheleth's search for wisdom. One can hardly speak of an *inclusio* (7:25; 8:1) on the basis of the repetition of חכם; this word occurs too often in the entire work. Or possibly 8:1a reflects back on the pessimistic conclusion in 7:29. A. Lauha's caution is commendable: "Verse 1 in chap 8 consists of two sayings without logical connection in the context." However, he is hardly justified in dismissing 8:1 as a gloss. M. Fox ends the unit in 8:1a, which is analyzed as a rhetorical question that recapitulates an earlier generalization (2:14b; 7:23f.). K. Galling would include 8:1 within the unit since 8:2 begins with a saying about a king. There is simply no certain solution. The wide-ranging differences of opinion on the length of the section illustrate the weakness of relying only on content to determine the structure. Our translation ends with 7:29 because of the occurrence of the telling phrase "find out" (see the remarks on *Form/Setting/Structure* above for 6:8–10).

Comment

25 Despite the admission that he has made in vv 23–24, Qoheleth describes his relentless search for wisdom in words that echo earlier phrases (תור, "investigate," in 1:11, 2:3; "folly," "madness" in 2:12a). Catch words for the following lines are also found: חשבון, "answer" (v 27); בקש, "seek" (v 27). The intensity of his engagement with wisdom is clear (see also 8:16), but the plethora of objects in v 25b obscures his intention. Are the goals merely enumerated in v 25b (so M. V. Fox), or does he have a program to find the connection between the various terms he uses (see note 25.c.)? More probably the latter (see *Comment* on 1:17). In any case, wisdom is known by its opposite, folly. The two לדעת, "to know," clauses are directed equally to wisdom (perhaps hendiadys in v 25a, "wisdom's answer") and to folly.

26 The reader may be caught off guard after the elaborate introduction to Qoheleth's search in v 25. The discovery seems to be merely an old *topos* celebrated in the wisdom literature (cf. Prov 2:16–19; 5:1–4; 7:22–23; 9:13–18; cf. also 22:15; 23:27–28): the adulterous woman. The description fits a certain type of woman against whom the sages railed; it is not a description of the female sex *per se*. H. Hertzberg rightly observes that Qoheleth does not condemn woman as such. But the sages exploited, one-sidedly, the dangers that women posed to men (without exploring the need to investigate the blame that attached to the males). In Prov 5:4 the "bitterness" inflicted by such a woman is compared to wormwood. The metaphor of the מצודים, "snare," is used in Prov 6:25 (תצוד). A different perspective of Qoheleth's view of woman emerges from 9:9. The description in v 26a has the ring of a proverbial saying about a particular type of woman, and it is expressed in parallelism.

The terms טוב, "good," and חוטא, "errant," are best understood as in 2:26, not as moral qualifications, but as designations of human beings in terms of the inscrutable divine will. Some will fall victim to this type of woman, but others will not, as God pleases. Even if one were to insist that there is a moral nuance to these words in v 26, the meaning would be consonant with Qoheleth's views. He shared the traditional Israelite values about sexual morality and would be merely reflecting these in the terminology of v 26: adultery is wrong and fidelity is good. In contrast, the concern of 2:26 is not morality but the mysterious actions of God.

27 The verbose style in which Qoheleth describes his inductive approach ("one to one") to "find" (מצא again) an answer makes his thought difficult to grasp. If "this" refers back to v 26, one is inclined to question the significance of the discovery, when the *topos* of the adulterous woman is so prominent in the wisdom tradition. Hence it seems better to understand "this" as pointing forward to v 28 (as does Michel, *Eigenart*, 229).

It would be most unusual for Qoheleth to speak of himself in the third person. Hence commentators are inclined to regard "says Qoheleth" as an editorial addition. K. Galling thinks it is an editorial insertion to indicate precisely that this is Qoheleth's private opinion, but this seems gratuitous.

28 The verse contains ambiguities. As indicated in note 28.a., the אשר that begins v 28a can be referred back to חשבון, "answer," and understood as the relative particle. According to our translation, it is to be considered as beginning a new statement indicating something that Qoheleth did not find, namely, the truth of v 28b. In 28b the figure of a thousand is merely a round number (cf. Job 8:3). The text says, literally, "one man (אדם) in a thousand I found but a woman in all these I did not find"; presumably "in all these" means an equal number of women as there were (a thousand) men.

The usual interpretation of this verse is that Qoheleth discovered one good man but no good woman. R. N. Whybray is correct in insisting that the verse "does not state what it is that the speaker has sought, and which he has, or has not, found." It is the context (vv 26 and 29) that justifies the assumption that the specific meaning deals with moral conduct: good, trustworthy, etc. Then the statement is reminiscent of Prov 20:6, "Who can find a man (איש) worthy of trust?" (cf. Prov 31:10). The alleged discovery of Qoheleth does not speak well for man (one in a thousand!), much less for woman. In support of this view many examples of misogynism from various ages and cultures could be instanced. It is true that Hellenistic Judaism shared in the general failure to appreciate women properly, and it would be no surprise to find Qoheleth a child of his time. But is the intent of v 28 to disparage women? Our translation indicates that he rejects a saying that is demeaning to women (see note 28.a.). V 29 contains his verdict on all human beings, men and women alike, and would be anticlimactic after a misogynistic statement. The series of "discoveries" in vv 26–28 seems to be threefold: (1) v 26 concerns the saying about the adulterous women (which can be duplicated in Proverbs and the wisdom tradition); (2) vv 27–28 deal with a saying about one in a thousand (man not woman), which is found *not* to be true; (3) v 29 presents a statement about humankind, which is found to be true. In this sequence there is a continual heightening of the "discoveries," leading to the conclusion of v 29.

29 Qoheleth asserts the basic sinfulness of all, male and female, even though God made them upright (ישׁר; cf. יפה in 3:10). This is his considered judgment upon humankind, and it exonerates him from the charge of considering women more evil than men. Indeed, v 29 is in dialogue with the saying of v 28b, which he found to be untrue. Rather, God created human beings as simple and just; perversion comes from their own doing, regardless of their sex. Qoheleth has found his answer (vv 25, 27, חשבון) in the devices (חשבנות) that human beings seek out (בקשׁ, vv 25, 28, 29).

Explanation

This is one of the more difficult and perhaps one of the more notorious passages in Ecclesiastes. It has usually been taken in the sense of misogynism, a popular trait in the Hellenism of the author's day and at various times since: Qoheleth found one good man among a thousand, but not one woman. In the *Notes* and *Comment* offered above, the charge of misogynism is rejected. At the same time, it is difficult to see the progression of thought from the stereotype of the wicked woman (v 26; the type of person that Prov 7 warns against) to a defense of women in v 28. The style of the entire passage is peculiarly redundant and complex, even for Qoheleth, and the sense remains obscure. No matter what solution is adopted, Qoheleth is expressing himself in a very labored manner, and other construals have been made.

M. Fox (*HS* 19 [1978] 31) argues that the relative clause that begins v 28 (אשר עוד, etc.) has no relevant or meaningful antecedent (not even חשבון of v 27). He changes the text (with Ehrlich) to read אִשָּׁה, "a (good) woman," for the relative particle אֲשֶׁר. This may be clearer Hebrew, but the result is the same; the misogynism remains.

In his commentary and in greater detail in *SagAT*, 259–87, N. Lohfink has proposed a new interpretation of 7:26–29. The issue is not the moral worth of woman as opposed to man, but the issue of death. He does not emend the text but allows certain meanings to be heard that traditional translations have not recognized. Thus Qoheleth finds woman stronger (מַר, which also means "bitter") than death (cf. Cant 8:6). What was originally a statement of admiration and astonishment in v 26a has been changed by v 26b into a derogatory saying, characteristic of a male-dominated culture. In vv 27–28 Qoheleth reflects somewhat "naively" on the immortality of woman. He has observed a thousand cases and in every instance woman dies—she is *not* stronger than death. The saying in v 26 had described the woman as a kind of war machine (instead of "snare," מְצוֹדִים can mean fortification; see 9:14, but not 9:12). In v 29 he plays with the double meaning of חֶשְׁבֹּנוֹת ("reckoning" or "sum" in vv 25 and 27, but in v 29, at least in a concomitant level of meaning, a "siege machine"; cf. 2 Chr 26:15). His point is that human beings (הָאָדָם in v 29 is collective) have brought death (by war, etc.) into God's creation. This stark resume does not do full justice to the complicated arguments that Lohfink offers. One may say broadly that the reader can detect a double meaning in the saying about woman; at first sight v 26 is apparently unfavorable (more bitter than death) until one hears the real issue (immortality).

In a spinoff from Lohfink's study, K. Baltzer (*HTR* 80 [1987] 127–32) interpreted the "thousand" (אֶלֶף) in v 28 as a military unit or brigade. He interprets the verse thus: "'One man only' or 'men alone' (*ʾadam ʾeḥad*) have I found among the brigades ('thousands'), but a woman among all these I have not found." His comment is "there are no women in the army; it is a male affair" (131). In this view Qoheleth's discovery is that women are absolved from any responsibility in death-dealing war. Woman is "stronger" (not "more bitter") than death. Baltzer shifts the emphasis from the common fate of death for humanity to the death that war inflicts.

Obviously the final word on this text has not been written. Thus far, it refuses to yield its secret.

Varia: Instruction and Reflections   (8:1–17)

Bibliography

Driver, G. R. "Problems and Solutions." *VT* 4 (1954) 225–45. Irwin, W. "Ecclesiastes 8:2–9." *JNES* 4 (1945) 130–31. Lohfink, N. "*melek, šallît* und *môšēl* bei Kohelet und die Abfassungszeit des Buchs." *Bib* 62 (1982) 535–43. Michel, D. "Qohelet-Probleme: Überlegungen zu Qoh 8:2–9 und 7,11–14." *TV* 15 (1979–80). 81–103 (rev. in *Eigenart.* 84–115). Serrano, J. J. "I Saw the Wicked Buried (Eccl 8,10)." *CBQ* 16 (1954) 168–70. Waldman, N. M. "The *DĀBĀR RĀʿ* of Eccl 8:3." *JBL* 98 (1979) 407–8. Wright, A. G. *CBQ* 30 (1968) 313–34.

Translation

1 Who is like the wise man,[a]
   and who knows the meaning[b] of a thing?
   Wisdom makes one's face shine,
   and hardness of face[c] is changed.[d]
2 [   ][a] Observe the command of the king,
   because[b] of the oath to God.
3 Do not hasten to leave[a] his presence;
   do not persist in a bad situation,
   for all that he wishes he can do.
4 Because the word of a king is powerful,[a]
   and who can say to him, "what are you doing?"

5 Whoever observes a command will not experience a bad turn,
   for a wise heart knows the time and judgment; [a]
6 Indeed,[a] there is a time and judgment for everything.
   But [b] misfortune lies heavy upon a person,
7 In that[a] no one knows what will happen,
   because[b] how it will turn out—who can tell him?
8 There is no one who has power over the breath of life[a] so as to retain it, and there is no one who has power over the day of death, or dismissal in war; but neither does wickedness save those who practice it.

9 All this I have seen and I have given my attention to every deed that is done under the sun when[a] one person has power over another so as to harm him.[b] 10 Then[a] I saw the wicked buried.[b] They used to come and go from the holy place![c] But those were forgotten[d] in the city who had acted justly.[e] This also is vanity. 11 Because sentence against an evil deed is not quickly executed,[a] therefore the human heart is set on doing evil.[b] 12 For[a] the sinner does evil a hundred times,[b] and yet prolongs his life[c]—although I know that those who fear God will be well off because they fear him, 13 and that the wicked person will not be well off, and will not prolong his shadowy[a] days because he does not fear God. 14 There is a vanity that is done on the earth: there are just who are treated as if they had acted wickedly, and there are wicked who are treated as if they had acted justly.[a] I said, this also is vanity. 15 So I praised joy because there is nothing better for a human

under the sun than to eat and drink and to be joyous. This can be his part [a] *for the toil during the days of the life which God gives him under the sun.*

[16] *When* [a] *I put my mind to know wisdom and to contemplate the task that is carried out on earth—even though neither by day nor by night do one's eyes have sleep* [b]—[17] *I looked* [a] *at all the work of God: no one can find out what is done under the sun. Therefore* [b] *humans search hard, but no one can find out; and even if the wise man says he knows, he cannot find out.*

Notes

1.a. The definite article in כהחכם has not been elided; this is unusual but by no means unheard of; cf. Joüon §35e. However, the Greek traditions read כה apart from חכם: "who is so wise?" οἶδεν of LXX is probably (Podechard) a corruption of ὧδε, found in Aq, while Sym has οὕτως. Syr, Vg, Tg, and Jerome support the MT.

1.b. פשר, "meaning," is a *hap. leg.*, but found often in the Qumran literature and in the Aramaic of Daniel; cf. Wagner, *Aramaismen*, §239.

1.c. עז פנים is read as עַז פָּנִים in Deut 28:50 (cf. Prov 7:13), and the ancient versions (LXX ἀναιδής) reflect the adjective in 8:1.

1.d. Although ישׁנא can be interpreted as from the verb "hate" (so LXX and Syr), it should be taken as from the root שׁנה, "change," conjugated on the analogy of ל"א verbs (GKC §75rr).

2.a. The MT seems to be corrupt, despite efforts to translate the opening אני as "I do" (NJV). The easiest conjectural change is to read את, the sign of the accusative. It is not likely that אמרתי is to be understood in this context. For another solution, cf. Whitley (*Koheleth*, 71–72), who proposes אנפי מלך, "in the presence of the king (take heed)."

2.b. ועל דברת supplies a motive for the command; the "and" is the *waw explicativum* (GKC §154, n. 1[b]).

3.a. Many commentators (e.g., Fox) follow the lead of LXX, Syr, and Sym in reading the initial admonition with the final words of v 2. However, תלך, "leave," can be interpreted as dependent upon אל תבהל (GKC §120c). Another translation is offered by L. Alonso Schökel: "do not be disturbed by him, yield."

4.a. שלטון, "power," is found only here and in v 8. The root, שלט, is a catch word in vv 4–9; see also 7:19, 10:5.

5.a. עת ומשפט is usually rendered "time of judgment." Perhaps the connective *waw* was lacking for LXX, which understands the phrase as hendiadys here, καιρὸν κρίσεως, but not in v 6 (καιρὸς καὶ κρίσις). R. Gordis translates משפט as "procedure," and also A. Barucq (*conduite à tenir*), who refers to Judg 13:12.

6.a. כי appears twice in this verse and twice in the next. The first כי continues the thought of v 5b and seems to affirm it: "indeed, verily." The thought is akin to what has been stated in 3:1.

6.b. The second כי clause goes counter to the tenor of the preceding lines by introducing an "evil" (cf. 6:1), which v 7 will explain as human ignorance. Hence it is in tension with the preceding lines, and כי can have an adversative force here; it is introducing a new perspective. On the usage of כי in vv 6–7 see Michel (*Eigenart*, 201–3).

7.a. The first כי is resultative (Williams §450), explaining what the misfortune is.

7.b. The final כי is causal and presents a reason for human ignorance.

8.a. In 1:16 and 11:4, רוח clearly means wind; in 1:19, 21; 12:7, it means life-breath, and both meanings are possible here; the ambiguity may be deliberate. Several commentators (Zimmerli, Hertzberg, Kroeber) opt for "wind," but the mention of the day of death in context suggests "life-breath."

9.a. עת is the accusative of time (GKC §118i) and can be translated as "when."

9.b. לו (לרע) can refer either to the agent (to his own harm), or preferably to another. There is no need to read ל(ה)רע (hipil) as reflected in LXX (τοῦ κακῶσαι) and some of the ancient versions.

10.a. The translation of this verse is very uncertain. If the MT is not corrupt, it is certainly ambiguous, as various efforts at translation demonstrate. בכן, "then," is formed from the preposition ב and the adverb כן; a Ugaritic equivalent, *bkm*, is alleged, but it is not unambiguous. *běkēn* occurs elsewhere (Esth 4:16) and may be an Aramaism; cf. Wagner §43.

10.b. "Buried" is supported by Syr, Vg and Tg. In the LXX the wicked are "brought" (מובאים) to the tombs (εἰς τάφους εἰσαχθέντας), and this is preferred by many commentators (Barton, Kroeber, Gordis). Others make further changes (קרב for קבר) and propose "approach and enter" (G. R. Driver, *VT* 4 [1954] 230).

10.c. מקום should be read (with many MSS) as absolute instead of construct, and construed with the preceding and following verbs. The going to and from the holy place (the Temple; cf. Lev 7:6) is better attributed to the wicked than to those (just ones) who are mentioned next.

10.d. This translates the MT; the Greek tradition and some Hebrew MSS reflect וישתבחו, "and they (i.e., the wicked) were praised."

10.e. אשר כן עשו is ambiguous. It can be translated as "who acted justly" and as "who (or, because they) acted thus." The solution depends on the way in which the previous words have been rendered ("forgotten" or "praised"). For further discussion of the entire verse, see the commentators; Whitley, *Koheleth*, 74–76; and J. Serrano, *CBQ* 16 (1954) 168–70.

11.a. The MT can be rendered "because sentence is not executed, the work of evil is quick." The Masoretic punctuation is unusual and should be changed. נעשׂה is vocalized as nipal feminine participle, although פתגם (derived from the Persian) is apparently masculine (Esth 1:20; cf. Ezra 6:11). Moreover, פתגם receives an accent separating it from מעשׂה רעה (literally, "work of evil"). מעשׂה can be read as the adverbial accusative and so joined with פתגם.

11.b. בהם can be construed with מלא (cf. בלבבם in 9:3) and is in itself redundant.

12.a. As with v 11, this verse also begins with causal אשר, which is found again in the final clause.

12.b. פעם is to be understood after מאת, which is surprisingly in the construct, although one would expect מאה. The MT is to be retained against the ancient versions, which go in different directions: LXX has ἀπὸ τότε, "from then" (reading מעז for מאת); Aq, Sym, and Theod have ἀπέθανεν (hence, מת).

12.c. מאריך (with ימים understood; cf. v 13 and 7:15) is construed with לו, an ethical dative. It is less likely that God is the subject of מאריך and that the divine patience is referred to.

13.a. There is not sufficient reason to follow the LXX (ἐν σκιᾷ) and change to בצל. See 6:12; כצל, "shadowy," can be taken to refer to either the subject or his days. A shadow is a natural symbol for expressing the transience of human beings (Job 14:2) or their days (Job 8:9).

14.a. The structure of this verse is striking, with the repetition of יש, אשר, and the double מגיע אלהם. מגיע (hipil participle) is used impersonally.

15.a. It is also possible to interpret ילונו (literally, "accompany him") in the indicative mood.

16.a. The structure of this verse extends into v 17, where the main verb ראיתי occurs, after a parenthetical remark about human sleeplessness.

16.b. The construction, "see sleep," is unique in the Bible, but can be matched by Terence *"somnum . . . hac nocte oculis non vidi meis"* (*Heauton Timorumenos* 3.1.82), and by Cicero, *"somnum non vidit"* (*Epistulae ad Familiares* 7.30). The pronominal suffixes in this phrase can be taken as indefinite (rather than referring back to אדם in v 15); this is a parenthetical remark that bears properly on the human effort described in v 17.

17.a. The main verb is introduced by the *waw* of apodosis (GKC §112oo).

17.b. בשל, "on account of which," is apparently a late form (cf. Jon 1:7, 12) and seems to be formed on the analogy of the Aramaic, (ד) בדיל. The LXX (ὅσα, "whatever") is probably an interpretation; cf. Vg, *et quanto plus,* "and so much the more." For a discussion of the entire verse, see Ellermeier, *Qohelet I/1,* 295–303.

Form/Structure/Setting

The length of this unit is set by the threefold appearance of the phrase "cannot find" in v 17. The subunits go their own way, although the theme might generally be described as authority, both human and divine. An instruction concerning conduct before the king is found in 8:1–4. In 8:5–8 is an observation upon divine authority and human reaction. Another reflection, on the abuse of authority as found in certain injustices, follows in 8:9–15. The final reflection deals with the human inability to know God's "doing" (8:16–17).

These units are carefully expressed with several repetitions and catch words. דבר רע in vv 2, 5 unites 1–4 with 5–8. The root חפץ (vv 2, 6) has a similar function, and v 1 ties in with v 2 with the repetition of the significant פָּנָיו, "presence." מַעֲשֵׂה, "doing," human or divine, binds together the vv 9, 11, 14, 17.

The dialectic pattern that was recognized in 7:1ff. is to be found here also. Vv 2–4 modify v 1; 6–12a modify v 5; 14–15 are in opposition to 12b–13. Vv 16–17 are a conclusion about the impenetrability of the divine design (or, the work of God) that strengthens the previous statements in the chapter. The first part (chaps. 7–8) of the second half of the book has dealt with what humans cannot "find out." The second half (9:1–11:6) deals with what will happen in the future; humans do not know what will happen to them. See A. Wright, *CBQ* 30 (1968) 325–26, 331.

Comment

1 This verse creates difficulties as to meaning (see the *Notes*) and context (Does it belong with 7:29 or 8:2? See the remarks on *Form/Structure/Setting* above for 7:25–29). Even the relationship between the two lines is obscure. NJV and Kroeber would understand v 1b as the referent of "word" (דבר) in v 1a ("who knows the meaning of the [following] saying:"). This seems less likely in view of the absence of the definite article. The rhetorical questions in v 1a are exclamatory, and they suggest the exalted task of the sage at the same time as the impossibility of that task (cf. 7:23–25). Thus they may be deliberately ambiguous. One answer to them is: only the wise person. But it will be seen from the analysis of vv 2–4 that Qoheleth is once more relativizing the value of wisdom.

V 1b is a proverbial saying about the effect of wisdom. Presumably it refers to the sage, but the king (cf. Prov 16:15, "In the light of the king's face there is life; his favor is like a rain cloud in spring) cannot be excluded. In the Bible it is God who causes the face to shine (הֵאִיר פָּנִים, "be gracious to"; cf. Num 6:25, etc.). Here it is wisdom that has a beneficent effect upon the sage. Commentators usually stress an ennobling effect, but R. Gordis speaks of dissembling: merely "*appearing* gracious." The meaning of v 1b is expressed by another image concerning the change of face (see the *Notes*). Wisdom changes the unpleasant appearance of a person. The thought is akin to 2:13–14; cf. also Sir 13:25.

The context for understanding v 1 is not specified. Alonso Schökel would not exclude that God may provide the context. God acts according to divine pleasure (Ps 135:6; cf. Eccl 8:2b), and who can ask an account of his actions (Job 9:12; cf. Eccl 8:4)? See also Eccl 5:1–2. Our translation presupposes that v 1 presents traditional wisdom, with which Qoheleth begins to dialogue in vv 2–4. It seems best to correlate it with the setting of a court, which emerges clearly in the following verses. In *Bib* 62 [1982] 540–41, N. Lohfink understands these verses to refer to a courtly situation. The advice would be for a student who can have a court career, not in Alexandria (which was hardly within the realm of possibility) but in Palestine. The terms מֹשֵׁל (9:17; 10:4) and שַׁלִּיט (10:5; cf. 7:19) should be understood of officials like the Tobiad Joseph in Jerusalem or Ptolemeus son of Thraseas in Ptolemais, who would have had a certain entourage of his own. Thus, while v 1 forms part of traditional wisdom, it is applicable to any situation of authority and subjects. It is pertinent advice to the courtier, who was expected to control his feelings.

2 We may regard the following verses (2–4) as traditional court wisdom, but also as having relevance for Qoheleth's own day. However, he is not simply transmitting a body of sayings. He is relativizing the role and prestige of the sage (v 1) by following up with (wise!) admonitions that in fact are humiliating for the sage at court, even if they also save him from trouble. The wise advisor, for all his gifts, is confronted by royal power and is totally dependent upon the royal pleasure. It is all very well to praise the wisdom of the wise (v 1), but one must attend to the risks they run at court (vv 2–4). Hence Qoheleth's admonitions serve to qualify v 1, even though they are themselves derived from traditional wisdom. He pits traditional wisdom against itself.

Reverent obedience to the king is part of the wisdom teaching (Prov 24:21). One is expected to respond to him with "honest lips" (Prov 25:6) and "to claim no honor in his presence" (Prov 25:6). Royal displeasure is frequently mentioned as something to guard against (Prov 14:35; 16:14; 19:12; 20:21). Qoheleth's command fits into this attitude. The reference to the "oath to God" is difficult to specify: a subjective or objective genitive? One can conceive of an oath of fidelity to the king, made before God, as suggested by 1 Kgs 2:43. H. Hertzberg understands אלהים as subjective genitive: God's oath has made the king a sacred person. Interestingly enough, Qoheleth never adverts to the fact that he has introduced himself as a king in 1:12.

3 The admonitions guard against precipitate action, but one should know when absence is prudent, even if Prov 16:14 claims that the wise person can pacify the king's wrath. N. M. Waldman (*JBL* 98 [1979] 407–8) argues that the דבר רע, or bad situation, in v 3 refers to conspiracy and rebellion against royalty, but it is difficult to be specific.

4 The words in v 4b reproduce almost exactly Job 9:12 (cf. Isa 45:9), where God is the referent. Hence there can be no question about the power of royal decree; see also Prov 20:2. The sage has little protection against the authority of his royal master.

5 This verse has the deceptive simplicity of a traditional wisdom saying. שומר מצוה, "whoever observes a command," is found also in Prov 19:16, where the word of the teacher is presumably meant, although the pertinence of the saying can change with the context. Many commentators point out that שומר in v 5 picks up the שמור in v 2. Moreover, דבר רע seems to be a catch word with the same phrase in v 3. Hence v 5 can be understood within the context of court wisdom supplied by the previous verses; so Hertzberg, Zimmerli, and many others. Zimmerli specifies that Qoheleth radicalizes Prov 19:16, which secured life to one who observes a command, by interpolating v 5b: a wise heart (cf. 10:2) knows that there is nothing secure, that "time and judgment" come mysteriously into play. However, v 5b does not necessarily indicate a smart awareness of the uncertainty of time and the arbitrariness of a king. Of itself it merely indicates the confident attitude that is associated with wisdom; the sage knows when and how to act.

One may therefore question whether v 5 is really to be associated with the context of the royal court. It can be understood with N. Lohfink as referring to the command of the wisdom teacher (Prov 19:16), or even, in a decidedly religious context, of the Law itself. It certainly promises the traditional sapiential value; the wise person will succeed. Hence v 5 introduces a new topic; the knowledge of the wise (ידע, twice) is commended in positive fashion. This is obviously not in harmony with Qoheleth's views; it is precisely the kind of statement that he can be expected to challenge. The dialectical style that is the trademark of chaps. 7–8 continues, and the following verses relativize the traditional wisdom saying of v 5.

6–7   The interpretation of these verses depends upon the understanding of v 5 and the meaning of כִּי (four times; see the *Notes*). If one assumes the context of the royal court, the following interpretation is in order: the one who obeys the royal order will succeed since even for the king there is a "time and judgment"; events will catch up with him (vv 5–6a). From this point of view, wickedness (רָעַת, v 6b) will rest heavily upon a king (so A. Lauha). Perhaps the phrase "time and judgment" refers to the courtier's style of conduct; he will know the proper time and manner of acting, since human weakness provides an opening to act (so R. Gordis). This interpretation presumes that these sayings are simply conveying traditional wisdom, intended to guarantee security to the careful and wise courtier.

On the other hand, Qoheleth can be interpreted as criticizing the traditional wisdom expressed in vv 5–6a. In contrast to the "wisdom" asserted in these lines, he affirms that the predicament of human beings is a bad one (v 6b) in that they do not know what the future holds for them (v 7; cf. 3:21; 6:12). Thus vv 6b–7 contradict vv 5–6a. The knowledge (twice in v 5) of the wise person is denied in v 7. V 7 makes explicit the misfortune (v 6b) that rests upon human beings: their ignorance of what is to come (cf. 3:22; 6:12; 10:14).

8   Qoheleth proceeds to illustrate the ignorance and helplessness of human beings (cf. v 7). The four following examples have in common that they escape control and manipulation: רוּחַ *rûah*, day of death, war, and even wickedness. Many commentators prefer to interpret רוּחַ as "wind," and this would be an apt reference. But it is preferable to understand it as the breath of life, in the context of the "day of death" that follows. As was said before, there is a time for birth and for death (3:2), and this is determined by God. The specter of death always remains in Qoheleth's consciousness. Release from war might be understood as an excuse from participating. But in that case there is no reason why a person should not have adverted to the legislation of Deut 20:1ff., which provides for excuse. It is better to understand the phrase as escaping from the usual evils of war, such as pillage, capture, death. NJV translates, "from that war," i.e., the battle between life and death.

The final instance deals with wickedness. Originally this example might have referred to the inescapable effect of sin upon the sinner, and many commentators (Lauha, Hertzberg) recognize this meaning here. However, it appears to be a sardonic observation: neither does wickedness prolong life! This is perhaps unexpected, but it fits into Qoheleth's many-sided views of life (cf. 5:5; 7:16–18). There is no textual basis to justify changing "wickedness" to "riches"(רֶשַׁע to עֹשֶׁר).

9–10   On the one hand, it is possible that v 9 is a conclusion to the preceding remarks about power and human ignorance (so D. Michel, *Eigenart*, 98–99). The appearance of the root שׁלט, "power," in vv 4, 8, 9 seems to bind these lines together. On the other hand, the phrase "all that is done under the sun" (cf. 1:13, 14; 2:17; etc.) usually has to do with divine sovereignty in human events, and vv 10ff., which also deal with abuse of power, will illustrate this. Humans may lack power (שִׁלְטוֹן, v 8) over the day of death, but they have power (שׁלט) to harm one another, no matter how wise one may be. A concrete example of injustice, indicated by "all this," follows in v 10 and refers to incidents in Jerusalem. The precise details in this verse remain uncertain (see the *Notes*). But it is clear that we are presented with another example of the old dilemma of Israelite wisdom: the good and the wicked do not receive what they deserve. LXX understood the entire verse as referring to the scandal of the wicked, who are accorded honorable burial and even praised in the city because they frequented the Temple. Our translation expresses a *contrast* between the fate of the wicked and the good. The wicked are given the honor of burial, and their hypocritical attendance at the Temple is noted. On the other hand, the just are forgotten. This is another example of vanity.

11 Qoheleth singles out a demoralizing factor: retribution for wicked deeds comes late (if ever)—with the dire effect that people are moved to commit evil (רע occurs three times in vv 11–12a). He obviously does not trust people to act justly in the face of blatant corruption; some kind of retribution is necessary to coerce them to do good. His observation can apply to civil affairs as well as to divine governance of the world.

12 V 12a supports v 11 with the hard fact that sinners survive prosperously despite all their sins. The statement implicitly questions the justice of God in the government of the world. A long life is a well-known symbol of happiness in the Bible, and especially in the wisdom tradition (Prov 3:2, 16).

As R. Gordis rightly points out, v 12b is a subordinate clause, which follows on the blunt statements about the lack of retribution for evil-doers. Moreover, it continues into v 13, and these lines affirm a distinction in the treatment of those who fear God and those who do not. In order to avoid an apparently crass self-contradiction, many commentators (Siegfried, Podechard, Galling, et al.) have attributed these lines to a glossator intent on toning down the message. But this is a desperate solution; one has no control over the alleged presence of such glosses. The text should be dealt with as it stands. It is better to understand "I know . . ." as introducing Qoheleth's awareness of the orthodox claim concerning retribution, that all will be well with those who fear God. One may hesitate to go as far as Gordis, who considers this a quotation and translates "though I know the answer that 'it will be well in the end . . .'" But his solution is basically correct in that it has caught the direction of thought. Zimmerli and Hertzberg describe this approach as "yes, but . . ." *(zwar/aber)*: Qoheleth knows the teaching about those who fear God, but reality does not square with it.

"Fear of God" dominates vv 12b–13, but it should be noted that it does not have the same nuance as in 3:14, 5:16, 7:18. In those verses, fear of God has a tough-minded quality of fidelity and devotion. Here it reflects the traditional attitude that is secure and certain, for it is tied in to clear divine retribution.

13 This verse continues the traditional thought of v 12b: sinners will not fare well for their lack of fear before God. Such a view claims a distinction between the fate of the good and that of the evil. But Qoheleth cannot understand the divine manner of action; he sees no evidence for it, and indeed he points to contrary evidence in v 14.

14 The "vanity" is, of course, that the just are treated in this life as if they were wicked, and the wicked as if they were just. Qoheleth points this out as a simple fact, which stands in tension with the affirmation of vv 12b–13. Such a fact is the shipwreck of the traditional view of retribution enunciated in Deuteronomistic theology, in Job by the three friends, and elsewhere in the Bible. It is not possible to align such facts with the simple claim that divine justice distinguishes between the righteous and the wicked.

It is not apropos to say with H. Hertzberg (175; 224–25) that Qoheleth, unlike Job who criticizes God, criticizes only the world. He does not separate the world from divine causality; he well knows that the "contradictions" in it are the divine responsibility. However, he refuses to deny that God is just, even if on God's own mysterious terms, nor does he disdain fear of God. Job does attack divine justice, but this must be seen within the total context of the book of Job.

15   These words are in startling contrast to 2:2, where Qoheleth deemed joy as madness, and to 4:2, where he "praised" the dead more than the living. The changing perspectives must be kept in mind. He is not espousing here a vapid life of joy, but showing an appreciation of the limited, day-to-day pleasure (שׂמחה) that can be one's "accompaniment" in a God-given life span. The conclusion is in line with 2:24–25; 3:12–13; 5:17–19.

16   The introductory formula is familiar from 2:12 and 7:25. In 1:13 Qoheleth already expressed his concern about "what is done under the sun" (in v 16, however, "on the earth"). In both instances it is described as עִנְיָן (see also 3:10), a troublesome occupation. In fact, עִנְיָן, "task," is closely parallel to חכמה ḥokmâh, "wisdom," in v 16; wisdom consists in trying to make sense out of what is done on the earth. It is clear from 1:13 and 3:10 that this task is a troublesome burden.

The observation in 16b (see the *Notes*) is unusual on two counts. First it is parenthetical, and describes by anticipation the restless striving to find out the work of God (v 17). Second it is strange; as K. Galling remarks: "The singular image of 'not seeing sleep' is understandable for night time under certain circumstances, but who seeks sleep by day?"

17   The main affirmation of vv 16–17 lies here; no one can find out the work of God. Qoheleth twice asserts this, and adds that even the claim of the wise person to know it is a failure. See also 3:11; 11:5.

One may ask about the connection between the "task" (עִנְיָן) that is carried out on earth" (v 16) and the work of God "that is done under the sun" (v 17). They seem to be two sides of the one coin; "ultimately, every question about the meaning of human action is always a question about the action of God" (Zimmerli).

The challenge to the "wise," who would claim to know the divine action, is symbolic of the entire book. Although he was regarded as a sage (12:9), Qoheleth was intent on purifying wisdom of its shortsighted claims, and on making clear to the wise a truth in their own tradition: "There is no wisdom, no understanding, no counsel, against the Lord" (Prov 21:30).

Explanation

It has already been indicated that many interpreters include 8:1 or 8:1a with the previous section. We find no reason to separate one part of the verse from the other. The same kind of dialogue with traditional wisdom that marked chap. 7 continues here. 8:1 is a traditional saying in favor of wisdom and is relativized in vv 2–4 by the hard facts indicated in the admonitions. Despite their prestige, the sages can be demeaned; they have to be cautious within their dealings with those in authority, such as the king. In 8:5–7 traditional wisdom is modified again. The sage who observes the traditional teaching should not experience a bad turn, for he has a knowledge of "time and judgment" (8:5–6a). But this avails little since he does not know what the future will hold (8:6b–7). Then Qoheleth illustrates human impotence, especially in the face of death.

D. Michel (*Eigenart*, 92–100) would interpret this slightly differently. For him 8:1–5 is "traditional" wisdom. It praises the sage who knows "time and judgment," and thus can deal successfully with authorities. Then vv 6–9, according to Michel, form Qoheleth's critical commentary on such traditional wisdom. His understanding of vv 6–9 can be paraphrased: yes, there is a time for judgment, but the "evil" that burdens human beings is that they do not know the future. This ignorance, human and inevitable, is illustrated in the contrast between the "power" of the king (v 4) and the lack of power in human beings (v 8). Such "quotation with a commentary added to correct it" (100) is found elsewhere, e.g., 7:11–12 in contrast to 7:13–14. One may quibble at times whether Qoheleth is actually "quoting" (esp. quoting himself, a *Selbstzitat*) a traditional saying, but there can be no mistaking a deliberate dialogue between his own views and the traditional teaching. Chaps. 7 and 8 are filled with this dialectic. At the same time, the delicate nature of this interpretation is clear from the differences between Lohfink and Michel. Is 8:2–4 a critique on 8:1, and is 8:6b–7 a critique on 8:5–6b (Lohfink)? Or does 8:6–9 correct 8:1–5 (Michel)?

Even though there was no longer any kingship in Israel, the references to king and to court are not simply harking back to traditional life settings of a courtier. Many Jews would have been aware of the traditional wisdom lore concerning the court, but they would also have been confronted by an alien culture of Hellenistic authorities.

In 8:9 Qoheleth moves on to another distortion of power: the injustice that characterizes "every deed that is done under the sun." As an example he cites the triumph of the wicked (v 10—whatever be the exact translation of this corrupt verse), and he notes the evil effect that such example has upon humankind (v 11). According to our interpretation, vv 12–14 begin and end on the same note: the scandal and injustice caused by the prosperity of the wicked, while the just go unrewarded. In these verses, 12b–13 have been singled out as a classical example of a glossator at work. They affirm a distinction in the treatment of the God-fearing person and the wicked (traditional wisdom teaching) that is contrary to Qoheleth's thought. Rather, they should be seen as an indication of his knowledge of the traditional teaching, with which he deliberately disagrees. M. Fox takes a more lenient view: "Although Qohelet 'knows' the principle of retribution and nowhere denies it, he *also* knows there are cases that violate the rule. It is because Qohelet generally maintains the axioms of Wisdom that he is shocked by their violation and finds the aberrations absurd." But there is more than "shock" in Qoheleth's quarrel with traditional retribution; he denies that it works, as 8:14 indicates in this very context (cf. 2:12–17; 7:15). As often before (2:24; 3:12–13; 5:18), he concludes his reflection with the resigned statement that joy should be prized as a kind of compensation for the hard life. It is understood, of course, that this possibility is entirely at the whim of God.

The conclusion of 8:15 is emphasized and elaborated in vv 16–17 by the claim that humans, even the wise, cannot understand the work of God (cf. 3:11). This is the work so often referred to as "done under the sun" (e.g., 1:13–14 and, in the present context, 8:9). The ending of chap. 8 serves as a transition to chap. 9.

Reflections   (9:1–12)

Bibliography

Ginsberg, H. L. "The Quintessence of Koheleth." In *Biblical and Other Studies*. Ed. A. Altmann. Philip W. Lown Institute of Advanced Judaic Studies: Studies and Texts, vol. 1. Cambridge: Harvard UP, 1963. 47–59. **Loretz, O.** Altorientalische und Kanaanäische Topoi im Buche Kohelet." *UF* 12 (1990) 267–78. **Michel, D.** *Eigenart*. 166–83. **Ogden, G. S.** "Qoheleth ix 1–16." *VT* 32 (1982) 158–69. **Savignac, J. de.** "La sagesse du Qohéleth et l'épopée de Gilgamesh." *VT* 28 (1978) 318–23.

Translation

[1] *Indeed, all this[a] I took to heart;[b] and all this I examined:[c] the just and the wise and their actions[d] are in the hand of God. Love from hatred human beings cannot tell; both are before them.[e]* [2] *Everything is the same for everybody:[a] the same lot for the just and the wicked, the good,[b] the clean and the unclean, the one who offers sacrifice and the one who does not. As it is for the good, so it is for the sinners; as it is for the one who takes an oath, so it is for the one who fears to take an oath.* [3] *This is an evil in all that is done under the sun: there is the same lot for all, and also the heart of human beings is set on evil, and folly is in their hearts during their lives. Then afterwards[a]—to the dead!* [4] *Indeed, who can be set apart?[a] For all the living there is hope, because "a live dog[b] is better off than a dead lion."* [5] *For the living know that they will die, but the dead know nothing! There is no longer any recompense for them because any memory of them has disappeared.* [6] *Their love, their hate, their jealousy, are long gone, and they have no portion ever again in all that is done under the sun.*

[7] *Go, eat your bread with joy and drink your wine with a merry heart because God has already accepted your deeds.* [8] *At all times let your clothing be white, and let no oil for your head be lacking.* [9] *Enjoy life[a] with a wife whom you love all the days of the vain life that are given you under the sun [   ],[b] for that is your portion in life, and for the toil with which you toil under the sun.* [10] *All that your hands find to do, do with might,[a] because there is no action, or answer, or knowledge, or wisdom in Sheol where you are going.*

[11] *Again I observed under the sun[a] that the swift do not win the race, nor the strong, the battle, nor do the wise have bread, nor the clever have riches, nor do those who know find favor; but a time of calamity[b] happens to them all.* [12] *For no one knows even his own time; like fish taken in a fatal snare or like birds taken in a trap, so people are caught[a] at a bad time when it suddenly falls upon them.*

Notes

1.a. The opening words (down to אשׁר) are uncertain, but the general meaning is clear. אֶת־כָּל־זֶה is redundant, but it is not to be deleted.

1.b. The more usual phrase (1:13, 17) is אֶל לִבִּי (not אֶל). However, the MT is reflected in the ancient versions (LXX, εἰς καρδίαν).

1.c. לָבוּר can be explained as the infinitive construct, continuing a main verb (GKC §114p), but the form is surprising. לָבוֹר (from ברר, "to sift"; cf. 3:18) would be expected; the verb is conjugated by analogy with ע"ו verbs. Others prefer to read "and my heart saw (all this)," on the basis of LXX (καὶ καρδία μου σὺν πᾶν εἶδεν τοῦτο) and Syr.

1.d. As vocalized, the singular of עֲבָדֵיהֶם would be עֶבֶד, a *hap. leg.* and an Aramaism.

1.e. הכל לפניהם has given rise to several interpretations. It can be rendered "all (both love and hatred) is before them" (referring to the collective humankind, האדם). "Before" is ambiguous. It can be understood temporally, as "before their time" (so Hertzberg; the phrase can refer only to the past, not the future, and it refers to divine predestination), or "in advance" (NJV). It can also be taken as "at their disposal" (Lauha). The reading of MT is dense and apparently repetitive; a popular emendation based on the LXX (cf. NRSV, NAB, and many commentators) is "all before them is vanity." This is derived from the first word of v 2, הכל, which is read as הבל.

2.a. הכל כאשר לכל is, literally, "all (is) as to all," i.e., everything turns out the same for everybody; the following words would then explain how this is true. However, LXX, Syr, Aq, and Vg joined v 2 to v 1. LXX read ματαιότης (הבל for הכל), and this has provided the grounds for the emendation proposed above for v 1. However, LXX itself is suspect, because it omits כאשר. Syr presents a conflate reading, and Vg reads *incerta*, "uncertain," apparently an interpretation of the first word of v 2. All things considered, MT is to be preferred, although הבל provides a smoother rendering.

2.b. The textual tradition for לטוב is uncertain. MT reads it, but LXX omits it. Syr and Vg add "and the evil." The word is redundant in view of the כחטא in v 2b.

3.a. אחריו, "after it [him]," can be understood adverbially "afterwards." The versions reflect other forms, or interpretations, of the text, such as "after them" (LXX, Syr), "their end" (Sym), "after these things" (Vg, Jerome).

4.a. The ketib has יבחר, "(who) is chosen?" This means "who can be excepted (from death)?" Many Hebrew MSS, and most of the ancient versions reflect יְחֻבַּר, "whoever is associated with (all the living)"—in the qere reading.

4.b. כלב is the subject in v 4b, and the *lamedh* before it is emphatic (cf. GKC §143e).

9.a. ראה חיים is, literally, "see life" (cf. "see good" in 3:13).

9.b. The repetitive "all your vain days" at the end of v 9a may be for emphasis (C. D. Ginsburg), but it is lacking in LXX, OL, Tg, Jerome, and seven MSS and should be omitted; see Podechard.

10.a. The punctuation of MT construes בכחך, "with your might," with לעשות, but several MSS, and LXX, Vulg, and Tg with the imperative, עשה.

11.a. For the opening formula, see 4:1, 7; here the infinitive absolute is used (GKC §113z).

11.b. "Time of calamity" is, literally, "time and event"; the event is to be taken as a misfortune; cf. עת רעה in v 12.

12.a. Although the *mem* before יוקשים, "caught," may have dropped out by haplography, the pual participle appears occasionally without it (GKC §52s).

Form/Structure/Setting

The second part of the second half of the book begins at 9:1 and continues to 11:6 (A. Wright, *CBQ* 30 [1968] 331). This part is characterized by the phrase "know/not know," which creates divisions at 9:12; 10:15; 11:2; and 11:5. It is hardly coincidental that two inclusions appear: אין יודע האדם and לא ידע האדם (vv 1, 12), and מקרה, יקרה (vv 2, 11). Verbal and conceptual connections between chaps. 3 and 9 have been pointed out by G. S. Ogden (*VT* 32 [1982] 158–69), e.g., מקרה in 2:14 and 3:19. However, it is not likely that the issue of God's love and hatred, raised in 9:1 is settled by the example in 9:13–16, in favor of the wise person, "for whom the outcome is always 'love'" (167).

The opening reflection (9:1–6) laments that human beings do not know whether God loves them or hates them, since things turn out the same for all. No distinction can be made between the treatment accorded to the good and that accorded to the wicked (cf. 8:14). Once again Qoheleth returns to the מקרה, "lot," of death, which all share (9:2–3; cf. 2:14–16; 3:14). This leads into an ironic praise of the dead, who are spared the troubles of those who live, for they no longer know love or hatred (v 6, an inclusion with v 1).

Another of Qoheleth's patented conclusions follows (9:7–10), as he vigorously commands the enjoyment of the normal pleasures that life may provide—in view of the fact that this will be impossible in Sheol.

A reflection about the "time of calamity" is offered in 9:11–12. It comes for everyone. Despite the talent and skill of human beings, they do not know when the evil time will "fall" upon them.

Comment

1 The initial כִּי, "indeed," is emphatic rather than causal. Qoheleth proceeds to sharpen his complaint concerning the inexplicable work of God (8:17). The "hand of God" is in itself ambiguous (cf. 2:24). It can be taken to mean a benign, protective divine providence (Wis 3:1; cf. Ps 31:6; Isa 50:2), or simply that God is in control of things (יָד, "power"; Prov 21:1; Isa 66:2). In view of what follows, it seems that Qoheleth understands it in the latter sense. Even were he to mean it in a benign way, it would be understood as a mere concession to common tradition. But he then goes on to point out that this is contradicted by harsh reality (vv 2–3). For him "the hand of God" is not a consoling thought or a sign of predilection; it merely designates divine power, from which there is no escape.

V 1b is ambiguous and its ending is textually obscure (see notes 1.e. and 2.a.). The ambiguity arises from the undefined nature of "love" and "hate." Is this divine (so that humans do not know whether God loves them or hates them?—so Fox, Levy, Lohfink, Podechard, NAB, NIV, NRSV, and others), or human? It is difficult to refer the love and hatred to human beings as agents. They would seem to *know* when they love and hate. Rather, one cannot know from experience, from the way things turn out, whom God truly loves since the same treatment is dealt out to the just and to the wicked alike (vv 2–3). The customary signs of blessing or curse have been displaced, since there is no comprehension of what God is about (8:17). Traditional wisdom recognized that man proposed and God disposed (Prov 16:1), but it still came down on the optimistic side of events. Qoheleth does not tolerate any easy conclusion.

Some interpret "love" and "hate" in an active sense (so Hertzberg, Lauha) in that they represent human activities. Hertzberg remarks: "humans do not even know whether and when the most common emotions will surface in them; one is not even completely master of one's own ego." But the inner life of humans hardly seems pertinent to a context that is dominated by divine power (v 1a) and by apparently "contradictory" retribution (vv 2–3). Nor are we dealing here with merismus (suggested by Whybray). Hebrew idiom expresses the idea of totality by opposites. But this is not the thrust of Qoheleth's remarks, as though he merely meant by love/hatred that humans know nothing. It is a particular agony that the divine love/hatred are not clearly defined in the events of a person's life.

R. Kroeber (54–55) points to the epilogue (ll. 545–50; 16.5–10) of Ptah-hotep's Instruction as a parallel to 9:1: "He whom God loves is a hearkener, (but) he whom God hates cannot hear" (*ANET*, 414). The love/hate contrast is divine, as it is in Qoheleth, but the meaning is quite different. Ptahhotep invokes divine retribution in favor of wisdom ("hearing"). It is because one hears (obeys) that God loves. But Qoheleth can see no rationale for the divine action.

The ending of v 1 is obscure and also uncertain. If the MT is retained, Qoheleth can be understood to say that the uncertainty of divine love/hatred is the possibility that human beings must face.

2 The first three words of v 2 ("everything is the same for everybody"; see note 2.a.) announce the lamentable fact of the one lot for all, and then particular cases are specified. If the text is corrected to "vanity" (for "all"), as in many current translations, there is little change in the general meaning. Because things turn out the same for all, Qoheleth had already passed the verdict of vanity in 2:15. If "vanity" is the correct reading in 9:2, it serves as a conclusion to v 1, preliminary to taking up the fate of individual classes of people.

Qoheleth presents the evidence for the claim made in v 1. There is one lot for the classes of people among whom there should be some differentiation. מקרה, "lot," is used in the sense of death in 2:14–17 and 3:19–21, where the lots of the wise/foolish and human/animal had been considered. Now Qoheleth approaches it from the point of view of retribution. His conclusion is that ethical considerations have nothing to do with the way things turn out for human beings. Although he may have held a strict ethical code, his interest does not lie here, but in the futility of ethical conduct as a guide to the divine will, or to the human condition.

3 The "evil" (cf. 5:12, 14; 6:1) consists in the fact that there is one מקרה, "death," for all, as Qoheleth has pointed out before (2:16–17). K. Galling, followed by A. Lauha, interprets v 3b as a "motivation," a moralizing explanation of human sinfulness as the reason for human mortality. Hence it is to be ascribed to a later editorial hand. This is unnecessary. Already in 8:11 Qoheleth had pointed out that the failure to execute justice moves people to do evil (cf. Ps 125:3). He is not moralizing; he is recognizing facts. His comment is biting; wickedness and folly (as he stated in 7:25) are madness, but they characterize life, and nothing is to be expected beyond it—only death. The journey to death was considered by the sages as the fate of fools (Prov 2:18; 5:5; 7:27; folly leads to Sheol and death), but Qoheleth emphasizes death as the unfortunate and common lot of all, good and bad alike. The expression is very abrupt: to the dead!

4 If the ketib is followed (see note 4.a.), there is a firm assertion that no one is exempt from the law of death: "who can be set apart?" This is what one would expect from Qoheleth; there is no exception from death. It is difficult to speculate why another reading (qere, whoever "is associated with [the living]") became attached to the verb. N. Lohfink thinks that later orthodoxy refused this denial of punishment for the wicked, and hence the qere (which is indeed rather flat) rendered the line "harmless."

Perhaps more important is the assertion about hope, the only time in the book that this note is sounded. The singling out of hope seems to be a startling reversal of 4:2, where the dead are praised as more fortunate than the living. There the context featured the oppression of the living; from that point of view, death would be preferable (cf. Job 3:13; 6:9). What is held out in v 4 is the experience of hope or trust (בטחון, occurring elsewhere only in 1 Kgs 18:19=Isa 36:4 and referring to Hezekiah's confidence in the face of the siege of Jerusalem). What kind of hope is meant? M. Fox answers forthrightly: "*Biṭṭāḥôn* is not 'hope' (knowing that one will die is not a 'hope') or a feeling of security, but rather something that can be relied on, something that one can be certain about (cf. Isa 36:4)."

Hence the certainty would be that of death. However, many commentators interpret this line in a positive manner. The living can hope that the joy that God gives (2:24–25, etc.) will somehow be theirs. Or at least there is hope associated with human activity, which the dead lack (9:10). N. Lohfink even questions if "perhaps" trust in God is meant. But Qoheleth gives no reason for the reader to think he is proposing a solution to the human predicament. Moreover, in the context of v 5 a bitter irony is seen to emerge: the advantage of the living is that they know . . . that they are going to die!

Qoheleth resorts to what was doubtless a popular saying in support of the advantage of being alive. The value of a dog in the ancient Near East is minimal if anything (1 Sam 7:43; 24:15). Hence the pungency of the comparison with the dead lion.

In connection with v 4, both R. Braun (*Kohelet*, 104) and N. Lohfink quote Euripides (*Troad.* ll. 634–35): "No, child! Do not compare life and death. Death means annihilation! The one who is still alive can hope." Braun has several other quotations from Hellenistic philosophers. But the degree of relevancy is the issue here. Perhaps Qoheleth's attitude to life is not as positive as that of Euripides, but he is arguing on a plane that is different from that of the Greek philosopher.

5 The irony of this verse is inescapable; the advantage of the living over the dead is that they know that they are going to die! If Qoheleth is not ironic here, he is speaking very abstractly (and some commentators construe him so). Such theoretical knowledge is hardly an advantage that the living have over the dead who know nothing. The description of the dead follows with a word play, שָׂכָר/זֵכֶר, "recompense"/"remembrance." Profit and remembrance have already been ruled out for the living (1:3, 11).

6 Love, hatred (these two words an inclusion with v 1), and jealousy are rhymed in Hebrew: קִנְאָתָם, שִׂנְאָתָם, אַהֲבָתָם; the latter word may bear the meaning "rivalry" as in 4:4. Elsewhere חֵלֶק ḥēleq, "portion," appears in connection with the recommendation to enjoy life (3:22; 5:17–18; 9:9), and it may retain a positive note here. But it is also associated with "all that is done under the sun" (an inclusion with v 3), which remains a disagreeable mystery for Qoheleth.

7 He now proceeds (vv 7–10) to develop the "portion" (a catch word, vv 6, 9) that humans *may* enjoy. The advice is similar to his other conclusions (2:24–26; 3:12–13, 22; 5:17–19; 7:14; 8:15), but it is sharper than most, inculcating *carpe diem* ("enjoy the day"). It lacks any introductory formula (cf. v 1, 11) and is expressed in commands. Bread and wine are staple food, and also symbols of life's joys as well as needs (Ps 104:14–15).

The meaning of v 7b is not immediately clear: in what sense has God already (or from a long time ago) רצה, "accepted," human actions? The verb is often used of divine pleasure in sacrifices (Deut 33:11; Amos 5:22, etc.). But in the context of Qoheleth's steady denial of any meaningful connection between human deed and divine reaction, this can only refer to divine largesse. The divine "pleasure" is manifested in that one is enjoying these gifts that Qoheleth is recommending. However, they are not "earned," for humans have no claim on them; they depend on the inscrutable will and generosity of God (2:24–26; 3:13). Lauha is inclined to derive 7b from the redactor's hand but finally allows it to stay as possibly expressing the idea of 5:19: the divine strategy is to keep humans occupied (Levy also refers to this passage). In v 7b the divine "pleasure" would seem to mean the mysterious approval and the gifts freely bestowed by God (cf. 2:26).

8 A change of clothes to festive attire (not necessarily white) is mentioned several times in the Bible (Esth 8:15; Judg 10:3). The use of oil or perfume is quite common (2 Sam 12:20). These occur here as symbols of joy and festivity (2 Sam 14:2; Ps 23:5).

9 The lack of the definite article before "wife" (literally, "woman") does not indicate that Qoheleth means any woman at all. He doubtless has one's wife in mind (cf. Prov 5:18–19). The usual irony is present; one is to accept this "portion," but without forgetting the perspective of "vain life" and its "toil."

These verses (7–9) find a striking parallel in the epic of Gilgamesh, where Siduri, the ale-wife, offers similar advice to the hero:

> Gilgamesh, whither rovest thou?
> The life thou pursuest thou shalt not find.
> When the gods created mankind,
> Death for mankind they set aside,
> Life in their own hands retaining.
> Thou Gilgamesh, let full be thy belly.
> Make thou merry by day and by night.
> Of each day make thou a feast of rejoicing.
> Day and night dance thou and play!
> Let thy garments be sparkling fresh,
> Thy head be washed; bathe thou in water.
> Pay heed to the little one that holds on to thy hand,
> Let thy spouse delight in thy bosom!
> For this is the task of [mankind]! (*ANET*, 90)

H. L. Ginsberg ("Quintessence," 59) remarks that "the proof that the Biblical passage must be literally (even if not directly) dependent on the Babylonian one is the identical order in which the ideas are presented." The sequence (noted also by E. Podechard) is fairly close: eat/drink, feasting, clothing, washing, wife; the child is not mentioned in Ecclesiastes. See also O. Loretz, *UF* 12 (1980) 267–78.

10 In view of Qoheleth's use of "find" as a key term in 6:10–8:17, where he never finds anything, the occurrence of the word here deserves attention. The meaning is quite casual: whatever activity one finds at hand—whatever one is able to do—one should pursue. This advice, to live intensely, is motivated by a dour but realistic perspective: in Sheol there is no real activity or life, so act now! This description of Sheol is a classic; it portrays a state of non-life.

11 Qoheleth now turns to a reflection upon the times of misfortune, or accidents, that thwart human endeavor. He enumerates five examples from different quarters: racing, war, livelihood, riches, and favor. The traditional wisdom was optimistic about the ability of human talents to achieve success in areas that corresponded to one's wisdom and skill ("Good sense brings favor" [חן], Prov 13:15). Running is not necessarily to be understood in the context of war, nor of the athletic games of the Greek period. It was also part of being an official courier (2 Sam 18:19–32). The final three qualities are tied together by wisdom terms: חכם, "wise," suggests either an artisan or a teacher; נבון, "clever," and ידע, "know," suggest influential counselors. Qoheleth maintains that, no matter what one's talents, because of events beyond human control, one never has a sure grip on success.

The "time of calamity" is an unfortunate time, a fortuitous event that happens when one cannot cope with it. It refers to death, but also to any serious adversity.

12 The background to this verse is 3:1–11, where Qoheleth singled out the key "times" determined by God, who "made everything beautiful in its time," but to which humans are not attuned. The comparison to the catching of fish and birds indicates the hopelessness of human beings when the evil time תִּפּוֹל, "falls," upon them. They have no control over "falling time." Lohfink calls attention to Homer's use of the image of the snare (*Odyssey*, 22.283ff.).

Explanation

The main concern of this section is clearly that of death, the great leveller, which comes to all. Although the recommendation to enjoy life is present, it is colored by the thought of death, which surrounds it in vv 1–6 and in 10b–14. D. Michel (*Eigenart*, 166–83) has interpreted vv 1–10 as a polemic against the hope that good deeds will be rewarded after death. He takes the opening verse as a quotation that affirms that the just are in the hands of God—*in the next life.* The phrase "love and hate" of v 1 is interpreted as God's reaction to humans (and Michel regards this as the minority opinion, e.g., Levy, Galling, Gordis, Lohfink), as opposed to a majority opinion, which would hold that humans cannot understand their own actions, nor have control over them (a view rejected above in the *Comment*). Qoheleth introduces nothing really new in vv 2–3; the inevitability of death for all has been mentioned before (e.g., 2:14–15; 3:19–22). The conclusions supposedly drawn in vv 4–6 by Qoheleth are: (1) the living differ from the dead in that they have hope; (2) the dead know nothing, but the living know at least that they will die; (3) the dead have no reward (שָׂכָר *śākār*) because remembrance (זֵכֶר *zēker*) of them is forgotten. The strong words in v 6, that love and hatred (cf. v 1) and jealousy disappear, continue the emphasis on death. Michel would claim that these words make sense only if Qoheleth is polemicizing against a view that would claim activity beyond death, a "portion" (חֵלֶק *ḥēleq*) that would involve life *on this earth* (cf. 9:6b). The recommendation to enjoy life in view of the inactivity in Sheol follows (vv 7–10),

What reception should be given to Michel's view? First of all, the evidence of the existence of a "quotation" is hard to come by (cf. M. Fox, *ZAW* 92 [1980] 416–31), and Michel has recourse to this device much too frequently in his interpretation of the book. If we suppose that there is no quotation in a strict sense, it might be possible that Qoheleth is alluding to a view that did proclaim some eschatological hope, as seems to be the case in 3:21 (a distinction between the life-breath of humans and animals—which Qoheleth denies!). The basis for an eschatology that Qoheleth is supposedly disputing lies mainly in his denials of any differentiation after death. But this is the usual biblical doctrine (Ps 104:29–30). He merely affirms the denial and uses it as a motif. He does not delineate the position of his alleged opponents. Indeed, his message is taken up with the affirmation of this life as the only theater of activity. One may readily concede that at various times in the post-exilic period a boost was given to eschatological hope. But there is no objective evidence that Qoheleth is tilting with such ideas. His vision is severely limited to what happens under the sun in this world, and that is a view that is genuinely attested to in the rest of the Hebrew Bible in general. (Dan 12 would be an exception.) One cannot base an argument on the similarity of 9:1a to the line from Wis 3:1, "the souls of the just are in the hand of God, and no torment shall touch them." The date for this book, at the earliest, might be around the middle of the first century B.C. Although it is a Jewish book in essence, it shows a remarkable openness to Greek thought. Michel (*Eigenart*, 180) thinks that Qoheleth is arguing against the proponents that preceded the Greek work. There is simply no proof of this. At most, he points to a few key words: know, hope, love, and portion, which also occur in the Book of Wisdom. These are fairly common words in dealing with the next life (and also with this life!) and simply do not constitute an argument for the existence of an eschatological party.

There is little to gain from postulating imaginary opponents of Qoheleth. He is in tune with the rest of the Hebrew Bible with his denial of life after death. His startling difference is that he does not go along with the resignation and acceptance of this fate, and that is uncharacteristic of an Israelite.

There is no need to be shocked by the love/hate statement in 9:1. The ignorance of the divine love/hate is almost obvious once one considers Qoheleth's view of God's work and human ignorance. He says that from the point of view of experience (the essential point of view of the sages), humans cannot say that good fortune and blessings are the result of divine love. This follows not only from experience but from Qoheleth's basic contention that God's ways with humans are inscrutable.

Such a view of divine retribution is not, of course, a view commonly expressed in the Bible. The Lord's ways are mysterious, no doubt, but the Law and the Prophets proclaim quite clearly that the divine love/hatred is generally geared to human conduct. On the other hand, "Jacob I have loved, but Esau I have hated" (Mal 1:2; cf. Rom 9:13) is a statement of divine choice; it does not bear directly on the love/hatred relationship envisioned by Qoheleth, but it is a statement of divine freedom which he acknowledged.

"The same lot for the just and the wicked" is a grief for Job and for Qoheleth. It was put well by the slave to his master in the "Dialogue of Pessimism" (*BWL*, 149; *ANET*, 601). When the master resolves against an action for the common good, the slave urges him,

> "Do not perform, sir, do not perform.
> Go up on to the ancient ruin heaps and walk about;
> See the skulls of high and low.
> Which is the malefactor and which is the benefactor?" (ll. 75–78)

This is quite close to the complaint of Qoheleth. Death makes no distinction between the good and the wicked.

Various Applications of Wisdom   (9:13–10:15)

Bibliography

Frendo, A. "The 'Broken Construct Chain' in Qoh 10,10b." *Bib* 62 (1981) 544–45. **Kottsieper, I.** "Die Bedeutung der Wz. ʿṣb und śkn in Koh 10, 9: Ein Beitrag zum hebr. Lexikon." *UF* 18 (1986) 213–22. **Leahy, M.** "The Meaning of Ecclesiastes 10,15." *ITQ* 18 (1951) 288–95. **Lohfink, N.** "*melek, šallîṭ* und *môšēl* bei Kohelet und die Abfassungszeit des Buchs." *Bib* 62 (1982) 535–43. **Michel, D.** *Eigenart.* 107–8. **Ogden, G.** "Qoheleth ix 17–x 20: Variations on the 'Theme of Wisdom's Strength and Vulnerability.'" *VT* 39 (1980) 27–37. **Piotti, F.** "Il rapporto tra ricchi, stolti e principi in Qoh. 10:6–7 alla luce della letteratura sapienziale." *ScC* 102 (1974) 328–33.

Translation

[13] *This also I observed under the sun: (an example of) wisdom[a] which seemed great[b] to me:* [14] *There was a small town with few men in it, to which a great king came. He surrounded it and invested it with great siegeworks.[a]* [15] *In it was to be found[a] a poor wise man who saved[b] the town by his wisdom, but no one had any thought for that poor man.* [16] *So I said, "better is wisdom than strength," but the wisdom of a poor man is despised and his words are not heeded.*

[17]   *The calm words of the wise[a] are better heeded*
            than the cry of a ruler among fools.
[18]   *Wisdom is better than weapons of war,*
            but one bungler can destroy a lot of good.[a]
[10:1] *Dead flies[a] corrupt and ferment[b] the perfumer's oil;*
            a little folly counts more than much wisdom.[c]

[2]   *The heart of the wise tends to the right,*
            the heart of the fool to the left.
[3]   *Also, when the fool[a] goes on his way,*
            he lacks any sense and he tells everyone that he is a fool.[b]

[4]   *If a ruler's wrath[a] rises against you,*
            do not yield[b] your place,
            for calmness[c] makes up[b] for great mistakes.
[5]   *There is an evil I have seen under the sun,*
            the kind[a] of error made by one who wields power:
[6]   *The fool[a] is placed among the exalted;*
            the great[b] and the rich dwell at the bottom.
[7]   *I have seen slaves on horseback,*
            and princes walking on foot[a] like slaves.

[8]   *Whoever digs a pit[a] may fall into it;*
            whoever tears down a wall a serpent may bite.
[9]   *Whoever quarries stones can be hurt by them;*
            whoever chops wood can be endangered[a] by it.

10 *If*[a] *the iron*[b] *is dull*[c]
      and[d] *the blade*[e] *has not been sharpened,*[f]
    one must exercise more strength;[g]
      but[h] *the advantage of skill*[i] *is (a matter of) wisdom.*
11 *If the serpent bites without*[a] *being charmed,*[b]
      then there is no advantage in being a charmer.[c]

12 *Words from the mouth of the wise win favor,*
      but the lips of a fool destroy[a] *him,*
13 *The words*[a] *of his mouth start with folly;*
      his talk ends in dangerous nonsense—
14   *for*[a] *the fool never stops talking.*
    No one[b] *knows what is going to happen,*[c]
      for,[d] *what will happen after him—who can tell him?*
15 *The*[a] *toil of a fool*[b] *wears him*[c] *out,*
      for[d] *he does not even know the way to town.*

Notes

13.a. חכמה means here an instance or example of wisdom, which is presented in the episode of vv 14–15.

13.b. The repetition and contrast of גדול, "great" (vv 13–14), and מסכן, "poor" (vv 15–16), in the story seem deliberate.

14.a. מצודים occurs in 7:26, meaning "snares"; cf. also מצודה in 9:12. Here the meaning of "siege works" is demanded by בנה עליה. But the meaning of מצוד remains uncertain (see the lengthy discussion of this word by N. Lohfink, *SagAT,* 285–86, esp. notes 85–87). The ancient versions (LXX, Sym, Syr, and Vg) understood here something like fortifications, but there is no hard evidence that they read מצורים (found in two MSS, presumably from מצור, "siege").

15.a. ומצא has an indefinite subject and is equivalent to the passive voice (GKC §144d).

15.b. In Hebrew the potential can be expressed by the perfect tense (ומלט; cf. GKC §106p; Judg 14:18; Esth 7:5). Hence translations differ: the man could have saved the city by his wisdom, but was then ignored—or he actually saved the city and was then ignored. M. V. Fox argues incisively for the fact: "It would be an entirely unpersuasive lesson for Qohelet to claim that this man *could* have saved the city but was not allowed to do so. The reader would certainly wonder how Qohelet could know that the wise man *could* have done this" (263).

17.a. Literally, MT has: "the words of the wise in calm are heard." There is an inherent ambiguity here: are the words spoken calmly or heard calmly? More likely the former.

18.a. טובה at the end of the verse seems to balance טובה, "better," at the beginning; hence, one should not separate out v 18b and join it to 10:1, as A. Lauha does.

10:1.a. זבובי מות, "flies of death," means dead flies, not flies that cause death (LXX, θανατοῦσαι). The plural, even with the singular verb, need not be changed to singular.

1.b. יאיש יביע are united asyndetically. The second verb is doubtful in this context; נבע has the meaning of "bubble." The tendency of commentators is to eliminate it as a gloss or even dittography (Barton, Zimmerli, Galling, Lauha, et al.), since it is omitted in Sym and Vg, and it appears as a noun in LXX ("preparation") and Syr ("vessel").

1.c. The translation of v 1b is uncertain. The Hebrew text reads, literally, "more precious (יקר) than wisdom, than honor, is a little folly." יקר can be interpreted out of Aramaic as "weighty," and probably should be given that meaning here (this in turn can suggest the meaning of "heavy" for כבוד). Many commentators join מחכמה מכבוד asyndetically as "massive wisdom" (NJV) or "an abundance of wisdom" (Gordis). LXX interpreted differently, "more prized is a little wisdom than the glory of great folly." The context suggests that v 1b is in synonymous parallelism with v 1a, and the meaning would be that a little folly outweighs a lot of wisdom.

3.a. The meaning is not affected by the choice between the qere, which does not read the article, and the ketib, which reads the article in כשהסכל. The choice of the noun סכל is in deliberate contrast with כסיל in v 2.

3.b. The translation, "he is a fool," retains the ambiguity of the text (see the *Comment*). The ancient versions go in various directions: καὶ ἃ λογιεῖται πάντα of LXX may be a corruption of καὶ λέγει τά πάντα(cf. A. McNeile, 165); Vg has "he considers all to be fools." The ambiguity stems from לכל, which can be interpreted as "to all," or "concerning all."

4.a. רוח here means "wrath" (cf. Judg 8:3; Prov 16:32).

4.b. There is a play on נוח in the sense of "leave" (v 4a) and "leave alone," "avoid" (v 4b). The precise nuance of יניח (which is not to be emended) remains unclear; LXX and Vg understood it in the sense of "assuage, give rest."

4.c. For the meaning of מרפא (the root is רפה), see Prov 14:30; 15:4; Sir 36:28.

5.a. The *kaph* before שׁגגה could also be interpreted as the asseverative *kaph* (so R. Gordis); cf. GKC §118x.

6.a. The MT vocalizes הסכל as the abstract instead of the concrete, "fool," that is reflected in the ancient versions.

6.b. It also associates רבים, "great," with מרומים, "high places," despite the fact that the latter has the definite article. It seems better to join רבים with the "rich" of v 6b.

7.a. על הארץ is best rendered in English idiom as "on foot," as in NEB.

8.a. גומץ is a *hap. leg.*, and probably a borrowing from Aramaic; it is equivalent to שׁחת (cf. Whitley, *Koheleth*, 86).

9.a. The nipal of סכן is a *hap. leg.*; the root is perhaps to be associated with Aramaic *skn*, "be in danger" (LXX, κινδυνεύσει); cf. Whitley, *Koheleth*, 86. I. Kottsieper (*UF* 18 [1986] 213–22) argues for "pierce" on the basis of a Ugaritic parallel *(sknt)*.

10.a. No translation of this verse is certain. The ancient versions seem to have read basically the same text as the Hebrew, but they are confused. For a range of interpretations, see C. D. Ginsburg and R. Gordis. Nevertheless, most modern versions agree that at issue is a dull instrument that has to be treated, unless one is going to use sheer strength.

10.b. ברזל means here an iron tool, such as an axe (cf. v 9).

10.c. קהה (occurring only here in the piel) is used in the qal (Ezek 28:2) of teeth that are blunt or dull.

10.d. והוא marks a change of subject from the previous clause and associates the agent with the subject of v 9.

10.e. פנים is interpreted to mean the face or edge ("blade") of the iron instrument, on the basis of Ezek 21:21.

10.f. קלקל is pilpel of קלל, "to be light." In the only other usage it seems to indicate shaking (of arrows, Ezek 21:26), and it is interpreted here as meaning the quick movements of sharpening an instrument.

10.g. The *waw* prefixed to חילים, "strength," is emphatic, like the *waw* of apodosis; cf. Joüon §177n.

10.h. The last three words are, literally, "and the advantage of making succeed is wisdom." A. Frendo (*Bib* 62 [1981] 544–45) translates, "the advantage of wisdom is success." In this view, יתרון is construed with חכמה, while הכשׁיר separates them.

10.i. הכשׁיר (qere) is the hipil absolute infinitive of כשׁר, which is found also in the qal (11:6, "succeed"; in Esth 8:5, "to be proper"). Here it presumably refers to making the instrument a successful one, i.e., sharpening it. The ancient versions had trouble with the line, but MT should be retained.

11.a. See בלא עתך in 7:17; the idea is that one is bitten before the words of the charm are uttered.

11.b. There is deliberate alliteration in נחשׁ/לחשׁ and נחשׁ לבעל הלשׁון and יתרון לבעל הלשׁון.

11.c. "Charmer" is literally "master of the tongue." One may question whether the tongue refers to the charmer or to the snake.

12.a. בלע means "swallow," hence "destroy"; the verb is feminine singular, despite the fact that "lips" is in the dual; cf. GKC §145 k, n.

13.a. The juxtapositional style characteristic of proverbial sayings marks vv 12–13, which find their logical conclusion in v 14a.

14.a. V 14a obviously continues the topic of foolish speech; the initial "and" has a causal meaning; cf. GKC §158a.

14.b. V 14b resembles 8:7. In context, the subject האדם can be understood to refer to the ignorant fool.

14.c. Except for Tg, the ancient versions seem to reflect מה שׁהיה, "what has been," so that the apparent tautology (יהיה) is averted. The MT is to be retained; cf. 8:7.

14.d. Again, the *waw* in ואשׁר is causal; cf. כי in 8:7.

15.a. Literally, the MT can be rendered "the toil of fools—(she) weakens him." The grammatical peculiarities are obvious but not insuperable. עמל is normally masculine, and here it is construed with the feminine form of the verb (which Whitley, *Koheleth*, 86–88, would explain as masculine, the preformative *taw* being explained, on analogy with Ugaritic, as pointing to the *taqtul* type).

15.b. The singular, "fool," seems to be reflected in important Greek MSS and Tg, but it is also possible to regard the *mem* as an enclitic added on to the old genitive case ending.

15.c. R. Gordis would explain the singular suffix, "him," as a distributive use; cf. GKC §145m.

Because of these grammatical difficulties, many commentators prefer the conjecture first offered by A. Ehrlich: הכסיל מתי ייגענו, "when will the labor of the fool weary him?" (Galling, Hertzberg, Lauha, NAB, NEB); this does not represent a change in *meaning* from the attempt to explain the MT.

15.d. אשׁר introduces v 15b and can be understood as the relative particle, or as "so that" (GKC §166b), or, more probably, as "because." This ambiguity enables some commentators (G. Barton) to construe it with v 15a, as a relative clause; but this is unnecessary.

Form/Structure/Setting

The length of this unit is determined by the occurrence of the key phrase "not know" in 10:14–15 (cf. A. Wright, *CBQ* 30 (1968) 313–14, and the remarks on structure in the Introduction, p. xl). Possibly "city" can be taken as an inclusion (9:14; 10:15).

There is a general recognition that Qoheleth treats of several disparate items and uses various forms toward the end of his book. For example, R. N. Whybray gives to 10:1–11:6 the title of "miscellaneous sayings" (9:13–18 is entitled "the limited value of wisdom"). This section can be compared with the sayings that begin 7:1ff. We have already seen that the division and interpretation of that chapter posed problems for every interpreter. The difficulties will be perhaps best appreciated if we lay out at the beginning the forms that this commentary recognizes in 9:13–10:15.

9:13–16 is an example story (vv 13–15) that is followed by a "better" saying in favor of wisdom (v 15a). This is immediately modified by the two-line saying in v 16b. Catch words in v 16: חכמה *hokmâh*, with v 15; טובה, with v 18 (where it occurs twice); נשׁמעים, with v 17; דברי, with v 17.

10:1 continues the theme of the vulnerability of wisdom in a saying that specifies the power of even a little folly to outweigh and even undo wisdom.

In 10:2–3, two sayings characterize the conduct of the fool. Catchwords: wise/wisdom in vv 1–2; fool/folly in vv 1,2,3.

10:4 is an admonition with a motive clause, concerning conduct before some kind of ruler (מושׁל, not a king).

10:5–7 contains an introduction (v 5) to two sayings (vv 6–7) that illustrate folly that the powerful (שׁליט, not מושׁל) are capable of: the rewarding of fools and slaves.

10:8–9 is made up of two sayings with a common theme.

10:10–11 comprises two sayings on the application of wisdom.

10:12–15 contains sayings about the dangerous folly of a fool's garrulity (vv 12–14a), followed by sayings on human ignorance and folly (vv 14b–15).

A conceptual unity is lacking to 9:13–10:15. G. Ogden (*VT* 32 [1982] 158–69) makes many useful observations about the text, but his "inclusions" strain under the weight attached to them. It seems better not to impose a logical unity upon these verses. The vulnerability of wisdom, a topic perhaps triggered by the example story in 9:13–15, keys into 9:17–18 (a little folly can spoil wisdom), but it is difficult to see this theme continued all the way through chap. 10.

Comment

13 Vv 13–15 constitute an example story (cf. 4:13–16). The point is expressed
in v 16: although wisdom may be better than strength, it does not secure victory,
as shown by the story of the poor wise man whose wisdom is not acknowledged.
Commentators have sought in vain to identify the "poor but wise" person of v 15.
Rather, this *is* a story, something typical that illustrates a point.

Qoheleth terms his story "wisdom" since a wise man is involved in it, but the
value of wisdom will be relativized by the story. This case was important (literally,
"great") to him because of the way the event turned out.

14–15 A terse description of the siege of a small town by a powerful army is
presented in this example story. The tradition emphasized the value of wisdom
in the prosecution of war (Prov 21:22, a wise man conquers a city). One may
presume that the poverty of the wise person mentioned in the story is the reason
he did not win proper recognition. The social disadvantages of poverty are frequently noticed by the sage (Prov 14:20; 18:23, and especially Sir 13:21–23). As
indicated in the *Notes*, it seems better to take this story not as a potential but as
what actually happened: the wise man delivered the city but was then disregarded.

16 The conclusion to the story is couched in a "yes, but" style: wisdom is
better than strength, but when it is not recognized, as in the case of the poor
man, it counts for nothing. V 16 has associated with it some sayings (vv 17–18):
the word נשמעים, "heard," in both verses is a catch word, and טובה, "better," in vv
16, 18 is an inclusion.

17 The hearing of the words of the wise (v 16) is picked up again. The advice
of sages is rated higher than the ranting of an official who has to deal with fools
(the meaning is not that the official is the prime fool). M. Fox would place the
emphasis on the *way* the words are communicated, quietly or raucously. The quiet
style is more effective than shouting. In any case, v 17 is a saying in favor of wisdom, typical of the tradition.

18 Verse 18a is clearly in the spirit of v 16a: the supremacy of wisdom in battle.
If taken with v 17, it continues the recognition of the art of wisdom, but both
verses then come up against reality in v 18b: one slip can undo everything. Thus,
vv 17–18a, with v 18b, constitute a "yes, but" saying. The second half of v 18 introduces the modification that wisdom can be undone by a single חוטא ("bungler,"
or "loser," rather than "sinner"; cf. 2:26). It is unnecessary to associate v 18b with
the examples that follow in 10:1 (a small item can spoil everything), as A. Lauha
does, by rearranging the verses.

10:1 Although the text is uncertain (see the *Notes*), the general meaning is
beyond doubt. A small thing, no matter how apparently insignificant, can spoil
one's efforts. Thus dead flies will spoil the perfume, and an ounce of folly can
undo wisdom. The idea of the vulnerability of wisdom is itself a compliment to
the wisdom tradition with which Qoheleth is so often at odds. It is another sign
that judgments about Qoheleth and wisdom ("bankruptcy" and other wholesale
judgments) have to be reconsidered. In many of the sayings that follow in chap.
10, there is a positive judgment in favor of the wisdom tradition. It is worth repeating that he never recommends folly, even if wisdom is found wanting.

2 לב, "heart," designates here not only the reason at work in arriving at a
decision but also the will and direction one takes. It occurs again in v 3, with *the*

meaning of (good) sense. "Right" and "left" mean more than that the wise and the fool differ. One does well, the other poorly. The right side is the side of prosperity and good fortune (cf. "Ben-Jamin," Gen 48:14; Matt 25:33), and the left that of disaster and ill omen. The saying is not unlike 2:14; in both a decision is made in favor of the wise person as opposed to the fool, along the lines of traditional wisdom. However, it is clear from Qoheleth's general critical attitude that such sayings are not to be absolutized.

3 It is better to understand דרך, "way," literally, not metaphorically (path of life). V 3b is ambiguous (see note 3.b.). It can mean that the fool tells everyone that he himself is a fool, or that he calls everyone else a fool. The former is more likely, and then one can understand this to mean that he advertises his foolishness by his foolish conduct.

Vv 2–3 are united by reason of content (the emphasis is on the fool) and catch words (לב, "heart"; כסיל/סכל, "fool").

4 In 8:2–3 the advice to courtiers was gauged to let them know their place before the all-powerful king; personal wisdom is controlled by royal power. The מושל here is not the מלך, "king," but some lesser official in authority, wherever this "court" may be; see N. Lohfink, *Bib* 62 (1982) 535–43 on the various terms for officials used in vv 4–5. Lohfink acknowledges that these sayings do not have a specific court for their setting. But there were lesser circles of authority, and it behooved a courtier to know how to handle various situations. This is typical of traditional wisdom advice, e.g., Prov 16:14; 27:1–3; 25:6–7. The admonition in this verse is less fearful than in 8:2–3, but no less diplomatic. At all costs, the courtier is to keep cool. Tranquillity is a regular topic in the wisdom tradition (Prov 14:30; 15:4; מרפא occurs in both verses). It is not clear whether the חטאים, "mistakes," are those of the ruler or courtier. A healing word and calm response can solve a touchy situation. V 4 can be loosely associated with vv 5–7, because of the officials envisioned: ruler, powerful, prince.

5–7 The introductory formula has appeared before (5:12; 6:1). Now it introduces a judgment upon the topsy-turvy conditions described in vv 6–7. The responsibility for this situation is attributed to one who wields power (שליט, not מושל as in v 4); he commits an "error" in allowing such a situation to obtain. The examples that follow seem to be a wisdom *topos* (Prov 19:10; 30:21–23; cf. R. C. van Leeuwen, "Proverbs 30:21–23 and the Biblical World Upside Down," *JBL* 105 [1986] 599–610). Similar instances from the admonitions of the Egyptian sage, Ipuwer, can be cited (*ANET*, 441–43), but they are actually describing a greater social chaos.

Vv 6–7 seem to be a disparagement of folly: the fool should not be exalted; the slave should not be treated as a ruler. There may be a middle- or upper-class scale of values reflected in these judgments. At the same time, they illustrate the uncertainty of the courtier, despite wisdom: things do not turn out the way one expects. The examples reflect the tangled politics and sociological conditions that can produce the situations that Qoheleth envisions.

8–9 These verses also deal with uncertainty; one never knows what may happen in a given activity. The use of the participial style (e.g., the one digging) is characteristic of wisdom sayings. The verbs can be translated with a modal nuance ("may"), rather than as declarative statements.

The maxim about digging a pit appears frequently elsewhere (Prov 26:27; Pss 7:16; 9:16–17; 35:7–8; 57:7; Sir 27:26). It is the parade example of the act-consequence view of retribution advocated by K. Koch: the evil-doer will/ should fall by the very evil that is perpetrated; wrongdoing is essentially corruptive for the wrong-doer, because it comes back upon him. It has been argued above (pp. lxi, lxvi) that this is a one-sided view of retribution in the OT. The Lord's personal agency is described as directly at work in the majority of cases. The act-consequence view of reality is not to be characterized simply as "Israelite mentality" (see the critique by M. Fox, 124–27, and also by E. Huwiler in R. E. Murphy, *BTB* 21 [1991] 31).

However, it should be emphasized that there is no reason to interpret v 10 as digging a hole precisely for another to fall into (pace J. Crenshaw). What Qoheleth has in mind is an accident: one may fall into a hole that one has dug. Similarly, it is possible to be bitten by a snake while tearing down a wall. These sayings illustrate the uncertainty and the unexpected in life's affairs. There is always the possibility of an accident, even in the most pedestrian activity. These sayings fit well with 9:11–12 and 10:14 about the "evil time" and human ignorance.

The reference to the serpent can be illustrated by Amos 5:19. The connection between walls and serpents is not at first obvious until one recalls that the "mortar" in ancient walls and buildings of Israel would be any kind of small loose fill, in which a serpent might readily lurk.

9   Two more examples of the theme of v 8 are provided: everyday activities can have unforeseen results: the potential for danger is present while quarrying rock or chopping wood (cf. Deut 19:5).

10–11   These verses are linked in a literary and conceptual unity. Both begin with an "if" clause, and both point up the need of using one's expertise, either with a dull blade or with a snake that can be charmed. As opposed to the uncertainties and risks in vv 8–9, the verses call for the exercise of wisdom. Of course, there is always a risk if one does not use one's skill, as in chopping wood (v 9).

Although the translation of v 10a is uncertain (see the *Notes*), the general meaning is clear: the difficulty of cutting with a dull blade. Despite the grammatical peculiarity of v 10b, it must mean in context that it is up to wisdom to remedy the situation that has just been described. Instead of increasing one's efforts, one should be wise enough to sharpen the instrument.

V 11 also calls for the use of technical skill, in this case, snake-charming. The point of the saying is that even the experts fail if they do not apply their skill. The "advantage" (יתרון *yitrôn*, a catch word in vv 10–11) lies in exercising one's ability. Snake-charming is mentioned several times in the Bible: Isa 3:3; Sir 12:13; cf. Jer 8:17; Ps 58:5–6. M. Fox thinks the saying can be generalized: "no one, *not even* the skilled man, can undo damage after the fact."

12   There seems to be no connection with the preceding sayings except that "tongue" occurs in v 11. V 12 begins with "words," which are certainly the topic of vv 12–15, although H. Hertzberg would try to unite 12–20 by pointing to "word" in v 20 as an inclusion.

The succinctness of v 12a makes for ambiguity. It could mean that the words of the wise are gracious, as in the phrase "the graciousness of his lips": (Prov 28:8; cf. Ps 45:3). However, the parallelism suggests that graciousness or favor (חן) is won for the wise by speech (Prov 14:3). The saying is completely in line with traditional wisdom. But it is clear from 9:11 (חן, again) that Qoheleth has already relativized the value of wise speech, which is not always successful. In the present context he is primarily concerned with the hopeless task of the fool, as v 12b (cf. Prov 18:7) and the following verses (13–14) indicate. For the *topos* of speech, see Prov 10:13; 12:18; 14:3 and passim.

13 The thought of v 12b is continued here in the juxtapositional style that is characteristic of proverbs ("the beginning—folly"). From beginning to end, the speech of the fool is a disaster. The "end" can be understood as the prolonged effect of his speech.

14 V 14a is to be considered as completing v 13. The folly of many words has been treated before (5:1–2, 6; 6:11).

The connection between v 14b and the preceding lines about foolish speech seems tenuous. Qoheleth picks up the thought, even the phrases, of 8:7 (cf. 6:12) and applies them in the present context to the fool. In these earlier passages, human ignorance is alleged in order to show the vanity of speech (no matter how wise). Now in v 14b ignorance is associated with the chatter of fools.

15 The catch word סכל/כסיל, "fool," is the only thing that ties this verse to the preceding lines. The conduct, and not the speech, of a fool is the concern, but the end result is the same. His conduct—he cannot even find his way to the city—is as futile as his words. His walk, as well as his talk, avails nothing; he merely tires from it all.

Explanation

Most commentators agree that this section contains relatively disparate units, and hence it is difficult to bring them under one overarching title. An exception to this view is N. Lohfink, who considers the end of the book, 9:7–12:7, as treating of ethics. He allows that the material consists mainly of sayings, but he finds an outer framework, 9:7–9 and 11:1–12:7 (dealing with enjoyment of life) and an inner framework, 9:10 and 11:4–6 (dealing with vitality of action as opposed to inactivity). These may appear to be a frail support to the varied contents of 9:11–11:3. He regards 9:13–10:7 as dealing with the opportunities of the wise in the political arena—in contrast to 10:12–11:3, which are concerned simply with personal security.

Lohfink allows that "ethics" may not be the right word for the content. His point is that traditional wisdom deals with reality, "the way it is." That is certainly correct; traditional wisdom deals with reality as well as morality: "the way it is," as well as "the way things ought to be." Many of the sayings in the Book of Proverbs are experiential, mere observations, and do not *per se* urge a course of moral action (cf. R. E. Murphy, *The Tree of Life*, 7–8).

This section also has a bearing on the oft-repeated charge that the book represents the crisis or bankruptcy of wisdom (e.g., H. D. Preuss, *Einführung in die alttestamentliche Weisheitsliteratur,* 53, 173, and passim). Such a charge is made possible by reducing wisdom to the alleged act/consequence interpretation that is supposedly torpedoed by Job and Ecclesiastes. But if one operates with a more flexible notion of what biblical wisdom is about, one will see from this section that Qoheleth leaves room for traditional wisdom, not as a panacea for life, but as reflecting part of reality. See M. Fox ["Qoheleth's Epistemology," *HUCA* 58 [1987] 137–54], who argues forcefully against Ecclesiastes being simply a polemic against traditional wisdom.

A Collection of Sayings   (10:16–11:2)

Bibliography

Ellermeier, F. *Qohelet I/1*. 252–61. **Michel, D.** *Eigenart*. 207–8. **Salters, R. B.** "Text and Exegesis in Koh 10,19." *ZAW* 89 (1977) 423–26. **Staerk, W.** "Zur Exegese von Koh 10²⁰ und 11¹." *ZAW* 59 (1942/43) 216–18. **Thomas, D. W.** "A Note on במדעך in Ecclesiastes X 20." *JTS* 50 (1949) 177.

Translations

16   Woe[a] to you, O land, whose king is a (mere) youth,
      whose princes dine in the morning.

17   Happy[a] the land whose king is noble,[b]
      whose princes eat at the proper time,
      with discipline, not in debauchery.[c]

18   Because of laziness[a] the roof sinks in,
      and because of slack hands the house leaks.

19   For enjoyment one prepares a meal,[a]
      and wine makes life happy,
      and money answers[b] for everything.

20   Even in your thought[a] do not curse the king,
      and in your bedroom do not curse a rich person,
      for a bird in the sky can carry the news,
      a winged creature can report[b] what is said.[c]

11:1   Send forth[a] your bread upon the waters[b]—
      after[c] many days you may have it back!

2   Divide what you have in seven or even eight ways—
      you do not know what misfortune may befall the land![a]

Notes

16.a. אוֹי=אִי, "woe"; cf. the textual note on 4:10.

17.a. For the form אַשְׁרֵי, see GKC §911.

17.b. בֶּן חוֹרִים is "a son of a freemen," i.e., one born to the position.

17.c. The last three words are, literally, "with strength, and not in drinking." Since the phrase qualifies the "proper time" for eating, "strength" is to be understood in the sense of self-control. But the succinctness of the phrase allows other nuances: "in a manly way, and not as drunkards"; "to gain strength, not for the pleasure of drinking."

18.a. עַצְלְתַיִם, "laziness," is a *hap. leg.*, and probably to be explained as the intensive dual of עצלה (cf. Prov 19:15).

19.a. The translation preserves the chiasm in v 19a. The phrase "make bread" is the equivalent of preparing a meal (Ezek 4:15), and the participle, עֹשִׂים, is to be construed with an indefinite subject rather than with the princes of v 17.

19.b. LXX and Vg interpreted the root ענה, "answer," in the sense of "hear, obey."

20.a. Although the general meaning is clear, questions can be raised. Because במדעך, "in your thought," is in parallelism with a noun indicating place, doubts have been cast upon it by commentators; see D. W. Thomas, *JTS* 50 (1949) 177. But rigidity in parallelism should not be expected.

20.b. The MT vocalizes יגיד as hipil jussive, for no apparent reason (cf. GKC §109i, k).

20.c. דבר, curiously, without the article, is parallel to "news" (הקול), with the article).

11:1.a. שלח does not mean "throw, cast"; it has the meaning of "let go, send."

1.b. *hammayim* and *hayyāmîm* (v 1b) form an alliteration.

1.c. כי, "for," can have various meanings (causal, asseverative, concessive; cf. Williams §§444–49), depending upon the interpretation of the verse. In view of the ambiguity (see the *Comment*), it could be left untranslated, as maintained by D. Michel (*Eigenart* 207–8), who argues for deictic כי.

2.a. The structure of v 1 is repeated exactly here: an imperative (which can be understood as condition or concession; cf. GKC §160a), followed by a כי clause.

Form/Structure/Setting

It may appear arbitrary to consider 10:16–11:2 as a separate unit. The justification is the consistent appearance of the phrase "not know," which occurs in 11:2 (cf. also 11:6) and serves to structure this part of the book (see A. Wright, *CBQ* 30 [1968] 330–32). The משלים, "sayings," that are assembled here seem to be relatively independent of each other, even if some coordination can be suggested by the context. Thus, 10:16–17 form a unit because of the blessed/woe contrast. Similarly, 11:1–2 are related to each other by way of contrast. In form, 11:1–2, 6 are admonitions with כי clauses attached. Vv 18–20 are only loosely, if at all, connected; they consist of two sayings (18 and 19a, followed by an ironic comment in 19b) and an admonition (v 20).

Comment

16 Vv 16–17 introduce a new topic; they form an apostrophe to a country about its rulers, the king and princes (cf. 5:7–8). What is presented is to be seen as something "typical," rather than a reference to a specific contemporary event.

נער, "youth," has here the meaning of "too young" (H. Hertzberg). The young king is unequal to the responsibilities of his office, as the conduct of the princes demonstrates.

Drinking at an early hour is a sign of debauchery (Isa 5:11) and a breakdown in leadership (cf. Isa 5:22–23).

17 Although בן חורים, "of noble lineage," is not in strict opposition to "youth," it conveys the idea that the king is fully in charge, that he lives up to the standards of a royal family, and is not a *parvenu*. The contrast between v 16 and v 17 lies in the style of the leaders, not merely in the age or lineage of the king. The danger against which these verses warn has already been pointed out in the advice to Lemuel (Prov 31:4–5).

18 This warning against laziness can perhaps be related by context to the preceding verses; dissoluteness usually involves neglect of duty, and laziness can lead to destruction. The theme of laziness is a common one in the wisdom tradition (Prov 6:6–11; 12:11; 24:30–38; 29:19; Sir 22:1–2). V 18 has the air of a separate saying (cf. Prov 20:4; 21:25), associated with rulers only by juxtaposition.

It should be recalled that the flat roofs in Palestine were covered with lime, which eventually cracked and allowed rain to seep in (cf. Prov 19:13; 27:15), since no run-off was provided.

19 Several commentators (e.g., H. Hertzberg) would associate this statement with the dissoluteness described in v 16. However, the saying can be easily understood as a recommendation of the good life (food and wine), which has been urged several times before by Qoheleth. In this case the final clause (19b) is a sharp reminder that this life style is impossible without money, apparently an ironic comment.

20 This admonition, like the previous verses, seems to be an independent unit. Silence is the sign of the sage (cf. 10:14; Prov 10:19, etc.), and Qoheleth applies this to dealings with the rich and powerful. Cursing the king (cf. Exod 22:27) has to be avoided—"not even in your thought," he adds with some hyperbole (see note 20.a.). He had already called for circumspection in dealing with royalty (8:2–4; 10:4), and he shows the same attitude here. It could be that such realistic advice was prompted by the role of Jewish representatives at foreign courts.

The bird motif ("a bird in the sky") occurs in Aristophanes (*The Birds*, 601.49ff.), and in Juvenal (*Satires*, 9.95f.). And in English there is the saying, "a little bird told me."

11:1 The multivalence of proverbs can hardly be better exemplified than in vv 1–2. Three interpretations need to be considered.

The traditional interpretation (already in Jerome and the Targum) understood v 1a as a recommendation of alms-giving, which eventually will be rewarded (v 1b). The enduring popularity of this interpretation can be seen from Goethe's lines in his *West-östlicher Diwan*: "Was willst du untersuchen wohin die Milde fliesst! Ins Wasser wirf deine Kuchen, wer weiss, wer sie geniesst." ("Why do you want to find out where charity flows! Throw your bread into the water—who knows who will enjoy it?" [author's translation]; see *West-östlicher Divan*, ed. H. A. Maier [Tübingen: Niemeyer, 1965] 111; in *Hokmet Nameh: Buch der Sprüche*, 6:10). However, the action of letting bread go upon the water does not of itself suggest alms-giving. For a critique of W. Staerk (*ZAW* 59 [1942] 216–18), see F. Ellermeier, *Qohelet I/1*, 256–59.

F. Delitzsch and others have understood the phrase to refer to commerce on the sea. This view finds support in Isa 18:2, "which send (שלח) ambassadors in the sea and (in) papyrus vessels upon the waters (על פני מים)." In Isaiah the reference is to traveling by sea, and here in 11:1 to commerce by sea (לחם; cf. Prov 31:14). Accordingly, despite the risk and daring of such a course, one is counseled to take a commercial risk that has some possibility, but not certainty, of success. תמצאנו can have a modal nuance: you *may* find it. The venture at sea can be understood literally, or metaphorically for any venture. In any case, the interpretation flows naturally from the meaning of v 1a, which involves a risk. Take a calculated risk, since there may be a good result from it (v 1b).

A third interpretation is also possible. Bread in the water is a metaphor for doing something that is really senseless. The bread merely dissolves. But this action, which is counseled, can nevertheless paradoxically lead to an unexpected successful result (v 1b). The reason for this action is that we are simply ignorant of the future and its possibilities (10:14b; 11:5).

Only the second and third interpretations are to be taken seriously, since the text says nothing about alms-giving. Which of the two is appropriate? The answer depends upon the interpretation of 11:2.

2 The structural agreement between v 1 and 2 is a sign that these lines must be related in meaning.

Those who interpret v 1 in the sense of alms-giving see here the admonition to share possessions in several (seven or eight) ways.

The second interpretation (F. Delitzsch, R. Gordis, et al.) understands the division into portions as a precaution against the misfortune that may occur. The meaning is similar to "don't put all your eggs in one basket." The practice followed by Jacob in Gen 32:8–9 would be a concrete example.

The third interpretation (K. Galling, H. Hertzberg, et al.) finds in v 2 an antithesis to v 1. If previously the paradox of a possible success was held out (v 1), now one is warned not to bank on taking precautions against mishap. These will do no good; the misfortune one knows not of may be lurking ahead.

The third interpretation is vintage Qoheleth. The uncertainties (which may just possibly go in one's favor, v 1) are such that one cannot rely on careful moves. Precautions will bring no security. As G. von Rad has remarked, one cannot rely even on uncertainty itself. "Thus, not even the outcome of insecurity can be taken for granted!" *(also nicht einmal auf die Unsicherheit ist Verlass!)*; cf. *Theology of the Old Testament* (New York: Harper & Row, 1962–65) 1:456–57.

Explanation

The discontinuous character of these sayings is in character with the rest of chap. 10, although a certain grouping was noted above for particular verses: the wise and the foolish (10:2–3); the fool and speech (10:12–15). There is also some grouping here (10:16–17 and 11:1–2). Attempts have been made to tighten up the sayings. Thus, could the "house" of 10:18 refer to the "house of state" that is the subject of vv 16–17 (a suggestion of N. Lohfink)? There is no way of knowing whether any of these are original with Qoheleth or merely formed part of the common fund of wisdom that was the patrimony of the wise. R. Whybray remarks that Qoheleth "appears here as a wisdom teacher. Some of the sayings would occasion no surprise if they occurred in the Book of Proverbs. In others, Qoheleth's characteristically critical attitude towards conventional wisdom shows itself clearly" (150).

On the other hand, A. Barucq finds some units in chap. 10: a royal theme (vv 4–5, 16–17, 19–20) and the wise/foolish opposition (vv 8–15, 18–19). But he allows that it is difficult to speak of unity with the variety of literary forms that Qoheleth is employing. Much depends upon how the verses are construed. Whereas others would despair of uniting vv 16–20, D. Michel (*Qohelet*, 164) construes these verses as the views of the fool mentioned in 10:15, whose "toil" is wearisome.

Living in Uncertainty and Ignorance   (11:3–6)

Bibliography

Ellermeier, F. *Qohelet I/1*. 262–68. Kugel, J. *The Idea of Biblical Poetry: Parallelism and Its History*. New Haven: Yale UP, 1981. Michel, D. *Eigenart*. 208–10.

Translation

3 When the clouds become full,
      they pour rain[a] on the land.
    Whether a tree falls to the south or to the north,
      wherever it falls, there it will remain.[b]
4 Whoever observes the wind will not sow,
      and whoever looks at the clouds will not reap.
5 Just as you do not know the way of the life-breath
      [in][a] the limbs within a mother's womb,
    So you do not know the work of God
      who does everything.
6 In the morning sow your seed,
      and in[a] the evening let not your hands be idle,
    For you do not know which will be profitable,
      or if both will be equally good.

Notes

3.a. The punctuation of the MT joins נשם with העבים, but it could also be understood as the object of יריקו.

3.b. יהוא is an apocopated form of the verb הוה, a jussive form with an anomalous *aleph*; (א) יהו is comparable to the frequent יהי; cf. GKC §23i. Whitley (*Koheleth*, 93) derives the word from הָוָה (הוה), to be vocalized יֶהֱוֵא on the analogy of תֶּהֱוֵה in Dan 2:20.

5.a. The *kaph* in כעצמים can hardly be considered a conjunction like כאשׁר; cf. GKC §155g. Yet many translate as if two comparisons were stated: ignorance of the way of the רוּחַ and of the limbs in the womb. The MT is supported by LXX (ὡς ὀστᾶ) and Vg (*qua ratione ossa*), but it is sounder to follow several Hebrew MSS and Tg and to read בעצמים. רוּחַ can mean wind, or life-breath/spirit.

6.a. לערב can mean "until evening," or "in the evening" (cf. Gen 8:17; 49:27).

Form/Structure/Setting

Human ignorance is consistently highlighted in chaps. 9–11, and this small unit ends with a threefold affirmation of ignorance. Most commentators take 11:1–6 as a unit. Following the structural motifs of A. Wright, these verses can be set apart from 11:2. The concluding line (11:6) provides a title for this section: you know not what good may happen. In a similar way, 11:2b provides a title for 10:16–11:2: you know not what evil may happen; see A. Wright in NJBC 31:33–34, p. 494.

Qoheleth adopts the form of the saying in vv 3–5, and they all deal with nature: rain, falling trees, sowing, gestation. V 6, in the form of an admonition, returns to the theme of sowing. It is difficult to judge whether these verses are all (especially v 5) poetry, but our translation records them in poetic form; on the difficulty of distinguishing Hebrew poetry from prose, see J. Kugel, *The Idea of Biblical Poetry*, 59–95. Catch words link vv 3–4 (עבים, "clouds") and vv 4–5 (רוח, "wind," "life-breath"). V 3 seems to be connected with the previous unit by the phrase על הארץ, "upon the land."

Comment

3   This verse is usually understood as pointing to certain inexorable events about which humans know nothing and can do nothing. Whether the end result concerning the action of the clouds and the trees is good or bad is not said. Attention is simply drawn to a process that has its own inner laws, beyond human control. It makes no difference that human industry can change the lie of a fallen tree, or even interfere with clouds; such considerations are beyond the point of saying.

However, one may well ask if v 3 says more than this. The "falling" of the tree recalls 9:12, which speaks of the evil time that "falls" on a person. E. Podechard understood v 3 in the light of the "misfortune" mentioned in v 2; there are certain inevitable evils. N. Lohfink finds a "yes, but" saying in v 3: one can recognize cases where causal connections are at work (v 3a), but there is also the incalculable chance event which is determinative. A. Strobel thinks that the following is implied: one must act *before* the rain comes (and not wait for the "right" time as v 4 warns about), and see to it that the tree falls in the right direction.

4   This saying rests on the fact that there is a propitious time for sowing (wind) and for reaping (dryness). But the "right" time is ever uncertain, and the danger is that if one remains always on the watch for the perfect moment, one will never act. Hence the saying is aimed at those who are paralyzed by their concern for the right time. Once again human ignorance and impotence are scored, but the observation will not tolerate simple inaction. One has to get on with living (cf. v 6 and also 9:10) and give up the luxury of being "certain."

5   If רוח *rûaḥ* is translated as "wind," the meaning it has in v 4, then Qoheleth is offering two examples of natural mystery (wind and gestation), which he compares to the "work of God" (3:11; 7:13; 8:17). However, it seems better to recognize only one term of comparison, the action of the רוח, or "life-breath," in the womb (see note 5.a.). The mystery that conception and birth held for the Israelite is indicated in Ps 139:14–16; Job 10:10–11; 2 Mac 7:22. V 5 is the pivotal assertion for 11:3–6, and it reflects a basic observation in the second half of the book: human ignorance, especially of the work of God (8:17).

6   The topic of sowing is taken up from v 4. In v 6a it is not clear if two sowings, *in* the morning and *in* the evening, are intended, or merely one sowing in the morning accompanied by diligent labor *until* evening (see note 6.a.). The first alternative is suggested by the phrase in v 6b (this [sowing] or that); the advice is then to sow at both times if one is uncertain. The second alternative (until evening) stresses the continuous diligence of the sower throughout the day. In this case v 6b would refer both to the morning sowing and the continuing labor. The statement in v 6b goes better with the first than the second alternative. Then the entire verse warns against assuming that any given time for action is the "right" one. One time may be as right as another. Success does not depend upon human ingenuity. Qoheleth puts negatively what the sages expressed positively: "It is the Lord's blessing that brings wealth, and no effort can substitute for it," Prov 10:33 (NAB). His advice is motivated by uncertainty. One can never know how things will turn out; the action of God is beyond human calculation. At the same time, the command of v 6a precludes inaction. One must get on with life (cf. 9:10). The verse thus serves as a transition to the opening lines of the poem that follows ("how sweet it is . . .").

Explanation

These sayings, at first sight so disparate, are given a certain unity by the admonition in v 6. Despite human ignorance about reality and especially about what is going to happen, one cannot remain inactive. Paralysis is out of the question.

But when the sayings are analyzed separately, several levels of meaning can be detected. To the interpretations presented in the *Comment* above on v 3 one can add other points of view. A. Lauha regards the rain and fallen tree as examples of simple determinism. K. Galling adds that the implication is that one should not ask for the cause of such happenings. R. Whybray points to the notes of inevitability and randomness in nature that are exemplified. The applicability of the proverb, as well as the mystery of proverb performance, is illustrated by these various interpretations.

V 4 is a saying that matches the admonition found in v 6. One cannot remain inactive under the pretext of waiting for the "best" time. Or it can be linked with 11:1 if that verse is interpreted as in favor of taking a risk. While the examples are specific, the applicability of the saying is broad. V 5 touches upon a central teaching in Ecclesiastes, the mystery of God's "work." Since the divine activity undergirds all that happens, mere humans are at a loss to comprehend events.

Instruction concerning Youth and Old Age   (11:7–12:8)

Bibliography

Bruns, J. "The Imagery of Eccles 12,6a." *JBL* 84 (1965) 428–30. **Busto Saíz, J. R.** "Estructura métrica y estrófica del 'poema sobre la juventud y la vejez': Qohelet 11,7–12,7." *Sef* 43 (1983) 17–25. ———. בוראיך (Qoh 12,1): Reconsiderado." *Sef* 46 (1986) 85–87. **Buzy, D.** "Le portrait de la vielliesse (Ecclésiaste XII,1–7)." *RB* 41 (1932) 329–40. **Crenshaw, J. L.** "Youth and Old Age in Qoheleth." *HAR* 10 (1988) 1–13. **Fox, M. V.** "Aging and Death in Qohelet 12." *JSOT* 42 (1988) 55–77 (reproduced in *Qohelet.* 280–98). **Gilbert, M.** "La description de la vielliesse en Qohelet XII 1–7 est–elle allégorique?" In *Congress Volume, Vienna, 1980.* VTSup 32. Leiden: Brill, 1981. 96–109. **Ginsberg, H. L.** "Koheleth 12.4 in the Light of Ugaritic." *Syria* 33 (1956) 99–101. **Leahy, M.** "The Meaning of Ecclesiastes 12,1–5." *ITQ* 19 (1952) 297–300. **Moore, G. F.** "The Caper–plant and Its Edible Products, with Reference to Eccles. XII,5." *JBL* 10 (1891) 56–64. **Ogden, G.** "Qoheleth XI 7–XII 8: Qoheleth's Summons to Enjoyment and Reflection." *VT* 34 (1984) 27–38. **Piotti, F.** "Osservazioni su alcuni usi parallel extrabiblici nell' 'allegoria della vechiaia' (Qohelet 12,1–7)." *BeO* 21 (1977) 119–28. **Sawyer, J. F. A.** "The Ruined House in Ecclesiastes 12." *JBL* 94 (1975) 519–31. **Strauss, H.** "Erwägungen zur seelsorgerlichen Dimension von Kohelet 12,1–7." *ZTK* 78 (1981) 267–75. **Witzenrath, H.** *Süss ist das Licht . . . : Eine literaturwissenschaftliche Untersuchung zu Kohelet 11:7–12:7.* MUSKTF. ATSAT 11. St. Ottilien: Eos, 1979. **Youngblood, R.** "Qoheleth's 'Dark House' (Eccl 12.5)." *JETS* 29 (1986) 397–410.

Translation

7   *Sweet is the light,*
      and pleasant it is for the eyes to see the sun![a]
8   *However*[a] *many years one lives,*
      one should rejoice in them all,[b]
   but remember
      that the days of darkness will be many;
      all that is coming is vanity.
9   *Rejoice, O youth,*
      while you are young.
   Let your heart be merry
      in the days of your youth.
   Walk where your heart leads you,
      and where your eyes look,[a]
   but know that on all these (counts)
      God will bring you to judgment.[b]
10   *Banish trouble from your heart*
      and remove suffering from your body,
      for youthfulness and black hair[a] *are fleeting.*
12:1 *Remember your creator*[a] *in the days of your youth,*
      before the days of misfortune come

and the years arrive, of which you will say,
"I have no pleasure in them";[b]

2 Before the darkening of sun and light,[a]
and moon and stars,
and the return of clouds
after the rain;

3 When the guardians of the house tremble,
and strong men are bent over,
and the women at the mill cease because they are few,
and the ladies who look out of the windows are darkened;

4 When the doors in the street are closed,
and the noise of the grinding mill is low,
and one arises[a] at the sound of a bird,
and all the daughters of song[b] are quiet;

5 When one has fear[a] of heights,
and terrors are in the road;
and the almond tree blossoms,[b]
and the locust is heavy,[c]
and the caperberry[d] is opened.[e]
When[f] humans go to their everlasting home,[g]
and mourners go about the street;

6 Before the silver cord is [torn],[a]
and the golden bowl is shattered,[b]
And the jar by the fountain is broken,
and the pulley is [shattered][c] on the cistern,

7 And the dust returns[a]
to the earth as it was,
And the life-breath returns
to God who gave it.

8 Vanity of vanities! says Qoheleth,
all is vanity![a]

Notes

7.a. The "and" that begins v 7 is omitted in translation (so also Syr and Vg). It need not indicate a continuation of the previous section. R. Gordis points out that *waw* often introduces a new theme or division (e.g., 3:16, 4:4, etc.). It can be interpreted as a strengthening particle (KB[3] *s.v.* #20).

8.a. Normally כי אם is exceptive; cf. 3:12, 5:10, 8:15. Here כי can be taken as asseverative or causal; see the discussion in E. Podechard.

8.b. Again there is a fluctuation in the use of the pronominal suffix: כלם (masculine) refers to "years" (feminine).

9.a. The qere reading in the singular, מראה, as in 6:9, is reflected in the ancient versions; the meaning is not affected.

9.b. The invitation to joy is tempered in glosses found in the Greek tradition, where ἄμωμος is added after "heart" and μή is inserted before "eyes." For the problems this verse gave to the rabbis, see *Midrash Rabbah, Kohelet,* on 1:3. Num 15:39 is quoted in opposition, but the ending of the verse ("judgment") helped to settle the difficulty.

10.a. שחרות is a *hap. leg.*, and it is to be derived from שחר ("black," not "dawn"), and hence "dark hair," as opposed to the white hair of the elderly. The parallelism suggests youthfulness. Both LXX and Syr have a mistranslation ("folly," perhaps due to the association of folly with youth). R. Scott has a felicitous rendering: dark-haired youth. הֶבֶל is best translated here as "transient, fleeting" (cf. 6:12; 9:9).

12.1.a. The form of "your creator" is plural: בּוֹרְאֶיךָ; it can be understood as a plural of majesty or even explained as a singular (a ל"א verb vocalized as a ל"ה; so Gordis). The ancient versions have the singular. Many commentators regard the reference to creator as unexpected and unlikely, and propose other readings: (1) בְּאֵרְךָ, "your well/spring"; cf. Prov 5:15 where בְּאֵר is a metaphor for one's wife; (2) בּוֹרְךָ, "your pit/grave," suggested by the context of death; (3) בְּרִיךָ, "vigor" (NJV); (4) an understanding of the root ברא in the sense of healthy, not creator; cf. J. R. Busto Saíz, *Sef* 46 (1986) 86–87. None of these interpretations has won general assent.

1.b. As elsewhere (e.g., 2:6, מֵהֶם), the masculine suffix in בָּהֶם refers to a feminine antecedent.

2.a. הַשֶּׁמֶשׁ וְהָאוֹר may be hendiadys (Gordis), but "light" is a separate entity in Gen 1.

4.a. The interpretation of יָקוּם, "arise," is problematical. The subject might be קוֹל, "voice," the only obvious antecedent. It seems better to interpret it impersonally, "one rises" (cf. LXX, ἀναστήσεται; Syr, *wnqwm*; Vg has the plural, *consurgent*, and Sym is aberrant, παύσεται, "will cease"). The implication is that here a person is being described, presumably elderly, who is awakened merely by the song of a bird. Many reconstructions have been proposed; only one respects the consonantal text and divides thus: וְיִקְמֹל קוֹל, "the sound decays." It seems best to keep the MT. It is clear that "arise" is in contrast to יִשַּׁחוּ, "stoop," "be low."

4.b. בְּנוֹת הַשִּׁיר, "the daughters of song," has been variously interpreted: (1) birds (cf. בַּעֲלֵי כְנָפַיִם in 10:20; בְּנוֹת יַעֲנָה for ostriches in Mic 6:8; Job 30:29); (2) female singers (cf. Ugaritic *bnt hll*, "daughters of praise"); (3) songs.

5.a. יִרָאוּ, "they fear," is to be interpreted impersonally. Vg and Syr (in the singular) understand the verb as "fear," in contrast to the "see" in LXX, Sym, and several Hebrew MSS. "Fear" provides better parallelism with חַתְחַתִּים, "terrors," a *hapax* noun derived from חתת.

5.b. The verbs in v 5a resist any certain translation, and our rendering attempts to stay open to the two dominant interpretations (see the *Comment* on 12:5). יָנֵאץ, "blossom," is imperfect hipil of נצץ, with an *aleph* in full writing (cf. GKC §73g, "incorrectly written for *yānēṣ*"); the ancient versions support the meaning of "bloom." E. Podechard and others argue that the root should be considered as נאץ, "disdain," "reject" in hipil or pual.

5.c. סבל means "carry, bear" and in the hitpael "be burdened"; hence the possible meanings: "dragging one's self," as of one who is heavily burdened, or "becomes heavy." LXX has παχυνθῇ, "fat"; cf. Vg, *impinguabitur*).

5.d. הָאֲבִיּוֹנָה is a *hap. leg.*, and the ancient versions understood it as caperberry (cf. G. F. Moore, *JBL* 10 [1891] 56–64). Its leaves were regarded as stimulants to the appetite.

5.e. תָּפֵר is hipil imperfect of פרר, "to break"; its meaning here is doubtful. A passive meaning (and perhaps hopal תֻּפַר) seems to be reflected in LXX (διακεδασθῇ, "be scattered"), Sym (διαλυθῇ, "be broken"), and Vg (*dissipabitur*, "be dissipated"). M. Gilbert (VTSup 32, 105, n. 15), with several modern commentators, interprets the line to mean that the caperberry no longer has any effect (on the appetite).

5.f. כִּי, opening v 5b, can have different meanings according to the interpretation of the previous line: "but" (in contrast to the revival of nature) humans die; or it can mean simply "indeed," or "when."

5.g. בֵּית עוֹלָם (literally, "eternal home") means the grave, and it occurs only here in biblical Hebrew; however, it is found also in Egyptian, Palmyrene, Punic, and post-biblical Jewish sources; see E. Jenni, "Das Wort *ʿōlāmim* Alten Testament," *ZAW* 64 (1952) 197–248, esp. 211–217, and 65 (1953) 1–35, esp. 27–29, for references. R. Youngblood's attempt to render this as "dark house" has not succeeded.

6.a. The ketib has יִרְחַק, "is distant," and the qere has יֵרָתֵק, "is bound, joined." Neither of these yields satisfactory sense. The *Vorlage* of the ancient versions remains uncertain, but all have a stronger verb (LXX, "overthrow"; Sym, "cut"; Vg, "break"). Hence it is reasonable to suggest יִנָּתֵק, "is torn," and this is widely adopted by commentators (pace J. E. Bruns, *JBL* 84 [1965] 428–30).

6.b. תָּרֹץ, "shattered" can be explained as qal imperfect of רצץ (GKC §67q), conjugated after the analogy of the ע"ו verb. A revocalization in the hipal, תָּרִיץ, is preferred by many commentators since the verb does not seem to have an intransitive meaning in the qal conjugation. The picture presented by "cord" and "bowl" is not clear; presumably the bowl (a lamp?) would be suspended by the cord.

6.c. וְנָרֹץ was interpreted by Vg, Sym, and Tg as from the root רוץ, "run," but רצץ, "break," is the correct root, and the imperfect וְיָרֻץ should be read in line with the other imperfect tenses in the verse. גַּלְגַּל means "wheel," and here presumably a pulley; others argue for "bowl." The picture is that of a well with a broken pulley and smashed jar that served to carry the water.

7.a. There is no explanation for the occurrence of the jussive form, וְיָשֹׁב, despite GKC §109k, especially since the normal imperfect occurs in the next line.

8.a. This verse is intended as an *inclusio* with 1:2, despite the fact that הבל הבלים occurs only once. The definite article with קהלת is unlike 1:2, but it agrees with the corrected text in 7:27.

Form/Structure/Setting

There is a broad consensus concerning the extent of this unit. It ends before the literary inclusion in 12:8 (cf. 1:2). Some commentators (e.g., D. Michel, *Eigenart*, 210) regard 11:7–8 as a conclusion to 11:1–6. One can point to the connective *waw* which begins 11:7 (see note 7.a.), and also to the catch word טוב in vv 6–7. However, the content of vv 7–8 is clearly different from the previous lines, which deal with the unknowability of the future. There are literary contacts that tie vv 7–8 with what follows: שמחה *śimḥâ*, "joy" (vv 8, 9), זכר, "remember" (v 8; 12:1), הבל *hebel*, "vanity" (vv 8, 10). The themes of the time (days, years in vv 8 and 12:1) and of light/darkness (vv 7–8 and 12:1) are a further bond. The entire unit betrays a remarkable weaving together of words and ideas.

Although the striking description of old age and death in 12:1–7 has tended to dominate the question of form, this is only part of the unit, which is properly an instruction. It is essentially a speech or address concerning life and death directed to a youth (11:9, the only time an addressee is specifically mentioned by Qoheleth). The speaker (or even the youth, for that matter) hardly appears; the material in the poem emerges as the topic of interest. Although the instruction begins by emphasizing enjoyment of life, the lengthy description of "the days" of darkness" (11:8) outweighs all else; זכר, "remember," casts a cloud over שמח, "rejoice." The twofold character of this section can be seen from the titles given to it. For M. Fox (277), 11:7–10 is characterized as *carpe diem*, "enjoy the day," and 12:1–8 as *memento mori*, "remember you must die." In a certain sense A. Strobel combines both notes: *Abschiedslied an die Freude*, "a good-bye to joy." H. Witzenrath (*Süss ist das Licht. . .* , 6) diagrams the frequent repetitions of terms that bind together each part: 11:8–10 repeat הרבה (*harbēh*, "many"), לב (*lēb*, "heart"), ימים (*yāmîm*, "days"), ילדות (*yalĕdût*, "youth/young"), הבל (*hebel*, "vanity"), and especially the key terms, שמחה (*śimḥa*, "rejoice") and זכר (*zēker*, "remember"). Repetition is also characteristic of 12:1–6 where, for instance, three word pairs occur: כסף (*kesep*, "silver") and זהב (*zāhāb*, "gold"); גלה (*gullāh*, "bowl") and כד (*kad*, "pulley"?); מבוע (*mabbûaᶜ*, "fountain") and בור (*bôr*, "cistern"). Other ways of uniting the entire section are also possible. Thus, G. Ravasi (diagram on p. 332) points out how 11:7–8 is dominated by שמחה and זכר, הבל at the end; 12:1–8 begins with זכר and ends with הבל. Perhaps the most striking structural mark, as nearly everyone points out, is the עד אשר לא, "before," which dominates 12:1–7 (vv 1, 2, 6). See also J. R. Busto Saíz, *Sef* 43 (1983) 17–25.

The poem occurs at a very appropriate time in the book. It sums up the tantalizing message of the author who has bound together the themes of joy and death throughout his work. There can be no mistaking that old age and death are the theme of 12:1–7. But at the same time the author has left a legacy typical of himself: what is the precise nuance of the symbolism that he uses to describe aging and death?

The passage extends from 12:1 ("remember. . .," and this continues the imperatives of 11:8–10) to 12:7, which is explicitly concerned with death. The structure is rather clear. It begins with an imperative and develops by way of three "before" clauses in vv 1, 2, 6. A lengthy portion, somewhat parenthetical, is governed by a "when" clause (בְּיוֹם, vv 3–5). The meaning of v 1 and v 7 is clear, but the references in vv 2–6 are obscure. There is a difference of opinion among interpreters as regards the precise topic and the nature of the language.

Death is explicitly mentioned at the end of the narrative (v 7), and G. Ogden argues that a single theme, death, holds the verses together. But it is more reasonable (with the majority of commentators) to suppose that the preceding lines deal with the "days of misfortune" (v 1b), which culminate in death. These days stand in opposition to the "days of your youth" (v 1a). It appears then that the intervening verses refer somehow to old age.

But the distinction between old age and death is minimal here; the really critical issue is the nature of the language in vv 2–6. Is it merely symbolical, describing the reality of old age under several different metaphors? Or is it properly allegorical, so that each detail in the description has a transferred meaning? Or is it a mixture of both with the allegory appearing only in vv 3–4a?

1. The metaphorical approach claims that the "evil days" (of old age) are symbolized by darkness, by the change of seasons (v 2), by a description of the deterioration of house and homestead (vv 3–6). There are some differences in detail among those who hold this view, but there is agreement that only simple metaphors are being used.

2. The allegorical approach argues that although Qoheleth is ostensibly describing something such as a house, the objects and actions portrayed represent the effects of old age. The allegory is physiological; specific parts of the body are associated with particular details (e.g., the ladies who look out the window would refer to eyes that grow dim, v 4). Because of the ambiguities in the description, allegorists differ in details: do the two doors of v 4 refer to the eyes or the lips? But the claim is that the passage is written as allegory. The allegorical approach derives from Jewish tradition (see the Targum; *Qoheleth Rabbah*; b. *Shabbat*, 131–32). Jerome in his commentary is also aware of this Jewish interpretation, although he also records (commenting on 12:1) the historical interpretation by which Israel itself is addressed and the exile is referred to. He begins his comment on 12:1 with the observation *tot sententiae, paene quot homines*, "almost as many opinions as there are people."

3. Some commentators (e.g., A. Lauha, K. Galling) limit the allegorical intent to vv 3–5, or parts thereof, and interpret the rest as merely metaphorical language. It is even possible that metaphor disappears in vv 4b–5 if a human being is being directly described.

The metaphorical approach is to be understood as literal; one is describing old age metaphorically. Thus O. Loretz (*Qohelet*, 189–193) calls this a *māšāl* that describes old age through the metaphor of winter (vv 2–5). He argues against Zimmerli's view of an allegory that nowhere else in the Bible is the image of an inhabited house ever used to designate parts of the body. C. D. Ginsburg sees the approach of a storm described here. Commenting on 12:2 he remarks that the author "passes over to the *approach of death*, which he describes, under the figure of a gathering storm," and the reactions of the "inmates of the house." For M. Leahy (*ITQ* 19 [1952] 297–300), this description records the reactions of humans to a thunderstorm. J. Sawyer (*JBL* 94 [1975] 519–31) prefers to see here the description of a house that falls into ruin. Recently M. Fox (*JSOT* 42 [1988] 55–77) has characterized this section as a description of a funeral: the dead person goes to the eternal home, and mourners are keening (vv 2–5). He admits that this funeral scene does not answer all the difficulties raised by the text. Yet there is a certain restrained eschatological symbolism that recalls death—the death of the reader, even though Qoheleth's first listener is the youth of 11:9. Thus there is a threefold reference: description of a funeral scene, eschatological overtones that point to the end of the world, the death of the individual (esp. 12:7).

In addition to this understandable difference of opinion, there are several textual problems within 12:1–6, and the solutions given to these are often guided by the overall interpretation that the commentator has already arrived at. Since there is no one key that has unlocked the secrets of vv 2–6, the *Comment* will take limited cognizance of various interpretations.

Comment

7 The light/darkness contrast is common in the Bible, and it appeared already in 2:13–14 in a description of wisdom. It is also basic to the metaphors used throughout 11:7–12 (cf. H. Witzenrath, *Süss ist das Licht . . .*, 20). The use of the phrase "under the sun" is generally a disparaging indication of human existence. Now, to "see the sun" conveys a certain fullness of life; cf. 6:5, 7:11. As E. Podechard remarks, it is impossible to neglect the quotation from Euripides, *Iphigenia in Aulis*, l.1218: ἡδὺ γὰρ τὸ φῶς λεύσσειν, "sweet it is to see the light."

8 Qoheleth has not reversed the earlier harsh statements about life (2:17, 23, etc.). Here he is emphasizing the present and contrasting it with the "days of darkness" (probably both old age, described in 12:2–5, and death, in 12:6–7). The tension between death and whatever joy this life can offer is always present; v 8b in effect relativizes v 8a (pace N. Lohfink). See also 5:17–19; 9:10.

9 One need not conclude from the address to a youth that Qoheleth dealt primarily with the young. The emphasis on youth is in deliberate contrast to the theme of old age that follows in chap 12. In 12:12 the editor will use the phrase "my son," which is typical of the wisdom tradition.

The recommendations in 11:7–10 are an ancient *gaudeamus igitur, juvenes dum sumus,* "let us rejoice while we are young," but they are not to be misunderstood, as though one could speak of hedonism here. Already Ptah-hotep had urged enjoyment while one lives:

> Follow your heart as long as you live,
> Do no more than already is required,
> Do not shorten the time of "follow-the-heart,"
> Trimming its moment offends the *ka.*
> (190) Don't waste time on daily cares
> Beyond providing for your household;
> When wealth has come, follow your heart,
> Wealth does no good if one is glum! (*AEL,* 66; 11th maxim)

Nevertheless, Qoheleth's words gave trouble early on. The phraseology about "heart" and "eyes" seemed to contradict Num 15:39, and the glosses in the Greek tradition ("without sin"; see note 9.b.) are futile attempts to rectify a faulty interpretation. But these lines are referred to in Jewish tradition as giving rise to doubts about the teaching of the book of Ecclesiastes (see note 9.b.). They sounded too much like the reprehensible views found in Isa 23:13 and Job 31:7. Sir 5:2–3 perhaps refers to Eccl 11:9 in arguing against presumption, and in 5:2b he makes explicit reference to "evil" delights. However, vv 7–9 are to be understood in the context of the joy that Qoheleth has already recommended several times (2:24–25; 3:12–13, 22; 5:17–19; 8:15; 9:7–10). There is an undeniable verve to these lines (cf. also 9:10a), despite the overarching verdict of vanity.

The authenticity of the final command (v 9b, "know . . .") is widely denied. It is usually attributed to an editorial hand because of the mention of judgment and the repetition of the phrase במשפט יביא, "bring to judgment," that is found in 12:14 where it is certainly part of an editorial addition. However, as far as divine judgment is concerned, Qoheleth never denies the *fact* (cf. 3:17). The Israelite tradition of divine judgment is too strong for him simply to negate it. But he can find no evidence of judgment, as this was understood in the tradition (cf. 8:5b–7). With regard to the similarity between 11:9 and 12:14, there is no reason why an editorial hand could not have deliberately chosen this phrase of v 9, and he would have meant it in his own, traditionalist, sense (see the *Comment* on 12:14).

10 כעס and רעה, "trouble" and "suffering," have occurred frequently (respectively, seven and thirty times) to describe various phases of the human condition. The elimination of these trials is a negative statement of the positive advice in v 9a.

V 10b is not to be considered as a gloss (against A. Lauha and others) that would neutralize v 10a. On the contrary, it is the constant horizon of Qoheleth's thought, expressed already in v 8b; elsewhere through the book he reminds his readers of the specter of death and Sheol (2:14b; 3:19–20; 9:10–12).

12:1 The chapter division at this point should not obscure the fact that Qoheleth is continuing the advice he began in 11:7. He cannot praise the time of youth without some reservations as in 11:8: God ("your creator," see note 12:1.a.) and the "days of misfortune," and unpleasant "years" that lie ahead. E. Podechard questions the logic of remembering the creator before the arrival of old age (the "days of misfortune"). But the mention of God as a caution in human activity is not foreign to Qoheleth's thought (cf. 5:6; 7:18; 11:9), and 12:7 describes death as the return of the life-breath to the creator. M. Gilbert (VTSup, 32 [1981] 100) has put this well: "Thus, in order to recall death, Qoheleth refers to creation. The circle is complete: the end is tied to the beginning. Hence one should not be astonished to see in 12:1 an explicit mention of the creator. Remembrance of him does not mean a return to the past in which one began but calls attention to the end in which the *rûah* given in the beginning will return to the one who gave it." He goes on to instance several other passages that, in effect, recall a future while remembering the past: Sir 7:36 (Hebrew text); 8:7 (Hebrew text); Tob 4:5. The most striking is in *Pirqe ʾAbot*, 3:1: "Keep in view three things and thou wilt not come into the power of sin. Know whence you comest and whither thou goest and before whom thou art to give strict account. Whence thou comest,—from a fetid drop. Whither thou goest,—to the place of dust worms and maggots: and before whom thou art, to give strict account,—Before the king of the kings of kings, the Holy one blessed be He" (R. T. Herford, *Pirkē Aboth*, 2nd ed. [New York: Bloch, 1930] 63).

Therefore, mindfulness of the creator conditions the enjoyment of youth. By opposition to "youth," the "days of misfortune" are best understood as old age with its attendant difficulties. Youth remains the best of times, but a full evaluation of life must consider the creator and the approach of death, the beginning and the end (cf. Eccl 7:1a).

2 The central idea of this verse is the coming of darkness (the opposite of 11:7–8). It is described in physical terms; the absence of sun, moon, and stars is heightened by the return of the clouds. Some commentators find here the suggestion of a storm, or the onset of the winter season (H. Hertzberg). Light and darkness are standard symbols for well-being and evil. Qoheleth is advising the enjoyment of life before the arrival of "darkness," which like the days of misfortune in v 1 seems to refer to the onset of old age with its troubles. There is no need to allegorize the details as in the Targum, where sun, moon, and stars are coordinated with parts of the body (e.g., the rain indicates "tears"). If there is allegory in vv 1–6, it does not begin here.

3 בַּיּוֹם (on the day, "when") controls vv 3–5, and the whole is integrated, somewhat parenthetically, into v 2. At first sight v 3 appears to be a description of a house and certain of its inhabitants: guardians, strong men, female servants at the mill, women looking through the window. They seem unable to cope with their situation. Coordinated with v 2, this verse portrays the distress that accompanies the darkness; so the guardians tremble, etc. There is a kind of desolation about the "house," but the picture remains fuzzy. Questions immediately arise: What is being described here? A house, or better, the inhabitants of a house? With M. Gilbert (VTSup, 32 [1981] 102–3) and E. Podechard, one must answer, the inhabitants, not the house itself (pace J. Sawyer, *JBL* 94 [1975] 519–31). Why are these particular groups singled out for mention and what is really said about them? For example, why should the women grinding at the mill cease simply because they are few, or how and why can the women looking through the window be said to be darkened? Such details concerning the inhabitants seem rather banal. One asks if perhaps there is more than meets the eye here, and the allegorical approach is put forth as an answer.

A transferred meaning can be applied to each of the principals mentioned in this verse. There is no particular identification that is universally agreed upon (are "the guardians of the house" arms or legs?). Was the author deliberately vague? Perhaps the most common and reasonable equations are the following: guardians=arms and/or (trembling) hands; strong men=legs; grinding maidens=teeth; ladies looking through the window=eyes. The verbs associated with these words indicate a falling off of some kind, if the reference is to appropriate parts of the body: firmness, straightness, activity and number (of teeth), and clarity of vision. However, it should be noted that precisely at this point the application of the physiological allegory shows a certain arbitrariness. There is simply no agreement on the specifics (arms or hands, etc.).

4 The description in v 4a seems clear; the (two) doors are closed, and the sound of the mill is low. The reason for the dual דְּלָתַיִם, "two doors," is obscure, since residences would normally have only one entrance. However, in the context of a description of a desolate house, or even of a storm, v 4a is intelligible.

If one approaches the text from the allegorical point of view, appropriate parts of the body can be supplied. The doors can refer to the two ears, or possibly lips. The noise of the mill can be the voice that weakens with age.

No translation of v 4b can be considered certain, and the passage remains obscure (see notes 4.a. and 4.b.). The MT can be interpreted to mean that one rises from bed when the birds sing. Obviously the reference must be to human beings, and supposedly to an elderly person who is unable to sleep. Neither would such a person find joy in songs (literally, "daughters of song"; see note 4.b.), whether sung by himself or by another. Some would interpret the "voice" of v 4a as the subject of "rise" and see here a reference to the bird-like sound of a human voice. H. Hertzberg understands this to mean the thin, high-pitched voice of an old man. Many commentators claim that with v 4b a direct description of an elderly person has begun, freed from the metaphors of the previous verses.

The physiological approach of allegory finds less support in v 4b than elsewhere, because the words more easily refer to a direct description of an elderly person, and certain terms remain obscure. R. Gordis notes that the "daughters of song" signify the throat (following Ibn Ezra), but this seems far fetched (see the *Notes*).

5 There is hardly need to interpret v 5a in allegorical fashion. This is a straightforward assertion about the fear of heights and the presence of "terrors" on the road. It can be easily understood as the uncertainties of an elderly person who is unsteady of gait and keeps to his room. However, it should be remembered that the existence of such a person has been *inferred* from v 4 (see note 4.a.). Allegorists may find here a reference to bodily decline, such as shortening of breath and stiffness of limbs (G. Barton).

The meaning of v 5ab is obscure. It is clear that there are three nouns: the almond, the locust, and the caperberry. The verbs attached to the nouns pose problems (see notes 5.b., 5.c., and 5.e.). One interpretation finds an awakening of nature. With some minor differences, this is advanced by F. Nötscher, K. Galling, H. Hertzberg, and A. Lauha. The almond blossoms, the locust becomes full by eating (or the elderly person is filled by eating locusts?), the caperberry breaks open (or fails to stimulate?). The opposing view, which lends itself more to an allegorical interpretation, understands the passage as a description of the dwindling powers of an elderly person. The almond causes disgust (root, נאץ), the locust drags itself along (or becomes too heavy for an elderly person to digest easily), the caperberry has no effect (on the appetite in general or specifically on sexual potency).

The first interpretation finds a contrast between the two lines: the uncertainties and fears of an old person increase, although nature is in the process of renewal. The second finds a continuation of the description of an aged person, whether in a literal sense (loss of appetite, etc.) or in an allegorical sense (e.g., the blooming of the almond is a reference to white hair; so R. Gordis, with Rashi and others).

The meaning of v 5b is fairly obvious. It registers the death of a human being who is deposited in the tomb ("everlasting home"), to the keening of mourners. However, this is not the final word. The structure of the text in v 6 ("before") shows that the recommendation begun in 12:1 continues into v 7. If vv 3–5 were originally conceived as a unit, the ending in v 5 is quite appropriate. In the context of 12:1–7 it appears to anticipate v 7. There is not sufficient reason to rearrange the text as A. Lauha proposes: 1–2, 6, 3–5, 7. It can be admitted that v 5b seems almost parenthetical; it does not need to be stated here. But it has an effect of its own, and it is in harmony with the images of death in vv 6–7.

6 The narrative returns to the phrase ("before") that structures vv 1–7. It is unnecessary and even inappropriate to pursue allegory here, as if parts of the human body were meant by "cord," "bowl," etc. The metaphors speak for themselves, and they are images for death. The only problem is the precise translation of the verbs (see the *Notes*) and the meaning of certain terms (especially גלגל, "pulley"? or "bowl"?). If v 6a is parallel to v 6b, as seems likely, both express metaphors for death: the light of the lamp is gone, and the water of the well is unavailable. This view recognizes two distinct images: a golden lamp and a broken-down cistern or well. Others would put these together in one picture, as M. Fox, who thinks that "the verse claims to picture three vessels suspended by a cord over a well. The cord snaps and the vessels fall and shatter." However, it is difficult to consider a golden lamp and silver cord as functioning at a fountain. The metaphor itself is a lamp that is presumably empty of fire, thus symbolizing death; as the biblical phrase has it, "one's lamp (נר) goes out" (cf. Prov 13:9). The image is thus different from the severing of the cord or thread (of life) in Greek mythology.

The figure of the jar and pulley (v 6b) points to a well that has presumably been abandoned and is in disrepair. Fountain and life are combined many times in the Bible (Ps 36:9; Prov 10:11; 13:14). The water that symbolizes life can neither be drawn up from the well nor carried in a broken jar.

7 The note of death continues. The process described here is the reversal of Gen 2:7. The end of life is the dissolution (not annihilation; the Israelites never speculated *how* the "I" was in Sheol; cf. Eccl 9:10). Humans return to the dust (Gen 3:19) whence they came, while the life-breath given by God returns to its original possessor. This is a picture of dissolution, not of immortality, as if there were a *reditus animae ad Deum,* "the return of the soul to God." There is no question of the "soul" here, but of the life-breath, a totally different category of thought. Hence there is no reason to deny this verse to Qoheleth. K. Galling, A. Lauha, and others argue that it must belong to a glossator because it contradicts 3:21, where Qoheleth denies the affirmation that the human רוּחַ *rûah* goes upward in contradistinction to the רוּחַ *rûah* of animals. But the context of 3:21 is polemical. Some assert there is a difference between life-breath in humans and animals; Qoheleth's query ("who knows?") denies any qualitative difference. But he certainly shares with the rest of the OT that God is the owner and donor of life, i.e., the life-breath (Ps 104:29–30; Job 33:4; 34:15; see also Sir 40:11b, Hebrew text).

8 It has already been pointed out (cf. 1:2) that this verse forms an *inclusio* for the book, and it may be the work of an editorial hand, as the mention of Qoheleth in the third person suggests. Only in 1:2 and here does the repetition of הבל *hebel,* "vanity," occur. In view of the many times the single word is used to express Qoheleth's verdict about the futility of various aspects of human existence, there can be little quarrel about this summary. Both G. Sheppard (*Wisdom as a Hermeneutical Construct,* 122–26) and K. Galling have singled this out as a "thematization" of the work. Like all generalizations, it fails to capture nuances. Thus it does not convey the probing efforts of Qoheleth, the fine balance with which he pits one point of view against another. Nor does it leave any room for the several stereotyped conclusions that he enunciates as good for humans to do (such conclusions as "eat and drink"). In fact, Sheppard claims, this is an over-simplification of the message of the book. It is an important guide to Qoheleth's thought, but it does not exhaust it. It is balanced by another, and also later, thematization in vv 13–14.

Explanation

Qoheleth's reflections end with this instruction concerning two poles of his thought: life and death. The emphasis on life ("to see the sun," 11:7) opens the instruction, but from the very beginning, it is tempered by ominous remarks (11:8b, 9b, 10b) that anticipate the poem on old age and death in 12:1–7. The whole unit is thus artfully conceived and executed. He has consistently urged enjoyment of life ("eat and drink," etc.; cf. 2:24; 3:12, 22; 5:17; 8:15; 9:7–9). These positive recommendations underscore his personal zest for life and the possibility that they may be also the lot of the reader. However, just as "vanity" and the mystery of the divine "work" had modified these happy views in the earlier chapters, so now the grim reality of death overshadows the optimism of 11:7–10.

The difficulty in understanding the details of the description in 12:1–7 is not crippling for a reader. There is no doubt that it is a description of old age, leading into death. Not all will agree with M. Fox's recent characterization of it as a description of the time of death and mourning (*JSOT* 42 [1988] 55–77), in other words, a funerary scene. All would agree that such a scene is explicitly expressed at the end of v 5 (the keening of the mourners). Fox is not urging a specific one-sided interpretation of the poem that would eliminate certain figures that represent the aging process. He refers (*Qohelet*, 295–96) to a Sumerian poem on aging that mixes figures and literal statements (thus, a possibility that Eccl 12:1–7 does that also):

> My grain roasting fails,
> Now my youthful vigor, strength and personal god
>   have left my loins like an exhausted ass.
> My black mountain has produced white gypsum.
> My mother has brought in a man from the forest;
>   he gave me captivity.
> My mongoose which used to eat strong smelling things
>   does not stretch its neck towards beer and butter.
> My urine used to flow in a strong torrent.
>   but now you flee from my wind.
> My child whom I used to feed with butter and milk,
>   I can no more support it.
> And I have had to sell my little slave girl;
>   an evil demon makes me sick.
> (from Bendt Alster, *Studies in Sumerian Proverbs* [Copenhagen: 1975] 93)

The "white gypsum" is the white hair of an old man who describes some of the difficulties of the aging process, without any obvious allegory. More important, and more telling and effective in the poem, is the manner in which the mood is expressed. This is a symbolic meaning that goes beyond the limitation of a given image (such as guardians or mill-grinders). As Fox puts it, "the imagery is unsettling in an almost surrealistic way. The luminaries and light itself are extinguished.

Clouds hang overhead. All is murky. Then we encounter a succession of images of distortion and despair: trembling, writhing, cessation of activity, darkening, shutting, silence, bowing, fear. What do all these people see that so disconcerts them? For whom are they mourning so intensely?" (*JSOT* 42 [1988] 63). His remarks about the inadequacy of the allegorical approach are telling. It presumes the reader already knows what the images are supposed to mean: "We can know that the strong men's quaking represents the legs' shaking (if this is indeed so) only if we know that legs grow shaky with age. It cannot be the poem's goal to inform us of this. . . . The poem's purpose is not to convey information; it is to create an attitude toward aging and, more importantly, death" (70–71).

Epilogue (12:9–14)

Bibliography

Baumgärtel, F. "Die Ochsenstachel und die Nägel in Koh 12,11." *ZAW* 81 (1969) 98. **Eissfeldt, O.** *The Old Testament: An Introduction.* New York: Harper and Row, 1965. **Fishbane, M.** *Biblical Interpretation in Ancient Israel.* Oxford: Clarendon, 1985. **Fox, M.** "Frame Narrative and Composition in the Book of Qohelet." *HUCA* 48 (1977) 83–106 (also in *Qohelet*, 311–21). **Goldin, J.** "The End of Ecclesiastes: Literal Exegesis and Its Transformation." In *Biblical Motifs.* Ed. A. Altman. Philips W. Lown Institute of Advanced Judaic Studies. Studies and Texts 3. Cambridge: Harvard UP, 1966. 135–58. **Loretz, O.** *Qohelet und der Alte Orient.* Freiburg: Herder, 1964. 139–43, 290–97. ———. "Zur Darbietungsform der 'Ich-Erzählung' im Buche Qohelet." *CBQ* 25 (1963) 46–59. **Murphy, R. E.** "The Sage in Ecclesiastes and Qoheleth the Sage." In *The Sage in Israel and the Ancient Near East.* Ed. J. G. Gammie and L. G. Perdue. Winona Lake, IN: Eisenbrauns, 1990. 263–71. **Pautrel, R.** "Data sunt a pastore uno (Eccl. 12,11)." *RSR* 41 (1953) 406–10. **Sheppard, G.** *Wisdom as a Hermeneutical Construct.* BZAW 180. Berlin: de Gruyter, 1980. 120–29. ———. "The Epilogue to Qoheleth as Theological Commentary." *CBQ* 39 (1977) 182–89. **Wilson, G.** "The Words of the Wise": The Intent and Significance of Qohelet 12:9–14." *JBL* 103 (1984) 175–92. **Wright, A.** "Riddle . . . Revisited." *CBQ* 42 (1980) 38–51.

Translation

[9]*Besides*[a] *being a sage, Qoheleth continued to teach the people knowledge; he weighed*[b] *and examined*[c] *and corrected many sayings.* [10]*Qoheleth sought to find out pleasing words and he [wrote]*[a] *true words carefully.* [11]*The words of the wise*[a] *are like oxgoads,*[b] *like fixed nails*[c] *are the collected sayings;*[d] *they are given by one shepherd.* [12]*As for more than these,*[a] *my son, beware; there is no end to the writing of many books, and much study*[b] *wearies the flesh.* [13]*The end of the matter,*[a] *when all is heard:*[b] *fear God and keep his commandments, for this is (the duty of) everyone.*[c] [14]*For God will bring*[a] *every deed*[b] *to judgment, over*[c] *all that is hidden, whether good or evil.*

Notes

9.a. וְיֹתֵר occurs at the beginning of vv 9 and 12. The Masoretic punctuation separates it from what follows in v 9. Thus, NJV renders by "A further word"; A. Lauha by *"Nachtrag"*; M. Fox by "furthermore." These understand the word literally: "and an addition (is) that . . ." Others prefer "Besides (being wise)"; so NRSV, NAB. See the discussion in C. D. Ginsburg.

9.b. The meaning, "weigh," for אִזֵּן occurs only here, where it is parallel to חִקֵּר and תִקֵּן. It is usually connected with מֹאזְנַיִם, "scales." But the ancient versions had difficulty with it and understood it in the sense of hear or listen, as though derived from אֹזֶן (cf. LXX, οὖς).

9.c. חִקֵּר and תִקֵּן are united asyndetically (so LXX), but Tg and Syr make the "and" explicit.

10.a. The MT vocalizes וְכָתוּב as the passive participle, "what is written" (so also LXX). The other ancient versions have an easier reading, "and he wrote," which could reflect either וְכָתַב or the infinitive absolute וְכָתֹב. It is preferable to revocalize the consonantal text as the infinitive absolute (cf. GKC §113z). F. Baumgärtel has tried unsuccessfully to interpret כָּתוּב יֹשֶׁר as referring to the manner of writing: oxgoads and nails would be the cuneiform wedges in which "the words of the wise" were written; cf. *ZAW* 81 (1969) 98.

11.a. The translation is uncertain. There seem to be two comparisons: "words of the wise" are compared to goads, and בַּעֲלֵי אֲסֻפּוֹת to pegs; the last three words (v 11b) indicate the giver (of wisdom).

11.b. דרבנות, "goads," is a *hap. leg.*, and the singular would be *דרבנה; cf. דרבן in 1 Sam 13:21, indicating a sharp instrument. The word may be chosen in view of the דברי that begins the verse.

11.c. משמרות, "nails" (and without the definite article), is spelled elsewhere (Jer 10:4; 2 Chr 3:9) with *samekh* for *šin*; the root is שמר. נטע, "plant," is not used with nails or pegs, but there may be a play on נתן; תקע would be the usual term.

11.d. The translation and meaning of בעלי אספות is uncertain. The first word designates "masters of" or "members of." אסף means "collect," and אספה, a *hap. leg.*, has been taken to mean "assemblies" (of people) or "collections" (of sayings). The Greek tradition favors collection (τῶν συνθεμάτων, Alexandrinus), and other versions are vague (Vg, *magistrorum consilium*). In the chiastic structure of the verse, the phrase is parallel to "words of the wise." Whether it is understood personally (overseers of the collected sayings) or impersonally (the collected sayings) makes little different for the general sense, but the parallelism favors "collected sayings." The suggestion of R. Pautrel (בער אספות, "pour le bien des troupeaux") has not been adopted; cf. *RSR* 42 (1953) 406–10.

12.a. ויתר מדמה poses problems (see note 9.a. above). Here the two words are to be joined in accordance with the Masoretic punctuation: "and besides these" (המה refers to the sayings of the wise in v 11). See the detailed discussion of various translations in C. D. Ginsburg. Podechard regards the יתר as an adverbial accusative: "as to what is more (than)."

12.b. להג is a *hap. leg.*, but is satisfactorily explained in the light of Arabic *lahija*, "apply oneself"; LXX has μελέτη, and Vg, *meditatio*. Others see here an emphatic *lamedh* before הגה) ה) (=study); cf. Whitley, *Koheleth*, 104.

13.a. סוף (an Aramaizing term for classical קץ) דבר can be taken as a nominal sentence ("the final word is:") or adverbially ("by way of a final word"). The absence of the definite article before דבר is unusual.

13.b. נשמע can be interpreted as the plural cohortative, "let us (all) hear"; so Vg. It is preferable to interpret it as nipal perfect tense or participle: "(all) is heard." This is a circumstantial noun clause; cf. GKC §156c.

13.c. זה כל האדם is difficult to interpret. Both LXX and Vg read the traditional Hebrew text, but their rendering is not helpful: "for this is every man." כל האדם means "every man" (cf. 7:2), and the juxtaposition with זה establishes a relationship, such as duty, goal, or the like; cf. Ps 45:9, "your robes myrrh," etc.; Ps 120:7, "I peace." Others have understood the phrase as "this is the whole of man"; cf. NIV, which inserts "duty" after "whole."

14.a. It is important to observe that the phrase "bring to judgment" occurs in 11:9.

14.b. On the absence of the definite article before מעשה, see GKC § 117c, and the discussion in Gordis.

14.c. על is to be construed with משפט.

Form/Structure/Setting

There is a broad consensus that 12:9–14 is an addition to the Book of Ecclesiastes. It is clearly separate from 12:8, since that verse forms an *inclusio* with 1:2. The tone of these verses suggests a backward view, looking back at the work of Qoheleth (including this book). Whether or not several hands are to be recognized in these verses (see *Explanation* below), they can be termed an epilogue or postscript.

There seem to be two main units, both introduced by ויתר: vv 9–11 and 12–14. The first section contains a description of Qoheleth's activity as a חכם, "sage" (not as a מלך, "king"; cf. 1:1, 12), and it concludes with a saying (v 12) in favor of the sages and their "words." The second unit picks up the ויתר and begins, "and more than these" (see the *Comment* below). What follows is an admonition, as the author addresses "my son" in typical wisdom fashion (this appears nowhere else in the book), cautioning him about overproduction of literary works and personal study. Vv 13–14 contain a command that carries two motivations. More will be said about the setting and significance of this epilogue in the *Explanation*.

Comment

9 The import of חכם *ḥākām*, "sage," is that Qoheleth belonged to the class of sages who cultivated wisdom. We have no real knowledge of the post-exilic setting in which they worked, but there must have been some kind of "school" (cf. Sir 50:23) to which the writer of this epilogue may well have belonged.

mĕšālîm is usually rendered by "proverbs." There is no reason to refer this to the canonical book of Proverbs. Proverbial sayings are not the primary concern of Qoheleth, who cultivates reflections and observations more than sayings. The latter are more or less restricted to chaps. 7–8 and 10–11. This verse describes his activity rather than his book. The total effect is to place him firmly within the wisdom tradition: weighing, examining, correcting the sayings, as illustrated by the dialectic in chaps. 7 and 8.

10 The description of Qoheleth as a sage continues, and in a laudatory tone. He used words of strength and style, of some esthetic value. The goal of the sage had always been to have the right word at the right time (Prov 15:23; cf. 16:24). "Truth" (אמת) is meant in the profound sense of capturing reality.

11 The phrase "words of the wise" recalls the titles in Prov 22:17 (emended text), 24:23; 30:1; 31:1, and here it refers to the general wisdom tradition. Qoheleth is being placed among the honored bearers of this wisdom.

Oxgoads were used to prod cattle, and hence the wisdom sayings are conceived as stimulating and directing those who would hear them. This is, of course, particularly true of Qoheleth's teachings. The precise meaning of the metaphor of nails (pegs) is not clear. They can be conceived as giving strength and firmness, and perhaps providing a foundation for life's activities, a basis for a responsible life style.

The translation "collected sayings" is uncertain (see note 11.d.). But the intention of the entire verse is to exalt the wisdom tradition.

The "one shepherd" has been identified with Solomon, Moses, and even Qoheleth himself, or simply "any shepherd" (Fox). However, it is also possible to recognize here an allusion to God, the source and giver of wisdom (Prov 2:6; Sir 39:6). The metaphor of shepherd is applied to God, even if often indirectly (cf. Ps 23:1; Isa 40:11, etc.).

K. Galling is probably right in classifying v 11a as a quotation; it deals with the class of the wise (plural) and not directly with Qoheleth himself. The final addition, about the shepherd, is important for the understanding that the epilogist has of wisdom writings.

12 ויתר מהמה means more than "furthermore" (see note 12.a.). It can be rendered, literally, "and in addition to these." The issue is: what is the referent of "these"? It suggests more than a general reference to "these matters" (so R. Gordis). It is probably too much to think that the reference is to some specific wisdom books as though they were already canonical. But Qoheleth's book, far more even than the general wisdom tradition suggested by the phrase "words of the wise" in v 11, is surely the topic of the epilogue, and hence part of the referent "these."

The epilogist addresses the reader as "my son," in typical wisdom style (Prov 1:8; 2:1, etc.). His warning is ambiguous. It can hardly be taken as a general warning against too many books and too much study. A. Lauha and many others regard it as a criticism of Qoheleth. In this view, one can do without books such as Ecclesiastes that are so troublesome and confusing. Then the epilogist allegedly

proceeds in vv 13–14 to contradict Qoheleth's teaching. Thus the reader is presumably protected against the upsetting doctrine offered in the book. However,
this inference is not at all necessary. It seems to reflect more the problem of
moderns who see the presence of the book in the canon as an exceptional thing
that must somehow be "explained." Were the ancients as easily scandalized as the
moderns? There is no reason why "these" cannot refer to the "words" already
mentioned in vv 10–11, and given high praise. Even if it is referred to the teachers—בעלי אספות is to be understood of the tradents—the effect is the same. The
epilogist warns that there is no need to add more to the previous collections of
wisdom writings. It is impossible to define these more specifically, but the work of
Ecclesiastes is surely one of them. Instead of being a criticism of Qoheleth, this
verse is in fact praising his work; there is no need of more wisdom writings! In
this view one should not postulate a second redactor responsible for vv 12–14.

13 Despite the varying interpretations of v 13a (see the *Notes*), it clearly introduces a significant conclusion of the epilogist. The precise combination of
fear of God and obedience to the commandments is not found in the book of
Ecclesiastes. Although the fear of God is explicitly recommended in 5:6 (cf. 3:14;
8:12–13), the commandments of God are never mentioned. The epilogue is obviously putting forth an ideal which has been developed elsewhere and which is
not a concern in Ecclesiastes. G. Sheppard has shown that both elements of this
"dual injunction" are to be found throughout the book of Sirach (see the *Explanation* below). In addition to Sir 1:26–30, other passages also parallel fear of God
with obedience to the commandments: Sir 10:19; 23:27. The task of wisdom is
joined with that of Torah: "Those who fear the Lord seek to please him, those
who love him are filled with the Law" (Sir 2:16). M. Fox points to a certain similarity between this verse and Sir 43:27.

14 The epilogist uses the phraseology of 11:9. Does he mean by "judgment"
the same thing that Qoheleth did? The manner in which this is introduced by v
13 suggests that he shares the views of Sirach and another generation. The emphasis on divine judgment is not strictly contradictory to Qoheleth's views, but it
is hardly possible that he would have expressed himself in this way. He recognized God as judge but nowhere does he attempt to explain this, much less to
motivate human action on the basis of divine judgment. For him the judgment
of God is a total mystery. Perhaps the epilogist catches something of this mystery
in his phrase "all that is hidden." It is somewhat ironic that the word for every
"deed" is מעשה, which is used in the book to indicate the inscrutable divine action ("work of God"; 7:13; 8:17; 11:6; cf. 3:11), or events that transpire in this
dreary human life (2:17; 4:3; etc.). Now the "work" or "deed" (human) is here
associated too easily to divine judgment. Hence v 14 gives a different tilt to the
phraseology of 11:9. The viewpoint of the epilogist may or may not have been
eschatological; in any case it goes beyond the perspective of Qoheleth. The orientation provided by vv 12–14 exercised great influence in the history of the
exegesis of Ecclesiastes.

Explanation

The *Comment* indicates clearly enough the position of interpreter(s) on 12:9–
14. The interpretation of this puzzling book began with the addition of these

verses. They are usually called an epilogue. This is, as it were, a postscript written by someone (the editor?). It can be viewed as a colophon, an addition that conveys information about the writing and authorship of a book. Thus Ben Sira provides his name and claim to authorship in Sir 50:27 (chap 51 seems to be an addition to the work). There are other examples within and without the Bible. M. Fishbane (*Biblical Interpretation in Ancient Israel*, 23–43) has pointed to the "summary colophons" that can be found in Lev 7:37–38 and 15:32–33 ("such is the ritual") and in other texts. Also Ahiqar is several times described as a wise and skillful scribe who gave counsel and advice to Sennacherib (cf. Ahiqar 1.1–4 and passim in Charlesworth, *OTP* 2:494–97). Although "colophon" can have a very technical meaning, the definition of it has varied, and it seems better here to use "epilogue" or "postscript" in a broad sense as containing information about the author and the writing of a work.

When one turns to Eccl 12:9–12, one finds what Fishbane (29–32) terms a description of a variety of "technical procedures" that can be illustrated by Assyrian and Babylonian colophons. Thus, Qoheleth was a *sage*, who *ordered, examined*, and *fixed* (edited?) the work in question. Such an addendum is in harmony with the colophonic practice in Assyrian and Babylonian sources; even the "making" of books (Eccl 12:12) seems to have an Assyrian counterpart. Fishbane regards it as "quite likely that the technical use of תקן in Eccles. 12:9 also means 'to edit' or to 'arrange' in some sense" (32).

In addition to these more or less factual data about Qoheleth in 12:9–11, there is the important evaluative notice beginning in v 12, and extending into vv 13–14. This goes beyond merely biographical matter and is significantly addressed to "my son," the typical wisdom address (cf. Prov 1–9, passim) of a teacher to a pupil. Modern research has raised several questions about the epilogue (12:9–14): how many epilogists are there? Just what kind of judgments have been passed on the book by these verses?

First of all, how many hands can be recognized in 12:9–14? The highest number has been three, proposed by O. Eissfeldt and H. Hertzberg. Eissfeldt (*The Old Testament*, 493, 499) considers 12:9–11 to be the work of the compiler of Ecclesiastes, who praises Qoheleth. There are two different additions: v 12 is a complaint about too many works, but a complaint in favor of Qoheleth—let the other books alone! Vv 13–14 are an emphatic recommendation of the fear of God and solid piety. Hertzberg attributes vv 9–11 to the epilogist, who in effect has written an apologia for the work. But v 12 goes in another direction: it is a kind of correction to vv 9–11, because Qoheleth's book has been unsettling. Finally, a third epilogist gave a direction to the book for its practical use by means of the edifying ending.

However, there is a more general tendency to recognize only two hands at work in 12:9–14; so for example, A. Lauha and W. Zimmerli, who separate vv 9–11 and 12–14. In general, the first addition is positive, in favor of the book. But the second is a criticism and a warning, which would supposedly indicate a lapse of time during which the book had been met with opposition. Hence it is to be read as a rejection of the troublesome message of Qoheleth and a suggestion of another reading of it that will satisfy (biblical) orthodoxy.

With regard to the appearance of two or even three hands in the epilogue, one might invoke the old philosophical principle: *entia non sunt multiplicanda,* "beings should not be multiplied." In other words, does one need to hypothesize so radically about the ending? Is it not possible that there is only one epilogist, who is *not* criticizing Qoheleth, but in fact is praising the book, while at the same time giving it an interpretation that is more in line with Sirach (see the *Comment* above). The freedom with which commentators have appointed "authors" to these few verses is astonishing! Moreover, if the intention of the epilogist(s?) was to tone down the message of Qoheleth and render it more acceptable as many commentators think, it was a total failure. The question that arises concerns modern interpreters, not the ancients. Within the wisdom tradition, Sirach and Wisdom of Solomon betray no dismay at the book of Ecclesiastes. We are those who have been "shocked" and have not allowed for the tensions that the ancients tolerated.

Some scholars (F. Delitzsch, R. N. Whybray, L. Alonso Schökel, O. Loretz [*Qohelet*, 139–43, 290–97], G. Ravasi, A. Barucq among them) affirm that there is only one hand at work in 12:9–14, that of an epilogist. Those who uphold this point of view raise a more interesting question than the hypothetical issue of the number of writers involved in these six lines. There is a general recognition that the epilogue has some relation to the rest of the Bible.

Three studies in particular have made an impact in considering the epilogue as a unit. In *CBQ* 42 (1980) 43–45, A. Wright pointed out that the six verses of the epilogue are a deliberate addition to the book, to bring the number of verses up from 216 (the numerical value of the *inclusio*, הבל הבלים הכל הבל) to 222, so that the book falls into two equal parts of 111 verses at 6:9–10. The number 111 is important because of the numerical value of הבל (37), which occurs three times in the inclusion: 37 x 3 = 111. He remarks also concerning ויתר that the consonant *waw* has a numerical value of six, and hence the word can also have the meaning of "six additional"—a sign that the editor is aware of adding six additional verses. Since the numerical value of דברי (*dibrê*, "words," vv 10, 11) is 216, he argues that "the editor appreciated the numerical value of the word as a title for a book of 216 verses" (44–45). The appendix, 12:9–14, thus supplies the six additional verses to arrive at 222.

G. Sheppard (*Wisdom*, 121–29) was the first to establish a strong basis for correlating Eccl 12:9–14 with the Book of Ecclesiasticus. He has shown that the epilogue (vv 13–14) contains an editorial thematizing that is in the spirit of Sirach (cf. Sir 1:26–30; 2:16; 43:27; Baruch 3:9–4:4). K. Galling pointed out the first thematizing, the "vanity of vanities" formula that underscores a basic idea in Ecclesiastes. Sheppard claims there are two thematizings, each "an oversimplification and a judgment concerning the essential intent of the entire complex of sayings." A new perspective is offered by the combination of fear of God, obedience to the commandments, and torah. Thus the epilogue "offers an interpretation of the relationship between biblical wisdom and the commandments of God in the Torah" (127). There is admittedly tension between the two "thematizations." While "vanity of vanities" encapsulates an unmistakable note in the book, it is nevertheless "a maxim more bloodless and doctrinaire than the book itself" (126). It fails to convey the probing mind and shifting perspectives of Qoheleth (e.g., one need only recall his many stereotyped conclusions about what it is good for humans to do). A broader theological understanding is at work, whereby the book is placed "in the domain of the biblical wisdom which has itself become a developed theological construct already functioning as an interpretive idiom in the context of a nascent Scripture" (127). However, it should be added that the second thematizing is also a re-reading. It short-circuits the skepticism of Qoheleth, although it may not be strictly contradictory to the book. The thematizing, one may conclude, is selective, and the reader is left with two differing perspectives, in the light of which the book can be read. An example from Sirach will illustrate the association of 12:9–14 with Sirach:

> If you desire wisdom, keep the commandments,
> and God will bestow her upon you;
> For fear of the Lord is wisdom and culture:
> loyal humility is his delight.
> Be not faithless to fear of the Lord,
> nor approach it with duplicity of heart . . .
> For then the Lord will reveal your secrets
> and publicly cast you down.
> Because you approached the fear of the Lord
> with your heart full of guile (Sir 1:26–30, NAB).

In addition to the views of G. Sheppard, another perspective has been offered by G. Wilson. He has argued that there is "sufficient evidence to suggest that the epilogue serves to bind Qoheleth together with Proverbs and provides a canonical key to the interpretation of both" (178; cf. *JBL* 103 [1984] 175–92). Several connections with Proverbs are to be noted. The phrase "the words of the wise" occurs only four times in the Bible: Prov 1:6; 22:17; Eccl 9:17; 12:11. Moreover, the phrase is parallel to the enigmatic בעלי אספות, a delimited and specific collection of wisdom sayings, which is not to be considered coextensive with Qoheleth, but rather in addition to the book of Ecclesiastes. Wilson points out the striking similarity of the editorial titles in Prov 1:1 and Eccl 1:1. Qoheleth is identified as "son of David," and the epilogue (12:11) reveals an awareness of a collection process ("the words of the wise"), which is now to be restricted (v 12). Furthermore, the introduction to the Book of Proverbs (1:2–7) shows similarity to the epilogue of Eccl 12:9–14, especially in the repetition of the phrase "the words of the wise" (1:6; cf. Eccl 12:1). "It is not impossible that the epilogist has purposely cast his description of Qoheleth in light of the exhortation of Proverbs" (181). Moreover, just as "fear of God" crowned the epilogue, so it is the origin of wisdom according to Prov 1:7. Even the connection of commandments and fear of God (Eccl 12:13) seems to receive an explanation from the implicit implications of the Deuteronomic understanding (Deut 4:6; 8:5–6; 30:15–18, etc.) of Prov 1–9. While the order of books is not really an argument, it is interesting to notice the association of Proverbs-Qoheleth in the various lists of books that have come down to us. Thus from the point of view of canonical shaping, the two books were seen to have a common purpose, and there is no cleavage between wisdom and Yahwism: "The canonical editor insists that the 'words of the wise[men]' cannot be rightly understood apart from the 'commandments of God/YHWH'" (192).

In the discussion above (p. xxxvi) on the structure of the book, the singular view of the epilogue by M. Fox was noted. It will be recalled that for him the epilogist (also responsible for "says Qoheleth" in 1:2 and 7:27) is "the teller of the tale," or the frame narrator. Qoheleth is really his persona through whom he speaks to "my son" (Eccl 12:12). His is the true authorial voice (although he keeps himself in the background as a mere transmitter), for he not only gathered but even composed what we read in the book. We read in the text of the person of Qoheleth who observed, reflected, and reported. But Fox considers the epilogist not only as redactor, but "for all practical interpretive purposes, the *author* of the book" (*Qohelet,* 312). To this end he can refer to very many examples in Egyptian and Mesopotamian wisdom literature (and one should note the narrator's voice in Deuteronomy, e.g., 1:1–5; 5:1; 28:69, etc.; and also in Tobit, 3:7ff. and 14:15). Other scholars have raised this issue and then skirted it somewhat. Fox refers to F. Delitzsch (430): "In the book, Koheleth-Solomon speaks, whose mask the author puts on; here, he speaks, letting the mask fall off, of Koheleth." Similarly, O. Loretz questioned the equivalence of the "I" of the book and the "I" of the author: "It is worthwhile analyzing whether the customary equivalence between the 'I' of the book and the personal 'I' of the author can be the point at which one should start the interpretation of the book. One must therefore determine whether Qoheleth speaks to us as an historical person or as a 'poetic personality' (Croce)" (*CBQ* 25 [1963] 48). In the end, however, Loretz's interest lay in denying that an autobiographical approach to the work was viable (cf. *Qohelet,* 165–66); the narrative "I" is merely a stylistic device.

The position of M. Fox is attractive and well thought out. But he admits that it "has only limited implications for interpretation of Qoheleth's teachings, because the author does not undermine the persona's ethos or subvert his teachings. . . . In any case, there is no ideological conflict between Qoheleth's teachings and the epilogue" (*Qohelet,* 315–16). Since it is virtually impossible to distinguish between the meaning of one voice and the other, the distinction between the author and persona makes little, if any, contribution to the exegesis of the book.

One may conclude with the ironic but apt observation that it was somehow not fitting that the enigmatic book of Ecclesiastes should come to an end without the subtlety and open-ended character that the epilogue shows.

Epilogue

Bibliography

Alter, R. *The Art of Biblical Poetry.* New York: Basic Books, 1985. Audet, J.-P. "Origines comparées de la double tradition de la loi et de la sagesse dans le proche-orient ancien." In *Acts of the International Orientalists' Congress.* Moscow, 1980. 1:352–57. Boström, G. *Proverbiastudien: die Weisheit und das fremde Weib in Sprüche 1–9.* LUÅ 30. Lund: Gleerup, 1935. Bryce, G. *A Legacy of Wisdom.* Lewisburg: Bucknell, 1979. Bühlmann, W. *Vom rechten Reden und Schweigen.* OBO 12. Fribourg: Universitätsverlag, 1976. Bultmann, R. *The History of the Synoptic Tradition.* New York: Harper & Row, 1963. Camp, C. *Wisdom and the Feminine in the Book of Proverbs.* BLS 11. Sheffield: Almond, 1985. ————. "The Female Sage in the Biblical Wisdom Literature." In *SIANE.* 185–203. Collins, J. J. "The Biblical Precedent for Natural Theology." *JAAR* 45/1 Supplement (March 1977) B:35–67. Couturier, G. "La vie familiale comme source de la sagesse et de la loi." *ScEs* 32 (1980) 177–92. Crenshaw, J. L. "The Sage in Proverbs." In *SIANE.* 205–16. Delkurt, H. "Grundprobleme alttestamentlicher Weisheit." *VF* 36 (1991) 38–71. Duesberg, H. and Fransen, J. *Les scribes inspirés.* 2 vols. Paris: Desclée, 1939. Dych, W. "The Achievement of Karl Rahner." *TD* 31 (1984) 325–33. Fontaine, C. R. *Traditional Sayings in the Old Testament.* BLS 5. Sheffield: Almond Press, 1985. ————. "The Sage in Family and Tribe." In *SIANE.* 155–64. ————. "The Personification of Wisdom." In *HBC.* 501–3. Gerstenberger, E. *Wesen und Herkunft des 'apodiktischen' Rechts.* WMANT 20. Neukirchen-Vluyn: Neukirchener, 1965. Gese, H. *Lehre und Wirklichkeit in der alten Weisheit.* Tübingen: Mohr/Siebeck, 1985. Golka, F. W. "Die israelitische Weisheitsschule oder 'des Kaisers neue Kleider.'" *VT* 33 (1983) 257–70. ————. "Die Königs- und Hofsprüche und der Ursprung der israelitischen Weisheit." *VT* 36 (1986) 13–36. ————. "Die Flecken des Leoparden: Biblische und afrikanische Weisheit im Sprichwort." In *Schöpfung und Befreiung.* FS C. Westermann. Ed. R. Albertz. Stuttgart: Calwer, 1989. 149–65. Gordis, R. "The Social Background of Wisdom Literature." *HUCA* 18 (1944) 77–118. Hermisson, H.-J. *Studien zur israelitischen Spruchweisheit.* WMANT 28. Neukirchen-Vluyn: Neukirchener, 1968. Jamieson-Drake, D. *Scribes and Schools in Monarchic Judah.* JSOTSup 109. Sheffield: Almond, 1991. Kayatz, C. *Studien zu Proverbien 1–9.* WMANT 22. Neukirchener-Vluyn: Neukirchener, 1966. Kloppenborg, J. "Isis and Sophia in the Book of Wisdom." *HTR* 75 (1982) 57–84. Koch, K. "Is There a Doctrine of Retribution in the Old Testament?" In *Theodicy in the Old Testament.* Ed. J. L. Crenshaw. Philadelphia: Fortress, 1983. 57–87. Lang, B. *Frau Weisheit.* Düsseldorf: Patmos, 1975. ————. *Wisdom and the Book of Proverbs: An Israelite Goddess Redefined.* New York: Pilgrim, 1986. Lichtheim, M. *AEL.* 3 vols. Berkeley: University of California Press, 1975–80. Mack, B. *Logos und Sophia.* SUNT 10. Göttingen: Vandenhoeck & Ruprecht, 1973. Marböck, J. *Weisheit im Wandel.* BBB 37. Bonn: Hanstein, 1971. Marcus, R. "On Biblical Hypostases of Wisdom." *HUCA* 23 (1950/51) 157–71. Maré, L. *Proverbes salomoniens et proverbes mossi.* Frankfurt: Peter Lang, 1986. Murphy, R. E. "The Kerygma of the Book of Proverbs." *Int* 20 (1966) 3–14. ————. "Wisdom's Song: Proverbs 1:20–33." *CBQ* 48 (1986) 456–60. ————. "Wisdom and Eros in Proverbs 1–9." *CBQ* 50 (1988) 600–603. ————. "Wisdom and Creation." *JBL* 104 (1985) 3–11. ————. *Wisdom Literature: Job, Proverbs, Ruth, Canticles, Ecclesiastes, Esther.* FOTL 13. Grand Rapids: Eerdmans, 1981. ————. *The Tree of Life: An Exploration of Biblical Wisdom Literature.* ABRL. New York: Doubleday, 1990. Preuss, H. D. *Einführung in die alttestamentliche Literatur.* Urban-Taschenbücher 383. Stuttgart: Kohlhammer, 1987. Pury, A. de. "Sagesse et révélation dans l'Ancien Testament." *RTP* 27 (1977) 1–50. Rad, G. von. *Old Testament Theology.* 2 vols. New York: Harper & Row, 1962. ————. *Wisdom in Israel.* Nashville:

Abingdon, 1972. **Rahner, K.** *Foundations of Christian Faith.* New York: Seabury, 1978. **Richter, W.** *Recht und Ethos.* SANT 15. Munich: Kösel, 1966. **Ringgren, H.** *Word and Wisdom: Studies in the Hypostatization of Divine Qualities and Functions in the Ancient Near East.* Lund: Ohlssons, 1947. **Schmid, H. H.** *Wesen und Geschichte der Weisheit.* BZAW 101. Berlin: Töpelmann, 1966. **Skehan, P. W.** "Structures in Poems on Wisdom: Proverbs 8 and Sirach 24." *CBQ* 41 (1979) 365–79. ————— and **Lella, A. di.** *The Wisdom of Ben Sira.* AB 39. Garden City: Doubleday, 1987. **Steck, O. H.** *World and Environment.* BES. Nashville: Abingdon, 1980. **Vanoni, G.** "Volkssprichwort und YHWH-ethos: Beobachtungen zu Spr 15:16." *BN* 35 (1986) 73–108. **Westermann, C.** "Weisheit im Sprichwort." In *Schalom: Studien zu Glaube und Geschichte Israel.* Ed. K.-H. Bernhardt. Stuttgart: Calwer, 1971. —————. *Wurzeln der Weisheit: Die ältesten Sprüche Israel und anderer Völker.* Göttingen: Vandenhoeck & Ruprecht, 1990. —————. *Forschungsgeschichte zur Weisheitsliteratur 1950–1990.* AzT 71. Stuttgart: Calwer, 1991. **Whybray, R. N.** *The Intellectual Tradition in the Old Testament.* BZAW 135. Berlin: de Gruyter, 1974. **Williams, J. G.** "The Power of Form: A Study of Biblical Proverbs." In *Gnomic Wisdom.* Semeia 17. Ed. J. D. Crossan. Chico: Scholars Press, 1980. 35–58. **Zimmerli, W.** "The Place and the Limit of the Wisdom in the Framework of the Old Testament Theology," In *SAIW.* 314–26.

The work of Qoheleth was graced with an epilogue (12:9–14) that explicitly described him as a wise man and teacher. Whatever view the reader takes of this puzzling book, it is clear that 12:9–10 are not only explanatory but even laudatory. The man who seems so iconoclastic to later generations is one of the teachers in Israel, one in a long line of wisdom practitioners. It is appropriate, then, that an epilogue be added here to provide more information about the tradition to which he belonged and which he felt free to criticize. It would be entirely too hypothetical to reconstruct a history of the wisdom movement within the Bible. However, a sketch that allows for the uncertainties while describing the current state of scholarly research will help the reader to appreciate the setting of Ecclesiastes within the Bible itself.

Although some scholars are uneasy with the term "wisdom" literature, especially for the extra-biblical examples found in Egypt and Mesopotamia, we shall adopt it here to designate a fairly unified group of books. Students of the Bible are generally unanimous in classifying Proverbs, Job, and Ecclesiastes as wisdom literature. The phrase is used here to designate not only these but also two important apocryphal works, Sirach (or Ecclesiasticus, perhaps meaning the "church" book) and the Wisdom of Solomon (written in Greek). Anyone who takes the trouble to read these apocrypha will agree that they form a continuity with the three biblical works. Although references to them may not be frequent, their importance for the Jewish communities of Judah and the Diaspora is not to be underestimated. A great deal has been written about wisdom influence on the rest of the biblical books (see R. E. Murphy, *The Tree of Life*, 97–110), but this will not be our concern here. The discussion of OT wisdom will be along these lines: origins, linguistic style, world view, ancient Near Eastern parallels, the personification of wisdom, and the theological value of Israelite wisdom and its relevance to modern life.

Origins

At the outset it is wise to distinguish between what came to be called wisdom literature and the wisdom movement or educative process that flourished in Israel.

A literature is not the same as the impetus behind it (the manner of teaching, the institutions from which the literature came). A piece of literature can be oral before it is written.

The picture of education in ancient Israel is complicated by the ambiguous evidence for writing that archeological investigation in Israel has uncovered. The French Semitist, André Lemaire (*Les écoles et la formation de la Bible dans l'ancien Israël*), has made much of the abundance of inscriptions on sherds and other durable material. In his view these were school exercises that point to the early dawn of writing in Israel, to the almost total neglect of an oral stage of communication. Indeed, he extended his hypothesis about early literacy to the OT and sketched a literary history of these books (77–83). Naturally, this presupposed existence of schools going far back in Israel's history.

For the most part, however, biblical scholars have taken a more modest position on the scholastic origins of wisdom. There is no clear physical evidence of the existence of schools in Israel. Hence the argument for such has been by way of inference. The bureaucracy of the monarchy, it is said, would have necessitated an institution to serve the training of courtiers for foreign service. The analogy for this is the historical precedent in the surrounding cultures. The Sumerian literature is associated with the "*e-dubba*," or "tablet house," in which many of the literary masterpieces of ancient Sumer were written and transmitted. At the other end of the Fertile Crescent, the activity of the Egyptian scribes in the production of their outstanding collections of wisdom compositions came gradually to be known in the course of the twentieth century, especially through the comparative study of Proverbs and the Instruction of Amenemope by the famous German Egyptologist, Adolf Erman (cf. G. Bryce, *A Legacy of Wisdom*). This marked the beginning of a tendency to interpret the Book of Proverbs as a kind of Israelite counterpart to the Egyptian Instructions. This approach was strengthened by the striking similarity of the thirty units of the Egyptian work to the "thirty sayings," which seems to be the correct reading in Prov 22:17 (NRSV, NIV, etc.). Many other parallels between Amenemope and Prov 22:17–23:11 were also seen. In addition, the concept of the Egyptian *ma'at* (almost untranslatable, but something like "justice," "virtue") was seen as influencing Israelite thought. After all, had not the author of 1 Kgs 5:9–14[4:29–34] extolled the wisdom of Solomon as surpassing the wisdom of Egypt? Everything in this scenario seemed to fit nicely. One came to speak of the Israelite "Enlightenment" (G. von Rad), when Israel was exposed to the rich culture of its neighbors, especially Egypt. There would have been a need for scribes to function in various offices of the new kingdom. If one followed the model of the training in Egypt, learning the language from a wisdom literature served not only to teach the art of writing but also how to be responsible courtiers. Hence the Book of Proverbs, at least for most of Prov 10–31, came to be seen as a school book associated with such training (e.g., H. Duesberg and J. Fransen, *Les scribes inspirés*, 77–118). The Achilles heel in this theory was that archeological evidence still remained lacking for the existence of schools (see further D. Jamieson-Drake, *Scribes and Schools* . . .). As one of its champions admitted, the argument is built basically on analogy (H.-J. Hermisson, *Studien zur israelitischen Spruchweisheit*, 97–136).

Other scholars looked elsewhere to explain the origins of Israelite wisdom. They analyzed the probable beginnings of sayings among a simple society, and they pointed to modern illiterate cultures that possess many comparable wisdom proverbs, as an analogy to the Solomonic corpus in the OT. Perhaps the first insight into this possibility belongs to J.-P. Audet ("Origines comparées"). He advanced the reasonable claim that the origins of wisdom lay in the distant undifferentiated past—indeed, that there was no felt distinction between what came to be expressed in wisdom sayings and also in societal laws. Only later were they categorized separately (and then not completely: several sayings in the Bible are also commandments, and have parallels in the law; cf. Prov 15:35; 23:10 and Exod 22:21; Deut 10:8 as examples of wisdom and law). This line of thought was pursued by G. Couturier, who argued strongly for origins of wisdom sayings in the family (*ScEs* 32 [1980] 177–92).

Similar ideas were expressed by W. Richter (*Recht und Ethos*) and E. Gerstenberger (*Wesen und Herkunft*) who both spoke of *Sippenethos*, or tribal ethos. Strictly speaking there seems to be a distinction here between the narrow unity of the immediate family (leadership of parents) and the broader family of the tribe, where the tribal leader would set the tone for conduct and life style. This distinction matters little since the influence would be mutual and the differences negligible. It is quite different from postulating a school origin for the sayings. In a similar way, G. Vanoni (*BN* 35 [1986] 73–108) traces the "Armenethos," or ethos in favor of the poor, back to an oral stage (103). He concludes that court and school were not the only institutions serving wisdom theology.

C. Westermann seems to have been the first to advance arguments against schools on the basis of oral transmission of sayings among illiterate peoples ("Weisheit im Sprichwort"), and he followed up with further evidence in *Wurzeln der Weisheit*. This approach has also been pursued by F. Golka (*VT* 36 [1986] 13–36; "Die Flecken des Leoparden," 149–65) and L. Maré (*Proverbes salomoniens*). F. Golka (*VT* 33 [1983] 258–62) has reviewed the early history of the research into school and education in Israel (A. Klostermann and L. Dürr), and he has exposed the weaknesses in the arguments in favor of the existence of schools. To A. Lemaire's evidence he responded that the epigraphic material can be equally well derived from family training as from a professional school (263, n. 19). We know little about the sociological background for education in ancient Israel, but the family system can be illustrated by the examples of the *sôpĕrîm*, or scribes, Elihoreph and Ahijah, sons of Shisha, who seems to have been a prominent scribe in the time of David (cf. 2 Sam 20:25; 1 Chr 18:16). In Jer 36 Elishama is called scribe (*sôpēr*) and has a room where important leaders, such as members of the Shaphan family, congregate (36:12–21). Shaphan is the father of Ahikam and Gemariah, and his grandson is the Micaiah who heard Baruch read the inflammatory Jeremiah scroll in the Temple (Jer 36:9–13). It is also possible that membership in the ruling class was a tight family concern. There has been no refutation of the seven conclusions (270) that Golka draws in favor of the family as the locus of wisdom lore. The proverbial sayings are to be seen as largely deriving from a concrete situation, and not from a teacher's desk.

Both C. R. Fontaine and C. Camp have each in her own way underscored oral transmission and family origins of biblical sayings. The specific title of Fontaine's article, "The Sage in Family and Tribe" (*SIANE*, 155–64), indicates as much. She describes the various roles: teaching (e.g., Prov 1:2–6), counseling (e.g., 12:15), planning (economic resources, 19:15), and so forth. A particularly vivid example

of transmission within the family is Prov 4:1–9, in which the teaching received
from one's father is mentioned in the transmission to a grandson:

> Listen, children, to a father's instruction,
>> and be attentive, that you may know insight . . .
> When I was a son with my father,
>> tender and unique in my mother's sight,
> He taught me and said to me:
>> Let your heart hold fast my words;
>> keep my commands, that you may live! (4:1–4)

Fontaine also remarks that Job's description of his former life in chap. 31 includes several roles of a sage in the family setting: dealing with household
complaints (vv 13–15) and distributing goods to the poor (vv 16–22).

There was also a place for the mother, who is mentioned frequently in Proverbs (1:8; 6:20; 30:17; 31:1–9, 10–31), and C. Camp has described the role of
"The Female Sage in Ancient Israel and in the Biblical Wisdom Literature"
(*SIANE*, 185–203). Two outstanding instances show the "wise woman" is a meaningful title: the discussion of the woman from Tekoa with David and the encounter
of the woman of Abel with Joab. Their sayings are in the style of proverbial wisdom: "We must all die . . . like water spilled on the ground" (2 Sam 14:14), and
"They used to say of old, 'let them inquire at Abel,' and the matter would be
settled" (2 Sam 20:18). As Camp remarks, these sayings point to a wisdom that
carried covenantal values, and not just secular wisdom. Moreover, the very activity of Lady Wisdom in Prov 1–9 suggests a motherly, saving, activity on behalf of
the naive simple ones against the wiles of Dame Folly. This should reflect a corresponding role expected of women in everyday activities.

J. L. Crenshaw is more mechanical in determining the teachers and the setting in
life. He locates the poems of Prov 1–9 in the instruction given in schools (cf. the
Egyptian "Instructions"), while the sentences or sayings (mainly in Prov 20–31)
are congenial to the home (cf. "The Sage in Proverbs," 205–16). This division is
perhaps too neat in view of our ignorance of the contexts of Israelite learning.

In *Wurzeln der Weisheit* C. Westermann offered some astute observations about
individual groupings of sayings that suggest oral rather than school composition
as the source and means of transmission. His comments on the relationship of
proverbs to laws ring true: "The public nature and effect of sayings give them an
advantage over the laws. They live on in the people and are spoken and heard
time after time. They are applied where they can have an effect. This kind of
effectiveness is not possible for laws (with the exception of the commandments).
Once the laws are written down, they are known only in small circles, as their
technical language also suggests. Sayings which characterize human beings and
their actions have a much greater potential for influence; these sayings come to
the attention of everyone, and in a continuous manner" (*Wurzeln*, 54). Our own
experience tells us how true this is; we quote proverbs, not laws; everyone recalls
a common fund of sayings.

Westermann (*Wurzeln*, 72–75) looks at the range of comparisons that are to be
found in the Book of Proverbs: phenomena of heaven and earth (weather, the
deep), existence on the land (wells, stones, dew), plants and animals, humans
and the various parts of the body (especially lips, mouth, tongue), clothing and

food, the nature of one's occupation (farmer) and sustenance (wine, honey), housing (door, lock), sickness (drunkenness, bad tooth), the weather, and so forth. Several more examples are given, but all leave one with the impression of experience in a village or a small settlement. Nothing suggests a great city or capital such as Jerusalem (and an alleged school); there is no mention of war, commerce, palace, and such topics as might lead one to think that the sayings derive from a higher social level. This would lay to rest the views of R. Gordis (*HUCA* 18 [1944] 77–118) and a wide range of scholars who regard the sages as an elite higher class. The profession of the sages and their legacy are far too diversified for such a generalization; all strands of society contributed to the wisdom movement.

The position of Audet, Couturier, Westermann, and others who support a broader base (the people) for the origins of wisdom over the narrow base (school) seems to have the better argument. Wisdom certainly existed in Israel before the time of the monarchy (cf. Fontaine, *Traditional Sayings*). Perhaps we can sum up the origins in two stages that may have been partially contemporary: the oral forms that would have flourished in home and hamlet generally and the written forms, productions of schools or literati that were gradually assembled and made into collections. It is not possible to draw a date line between these two stages; there is doubtless an overlap, and at some point the oral transmission ended with literary expression. There is no need to question the implications of Prov 25:1 about the role of the men of Hezekiah in the transmission of a wisdom corpus; but that verse does not imply school (courtly) origins, or even that courtiers were the chief architects of wisdom.

It is useful to recall here that most of the biblical wisdom that has come down to us is of demonstrably post-exilic origin: Ecclesiastes, Sirach, and the Wisdom of Solomon. In addition, it is probable that Prov 1–9 is post-exilic and thus provides a hermeneutical key (Prov 1:1–6) for the interpretation of the various collections within the book. While the date of Job cannot be fixed with certainty, the majority of scholars puts the final composition in the post-exilic period. It is clear from Eccl 12:9 that Qoheleth was recognized as a "sage," presumably belonging to a certain stratum of society, because he "taught the people." By the third century, the likely date for Qoheleth, education seems much more formal. And Ben Sira, who can be securely dated at the beginning of the second century, issues an invitation to the untutored to come to his "house of instruction" (בבת מדרשי, as MS B of Sirach reads 51:23), which is a school of some kind.

More interesting than the prickly question of origins is the changing face of wisdom as it grows. With this come new meanings and also new applications. It is not really true that "a proverb in a collection is dead." Rather, its original "proverb performance" (cf. C. R. Fontaine, *Traditional Sayings*, 71–76), or application, may be irrecoverable, but the saying has taken on a life of its own, and new meaning(s) accrue to it. The "after-life" of a proverbial saying is a rich one. For example, "You can lead a horse to water, but you cannot make it drink," whatever its original form and meaning, has several applications and meanings in our culture.

The ambiguity and liveliness of proverbial sayings have been given a singular illustration by R. Alter. He reminds us of the manner in which we understand today "Fools rush in where angels fear to tread" as indicating a foolhardy undertaking. This is possible only because we have "lost" the context, a full statement, which goes this way: "Nay, fly to Altars, there they'll talk you dead; "For Fools rush in where Angels fear to tread" (Pope's "Essay on Criticism," 3:624–25), quoted in Alter, *The Art of Biblical Poetry*, 165). What Pope had in mind were certain literary critics that would pursue the victim of their criticism even into a holy place. The attractive ambiguity and polyvalence of the proverbial saying call for a more detailed analysis of the linguistic style.

Linguistic Style

For most of the wisdom literature, there is a ready understanding of the literary forms that are employed. Relatively few proverbial sayings occur in the book of Job (e.g., 5:5–6). The work is composed of prose prologue and epilogue, with speeches being the main form of expression. Qoheleth has his own style of "reflections" upon life (cf. above, pp. xxxi–xxxii; R. E. Murphy, *The Tree of Life*, 50–51). But he also puts forward several sayings (e.g., chap. 7) that are not easy to comprehend within the overall purpose of his work. Within Sirach there is a certain air of continuity, achieved by his concentration on specific topics (e.g., death, 4:11–19; 38:16–23). These longer units doubtless contain proverbial sayings, but they are blended into the whole. He moves his thought along by interlacing various proverbs and types of saying (e.g., "better" sayings, etc.). The unity of the topic often diverts attention from the sayings; for example, Sir 20:5,

> Some who keep silent are thought to be wise;
> others, who talk, are disliked. (cf. Prov 17:28)

This fits in perfectly with the other verses, some of them also sayings, in 20:1–8. In Sirach there are several poems of twenty-two and twenty-three lines in length, imitating the number of letters (twenty-two) in the Hebrew alphabet (cf. P. W. Skehan and A. di Lella, *The Wisdom of Ben Sira*; index on p. 613, under "twenty-two"). Preoccupation with the alphabet was a characteristic of later Hebrew poetry, as evidenced by the Book of Lamentations and Prov 2:1–22 (see R. E. Murphy, *Wisdom Literature*, 56, 172–73). The Wisdom of Solomon neglects proverbial sayings and develops its topics in a very forthright way. Many colorful comparisons betray its wisdom origins (cf., e.g., Wis 2:7–8; 5:14).

The customary two-line (at times, three-line) Hebrew parallelism is typical of the proverbial saying. This medium allows for extension in a somewhat synonymous style (if A, then more so B), or by contrast (the antithetic parallelism that characterizes Prov 10:1–15:32), or even by a story that teaches by example (Prov 24:30–34; Eccl 4:13–16). A mere description fails to convey the excitement (as well as the banality at times) of the saying. Striking ideas (a soft tongue can break a bone, 25:15b; the bitter turns out to be sweet, 27:7b) are fairly frequent. On the other hand, there is a large majority of sayings that seem to be tedious developments of the contrast between the righteous and the wicked, especially in chaps. 10–15 of Proverbs. C. Westermann (*Wurzeln*, 100) counts some 117 sayings about the righteous and the wicked—usually contrasts in their activity and in their lot in life. They pronounce in a very theoretical and universal style and fail to get into the concrete details of a situation that is a characteristic of the typical proverb. In a sense this style constitutes a teaching or a system; at bottom there is really only one theme: an affirmation of the basic difference in the conduct and fate of the righteous and the wicked. Indeed, the point of view favorable to the righteous is a conviction already prevalent before the sayings are formed. This is wisdom in a (heavy-handed?) teaching mode, not searching for new experiences. For this reason Westermann is inclined to say that they are not really proverbial sayings in the proper sense; they are secondary, thematic formulations that served the purpose of wisdom teachers ("Weisheit im Sprichwort," 84–85, n. 33; *Wurzeln*, 91–101).

Were the proverbial sayings formed originally as two lines or as one line? It is difficult to set up a criterion that would cover all the cases. We do not have any historical entrée to the "making" of a saying. Both the one-liner and the two-liner seem possible. Westermann is inclined to recognize many original one-liners (*Wurzeln*, 51, e.g., 16:27–30; see also pp. 77–78). In favor of his view, one can point to the study of proverbial sayings in a narrative context, as found in C. R. Fontaine's *Traditional Sayings*: Judg 8:2, 21; 1 Sam 16:7; 24:14; 1 Kgs 20:11 (although perhaps one could argue that 1 Sam 16:7 and 1 Kgs 20:11 are two-liners). The point of the proverbs is clear and precise, and the expression is concise. The words are to the point, without further elaboration. Moreover, this style of one-liner befits the oral stage of transmission of sayings that Westermann argues for. The form of parallel lines is what one would expect from further reflection and expression, perhaps in writing rather than in the oral phase of transmission. Hence in *Wurzeln* (51) he cites Prov 16:27–30; he thinks each of these proverbs was originally cast in one line, to which another parallel line was added:

> A scoundrel digs up (?) evil,
> and on his lips there is (like) a scorching fire.
> A plotter causes strife,
> and a talebearer separates friends.
> A violent person deceives his neighbor,
> and leads him along a way that is not good.
> Whoever winks the eye plans trickery;
> whoever purses the lips pursues evil.

It remains difficult to prove that the two-liner was created by parallelism with an original one-liner (see other examples in *Wurzeln*, 77–78). Each case would have to be considered, and the conclusion cannot always be firmly drawn. Perhaps the transition from an oral to a written stage is the most persuasive argument for this development.

Parallelism, however, is perhaps the least imposing characteristic of a proverbial saying. The real subtlety lies in certain tricks of speech such as onomatopoeia (hardly to be reproduced in translation), paradoxes, and clever juxtapositions. These phenomena have been studied by J. G. Williams in "The Power of Form."

An adequate rendering of Hebrew proverbs is very difficult to achieve. Most English translations are lame—a common affliction of other versions as well. So many sayings lose their pungency when they are rendered into another idiom. This is especially true in the case of the idiomatic use of juxtaposition in the Hebrew—juxtaposition within a line and also between two lines (cf. J. G. Williams, "The Power of Form," 40–42). A literal rendering of the following proverb illustrates this:

> Hope deferred—sickness of heart;
>> but (and) a tree of life—desire fulfilled. (Prov 13:12)

Several points deserve notice. First there is no verb connecting the topics; they are simply juxtaposed. Second, they are arranged in a chiasmus, or the form of X: sickness corresponds to life, and hope to desire. Third, the second line is in parallelism with the first in an antithetical manner; hence the simple "and" of the Hebrew may be rendered "but." Not all proverbial sayings have this inner-line juxtaposition and juxtaposition of whole lines. But many do, and when they are translated literally, they are even more striking than when they are found in an elegant translation.

One can also compare 15:32:

> Rejecter of discipline—despiser of his soul;
>> but (and) hearer of reprimand—gainer of mind.

The structure is similar to 13:12, but there is no chiasmus. One should also note the idiomatic use of heart in Hebrew to indicate the mind and, even broader, the inner spirit of a person.

English style will not permit translators to reproduce this juxtaposition, at least within a line; the rhythm would be too jerky. But the synonymous or antithetic character is easily seen—and it is best rendered by the choice of "and" or "but," as the case may be. Overall, the starkness and punch of the Hebrew poetry lose something in a "correct" translation.

Moreover, the reader of a proverbial saying must recognize the inevitable generalization implicit in the sentence. While based upon experience, no proverb can capture all of experience, all the exceptions, all the nuances. It is a relatively narrow slice of life that is captured and offered for consideration. Two perfectly valid proverbs can be on a collision course with each other, such as "the one who hesitates is lost" compared with "look before you leap!" Obviously if one looks for too long a time, opportunity may vanish. It is worth noting here that these sayings strive for a certain effect within English pronunciation: the combination of *st* in the first saying and the *lk*/*lp* in the second. Assonance and alliteration are characteristic of Hebrew sayings as well (e.g., Eccl 7:1), although this is hardly possible to convey in translation. Sometimes the opposition between two sayings seems to be absolutely contradictory (even if not so), as in the famous "Answer the fool/Answer not the fool" in Prov 26:4–5.

Finally, it would be a mistake to underrate a proverb. When one proverb follows constantly upon another, it may happen that the reader's eyes glaze over. They should be read in small doses, in order to savor their subtlety. Many paradoxical observations are sprinkled throughout the collections. Thus Prov 11:24:

> One person is lavish, but grows richer
> another spares, but grows poorer.

There is no moral intended here about the use of riches; this is an observation of a fact that in a sense defies explanation. How is it that one who spends is the richer for it? In general, a reader must beware of "moralizing" proverbs when they are simply experiential statements.

Robert Alter aptly entitled his chapter on Proverbs "The Poetry of Wit" (*The Art of Biblical Poetry*, 163–84). It is borne out by the examples cited, and also by the explicit judgment of the sages in such sayings as the following:

> An apt response is a joy to anyone;
> > and a word in season, how good it is! (Prov 15:23)
>
> Pleasing words are a honeycomb,
> > sweet to the taste and healthy for the body. (Prov 16:24)

When Qoheleth is described as searching for pleasant words (Eccl 12:10), this means an expressive literary style that matches his wisdom, not words that will necessarily "please" or bring joy to all who hear them.

It is not surprising, then, to be confronted with countless sayings that deal with the organs of speech (mouth, lips, tongue). Corresponding to these is the duty of "listening." This is not a passive but an active listening, an obedience to the teaching. The obligation to "listen," "hear," is firmly taught in the Egyptian Instructions (see, for example, the epilogue to the Instruction of Ptah-hotep, *ANET*, 412–14). It is this intelligent hearing that enables the docile to learn from reproof and reprimand (Prov 12:1). No one is born "wise." The wisdom of a person depends to a great extent on control of the tongue, when to speak and when to keep silent. Over sixty sayings about proper speech in the Solomonic collections have been studied by W. Bühlmann (*Vom rechten Reden und Schweigen*), and he does not treat the many proverbs about improper speech. Correct speech is praised as precious, gentle but reproving, honest, timely—in other words, only good effects can come from it. But one must know when to speak, and how (silence and its virtues). At the same time, the sage was aware of the ambiguities: silence could be misunderstood as a sign of intelligence because one has nothing to say, or understood properly as a sign of intelligence because of the care with which one speaks (Prov 17:28–29). There is a delicate balance to be observed, and whoever thinks oneself to be wise is in the worst situation of all; there is more hope for a fool than for such a person (Prov 26:12).

The World View of the Sages

The world view expressed in the wisdom literature is not exclusive to the sages, or else their teaching and writings would not have been understood. They spoke from experiences that their hearers also shared but were not all as able to articulate. Over long years, a treasury of wise insights was built up. Experience spoke forcefully, but sometimes with a forked tongue, and it was not always easy to discern the right path. As we have seen, one saying could correct another, and there was an underlying sense that a proverb could not be pushed too hard. The succinct, terse form of expression did not lend itself to distinctions. Thus the saying itself harbored ambiguities, or at least limitations, in the recesses of itself. The dogmatic appearance of a proverb had its own power of persuasiveness, but it had to sacrifice many exceptions for the sake of this ideal. The sages were well aware of their limitations, as the use of paradoxes demonstrates. But the greatest paradox was the Lord of Israel:

> There is no wisdom, no understanding, no knowledge,
> that can prevail against the Lord. (Prov 21:21)

This profound limitation will be reiterated again and again by Qoheleth (e.g., 3:11; 7:13; 8:17).

While the views of Israelite wisdom were shared by all (whether or not they agreed is another matter), it has long been a trademark of wisdom that daily human experience, not the sacred national traditions such as the promises to the patriarchs, the Exodus event, Sinai, formed the teaching of the sages. This is true in that the wisdom literature that has been preserved does not explicitly refer to these historical events—whether by way of motivation or exemplification. But one may not think that the God of Israelite wisdom was merely a "god of origins" or some distant "high god" whom the Israelite separated from the God of the Exodus. H. D. Preuss (*Einführung in die alttestamentliche Weisheitsliteratur,* 174–75) has argued vigorously for the recognition of such a divinity, and hence has taken an altogether dim view of the literature that is allegedly influenced by such theology. In fact he speaks of a "Polyyahwism," using Jer 2:28 as a basis for the "paganization" of the Lord, among which he counts "a kind of sapiential YHWHreligion," cultivated by the sages and the educated (60; cf. 163). It is no answer to Preuss's claim to say that the sacred name, *YHWH,* appears in many sayings (e.g., Prov 15:25–16:11); this can be a matter of editing. Rather, his judgment seems to be guided simply by the historical character of Israel's religion, to the exclusion of human experience. It is difficult to maintain such a distinction, since the teachers in Israel were obviously never ostracized as unorthodox. On the contrary, their teaching was preserved and understood as not opposed to the sacred tradition, however mysterious God appeared to Qoheleth and others.

Behind Preuss's caricature of wisdom theology are several presuppositions that need not be examined here (e.g., that revelation is to be viewed only on the axis of history). But some presuppositions deserve further investigation: (1) Is the goal of the wisdom movement the detection of an order that God has implanted in the world? (2) Is retribution (reward/punishment) to be viewed solely as a mechanical correspondence between the nature of the action (good or bad) and the result (good or bad)? (3) Can one properly speak of a "crisis" in the wisdom movement?

1. It is commonly assumed (e.g., H. H. Schmid, *Wesen und Geschichte der Weisheit*) that the goal of the sages was to find the order of things established in the world of nature and human experience and to be guided by it. One must fit into this order for it was established by the creator. Such a view resembles closely the Egyptian understanding of its own wisdom instructions. The primary concept is *maʿat,* "justice" or "righteousness," which is imprinted in society and in nature by the creator and is to be preserved and, as it were, completed by the human conduct that corresponds to it (cf. R. E. Murphy, *The Tree of Life,* 115–18). There is evidence in Prov 1–9 of the influence of the figure of *maʿat* (who is a goddess as well) on wisdom; cf. C. Kayatz, *Studien zu Proverbien 1–9.* For example, life is associated with both *maʿat* and wisdom; the goddess *maʿat* is pictured with the *ankh* sign (= life) in one hand and the scepter (= royal power) in the other. So Prov 3:18 describes wisdom as having long life in her right hand, and in her left, riches and honor. Many other examples of an Egyptian flavor could be cited (cf. C.

Kayatz, *Studien zu Proverbien 1–9*, 98–102). But this does not necessarily imply that the world view regarding *ma'at* is to be simply transposed to wisdom in Israelite thought. Yet, the advocates of wisdom as a search for order seem to do that very thing. Yes, there are rules of conduct, and also comparisons with the "order" in nature in the Israelite wisdom literature (as well as in the prophets!). But to conceive of the wisdom literature as an expression of a quest for order is mistaken. The sages were searching for immediate and also the ultimate meanings, insofar as these can be reached by human experience. The sages framed sayings that regulated conduct; they listened to experience and drew conclusions based on consistency and frequency. But there is no reason to impose upon Proverbs or Job a search for "order." The issue of retribution, as we shall see, brings up the question of the "order" that should obtain between wisdom/virtue and folly/wickedness. Retribution is a key concept in Israelite wisdom and it resists any reduction to an order that is peculiar to itself; the doctrine of retribution in Proverbs is thoroughly in harmony with Deuteronomic theology, which no one has ever accused of being concerned with order.

2. Klaus Koch designed the theory of "act/consequence," or "the fate-producing action" (cf. the nearly complete English translation of his article in J. L. Crenshaw (ed.), *Theodicy in the Old Testament*, 57–87). He was able to cite many passages from various parts of the OT (not merely from Proverbs or Job). These allegedly illustrated a mechanical correspondence between deed and result. A good deed produced a good result (blessing, etc.); a bad deed produced a bad result (suffering, etc.). This order of things is intrinsic to human activity and established by God, who is the "mid-wife," watching over the way things are played out. A typical example can be taken from Ps 7:15–17[14–16].

> See how they conceive evil,
>   and are pregnant with mischief,
>   and bring forth lies.
> They make a pit, digging it out,
>   and fall into the hole that they have made.
> Their mischief returns upon their own heads,
>   and on their own heads their violence descends. (NRSV)

In a similar way, the success of the wise/virtuous is guaranteed:

> The just will never be disturbed,
>   but the wicked will not remain in the land. (Prov 10:30)

Obviously there is evidence for Koch's reconstruction of the correspondence theory. But there are at least two considerations to be made. The first is that just as often, if not more often (but the question is not to be settled by numbers), the Lord is described as the direct agent of a good/bad result. The Lord rewards and punishes (cf. Amos 3:6; Isa 45:7). There is no further intimation that this is arranged by an order of mechanical correspondence. So it is quite legitimate to conclude that both mentalities (deed-consequence and the divine intervention) may have been operative.

Second, if one grants such a "deed-consequence" mentality, was its operation as thorough and mechanical as propounded in Koch's theory? Were the sages so obtuse that they failed to note the constant breakdown of such a theory in their daily experience? Really, does the one who digs a pit for another (harms another) inevitably fall into the pit or trap that was prepared? How many times would a person have to witness the breakdown of this "order" to become unconvinced of it? If the wit and perception displayed by the teachers in Israel are widely acknowledged, the theory of mechanical correspondence between act and result has to be recognized as a gratuitous generalization that suffers from countless exceptions. Perhaps the view was nourished by a strong desire to see appropriate justice done in the case of moral action ("virtue is its own reward" or "evil corrupts"). In a sense it overreaches itself and can hardly be considered a hard and fast law or world view. See also H. Delkurt, *VF* 36 (1991) 61–63.

3. Wisdom literature is almost never mentioned without bringing up its "crisis." Many scholars claim that the collapse of the act/consequence view results from the books of Job and Qoheleth; these works led to the much vaunted "crisis" of wisdom. H. Gese (*Lehre und Wirklichkeit in der alten Weisheit*, 78–89) and H. D. Preuss (*Einführung*, 69, 88–89) share this point of view. According to Gese, the victory was achieved by yahwism breaking through the gridlock of retribution current in the ancient Near East. In the book of Job, the mechanical correspondence is defeated by a theology of transcendence; Job demands to see the justice of God, who is above and free of any "order" of things. The Israelite belief in the justice and fidelity of a personal God triumphed. Again, one must ask if the sages of Israel could have remained captive so long to this view, or interpreted it in as rigid a manner as modern scholars understand it. One gets the impression that this "crisis" of wisdom was greater than that precipitated by the fall of Jerusalem in 587 (cf. Ps 89; Ezekiel). This is a total loss of perspective.

The oldest wisdom (generally recognized to be the major portion of Prov 10–31) was undoubtedly upbeat and optimistic. Like all teachers, the sages displayed their wares with too much reliance upon what they considered the generosity of divine retribution and upon a belief that good must somehow prevail and evil be punished. This is at least understandable, and in fact it is never lost, as the Books of Sirach and the Wisdom of Solomon manifest by their optimistic views of retribution. Can one truly speak of a "crisis" of wisdom, a "breakdown"? The continuation in these two books shows that the recovery, if there was a crisis, was remarkable. It was a recession, if you will, a purification, of the wisdom movement that is achieved by the Book of Job, and even by Qoheleth, who leveled the most radical criticism against traditional wisdom. Whatever "crisis" there may have been, wisdom reached a greater certainty that retribution is part of God's mystery into which humans cannot pry too closely. This also came from the recognition that wisdom in general has its limitations—a point already recognized in the oldest wisdom (Prov 21:30–31). Could it be that the personification of Wisdom, its exaltation and mysterious nature (Job 28; Prov 8, etc.), is prepared for by the purification of wisdom (rather than "crisis") that takes place on the journey from Proverbs to the Wisdom of Solomon?

Ancient Near Eastern Parallels

There are several good English translations of the pertinent texts (see the bibliography for the works of J. Pritchard, M. Lichtheim, W. K. Simpson, and up-to-date summary in R. E. Murphy, *The Tree of Life*, the appendix on pp. 151–79). Hence there is no need here to go over well-trodden ground. The Introduction above, pp. xli–lviii, treats Ecclesiastes and parallels in more detail. Here we merely offer a few considerations about the significance of parallels in international wisdom. For wisdom is international, and Israel is only one relatively small contributor in the arc that swings from Egypt to Mesopotamia.

Just how much does one really learn from the examination of biblical wisdom in the light of international wisdom? The association between Prov 22:17–23:11 and the Instruction of Amenemope is probably the most striking parallel. Whatever was the precise type of influence of the Egyptian upon the Hebrew, this resemblance is undeniable. But one also has the impression that there is nothing in these chapters of Proverbs that is distinctively Egyptian, nothing that is foreign to Israel's own wisdom. They seem to testify that Israel recognized a wisdom cognate to its own and adopted it. And this is precisely what is to be expected in a type of literature that deals with human experience. Human beings do not differ all that much from one another, and particularly the residents of the Fertile Crescent shared much in common. Much of that is a result of the universality of human experience.

Although *ma⁽at* was deified in Egypt as a goddess and one can point to some undeniable evidence of influence upon the figure of Wisdom, it should be said that the extensive personification and extraordinary role of Lady Wisdom, which is next to be considered, is unique. A parallel from the sayings of Ahiqar has been alleged (Ahiqar, ll. 94–95; cf. *ANET*, 427–30), but the text is uncertain, and the figure of wisdom is quite modest compared to Lady Wisdom in the Bible. The discovery of similarities between the wisdom of Ahiqar and that of *ma⁽at* and Isis of Egypt does not cancel the striking originality of the personification of biblical Wisdom.

The Wisdom of Solomon presents a unique case. It was written originally in Greek, perhaps in Alexandria, coming from the large Jewish and grecophone community living there. The Greek influence is palpable (cf. the discussion in R. E. Murphy, *The Tree of Life*, 83–96). Yet there is a distinctively Jewish voice to be heard throughout, and not merely in the treatment of the plagues (related in Exodus) in chaps. 11–19. It is unquestionably the wisdom book that is most heavily influenced by foreign culture.

Perhaps the most satisfactory recommendation concerning comparisons between biblical wisdom and the ancient Near Eastern parallels is simply to invite the reader to scrutinize carefully the texts and mentality that are manifested in each of the two areas. Biblical wisdom will fare well, not in the sense of superiority as much as in its particular orientation, the characteristic sense of values that is proper to it.

The Personification of Wisdom

It may be asked at the outset if personification is the correct term to be used in this discussion. Many scholars use the word hypostasis and speak of hypostatization. Because hypostasis carries heavy theological freight (witness the later christological discussions that Prov 8 gave rise to), it is better avoided here. Another reason is the difficulty of giving a definition of hypostasis that is commonly accepted. H. Ringgren adopts a broad definition of hypostasis: "quasi-personification of certain attributes proper to God, occupying an intermediate position between personalities and abstract beings" (*Word and Wisdom*, 8). But this itself needs definition: what is a quasi-personification? Perhaps the simplest definition is this: personification is the process of attributing human or divine characteristics to something that is abstract. Thus certain attributes, justice or wisdom, can be spoken of as independent beings, whether human or divine. This is a literary process; whatever reality may in hard fact be attached to the object (divine or intermediate between human and divine) remains to be determined. But some definition of the term, which is used in such widely different senses, is needed here (cf. R. Marcus, *HUCA* 23 [1950/51] 157–71).

There is no personification in the entire Bible that is comparable to the figure of personified Wisdom. This is not to say that she will not appear with traits that appear to be drawn from various sources, even foreign divinities (such as *maᶜat* or Isis). But the ever-recurring figure of Lady Wisdom is simply without equal. Elsewhere in the Bible personifications are quite modest: e.g., kindness and truth (Pss 89:15[14]; cf. 96:6; 97:2). In Prov 20:1, wine and intoxicating drink are personified by the rowdy effects they produce in those who consume the beverage. But for wisdom, there is a superabundance of texts that employ the personification: Prov 1:22–33; chap. 8; 9:4–6; Sirach, chap. 24; Baruch, 3:9–4:4; Wisdom of Solomon, chaps. 7–9. In all these places Wisdom is personified as a woman.

In the twenty-eighth chapter of Job, Wisdom is personified, but not clearly as a woman. The search for wisdom is contrasted with the search for precious minerals. The latter can be found by human industry. Then comes the question in the key verses, a kind of refrain, 28:12, 20: where is wisdom to be found? Several verses describe where wisdom is *not* to be found: not in the Deep, or the Sea, or Abaddon, or Sheol. The answer begins to emerge in vv 23–27. Only God knows where wisdom dwells, because nothing can escape the divine vision that sees everything under the heavens. God calculated various forces on the earth, such as the rain and the thunderstorm, and appraised wisdom carefully. But the tantalizing thing is that the author does not tell the reader where God located wisdom. The final verse of the chapter, which seems clearly separate from the mysterious whereabouts of wisdom in vv 1–27, is a straightforward traditional statement about what the "beginning" of wisdom is (not where wisdom dwells): "fear of the Lord," "the avoidance of evil" (cf. the description of Job in 1:1, 8 and also Prov 1:7). This is a very tantalizing ending, and the usual verdict of commentators is that v 28 is a later addition to the poem about wisdom. Be that as it may, what is the meaning of the previous few verses about the divine measuring and the appraisal of wisdom? No real answer is given to the refrain questions. God must have put wisdom somewhere, presumably in the world that God is preoccupied with in vv 24–27. In the context of the book, the chapter serves to contribute to the problem of retribution (why does innocent Job suffer?) only in a negative way. The wisdom necessary to understand all this is not available to humans.

The most one can gather from Job 28 is that Wisdom is with God. However, there is a further development in Sirach that is little noticed:

> All wisdom is from the Lord,
> and with him it remains forever.

The sand of the sea, the drops of rain,
    and the days of eternity—who can count them?
The height of heaven, the breadth of the earth,
    the abyss, and wisdom—who can search them out?
Wisdom was created before all other things,
    and prudent understanding from eternity.
The root of wisdom—to whom has it been revealed?
    Her subtleties—who knows them?
There is but one who is wise, greatly to be feared,
    seated upon his throne—the Lord.
It is he who created her;
    he saw her and took her measure;
    he poured her out upon all his works,
Upon all the living according to his gift;
    he lavished her upon those who love him. (Sir 1:1–10, NRSV)

In words that are reminiscent of Job 28:26–27 ("saw her and took her measure"), Sirach actually locates wisdom somewhere: she is poured out on all God's work, and specifically "on all the living" (including Gentiles) and upon the Jews, who are to be understood as "those who love him." Sirach has answered the questions of Job 28:12, 20 more clearly than anyone else has. As will be seen later, he has a specific locus for wisdom in Israel.

In the Book of Proverbs, the figure of Wisdom is clearly more diversified. In chap. 1 she appears as a prophet, excoriating in public those fools who failed to heed her words (cf. R. E. Murphy, *CBQ* 48 [1986] 456–60). The tone is in contrast to that usually employed by the sage: the calamity to come upon fools will be the occasion of mocking laughter on the part of Wisdom. Personified Wisdom here speaks with ridicule and venom usually reserved for the dire threats delivered by prophets.

The tone of chap. 8 is quite different. The message to all who will listen is very positive; Wisdom describes her own genuine message—one that is beyond the value of any riches, beyond all compare. She is fit company for all rulers and an ardent suitor: "Those who love me I love and those who search for me find me" (8:17). Those who love her will encounter her in the paths of righteousness and receive riches and honor. Then she lays claim to divine origins. The Lord created her before the rest of creation—a point reiterated over and over in vv 22–26, "I was brought forth." She affirms her presence as the Lord goes about the establishment of the world (heavens, foundations, etc.), and finally indicates her role:

"then I was beside him, like a master worker;
    and I was daily his delight,
    rejoicing before him always
rejoicing in his inhabited world
    and delighting in the human race." (8:30–31, NRSV)

There are some tantalizing difficulties in this text. The term ʾāmôn, rendered as master worker, craftsman, nursling, confidant, in various versions, remains unclear. There are two general implications: either Wisdom had some participatory role in creation or she was a spectator, playing as a child, as creation went on. In either case, she affirms her delight to be with human beings. After this remarkable description of herself, she issues an invitation to the "children" to heed and pursue her, because "the one who finds me, finds life" (8:35).

A role in creation has been ascribed to wisdom elsewhere (Prov 3:19, "The Lord founded the earth by wisdom"; Wis 7:22, "Wisdom, the fashioner of all things"). More striking in Prov 8 is the statement that Wisdom is all delight (there is no "his" referring to God in the Hebrew text of 8:30) and finds delight among human beings. The perspective of the whole chapter is one of love and attention to her (vv 17, 34), with the astonishing proclamation that to find her is to find life (v 35).

It has long been recognized that the kerygma of Wisdom is life. In every way, the goods of this life are associated with her and seen as a sacrament of her presence, a sign of her love (cf. R. E. Murphy, *Int* 20 [1966] 3–14). Hence, this assurance from Wisdom is not surprising. Rather, one is taken aback by the unparalleled claim to divine origins and to an age that precedes creation (leaving aside the reasonable interpretation that she actually played a role in creation; cf. Prov 3:19). It is difficult to say what prompted such an outpouring. B. Lang (*Wisdom and the Book of Proverbs*) has argued that Lady Wisdom is a relic of Israel's polytheistic past when she figured as a goddess, and in the Book of Proverbs she has been demythologized as it were, being merely a personification of wisdom teaching. However, the existence of the goddess Wisdom in Israel is totally hypothetical. Second, this elaborate and powerful personification is entirely too strong a vehicle to represent wisdom teaching, simply. Perhaps one can understand the figure of Wisdom as a prophetic persona in chap. 1 as a personification of wisdom teaching, but the exaltation of her in chap. 8 as divine, and in a sense eternal, is out of all proportion to the role of, and the importance attached to, wisdom teachers in Israel. In a sense, the narrative of the Sinai theophany and the giving of the Torah pales in comparison with the poetic heights reached by Wisdom in chap. 8. If this were the only example, one might write it off as simply an oddity, but it will appear again in force in Sir 24. Indeed, the personification is continued in chap. 9 of Proverbs.

In Prov 9:1–6 Lady Wisdom's invitation to dinner is in stark contrast to that of Dame Folly (9:13–18). Wisdom's industry in the preparation of the meal and the use of her servants to announce the invitation is directed to life (v 6). The invitation issued by Dame Folly to passersby to turn in to her abode promises that "stolen water is sweet." The comment of the author (9:18) is loaded with meaning—this is an invitation to death, to Sheol (see also 2:18–19; 5:5; 7:27). The description of Lady Wisdom is remarkably restrained in comparison to the claims made by her in chap. 8. One can understand this dinner invitation (cf. Isa 55:1–2) as a clever personification in the duel between Wisdom and Folly. It is precisely this "ordinary" quality of the presentation in chap. 9 that highlights the description in the previous chapter.

The issue of life and death is clearly presented by the choice of Wisdom or Folly. What is especially striking is the role of eros in these chapters. Over sixty verses have sexual overtones, some more than others. There is clearly a warning against sexual misconduct, especially in chaps. 5–7. One begins to suspect that a deeper meaning underlies this, that a symbolism attaches to the sexual encounter (R. E. Murphy, *CBQ* 50 [1988] 600–603). G. Bostrøm (*Proverbiastudien*) argued that behind the figure of the "strange woman" lurked the worship of foreign goddesses (in the style of Ishtar), as opposed to fidelity to Israel's traditions. It is striking that simple adultery plays a relatively small role in the rest of the admonitions in the book (cf. Prov 22:14; 23:27; 31:3). But in chaps. 1–9 it seems to become the touchstone of orthodoxy; there is a clear choice between life and death. It is really not possible to determine the exact historical background of these warnings. However, they provide an excellent example of the multivalence of this symbol (and there are others, such as the motifs of the tree of life, water, etc.) in the book. Moreover, one should keep in mind that the personifications of Wisdom in Sirach and the Wisdom of Solomon have yet to be considered. At the very least, the ennobling character of wisdom in these two books continues the lofty meaning of Wisdom.

B. Lang (*Frau Weisheit*, 148–54; *Wisdom and the Book of Proverbs*, 126–36) has presented a rather complete survey of opinions regarding the possible sources at the origin of the personification of wisdom (and its meaning) in chap. 8. We might here consider the rather unique solution of G. von Rad. In *Wisdom in Israel* he entitled his treatment of personified Wisdom as "the self-revelation of creation." In other words, he interpreted Lady Wisdom as the world order turning "as a person, towards men, wooing them and encouraging them in direct address. What is objectified here, then, is not an attribute of God but an attribute of the world, namely that mysterious attribute, by virtue of which she turns towards men to give order to their lives" (156). One cannot escape the feeling of a disappointment. Lady Wisdom is simply the order of creation? Von Rad was closer to the mark in his earlier work, where he wrote: "So wisdom is truly the form in which Jahweh makes himself present and in which he wishes to be sought by man. 'Whoso finds him finds life' (Prov viii.35). Only Jahweh can speak in this way" (*Old Testament Theology*, 1:444). We might summarize the point of Prov 8 by saying that in it Wisdom is a communication of one of God's most intimate gifts (because born of God) that could be bestowed upon human beings among whom she finds it a joy to live.

The origins of this figure of Wisdom remain unknown to us, although scholarly guesses have not been lacking. C. R. Fontaine gives a brief summary of the scholarly efforts along this line and concludes: "The unanswered question of this scholarly reconstruction is the manner in which Israelite sages would have borrowed material from traditions so roundly condemned elsewhere in the canon, even though such borrowing and free adaptation is in keeping with wisdom's international spirit and origins. Still, it may be that by 'co-option' of surrounding goddesses to create the Yahwistically subordinated figure of Woman Wisdom, Israel met its own psychological need for female imagery of the divine without serious compromise of patriarchal monotheism" (*HBC*, 502).

C. Camp has made a case for regarding Lady Wisdom as the culmination of the various roles performed by the Israelite woman in society: as wife and mother, lover, adulteress, as the "wise" woman, etc. (*Wisdom and the Feminine*, 79–123, 285–91). Israel's experience of women in all these roles provides a background for conceiving of the ideal Lady Wisdom, with all her arts. The manifold examples of female wisdom in the rest of the OT are thus factors leading up to the personification of Lady Wisdom. She is not merely a literary device that represents "order" in creation, appealing to young men; that is a flat and unimaginative approach to the text. Whatever the contributing factors to the figure of Lady Wisdom, she became a powerful symbol that continued to live, especially in the work of Ben Sira.

Within the canonical books, the personification of Wisdom ceases with the Book of Proverbs, but Lady Wisdom continues to be a powerful symbol among the Jews, as evidenced in the so-called apocrypha. Sirach has already been mentioned above in connection with Job 28 (cf. Sir 1–10). This book has more references to personified Wisdom than does any other work; see Sir 4:11–19; 6:18–37; 14:20–15:10; 51:13–30 (all according to the NRSV numbering of verses). But the most extraordinary development is in chap. 24, modeled after Prov 8, and yet pursuing its own way in extolling this mysterious figure.

The address of Lady Wisdom in Prov 8 was delivered in the public square. In Sir 24:2 she appears "in the presence of his hosts," presumably in the heavenly court among the sons of God, to tell her story. Again, divine origin is claimed ("I came forth out of the mouth of the Most High"). She seems to have a twofold mission: she has dominion over the world, but at the same time she is looking for a place to take up residence. Her choice is determined by order of the Creator: "make your dwelling in Jacob, in Israel your inheritance" (24:8). She makes the same boast (as in Prov 8:22–26) of divine origins—created by God at the beginning—and adds that she will never cease to be, and then she takes root among the people of God in Zion, where she performs liturgical worship, "ministering" to the Lord. After comparing herself to majestic trees and exotic plants, she issues an invitation to all who will listen to come to her to eat of her fruit. This description adds several details to Prov 8, but both come together in the invitation to the audience to listen and obey her (24:22; Prov 8:34).

However, in this case the mystery of Lady Wisdom is partially revealed. Sirach identifies her explicitly with the Law: "the book of the covenant of the Most High God, the law that Moses commanded us" (24:23). If one accepts Audet's thesis mentioned above, we can see that this turn of events brings wisdom and law, after having separated and traveled separate paths, back together again. The connection with Sinai and Law is furthered by reference to the "pillar of cloud" (Exod 13:21–22). But the main emphasis is on Wisdom's origin from God (v 3a) and especially on creation. She covers the earth "mistlike" (v 3), a reference to Gen 2:6, and her "covering" recalls the imagery of the spirit of God that swept over the waters (Gen 1:3). Although Prov 8:15–16 had indicated her importance for royal rule, in Sirach (24:4–5) she is portrayed as ruling over all things: heaven, the abyss, peoples on earth. Obviously it is not an absolute rule, since her Creator orders her to dwell in Jacob. Wisdom appears as the Lord's vice-regent and high priest (v 10), ruling from Jerusalem. Her relationship to the people is reminiscent of her invitation to the banquet prepared in Prov 8: "eat your fill of my fruits." The erotic overtones of Wisdom's invitation (compare Dame Folly in Prov 9:13–18) is expressed also in Sir 15:2–3, but here it should be noted that the banquet is "the bread of understanding" (15:3). While Ben Sira was guided by the description of Wisdom in Prov 8 (cf. P. W. Skehan, *CBQ* 41 [1979] 365–79), he is quite creative in his own treatment, and he regards his contribution as giving instruction, "teaching like prophecy," serving "all who seek wisdom" (24:30–34).

The identification of Wisdom and Torah by Sirach gave a direction to wisdom that was never to be lost (continued by the *Sayings of the Fathers* and the "sages" of

Judaism). The Book of Baruch is a collection of poems that are difficult to date—perhaps shortly after the work of Sirach. One of these poems (Bar 3:9–4:4) continues the thought of Ben Sira: Wisdom is "the law that endures forever" (4:1). The author imitates the style of Job—where is wisdom to be found (cf. 3:15 and Job 28:12, 20)? The answer, of course, is God, who gave her to Israel: "Afterward she appeared on earth and lived with humankind" (Bar 3:37), just as in Sirach Wisdom sought a resting place and received from God the "dwelling in Jacob" (Sir 24:8).

The personification of Wisdom does not stop here. There is a distinctive Hellenistic flavor given to Jewish Wisdom in the late (perhaps 50 B.C.?) Wisdom of Solomon, another deuterocanonical work that carries on the wisdom tradition. Chaps. 6–9 constitute a lengthy dissertation on Lady Wisdom, given by "Solomon" to those who rule and judge the earth (the Jews themselves in the Diaspora?). Pseudo-Solomon has a right to speak about her since he loved her from his youth and sought her for his bride (8:2): "I prayed, . . . I called on God, and the spirit of wisdom came to me" (7:7). This spirit of wisdom is described in twenty-one terms (7:22) that defy any simple explanation: "intelligent, holy, unique, manifold, subtle, mobile," etc. Her association with God is even more mysterious than the usual divine origin attributed to her: "a pure emanation of the glory of the Almighty," "a reflection of eternal light," "a spotless mirror of the power of God" (7:25–26). For the influence of Isis upon $\sigma o\phi\iota a$ in these chapters, see J. Kloppenborg, *HTR* 75 (1982) 57–84.

Again the association of eros and Wisdom is affirmed: "I loved her and sought her from my youth; I sought to take her for my bride, and became enamored of her beauty" (8:2). Of course, she is loved by God (8:3) and sits by his throne (9:4), as it were, the divine consort. The ambiguity of Wisdom's role in Prov 8:30 (the uncertain meaning of *ʾāmôn*: "artisan" or "nursling"?) is clearly resolved. She was indeed present when God made the world (9:9), and she is called the *technitis*, the "artisan" (of all things) in 7:22. Hence she had a prominent role in creation, but God remains the "guide" of Wisdom (7:15). Her role in creation is a continuous one because she "reaches from end to end mightily and governs all things well" (8:1), and that is because by her purity she penetrates all things (7:24).

This brief survey of the biblical data indicates the complexity of personified Wisdom. We are unable to determine why or how Israel moved from proverbial sayings to the personification itself. Despite all the efforts made to identify the sources that led to this figure, and to identify her, uncertainty prevails. How can one hold together the sayings of Proverbs, the disputes and retribution problem of Job, the skepticism of Qoheleth, not to mention the remarkable development of Wisdom in Sirach and the Wisdom of Solomon? One can begin by seeing her as an "innocent" personification of the wisdom that the sages in Proverbs intended to inculcate. But how explain the divine origins, and the wide-ranging claims made in her name? One can at least classify these various "wisdoms"—wisdom from above and wisdom from below (J. Marböck, *Weisheit im Wandel*, 127–33), or "hidden" and "near" (B. Mack, *Logos und Sophia*, 21–32). The description of Lady Wisdom by Mack is succinct and to the point: "She is a teacher, one who shows the way, a preacher and a disciplinarian. She seeks out human beings, meets them on the streets and invites them in for a meal. The bewildering sexual aspects include sister, lover, wife and mother. She is the tree of life, the water of life, the garment and crown of victory. She offers to human beings life, rest, knowledge and salvation" (*Logos und Sophia*, 32), and even this description omits important dimensions of Lady Wisdom, especially her relationship to God. But it is enough to underscore the difficulty of identifying this mysterious woman. She retains her mystery. Although her admonitions and encouragement are clear, we are far from understanding the implications of her person. At best the following points particularly call for more explanation. What are the implications of her (1) divine origins, (2) association with creation, (3) identification with the Torah, (4) identification with the spirit of the universe, permeating all things, while also seated at God's throne? Just those four items—how can one hold them together? One might reply that there is a common thread in all these: communication—God's communication. Lady Wisdom is certainly that, and she has assumed various forms in fulfilling that task through the ages.

In the midst of this development of biblical wisdom, Qoheleth seems to be a discordant voice. He has nothing of the poetic flights about wisdom that characterized some of his co-religionists. This does not mean that he was unaware of the prominence of wisdom in Israelite thought. He explicitly says that he tried to acquire wisdom (Eccl 7:12) and that he failed. Pure mystery on this score confronted him. He is closer to the questions in Job 28: where is wisdom to be found (cf. Eccl 7:24, "who can find it out?")? Since he was unable to find true "wisdom," reality and the meaning of reality, he frankly admitted his failure. He was ready to admit mystery and ignorance, but he seems to have been impatient with any poetic exaltation of the reality that he could not grasp.

A Theological Assessment of Biblical Wisdom Literature

Christian theology has not treated the wisdom literature in a creative fashion. At the risk of generalization, one may say that the punch of Qoheleth was deflected by the Christian ascetical interpretation: everything (in this world) is mere vanity. The influence of Jerome was very pronounced here. The agony of Job was overcome by the exuberant eschatological view of Christianity, and the Vulgate translation of Job 19:25 ("I know that my Redeemer liveth and in the last day I shall rise out of the earth") diminished its power to raise questions among Christian readers. Christology and eschatology found support in Sirach and the Wisdom of Solomon. Thus, Proverbs, Job, and Ecclesiastes found little *genuine* echo in Christian tradition. The Book of Proverbs has exercised powerful influence upon the proverbial literature of Europe, and it has also served as a kind of moral handbook. But in general, the approach to OT wisdom remained under the heavy hand of NT "superiority." Even the dimensions of Jesus as a wisdom teacher and his continuity with the OT sages were neglected until relatively recent times (see R. Bultmann, *The History of the Synoptic Tradition*, the chapter entitled "Logia [Jesus as the teacher of wisdom]," 69–108).

Even the personification of wisdom seems to have promised more than it delivered. In the early Christian church, the Arians turned to Prov 8:22 as a text for the doctrine they had evolved. The Greek form of 8:22 read ἔκτισε, (God) "created" Wisdom, and since σοφία and λόγος were identified, the text was referred to the Arian understanding of the relationship between the Father and Son. Such a Christian reading of an OT text is simply not viable in modern theological discourse. The shift from Lady Wisdom to Christ was possible only within the framework of the patristic vision of the relationship between the Testaments. Although there is today a more sophisticated discussion of such biblical roots of Christology, the personification of Wisdom is not at the forefront except as a backdrop to the first chapter of the Gospel of St. John. Thus it feeds Christology "from above," and not "from below," where most of the action seems to be in recent years.

One would think that any "theology" that the wisdom literature has to offer would derive in the main from a Wisdom that has divine origins, offers life, and somehow speaks to human beings for God. We have seen above that more has been written about the origins and influences (from *ma'at* to Isis) upon Lady Wisdom than about her theological significance. Perhaps this can be attributed to the successive identifications of Wisdom in the various books: a crafts(wo)man (or nursling?) of divine and "eternal" origins that found pleasure in human society (Proverbs), the Torah (Ben Sira), a world spirit (Wisdom of Solomon). Even to say that she is a gift, a communication of God, seems insufficient; it is difficult to see the connection of all this to the hard-headed observations about human behavior in Proverbs and Sirach. Yet there is no one more lyrical in his description of Wisdom than Ben Sira (Sir 24), who identified her with Torah (Sir 24:23), but who also wrote:

> The first man did not know wisdom fully,
>   nor will the last fathom her. (Sir 24:28)

What about the rest of the wisdom literature? What do the sayings of the sages (with all their limitations?), the various reflections in the book of Job, the skepticism of Qoheleth, the comfortable devotion of Sirach, the enthusiastic praise and encouragement of the Wisdom of Solomon, have to contribute to theology? Are they somehow, in some mysterious way, the outpouring of Lady Wisdom?

Several scholars consider wisdom to be bankrupt. Thus, H. Preuss (*Einführung*, 172–98) denies any theological importance to these books; at best, they may serve as a subjective means for an individual to be aided toward faith in Christ. Of course, when biblical wisdom is reduced to a search for world order, to the rigidity of the deed-consequence mentality, and to a "polyyahwism" (a form of worship of the God of Origins), it becomes a red herring that is easy to dismiss. The echoes of "*Christum treibet*" of Martin Luther (Preuss, *Einführung*, 193), a much too narrow focus on the "essence" of the Bible, can be heard in such an assessment.

One of the more successful efforts to find a place for wisdom in theological exploration was the study of W. Zimmerli (*SAIW*, 314–26), who interpreted the wisdom enterprise as an extension of Gen 1:28, "fill the earth and subdue it . . . ." Thus wisdom was made "respectable" by being associated with the Torah and salvation history. More important, as we shall see, was Zimmerli's emphasis on wisdom theology as creation theology. G. von Rad advanced a firm and clear view (*Wisdom in Israel*, 307): "The wisdom practiced in Israel was a response made by a Yahwism confronted with specific experiences of the world. In her wisdom Israel created an intellectual sphere in which it was possible to discuss both the multiplicity of trivial, daily occurrences as well as basic theological principles. This wisdom is, therefore, at all events to be regarded as a form of Yahwism, although—as a result of the unusual nature of the tasks involved, an unusual form and, in the theological structure of its statements, very different from the other ways in which Yahwism reveals itself." As we shall see, von Rad's observation about the "multiplicity of trivial, daily occurrences" is particularly relevant to the evaluation of the theological implications of wisdom literature. Our understanding of the problem of theology and wisdom will be helped by a brief reminder of the historical development of this literature.

We have already sketched the likely origins of traditional sayings (Book of Proverbs, chaps. 10–31 in general) in the family, and at an oral level. It would appear, on the strength of Prov 25:1 and the clear association of the teaching of Amenemope and Prov 22:17–23:11, that the court had a hand in the preservation (in written form) of these and other sayings. The best guess is that Prov 1–9, which breathes a different air than the "sayings" was written in the post-exilic period and was prefaced as a kind of introduction to the work. Prov 1:1–6 is clearly an introduction (which forms one sentence in Hebrew) to what follows. The summons to acquire wisdom (chaps. 1–9) is matched by the concrete and down-to-earth recommendations on how to achieve this goal (chaps. 10–31). The positive promise of blessing, success, and prosperity is going to have a rough road within the Bible because the realities of life cannot be so easily squared with these recommendations. That Wisdom was destined to this tortuous path can be seen by anyone who takes the trouble to compare the optimism of Ps 37 (every verse of which could be fitted into the Book of Proverbs) with the faith-struggle of the writer of Ps 73.

It is difficult to escape the conclusion that the Book of Job is in conflict with the Book of Proverbs. This does not imply any necessary date for either book. The doctrine of the Book of Proverbs harmonizes with that of Deuteronomy, but the Book of Job scuttles any such optimism. The view of wisdom exemplified by the three friends simply does not fit the case of Job, and the author was set upon moving the discussion a notch higher. The stakes are even higher in the Book of Ecclesiastes, where the realities of life are seen to amount to "vanity," or הבל *hebel*. Yes, there may be exceptions—the joy and satisfaction that life may bring, but only by the inscrutable divine will. The starkness and bleakness of this life is emphasized, and the mystery of the presiding God stands out.

With Sirach and the Wisdom of Solomon, the traditional association of wisdom and (the good) life returns. There also appears an entirely unexpected development: wisdom and Israel's sacred history. Sirach identifies wisdom and law and provides a catalogue of Israel's heroes in chaps. 44–50. The Wisdom of Solomon puts together wisdom and (eternal) life as the great gift of God and rehearses the plagues of Egypt, adapting the events to the needs of the diaspora community.

This sketch of the path followed by wisdom serves as a necessary reminder as we attempt to describe the theological potential of these books. There is little profit in looking for some contrived "unity" within them. For example, one could point to the theme of life as a bond of unity. The life that is envisioned is this life, seen from various perspectives. In the broadest sense, wisdom achieves the good life, folly leads to non-life. Implicit in this statement is a moral edge to wisdom praxis. But it would be a mistake to turn the literature into moral exhortations in the style of Epictetus or Marcus Aurelius. Another argument against any unified synthesis is the danger of muting one or another of the books, for example, hearing

Proverbs without Job and Ecclesiastes (or other possible combinations of these books). But perhaps we can find some "neutral" ground in the area of human experience that is such a dominant characteristic of wisdom.

We can use Zimmerli's phrase with profit and call this "creation theology." This is the description of Israel's attempt to understand and cope with reality—what G. von Rad called Israel's understanding of reality: that we are "in a quite specific, highly dynamic, existential relationship" with our environment (*Wisdom in Israel*, 301). This observation seems to be obvious, and not subject to contradiction. In Israel's case, the arena of experience was not perceived to be foreign to their faith. We may apply the term "revelation" to it, in the sense that the Lord (the God worshiped by orthodox practice, despite the fluctuating character of Israel's fidelity) communicated self to the people through creation and the experience of creation, and not only with or through the prophets. If this human experience is not recognized as a channel of divine communication, a considerable portion of the OT is removed from the canon, in effect. Wisdom literature becomes a kind of Hebraic philosophy, analogous to any other ancient system of thought, that can be relegated to the realm of "natural theology." This situation is posed most sharply by considering a study of John J. Collins (*JAAR* 45/1 Supplement [March 1977] B:35–67), which judges wisdom literature to constitute a "biblical precedent" for natural theology. He describes revelation in the wisdom books as "a religious experience but not (or only exceptionally) a direct encounter with a personal God. It is found rather in the depth dimension of the common human experience of the world and of life" (44). This is not adequate. Wisdom literature provides examples of experiences of the Lord *through* the world and life. We may not restrict revelation to direct encounters (of Moses, Isaiah, or of whomever else), nor should the Sinai revelation be considered "special" (which some would understand as the "only" revelation). The categories of natural and supernatural are not easily applicable to the OT. The words of Karl Rahner are appropriate here: "From a theological point of view, the concrete process of the so-called natural knowledge of God in either its acceptance or its rejection is always more than a merely natural knowledge of God. . . . The knowledge of God we are concerned with, then, is that concrete, original, historically constituted and transcendental knowledge of God which either in the mode of acceptance or of rejection is inevitably present in the most ordinary human life. It is at once both natural knowledge and knowledge in grace, it is at once both knowledge and revelation-faith" (*Foundations*, 57).

This would be directly contrary to the views of A. de Pury (*RTP* 27 [1977] 1–50), who separates wisdom (the realm of cosmic order, to which one should adapt) and revelation. Revelation achieves a personal relationship to God, a "faith" encounter, which is not available to the experience of everyday life, to the kind of experience, for example, that Qoheleth limited himself to in his writing.

Can one seriously exclude the daily living experience from the revelatory touch of God? G. von Rad answered this effectively: "the experiences of the world were for her [Israel] always divine experiences as well, and the experiences of God were for her experiences of the world" (*Wisdom in Israel*, 62). It is also the view of Karl Rahner that has been encapsulated in the phrase "mysticism of everyday things" and compactly described by his student, W. Dych (*TD* 31 [1984] 325–33): "The God experienced in this 'mysticism of everyday things' is not the distilled essence of things, not the highest abstraction from the world, but the experience of God's life at the very heart of the world, in flesh, in time and in history. Perhaps the greatest dualism that Karl Rahner overcame is that between God and the world. For him they are never identical, but neither are they ever separate, so that God and the world are experienced and known together. Presence to self, presence to world and presence to God are all aspects of one and the same experience of God's real presence in the world which he created to be his real symbol" (332). A German OT scholar expressed the dialogue between Israel and God in the world in these words: "To be exposed to Yahweh in absolutely everything, to encounter him, to find meaningful existence solely in orientation toward him, in what he gives and what he takes away, in his reliably revealed activity and in the activity that is mysteriously unexplorable—this was the determining background against which Israel perceived the natural world and environment, perceived it in experience, knowledge, and formative activity" (O. H. Steck, *World and Environment*, 187). This unity of everyday experience and biblical wisdom has been stated also by J. Marböck (*Weisheit im Wandel*, 104): "Wisdom in the sense of God's presence, of an intimacy and community with God, is not separate from the world, but is in the midst of everyday life with its customary, even petty events. At the same time this world, which is accepted with its own cleverness and wisdom, receives a midpoint, a secret center: the Wisdom of Israel's religion."

This understanding of Israel's wisdom has far-reaching implications. It means that biblical wisdom is properly a faith experience, faith in the *YHWH* whom Israel worshiped in the Temple, whose saving acts were proclaimed and transmitted from generation to generation (Exod 13:14–16; Deut 26:1–11). It is not possible nor desirable to limit a description of faith to historical traditions, or to separate out what is "yahwistic" in the experience of the wisdom writers. The old saying that associated wisdom and the fear of the Lord (Prov 1:7; cf. 9:10; Job 28:28; Ps 111:10; Sir 1:14) captured a profound theological insight: Wisdom experience and *YHWH* belong together.

Index of Authors Cited

Index of Biblical Texts
The Old Testament

Apocrypha

The New Testament

Index of Principle Subjects

Index of Hebrew Terms